By Common Confession

Essays in Honor of James M. Renihan

EDITED BY

Ronald S. Baines
Richard C. Barcellos
James P. Butler

RBAP

Palmdale, CA

Requests for information should be sent to:

RBAP
349 Sunrise Terrace
Palmdale, CA 93551
rb@rbap.net
www.rbap.net

Printed in the United States of America.

Cover design and formatted for print by Cameron Porter.

Paperback edition

ISBN-13: 978-0-9916599-3-7
ISBN-10: 0-9916599-3-7

Praedicatio Verbi Dei Verbum Dei est.

The preaching of the Word of God

is the Word of God.

~ Heinrich Bullinger

Contents

Exegetical and Biblical Theology

Symbolic and Systematic Theology

Pastoral Theology

Tributes

Appendix

Preface

The origins of this book go back at least one year from its publication. Two men on opposite coasts of the United States, who have both been influenced tremendously by Dr. Renihan, came up with the idea without knowing what the other was thinking. At different times, each man contacted the publisher to see if there would be interest in such a project. Needless to say, there was both immediate interest and enthusiastic approval of the project. Both men were in the midst of writing their dissertations and thus their time was limited. Because one of them could not help with the process of publication due to prior commitments, the publisher (and editors) would like to thank Stefan Lindblad for communicating the initial idea for this project and helping it get off the ground in its early stages. The other man was Ron Baines. Ron took the ball and ran with it, though a very busy man. Thank you Ron. Thanks are due as well to Jim Butler. Jim took over editorial duties when Ron had to tend to his dissertation.

This volume of essays is offered in honor of Dr. James M. Renihan. Because he is a historical theologian, most of the essays cover issues in that field of study. But because he is much more than a historical theologian, colleagues and friends of Dr. Renihan were asked to contribute essays covering the various branches of the theological encyclopedia. The efforts here reflect the contributors' esteem for their brother and the impact he has had in a wide range of theological inquiry and praxis.

The publisher is pleased to present these essays in honor of an esteemed friend and teacher. Many have been helped tremendously by Dr. Renihan's friendship, scholarship, counsel, and faithfulness to Christ and his calling as pastor and theologian.

The Publisher
September 2015

Introduction:

A Biographical Sketch of James M. Renihan

If one were looking for an ambassador for Reformed Baptists in the twenty-first century, there would be few candidates that would match James M. Renihan. To be sure, there are some prominent men, past and present, who are clearly well-known and have been hugely influential in grounding and growing Reformed Baptists from the start. Twenty-first century Reformed Baptists are aware, like any other group of this nature, that we stand on the shoulders of many men who have gone before, for whom we are thankful. Furthermore, as with any movement of this sort, the growing body of those who self-consciously identify as Reformed Baptists has become more wide (world-wide really) and more diverse. However, among this wide and diverse body, Dr. Renihan stands as one who has both embraced the movement in its early resurgence, and helped shape and enrich that movement as it has matured. This volume stands as a tribute to this pastor, theologian, scholar, brother, colleague, and friend from many within the movement and several friends of the movement.

Education and Pastoral Ministry

James M. Renihan was born the son of an Irish father and a Swedish mother in October 1955, in Worcester, Massachusetts. James came to faith and was baptized as a young teen. After completing high school he attended Liberty Baptist College where he earned a B.S. in 1978. Desiring to heed the call to the pastoral ministry, he entered Trinity Ministerial Academy where he came under the influence of a number of men in the nascent resurgence of Reformed Baptists in the United States. He completed his studies at Trinity Ministerial Academy in 1983.

In 1984 he took his first pastorate at the Mohawk Valley Bible Church of Herkimer, New York. Amidst the labors of pastoral ministry in this Upper State community, James also began to evidence those characteristics that would make him the Reformed Baptist ambassador he has become. Gathering frequently in the basement of this small church was a group of area pastors who were coming to embrace the doctrines of grace and had formed a fraternal. It was a fraternal in which James quickly emerged as a friend and a leader.

In 1987 James took the pastoral charge of Grace Reformed Baptist Church of Amesbury, Massachusetts. Amesbury is a few miles northeast of James' boyhood home of Worcester, which proved providential. As James was maturing as a pastor he was also developing as a scholar. Desirous of further ministerial and academic pursuits, he completed his M.Div. at Worcester's recently established Seminary of the East. He was attracted to this school due to its combined emphasis on pastoral ministry and scholarship, and it prepared the way for further service in both venues.

Growing in his desire to further his scholarly interests, James entered the doctoral program at Trinity Evangelical Divinity School (TEDS) in Deerfield, Illinois, in 1993. TEDS proved a fitting environment for James' scholarly interests to flourish. Combining his love for Scripture, his heart for Reformed Baptist theology, and his desire to explore the historical roots which birthed the Baptist Confessions of 1644 and 1677/89, he completed his dissertation on *The practical ecclesiology of the English Particular Baptists, 1675-1705: The doctrine of the church in the Second London Baptist Confession as implemented in the subscribing churches,* under the watchful eye of Dr. Tom Nettles.

Trinity proved important for at least two reasons. The first is that it provided James the opportunity to exercise his academic gifts. His future ministry would be predominantly directed at teaching pastor/teachers and his time here would prove advantageous to that end. Second, the dissertation provided him with the opportunity to study many of the original sources of the seventeenth-century English Particular Baptist signatories of the Confession which became central to late twentieth-century Reformed Baptists. His deep appreciation for the Second London Confession of Faith of 1677/89 (2LCF) was richly fueled by this study and the central focus of his future teaching ministry would revolve around helping Reformed Baptists more fully reclaim their English Particular Baptist theological and practical roots.

Academic Career and Pastoral Ministry

In 1994, while James completed his dissertation, he returned to Worcester, took the pastoral charge of Heritage Baptist Church, and began his teaching career by offering a class in Baptist History at a nearby extension campus of Southern Baptist Theological Seminary. His future would be marked by this rich combination of local church pastoral ministry and the academic and pastoral education of future ministers. During this time he was also involved with a number of other Reformed Baptist pastors in the founding of a North American body of Reformed Baptist churches birthed on March 11, 1997, as the Association of Reformed Baptist Churches of America (ARBCA).

Soon after ARBCA's founding, the Association made its first step in providing ministerial education for future pastors—the founding of the Institute of Reformed Baptist Studies (IRBS) in Escondido, California. In 1998, Dr. Renihan was asked to become the founding dean and associate professor, now full professor of Historical Theology at IRBS. He also helped form and now serves on the eldership of Christ Reformed Baptist Church of Vista, California. Dr. Renihan continues to serve the Association, its churches, and Reformed Baptists world-wide from this venue.

Since 1998, Dr. Renihan has been active in teaching and preaching on at least five continents, and has been especially instrumental in lecturing on the history and theology of the 2LCF. Furthermore, many of the students who have graduated from IRBS now serve confessional Reformed Baptist churches and Dr. Renihan's scholarship and leadership have spawned a group of younger men eager to explore the seventeenth-century history and theology of the English Particular Baptists. All of this gives much promise for the future that twenty-first century confessional Reformed Baptists will be even better informed and grounded in the Confession which has come to largely define the movement.

This Volume

This volume serves as a tribute to Dr. Renihan on his 60th birthday. It is also an exemplar of his influence among those within and outside of Reformed Baptist circles. His careful scholarship, irenic spirit, and warm friendship are behind the essays and tributes contained herein. The editors are especially mindful of Dr. Renihan's warm friendship and scholarly example on a personal level. Few men living or dead equal the influence he has had on our lives and ministries. It is a privilege to have had opportunities to sit under his tutelage, to labor alongside him in occasional venues, and to be within the circle of men he calls friends.

The Editors
September 2015

Chapter 1

Chaucer, the Medieval Nominalist Doctrine of Justification, and the Reformation

J. V. Fesko[*]

Within the realm of Protestant theology there are a few well-known allegories informed by theological ideas, such as C. S. Lewis' *The Lion, Witch, and the Wardrobe*, or John Bunyan's *Pilgrim's Progress*. But few are aware that Geoffrey Chaucer (ca. 1343-1400), famous for his *The Canterbury Tales*, wrote a brief allegory of his own that showcases the late-medieval doctrine of justification, namely the *Clerk's Tale*. Allegories possess both strengths and weaknesses given their imprecise nature—razor sharp theological distinctions can be lost in the effort to tell a story. What might make for a good story does not necessarily preserve important theological points. At the same time, allegories have the potential to take complex theological arguments and present them in a simplified manner—one need not be trained in the finer points of the theology to understand the overall thrust of an argument. Chaucer's the *Clerk's Tale* falls into this latter category.

Very few people in the church are directly familiar with one of the more common understandings of justification in the Middle Ages, but Chaucer's allegory offers a simplified view. But one should not be too easily misled by the apparent simplicity of the tale, as a number of key theological concepts lie beneath the surface such as the medieval ideas of the *potentia Dei absoluta et ordinata* ("the absolute and ordained power of God"), the doctrine of covenant justification and the medieval maxim of *facientibus in quod se est, et Deus non denegat gratiam* ("Do what is in you and God will not deny his grace"), as well as the idea of an initial and final

* J. V. Fesko, Ph.D., is Academic Dean and Professor of Systematic and Historical Theology, Westminster Seminary California, Escondido, CA.

justification. At the same time, Chaucer's tale not only reveals key elements of a medieval doctrine of justification but also provides a window into how a number of scriptural texts figured into this doctrine.

There are a number of allusions, particularly to Old Testament texts, that provide the reader with an interpretive index to compare and contrast with later Reformation interpretations. By comparing later Reformation interpretations of some of these key texts, one then has the basis upon which to understand how Protestant theologians arrived at a very different doctrine of justification in comparison with the medieval view that Chaucer presents in the *Clerk's Tale*. Hence, this essay will proceed with an examination of the *Clerk's Tale*, followed by an analysis to expose the doctrine of justification beneath the allegory. Subsequently, the essay will then compare and contrast key scriptural allusions in the allegory with later Reformation interpretations, primarily through the work of Martin Luther (1483-1546) and John Calvin (1509-64), to explain how the Reformation doctrine of justification differs from this medieval variant.[1]

The *Clerk's Tale* Summarized

The *Clerk's Tale* begins with the introduction of one of the chief characters, Walter, the Marquis of Saluzzo, Italy. Walter is lord of the land, and all of its inhabitants, both rich and poor, were obedient and loyal to him. But the people of Saluzzo were distraught because the Marquis was a bachelor and they wanted him to take a wife. Walter, however, was reluctant to take a wife because as a bachelor he was free to act as he pleased — he did not want to be bound by marriage. Nevertheless, the Marquis

---

[1] There were other views of justification in the middle ages, such as in the theology of Thomas Bradwardine (1290-1349) and Gregory of Rimini (d. 1358). See Thomas Bradwardine, "The Cause of God Against the Pelagians," in *Forerunners of the Reformation: The Shape of Late Medieval Thought*, ed. Heiko Oberman (Cambridge: James Clark & Co., 1967), 151-64; idem, *De Causa Dei, Contra Pelagium et De Virtute Causarum, Ad Suos Mertonenses* (London: Ex Officina Nortoniana, 1618); Gregory of Rimini, *Super Primum et Secundum Sententiarum*, ed. Elgius Buytaert (1522; St. Bonaventure: The Franciscan Institute, 1955). For an overview of the medieval period, see Alister E. McGrath, *Iustitia Dei: A History of the Christian Doctrine of Justification*, 3rd ed. (Cambridge: Cambridge University Press, 2005), 55-207.

voluntarily consented to find a wife and discovered a poor woman of the lowest social order, Griselda. Even though Griselda was of little means, she was rich in virtue and diligence, which commended her to the Marquis. Walter chose Griselda to be his wife, fitted her with royal garments, married her, and she eventually gave birth to a daughter.

Several years passed before the Marquis desired to test the fidelity of his wife and so he instructed one of his servants, the Sergeant, to take his daughter and inform Griselda that she would be put to death. The Marquis had no intention of harming the child and instructed the Sergeant to hide his daughter in Bologna with the Marquis' sister. But as far as Griselda knew, her daughter was to die, but she was nevertheless faithful to her husband, Walter, and voluntarily turned her daughter over to the Sergeant. Four more years passed and Griselda gave birth again, this time to a son. Once the boy was weaned, the Marquis wanted to put his wife to the test again. He instructed the Sergeant to take the child and informed Griselda that he would be put to death; the boy was also taken to Bologna to be raised with his sister. To the Marquis' amazement, Griselda patiently and faithfully suffered this second apparent loss. The Marquis decided to reveal the truth to Griselda but not before one last test of fidelity.

The Marquis sent for his daughter and son, ages 12 and 7, and informed his wife that the people of Saluzzo were discontent with her service and thereby required the Marquis to take another wife. Griselda, resolute as ever in her love and devotion to the Marquis, considered herself blessed to have been his wife and resigned herself to return humbly to her father's house. The Marquis intensified the level of the test by informing Griselda that she had to serve as a lady-in-waiting to his new wife and she had to plan and execute the wedding festivities. Once again Griselda was unflinching in her loyalty and devotion to the Marquis, regardless of what he asked her to do, and the Marquis was ultimately convinced of her unwavering fidelity. The Marquis revealed the true nature of the tests and Griselda was so overcome with joy that she nearly fainted. She was stripped of her tattered clothing and dressed once again in royal garments, and Griselda and the Marquis afterward lived together for many years.

Analysis of the *Clerk's Tale*

At first glance, the *Clerk's Tale* seems like a horrible story given Walter's penchant for cruel tests for his faithfully devoted wife, Griselda, and it hardly appears to bear any resemblance to a theological discourse of any sort. Yet a number of studies on *The Clerk's Tale* situate it within the milieu of late-medieval Oxford University where Chaucer was exposed to a number of nominalist works, such as those written by John of Salisbury (ca. 1120-80) and William of Ockham (ca. 1300-49).[2] One of the chief ways in which medieval nominalism appears in the *Clerk's Tale* is in Walter's attitude towards marriage. The people of Saluzzo approached the Marquis to encourage him to marry because they were concerned that his royal line would not continue. But the Marquis did not want to enter into marriage: "I always have enjoyed my liberty; That's hard to find once marriage shall intrude. Where I was free I'll be in servitude" (145-47).[3] But the Marquis was nevertheless willing to enter into marriage with a proviso: "Yet I see how sincere is your intent, And will as always trust in what you say; Of my free will I therefore will assent, To take a wife as quickly as I may" (148-51).

As a bachelor, the Marquis stands outside of the covenant of marriage but of his free will binds himself to it. Hence, no outside power was able to impose any conditions upon him; the conditions of the covenant were only those that he willingly imposed upon himself.[4] The Marquis' interaction with his people and the prospects of entering the marriage covenant parallel the theological categories

---

[2] J. Mitchell Morse, "The Philosophy of the Clerk of Oxenford," *Modern Language Quarterly* 19 (1958): 4-7, 10-14; Robert Stepsis, "*Potentia Absoluta* and the *Clerk's Tale*," *The Chaucer Review* 10/2 (1975): 129-46; Geoffrey Shepherd, "Religion and Philosophy in Chaucer," in *Writers and Their Background: Geoffrey Chaucer*, ed. Derek Brewer (Athens: University of Ohio Press, 1974), 275, 279.

[3] All quotations of *The Clerk's Tale* are taken from Geoffrey Chaucer, *The Canterbury Tales including Melibee and The Parson's Tale: Translated into Modern English*, trans. Ronald L. Ecker and Eugene J. Crook (Palatka, FL: Hodge & Braddock, Publishers, 1993). The parenthetical reference indicates the part with a Roman numeral, followed by line numbers.

[4] David C. Steinmetz, "Late Medieval Nominalism and the *Clerk's Tale*," *The Chaucer Review* 12/1 (1977): 42; also Lynn Staley Johnson, "The Prince and His People: A Study of the Two Covenants in the *Clerk's Tale*," *The Chaucer Review* 10/1 (1975): 19-20.

of the *potentia Dei absoluta et ordinata* and a medieval nominalist doctrine of the covenant.[5] According to these ideas, God is completely unbound and even *ex lex* ("outside the law") — he is free to operate according to his absolute power. But God willingly binds himself to his creation and to humanity through a covenant, which is a manifestation of his ordained power.

God's dependability rests in his voluntary covenantal activity with the world through his covenants with Adam and Noah, and especially with the church. In this second covenant, God commits himself to a process of salvation, which despite the sinfulness of humanity, he nevertheless upholds.[6] The specifics of this process entail that God has agreed on the basis of his ordained power and according to the terms of his covenant that he will justify every sinner who does what is within him to love God.[7] Here we may invoke the medieval maxim: *Facientibus quod in se est, et Deus non denegat gratiam* ("Do what is within you and God will not deny his grace").[8] The medieval nominalist Gabriel Biel (1425-95) made this medieval maxim famous.[9]

Given these theological anchors, the *Clerk's Tale* takes on a greater degree of clarity when we consider Walter's (read God) marriage to Griselda (read fallen sinner). Chaucer places the greatest amount of social distance between the Marquis and his wife to highlight the differences between God and sinful humanity.[10] The

---

[5] For definitions of these terms, see Richard A. Muller, *Dictionary of Latin and Greek Theological Terms: Drawn Principally from Protestant Scholastic Theology* (Grand Rapids: Baker, 1985), s. v. *potentia absoluta* (p. 231) and *potentia ordinata* (p. 232).

[6] William J. Courtenay, "Covenant and Causality in Pierre D'Ailly," *Speculum* 46/1 (1971): 117; also Heiko A. Oberman, *The Harvest of Medieval Theology* (1963; reprint, Grand Rapids: Baker, 2000), 30-56.

[7] Steinmetz, "Medieval Nominalism and the *Clerk's Tale*," 44; see also E. J. Dempsey Douglass, *Justification in Late Medieval Preaching: A Study of John Geiler of Keiserberg* (Leiden: Brill, 1989), 129-61; and Charles P. Carlson, Jr., *Justification in Earlier Medieval Theology* (The Hague, The Netherlands: Martinus Nijhoff, 1975).

[8] Steinmetz, "Medieval Nominalism and the *Clerk's Tale*," 45; Oberman, *Harvest*, 132-34; idem, *Forerunners of the Reformation: The Shape of late Medieval Thought* (Cambridge: James Clark & Co., 1967), 123-41.

[9] Gabriel Biel, *Collectorium in IV Libros Sententiarum Guillelmi Occam* (1501; reprint, Hildesheim, Germany: Georg Olms Verlag, 1977), b. II d. 27 q. 1 art. 3 dub. 5.

[10] Steinmetz, "Medieval Nominalism and the *Clerk's Tale*," 43.

Marquis found his wife "among the poor folks" and in particular, with one "who was considered the poorest of them all" (204-05). But despite Griselda's poverty and low social station, she was marked by "virtuous beauty," and "inasmuch as virtue was her pleasure, She knew about hard work, not idle leisure. . . . Inside her virgin breast was found to be, A heart that was both sober and mature. She cared, with great respect and charity, For her poor aged father" (216-21). These elements of the *Clerk's Tale* reflect a common medieval understanding of election, whereby God chooses those who are worthy and rejects those who are unworthy.[11] Ockham, for example, argues that there is a cause of predestination originating, not in God, but in the one who is predestined: "'He will persevere to the end; therefore he will be predestinate.' For just as God is not a punisher before a man is a sinner, so He is not a rewarder before a man is justified by grace."[12]

When the Marquis deigns to marry Griselda, this woman of lowly estate, he clothes her in regal garments, which parallel the concept of the infusion of divine habits in a person's initial justification:

> This marquis, though had had his craftsmen make, Of gems, in gold and azure set, a treasure, Of rings and brooches for Griselda's sake; To fit her for new clothes, he had them measure, A maiden of like build; they had not leisure, That his bride be adorned in such a way, As would befit so grand a wedding day (253-59; cf. 654-58).[13]

But Chaucer is not primarily interested in the sinner's initial justification, reflected in Griselda's investiture, but rather in the life-long process of becoming more just, which culminates the second or final justification at the consummation.[14] A person's status is always

---

[11] Steinmetz, "Medieval Nominalism and the *Clerk's Tale*," 45; Oberman, *Harvest*, 185-216.

[12] William of Ockham, *Predestination, God's Foreknowledge, and Future Contingents*, ed. Marilyn McCord Adams and Norman Kretzmann (Indianapolis: Hackett Publishing, 1983), 77.

[13] Steinmetz, "Medieval Nominalism and the *Clerk's Tale*," 49.

[14] Steinmetz, "Medieval Nominalism and the *Clerk's Tale*," 47; cf. Oberman, *Harvest*, 134-35; "Council of Trent, sess. VI, 13 Jan 1547: Decree on Justification," in

unknown and indefinite until his death and appearance before the divine bar because at any moment he can fall into mortal sin and lose his justified status. Interest in final justification is especially evident in the mounting tension that builds throughout the story when the Marquis tests Griselda with greater and greater incomprehensible absurdity—surrendering her first child presumably to death, surrendering her second child to the same fate, being cast off for another woman, and then being asked to plan and execute her husband's wedding to this other woman. Many a woman would instead want to plan and execute her cruel husband rather than a wedding.

Yet, in the face of each test, Griselda responded with joy, humility, and diligent obedience and love for her husband. She was willing to suffer humiliation and renunciation of all social status, and perhaps even death itself (though this is never asked) rather than refuse to obey her husband's every desire, no matter how absurd.[15] But Griselda's seemingly meaningless suffering gives way to the revelation of her vindication. Griselda discovers that her children are alive, that the Marquis still wants to remain married to her, and that the purpose of all of these tests was to reveal "your every purpose, all your will" (1077). The final revelation, a final judgment, if you will, disclosed the fact that in the face of tremendous tribulations and tests, Griselda was faithful the entire time and never failed to love her seemingly cruel husband. Chaucer concludes the tale with the following words: "So patient was a woman to the end, Toward a mortal man, the more we ought, To take without complaint what God may send" (1148-50).

Before we conclude the analysis of Chaucer's allegory, one other dimension of the tale should be taken into account, namely the people of Saluzzo. While Chaucer undoubtedly draws the reader's attention to the interaction between Griselda and the Marquis, the people of Saluzzo play an important and contrasting role in the narrative. Covenantal elements appear in the agreement between the people and the Marquis when he consents to find a wife. The

---

Heinrich Denzinger, ed., *Compendium of Creeds, Definitions, and Declarations on Matters of Faith and Morals*, 43rd ed., ed. Peter Hünermann (San Francisco: Ignatius Press, 2012), 374-88.

[15] Steinmetz, "Medieval Nominalism and the *Clerk's Tale*," 48.

Marquis tells the people: "And furthermore, this you will swear to me: Against my choice you'll not complain or strive . . . With hardy will they swore, gave their assent, To all of this, not one of them said 'Nay'" (169-77). With these words the Marquis sealed the covenant with the people.[16] Even though the stipulations of the covenant were clear — no complaints or action against his choice of a wife — the people were quite dubious and fickle throughout the narrative.

The people questioned the Marquis' honesty and intention to wed (252), they could not recognize Griselda when she was dressed in her regal garments (384-85), which demonstrated they judged things merely by appearances because "Is virtue often hidden, folks opined" (426). When the children disappeared their professed loyalty to the Marquis turned to hatred: "Because of this, where all the folks before, had loved him well, his scandalous ill fame, Was something they began to hate him for" (729-31). When the children returned to Saluzzo the people flocked around them: "And when such a rich array they had espied, among themselves they quickly would decide, That Walter was no fool to have expressed, The will to change his wives, for it was best" (984-87).

In the end when the Marquis vindicates Griselda, he offers stinging words of rebuke for the people:

O stormy people! Fickle, never true! As changeable as is a weather vane! In rumors you delight, whatever's new, Just like the moon you ever wax and want! You're full of chatter, never worth a jane! Your judgment's false, your constancy will cool, Whoever trusts you is an utter fool (995-1001).[17]

To say the least, there is a stark contrast between the two covenants, one with the people and the other with Griselda. Within the framework of the allegory, the different responses to the covenants with the Marquis parallel the old and new covenants of the Bible as they were understood by medieval theologians.[18] Under the old

---

[16] Johnson, "Two Covenants," 18.
[17] Johnson, "Two Covenants," 18-19.
[18] Oberman, *Harvest of Medieval Theology*, 112-18.

covenant, which was stricter, the people of Israel were fickle, disobedient, and unfaithful. Under the new covenant, Jesus is a gentler and kinder Moses, and with the proviso that sinners merely need to do what is in them, offer their best effort, one's attitude towards the will of God, no matter how seemingly absurd, will in the end secure justification.[19] Again, the people are fickle and Griselda has an unswerving love for the Marquis, something the people lack. In terms of the narrative, the message is clear — formal obedience and lip service are insufficient — faith must work through love to secure one's justification.

When we strip away the story and look allegorically at its climactic outcome, the medieval nominalist doctrine of justification continues to emerge, as those who are faithful to the end, and do what is in them to love God (*facientibus quod in se est*), will be finally justified. David Steinmetz explains:

> The Clerk has elaborated on an allegorical level the main elements of the nominalist doctrine of justification, but he has done so in order to press home a tropological point. Those men and women who faithfully keep the terms of God's covenant with them, although it involves joyless obedience in unexpected and wholly undeserved adversity, will find that obedience vindicated. Conformity of our will to the will of God, not in order to obtain temporal or eternal benefits from Him but out of love for Him alone — a love which is not turned aside when God Himself seems to be the very one who opposes our obedience and is the apparent cause of our adversity — will be rewarded at long last.[20]

With this theological goal in view, the point of the *Clerk's Tale* comes into focus — the story is ultimately about fidelity through the process of justification, which culminates in final vindication and consequent reward before the divine bar.

---

[19] Johnson, "Two Covenants," 24-25.
[20] Steinmetz, "Medieval Nominalism and the *Clerk's Tale*," 50.

Comparison and Contrast

1. Optimistic and pessimistic anthropologies

Anyone vaguely familiar with the Reformation doctrine of justification can immediately detect significant differences with the doctrine presented in the *Clerk's Tale*. A number of Protestant confessions reveal an entirely different principle at work — for Chaucer, Griselda's faithful obedience is front and center, but for the Reformers, Christ's obedience takes center stage in the drama of redemption.[21] The differences between the medieval and Reformation views most strikingly appears in Chaucer's allusions to various biblical texts throughout the *Tale*. One can begin with Chaucer's characterization of Griselda, a woman of virtue despite her lowly estate. Despite her poverty, Griselda is nonetheless rich in virtue *before* she is chosen by the Marquis. If Griselda is an avatar for an optimistic medieval view on anthropology and of fallen humanity's abilities, then Gomer, the adulterous wife of Hosea the prophet, would be the personification of sinful humanity for the Reformers. Though opinions were divided over the precise nature of Gomer's harlotry, Calvin's characterization of Hosea's wife reflects the idea that her adulterous ways were presented "as in a living portraiture" so that people could see "their turpitude and perfidiousness."[22] To say the least, the Reformers took an opposing view of fallen humanity in comparison to the view reflected in Chaucer's tale.

In his *Lectures on Romans*, Luther takes aim at a number of medieval nominalists, including John Duns Scotus (ca. 1266-1308),

---

[21] See, e.g., Augsburg Confession, IV; Smalcald Articles, I; Formula Concord, III; Belgic Confession, XXII-XXIII; Heidelberg Catechism, qq. 61-64; Second Helvetic Confession, XV; The XXXIX Articles, XI; Irish Articles, XXXIV-XXXVIII; Westminster Confession of Faith, XI; Westminster Shorter Catechism, q. 33; Westminster Larger Catechism, qq. 72-73. For these confessional documents see Jaroslav Pelikan and Valerie Hotchkiss, eds., *Creeds and Confessions of Faith in the Christian Tradition*, vol. 2 (New Haven, CT: Yale University Press, 2003).

[22] John Calvin, *Commentary on Hosea*, in *Calvin's Commentaries*, Calvin Translation Society, vol. 13 (Grand Rapids: Baker, 1993), 45; Steinmetz, "Medieval Nominalism and the *Clerk's Tale*," 45.

Ockham, Biel, and their optimistic anthropology. Luther argued that these nominalists took no account of original sin in their anthropology and did not echo earlier church fathers, such as Augustine (354-430) and Ambrose (ca. 340-97), but instead reflected the pagan views of Aristotle (384 BC – 322 BC). In his reflection upon this nominalist anthropology, Luther writes:

> It is plain insanity to say that man of his own powers can love God above all things and can perform the works of the Law according to the substance of the act, even if not according to the intentions of Him who gave the commandment, because he is not in a state of grace. O fools, O pig-theologians (*Sawtheologen*)![23]

Luther offers similar criticisms in his 1517 *Disputation Against Scholastic Theology*.[24]

2. Faith working through love v. faith alone

When the Marquis presented Griselda with the prospect of surrendering her daughter to be put to death, she willingly consented given that it was the will of her husband (491-504). At first glance such a request might seem over the top, but if the allegorical framework provides an interpretive key, then Griselda's surrender to her husband's will echoes the sacrifice of Isaac (Gen. 22). God commanded Abraham to sacrifice his only son, Isaac, upon Mt. Moriah. This text has been historically connected to the doctrine of justification through its subsequent interpretation in the book of James: "Was not Abraham our father justified by works when he offered up his son Isaac on the altar" (James 2:21)? Calvin engages the "sophists" who "leap on the word 'justification', and sing out in triumphant chorus that part of justification depends on works." Important to note is that by the term *sophists*, Calvin has Roman

---

[23] Martin Luther, *Lectures on Romans*, Luther's Works, vol. 25, ed. Hilton C. Oswald (St. Louis: Concordia, 1972), comm. Rom. 4:7 (p. 261).

[24] Martin Luther, *Disputation Against Scholastic Theology*, Luther's Works, vol. 31, ed. Harold J. Grimm (St. Louis: Concordia, 1957), 9-16; Carlson, *Justification*, 75.

Catholic theologians of the Sorbonne in mind, advocates of this nominalist medieval view of justification.[25] Calvin counters their claims:

> A sober exegesis must be sought from the circumstances of the present passage. We have said that James is not here dealing with the source or the manner of man's attainment of righteousness (as is evident to all), but is stressing the single point, that good works are invariably tied to faith: so when he states that Abraham was justified by works his words are in confirmation of the justification.[26]

Evident throughout the Reformer's exegesis of the life of Abraham was that his works were evidence of his faith, not that they constituted the ground or cause of his justification. This conclusion is no more evident than in Calvin's explanation of Romans 4, when he writes that Abraham was not in any way justified by his works. Calvin contends that Paul's expressions can be reconciled with James by acknowledging, "That those to whom righteousness is imputed are justified, since Paul uses these two expressions as synonyms." And what, according to Calvin, is the source of this imputed righteousness? "It is necessary," writes Calvin, "that Christ should be seen to be the one who clothes us with His own righteousness."[27]

By way of contrast, medieval exegetes interpreted Romans 4

---

[25] Cf. John Calvin, *Institutes of the Christian Religion*, trans. John Allen (Grand Rapids: Eerdmans, 1949), III.xv.7, III.xvii.3, III.xviii.4; Richard A. Muller, *The Unaccommodated Calvin: Studies in the Foundation of a Theological Tradition* (Oxford: Oxford University Press, 2000), 50-52, 56-57.

[26] John Calvin, *A Harmony of the Gospels Matthew, Mark & Luke and James & Jude*, Calvin's New Testmaent Commentaries (1960; reprint, Grand Rapids: Eerdmans, 1996), 285.

[27] John Calvin, *Romans and Thessalonians*, Calvin's New Testament Commentaries (1960; reprint, Grand Rapids: Eerdmans, 1996), 84; idem, *Genesis*, Calvin Translation Society (Grand Rapids: Baker, 1993), 404-10; idem, *Sermons on Genesis: Chapters 11-20*, trans. Rob Roy McGregor (Edinburgh: Banner of Truth, 2012), serms. LXVII-LXX (pp. 309-88); cf. Barbara Pitkin, *What Pure Eyes Could See: Calvin's Doctrine of Faith in Its Exegetical Context* (Oxford: Oxford University Press, 1999), 41-55; David Steinmetz, *Calvin in Context* (Oxford: Oxford University Press, 1995), 64-77.

somewhat differently. Though his views were representative of earlier realist medieval theology, Thomas Aquinas' (1225-74) explanation of the function of faith presents a view commonly shared among both nominalist and realist doctrines of justification. When Paul explained that Christians were justified "apart from works of the law" (Rom. 3:28), Aquinas argues that Paul has something very specific in view, namely the works of the ceremonial law. Aquinas writes that not only are ceremonial works of the law excluded from consideration in our justification, but also the moral precepts of the law prior to a person's conversion. However, based upon his understanding of James 2:26, Aquinas contends that works subsequent to a person's conversion are necessary for justification.[28] Thomas' explanation of the nature of faith in his exegesis of Romans 4 further reveals his commitment to the necessity of works for justification when he argues that the end of faith is charity, which echoes the medieval maxim of *fides caritate formata* ("faith formed by love").[29] Aquinas elsewhere explains that the act of faith

> depends on the intellect and on the will moving the intellect to assent. Hence, the act of faith will be perfect, if the will is perfected by the habit of charity and the intellect by the habit of faith, but not if the habit of charity is lacking. Consequently, faith formed by charity [*fides formata caritate*] is a virtue; but not unformed faith.[30]

For Aquinas, the believer's good works are not precluded from consideration in justification but are absolutely necessary for the whole process, as charity forms the core of a justifying faith.

---

[28] Thomas Aquinas, *Commentary on the Letter of Saint Paul to the Romans*, trans. F. R. Larcher, O.P., ed. J. Mortensen and E. Alacrcón (Lander, WY: Aquinas Institute for the Study of Sacred Doctrine, 2012), § 317 (p. 106).

[29] Aquinas, *Commentary on Romans*, § 327 (p. 111); idem, *Summa Theologica* (Allen, TX: Christian Classics, 1948), IIa IIae q. 4 art. 4; cf. Peter Lombard, *Sentences: Book III*, trans. Giulio Silano (Toronto: Pontifical Institute of Medieval Studies, 2008), III.xxiii.4, 5; Muller, *Dictionary*, s. v. *fides caritate formata* (p. 116).

[30] Aquinas, *Romans*, § 106 (p. 38); cf. Thomas Aquinas, *Commentary on the Letters of Saint Paul to the Galatians and Ephesians*, trans. F. R. Larcher, O. P. and M. L. Lamb, ed. J. Mortensen and E. Alarcòn (Lander, WY: The Aquinas Institute for the Study of Sacred Doctrine, 2012), §§ 285-86 (p. 128).

3. Job and the place of obedience in justification

Another scriptural allusion appears in Griselda's divestiture. When the Marquis informs Griselda that she will no longer be his wife, she immediately returns her royal garments, wedding ring, and jewelry, and states: "Naked out of my father's house I came, And naked I must now return" (871-72). Chaucer echoes a statement from Job: "Naked I came from my mother's womb, and naked shall I return. The LORD gave, and the LORD has taken away; blessed be the name of the LORD" (Job 1:21). Chaucer evidently believes Job's words are suitably placed upon the lips of the suffering believer, which from one vantage point falls within the scope of a Reformation understanding of Christian suffering exemplified in Job. In his sermons on Job, for example, Calvin explains to his congregation that Christians should always recognize that everything they receive from God is by his free grace:

> I was not able to helpe my selfe, nor to ridde mee of the povertie wherein I was, so as I must needs have perished altogither, if I had not ben succoured by others: so it please God too foster me, and to intertayne mee even too this hour, and too give mee of his gracious benefits without number. And therefore if it please him now to scourge me, it is good reason I shuld beare all paciently, seying it comment from his hande.[31]

But Calvin also has a periodic inclination to view Job as a priestly figure and hence as one who pointed to Christ, even in spite of his tendencies to shy away from a christocentric reading of the Old Testament.[32]

Throughout his sermons on Job, Calvin repeatedly beats a steady drumbeat that sinners should seek the forgiveness of their

---

[31] John Calvin, *Sermons on Job* (1574; reprint, Edinburgh: Banner of Truth, 1993), serm. VII (p. 30-31); idem, *Sermons sur le livre de Job* (Geneva: François Perrin, 1569), 32.

[32] Derek Thomas, *Calvin's Teaching on Job: Proclaiming the Incomprehensible God* (Fearn, Scotland: Christian Focus, 2004), 305-21; cf., G. Sujin Pak, *The Judaizing Calvin: Sixteenth-Century Debates over the Messianic Psalms* (Oxford: Oxford University Press, 2010).

sins, and hence their justification, solely in Christ. Calvin writes against the "Papists," who

> know what is righteousnesse after the maner of the heathen Philosophers. For if a man aske an heathen Philosopher what righteousnesse is: It is a life wel ruled in al vertuousnesse, will he answere. And even so also do the Popish divines reason of it. We say that the same is true in it selfe: but we must steppe yet further: that is too wit, to another righteousnesse which is not in men, and whereof there is not one drop to be found there. Then must they be sayne to have an other righteousnesse, which is, that having condemned us in our owne persons, should take us too mercie for oure Lorde Jesus Christes sake: that by hys meane we may be acceptable and holy to him, forsomuch as the obedience which Jesus Christ yielded unto him is set over unto us.[33]

The difference between the two trajectories is palpable: Chaucer applies Job's words to Griselda because her obedience forms the core of the ongoing process of justification. Whereas for Calvin, Job's words can certainly be applied to Christians but only when one first lays hold of and builds upon the foundation of the obedience and righteousness of Christ.[34] According to Calvin, the believer's good works are not constitutive of his justification.

For medieval commentators such as Aquinas, the book of Job was not primarily about God but about the Christian's patient suffering in the midst of trial.[35] Aquinas anticipates a number of elements from the *Clerk's Tale* when he writes about the intent and nature of the Joban account: "Now one should consider that God not only orders the life of just men to their own good but also makes it conspicuous to others."[36] Concerning Job 23:10, "when he has

---

[33] Calvin, *Sermons on Job*, serm. XLII (p. 199); Thomas, *Calvin's Teaching on Job*, 316.

[34] Calvin, *Institutes*, III.xi.1.

[35] Susan E. Schreiner, *Where Shall Wisdom Be Found? Calvin's Exegesis of Job from Medieval and Modern Perspectives* (Chicago: The University of Chicago Press, 1994), 117.

[36] Thomas Aquinas, *The Literal Exposition on Job: A Scriptural Commentary*

tried me, I shall come out as gold," Aquinas explains this Joban theme of revealing the Christian's character (faith working through love) in trial and adversity:

> And here for the first time he manifestly explains the reason for his adversity, which was brought upon him so that he might appear to men to have been proved as a result of it, just as gold which can withstand the fire is proved. And just as gold does not become true gold but its genuineness is manifested to men as a result of the fire, so Job has been proved through adversity not so that his virtue might appear before God but so that it might be manifested to men.[37]

One can summarize Aquinas' view of Job as the final revelation of the Christian's faith working through love; the believer's works are therefore constitutive of his justification. These are themes that emerge quite clearly in the *Clerk's Tale* — Griselda's continual fidelity and obedient love to her seemingly cruel husband is finally unveiled for all to see.

4. The timing of justification

If one thing is clear from the *Clerk's Tale*, Griselda's status is never certain until the end. The Marquis harbors a steady suspicion of Griselda's true intentions and questions her fidelity. If it were not enough to surrender two children to execution and death, the Marquis still presses her with divorce and planning his wedding to his new bride. Viewed through the lens of the allegory, one never knows if the initially justified Christian will persevere to the end to be finally justified. Humanly speaking, this soteriological uncertainty is compounded by two factors: (1) for medieval nominalists predestination is based upon God's foreknowledge of a

---

Concerning Providence, trans. Anthony Damico (Atlanta: Scholars Press, 1989), comm. Job 1:7-9 (p. 81).

[37] Aquinas, *Exposition on Job*, comm. Job 23:8-13 (p. 303); also Schreiner, *Wisdom*, 76-77.

person's worthiness; and (2) a person must continually ensure that his faith is working through love—he must do what is in him. In other words, a person cannot appeal to the doctrine of predestination as a source of hope because in the end, the "believer" may not persevere and therefore ultimately not be elect. And a person might fall away and fail to do what is in him. According to these nominalist presuppositions, justification must await the consummation.

For Protestants, on the other hand, the believer's justification by faith alone based upon the righteousness of Christ alone means that the consummation, the final judgment, has been brought forward into the present. The famous dictum attributed to Luther, that Christians are *simul iustus et peccator* ("simultaneously righteous and sinners") reflects the believer's settled judicial status. In other words, for medieval nominalism, justification is a process, a journey, whereas for Luther and Protestantism justification is a defining moment.[38] The competing conceptions of faith explain the differences between the mature Luther and medieval nominalist views. For medieval nominalists, faith works through love—charity is the form of faith. For Luther, Christ is the form of faith:

> Faith takes hold of Christ and has Him present, enclosing Him as the ring encloses the gem. And whoever is found having this faith in the Christ who is grasped in the heart, him God accounts as righteous. This is the means and merit by which we obtain the forgiveness of sins and righteousness. 'Because you believe in Me,' God says, 'and your faith takes hold of Christ, whom I have freely given to you as your Justifier and Savior, therefore be righteous.' Thus God accepts you or accounts you righteous only on account of Christ, in whom you believe.[39]

Hence, though the Christian still struggles with sin, the *peccator* side of Luther's maxim, his judicial status is secure because it does not

---

[38] Daphne Hampson, *Christian Contradictions: The Structures of Lutheran and Catholic Thought* (Cambridge: Cambridge University Press, 2001), 24-29.

[39] Martin Luther, *Lectures on Galatians 1535 Chapters 1-4*, Luther's Works, vol. 26, ed. Jaroslav Pelikan (St. Louis: Concordia, 1963), 132.

rest upon faith working through love but upon Christ.

Given that justification rests upon the perfect obedience of Christ, it means that God has never lowered the standard of his law. For Luther and the Reformation justification can never be *facientibus in quod se est*, because the demands of God's law and his righteousness (*iustitia Dei*) are too steep. But as Heiko Oberman explains, herein lies the key difference between Reformation and medieval views on justification:

> One can summarize, therefore, Luther's discovery in the following sentence: *the heart of the Gospel is that the iustitia Christi and the iustitia Dei coincide and are granted simultaneously.* It is on the basis of this view that the disciples of Occam are not presented or unmasked as Pelagians as such, but rather as 'worse Pelagians,' as those who 'postea subinde peiores facti sunt!' It is not the task of those who are justified to implement the iustitia Christi by relating themselves in an optimal fashion to the iustitia Dei. The Pauline message is the Gospel exactly because the iustitia Dei—revealed at the Cross as the iustitia Christi—is given to the faithful per fidem. The 'fides Christo formata' replaces the medieval 'fides charitate formata'; in other words, 'faith living in Christ' has come in the stead of 'faith active in love' as it had been formulated and defined in a unanimous medieval tradition and as it can be found with Thomas Aquinas, Duns Scotus, Gabriel Biel, et al., including the Council of Trent.[40]

Given, therefore, the change in judicial grounds for one's justification, the outcome of the final judgment is already decided the moment a person trusts in Christ according to Luther.

Along similar lines, Calvin offers his own criticism of the common medieval doctrine of justification in his sermons on Genesis, particularly as it concerns the initial and final justifications. Calvin notes that "papists" argue that the believer's initial

---

[40] Heiko A. Oberman, "'*Iustitia Christi*' and '*Iustitia Dei*': Luther and the Scholastic Doctrines of Justification," in *The Dawn of the Reformation* (Grand Rapids: Eerdmans, 1992), 120.

righteousness and justification comes from faith through baptism, but he also explains its incomplete nature: "It is true they add that we cannot be completely righteous at any time, and they have to be aware of that whether they like it or not, and experience also keeps them convinced they are indebted to God in many ways." Calvin characterizes the process of justification as a journey:

> Jesus Christ opens the door for them, but it is up to them to enter, they say, and complete the trip. . . . They say we are justified at the outset by the pure grace of Jesus Christ, and then by faith. And then again they say we are justified by our works, in part by our satisfactions, which serve to appease God and acquit us of all of the offenses we are guilty of.[41]

To counter this claim Calvin asks the question: At what point was Abraham justified?[42] This is an important question vis-à-vis the timing of justification in the application of salvation (*ordo salutis*) but also for the final judgment (*historia salutis*). Calvin explains that works must be completely excluded from our justification because they are always soiled by sin.[43] Calvin asks a question, which is especially relevant given Chaucer's allusions to Genesis 22 in the *Clerk's Tale*:

> Has there ever been a better work than Abraham's, when he was ready to kill his son? And yet it is certain he harbored many regrets, which betray his weakness. So even that work is soiled in God's eyes and cannot be imputed as merit.[44]

For Calvin, "there is not a single work which is not filled with a vice when it comes to being judged according to the worth God finds in it."[45] "If a wine," writes Calvin, "is the best in the world and it is put

---

[41] Calvin, *Sermons on Genesis*, 324-35.

[42] Calvin, *Sermons on Genesis*, 325-26.

[43] Calvin, *Sermons on Genesis*, 338.

[44] Calvin, *Sermons on Genesis*, 353; cf. idem, *Genesis*, comm. Gen. 22:15 (pp. 571-72).

[45] Calvin, *Sermons on Genesis*, 358.

in a foul-smelling cask or in a dirty bottle, the wine is ruined. That is the way it is with all our works."[46] Hence, "faith and only faith must justify us."[47] Even at the final judgment, the believer's works are not judged in and of themselves but are covered by the righteousness of Christ and only appear righteous purely by faith: "Therefore, God approves that because it is from him, but let us note that he justifies us in our persons and even justifies us in our works by pure faith."[48] Like Luther, Calvin believed that Christians were *simul iustus et peccator*.[49]

The difference in the two readings of Job, and hence, the respective doctrines of justification, lies in merging justification and sanctification for Chaucer and numerous medieval theologians, versus recognizing that justification and sanctification are inseparable but nevertheless distinct soteriological benefits for the Reformation.[50] For Chaucer, justification is by grace through faith working through love. The Marquis did not have to marry Griselda—he could have left her in her poverty. But by his grace he chose and entered into the covenant of marriage with her by his free will. Griselda did what was in her to show her love for her husband. For the Reformation, on the other hand, obedience and sanctification do not contribute to a person's justification but rather are the fruits of it.

Conclusion

Reading Chaucer's allegory leaves an indelible impression, one where the seemingly absurd suffering of Griselda regularly

---

[46] Calvin, *Sermons on Genesis*, 360.

[47] Calvin, *Sermons on Genesis*, 358.

[48] Calvin, *Sermons on Genesis*, 360.

[49] The *simul iustus et peccator* explicitly appears, e.g., in André Rivet, *Catholicus Orthodoxus, Oppositus Catholico Papistae* (Leiden: apud Abrahamm Commelinum, 1630), IV.xviii (p. 512); and William Twisse, *Vindiciae Gratiae, Potestatis, Ac Providentia Dei* (Amsterdam: apud Ioannem Ianssonium, 1632), II.xiv.4 (p. 104). Twisse, for example, like Calvin and Luther, explains that the Christian is a sinner through his actions or disposition as one still inhabited by sin, but is nonetheless righteous through the imputed alien righteousness of Christ.

[50] It should be noted that at certain points, according to Schreiner, Calvin echoes the nominalist *potentia Dei absoluta et ordinata* distinction (Schreiner, *Wisdom*, 105-20).

confronts the reader like repeated splashes of cold water upon the face. When we remove the narrative veil and uncover the medieval theological presuppositions, the hyperbolic suffering takes on a different cast. Set upon the backdrop of a medieval nominalist doctrine of justification and its attending features, such as the *potentia Dei ordinata et absoluta* as well as the *facientibus in quod se est*, Griselda's suffering provides an interpretive index as to how a number of alluded and echoed biblical texts function within Chaucer's understanding of justification.

Chaucer's allegory provides a perfect foil to contrast at a number of key points such as the theological differences between medieval and Reformation understandings of justification, but also the interpretive grids through which a number of scriptural texts were read to reach their respective theological conclusions. While one can take a point-by-point analysis of Chaucer's tale and explore each scriptural allusion and compare it with later Reformation exegesis, in true medieval fashion one can apply Ockham's razor and ask one question: Where is the Christ-figure in the *Clerk's Tale*? Griselda represents the fallen but nevertheless virtuous sinner, and the Marquis represents God, who willingly enters into a covenant with the sinner. The Marquis repeatedly tests Griselda and she does what is in her and, in the end, the Marquis does not deny her his grace. But in the course of allegory a Christ-figure never appears.

Were the Reformers to read this story they would likely re-write it along the lines of the prophet Hosea. Griselda would be an unworthy adulterer and the Christ-figure would be the prophet who, despite the profound wickedness of his wife, pursues and ultimately redeems her. While allegories can cloud important theological points, they can also sometimes illuminate and explain complex theological points. Such is the nature of Chaucer's the *Clerk's Tale*.

Chapter 2

The Abrahamic Covenant
in the Thought of John Tombes

Michael T. Renihan, Ph.D.[*]

Individual anecdotes are not normative, but illustrative of the fruit of men's labors. The fruit of a belief will be seen in how it manifests itself in practice. Ideas have consequences. Let me illustrate. A friend with whom I attended seminary called me to discuss a matter affecting the life of the church he pastored. The church is Presbyterian. My friend has always been a traditionally conservative Presbyterian pastor holding to all of the Westminster Standards—even the Directory for Publick Worship. His recent experience struck at the heart of how the infant's interest in the covenant of grace via the Abrahamic covenant is working itself out in *some* covenantal Presbyterian or paedobaptist circles. A young woman in her late teens had become a nightmare to her Christian parents. She was disruptive at home and rebellious to the authority figures in her life. Her church prayed for her regularly over the course of almost two years. In fact, they prayed so regularly that it seemed to the pastor that the congregation had given her over as a hopeless cause. They had become desensitized through familiarity with her condition. A Christian friend of this young woman, however, also showed concern for her. She "reached out to her with a lifeline" (as the evangelical cliché says). This friend invited her to a church other than her family's where there were special summer evangelistic meetings. She agreed to attend. The rebellious one was

---

[*] Michael T. Renihan, Ph.D., is pastor of Heritage Baptist Church, Worcester, MA, and author of *Antipaedobaptism in the Thought of John Tombes: An Untold Story from Puritan England*. This chapter appeared in *Recovering a Covenantal Heritage: Essays in Baptist Covenant Theology* (Palmdale, CA: RBAP, 2014) and is used with permission.

struck by the force of the preaching and made a public profession of faith. (Let's not get lost in a visceral reaction to methodology at this point.) Late that night, she announced to her parents with tears of repentance interspersed with her words that everything was going to be okay from now on because she was now a Christian. Sounds good, doesn't it?

Her father went into a tirade. He had presumed his daughter was already regenerate by virtue of her election and her place as a "covenant child." He would not be shown to be wrong. His hyper-covenantal theology blinded him to the possibility that his daughter might have been unregenerate. In his view, she had "broken the covenant again" by making such a public profession of faith. After all, he had professed faith for her at her baptism sixteen or so years earlier. What might have been a merciful answer to the church's prayers was perceived as a greater evil than her two years of rebellion. For this act she was cast from the home. It was the proverbial last straw. The father's real grief was that his child had become "a [expletive deleted] Baptist." In those words the father conveyed his horror to his pastor, my friend. For the first time in his ministry, my friend saw the consequences of "pressing too much out of covenant theology." He asked in desperation, "What's a pastor to do?" Since he knows my dry sense of humor, I replied, "Become a Reformed Baptist." I also sent him John Tombes' work on the Abrahamic covenant.

Tombes' Measuring Rod for Doctrine and Practice

For Tombes, the positive, codified law of God found in Scripture was the measuring rod for all doctrine and practice. He used regal language to illustrate the responsibility of those who would carry forth the sovereign Lawgiver's decrees:

> For as it is a perogative of a King to appoint the wayes of his owne service and honour, and he should be taken to be very presumptuous and arrogant that should take upon him to prescribe a fashion of attendance, suite, and service to his prince without consent, when he hath otherwise declared his

will; so is it much more intolerable pride, and presumption in a mortall man, to appoint a way of service to God, which he never consented to, but hath otherwise directed his owne service. And for the same reason it is a transferring of God's perogative on a man, when he doth servilly consent by subjecting his conscience to such usurpation.[1]

Tombes' view of the church and her need for divine governance accentuates the spirituality of the church over against her material existence alone. The church was more than a human society of people with mutual beliefs and concerns. It was God's domain on the earth, a realm in which God ruled, subduing the hearts of men in order to make them different—his unique people. In a summary of the practical issues as regards his regulating principle of God governing his church by the Scriptures, Tombes concluded:

And although I know Ceremonies invented by men are pretended to serve for edification, yet I must professe that I never found in my reading, or experience, that ever any person by such rites and observances was wonne to the profession of Christ, or brought to any spirituall knowledge of Christ, any true faith or sincere obedience to him. Possibly they may beget some kinde of raptures of carnall delight, through melodious soundes or pleasant sights, some kinde of womanish pity, and teares, such as the acting of a stage play will draw from some persons: but that ever they begat sanctifying knowledge, sound repentance, holy mortification of sinne, lively faith, fruitfull living to God, I assure my selfe cannot be shewed: But it is certain on the contrary that the teaching for doctrines commandments of men hath occasioned men to oppose the principall point of the Gospel of Christ, to wit, justification by faith in him, and contrary to the covenant of grace in Christ to conceive a righteousnesse in themselves by the observation of men's commands, as in the Pharisees and Papists, and all sorts of superstitious

---

[1] *Fermentum Pharisaeorum or, The Leaven of Pharisaical Will-Worship: declared in a sermon on Matth.xv., November 24, 1641, at Leominster in Herefordshire* (London: 1641), 6.

persons it doth abundantly appear.[2]

Tombes, then, was no iconoclast. He was concerned with evangelical concerns for the ultimate well-being of the souls of those who attended the church's worship. His deeply held concern was that people realize the effects of sin and find themselves eclipsed by the power of God found in the Christian gospel (Tit. 2:11-14). He also labored that God's glory would not be obscured by some novelty of man's creative mind. A rigid application of this principle drove Tombes to examine everything in his Christian belief system by the standard of Scripture alone, aided by reason, including baptism.

The recovery of right baptism was Tombes' personal, yet godly, obsession. He was concerned with the right practice of this ordinance for the good of men's soul, not to win a theological point. The debate that raged in the seventeenth century was more than the mere academic production of print on paper. Tombes really believed that the right doctrine would have major repercussions in the church-at-large. I believe that Tombes was right on target. These ripples still affect the churches of our day.

Tombes' Starting Point and the Argument from Genesis 17:7

The first argument is one that examines the case for infant baptism from the interest of believers' children in the promise given to Abraham in Genesis 17:7. It also serves as the all-important starting point for Tombes' theological reflection:

> Major premise: That which hath no testimony in Scripture for it, is doubtfull.
> Minor premise: But this Doctrine of Infant-Baptisme, hath no testimony of Scripture for it;
> Conclusion: *Ergo*, it is doubtfull.[3]

---

[2] *Fermentum Pharisaeorum*, 7.

[3] Tombes, *Exercitation*, 1. See also, John Tombes, *An Apology or Plea for the Two Treatises* (London, 1646), 6.

Tombes' first exegetical argument is a comprehensive, yet properly basic argument designed to examine any and all of the biblical evidence for infant baptism. The remaining arguments are applications of the first argument to specific Scriptures, theological constructions, or historical precedents. Tombes then used his conclusions to support the doctrine or practice. However, in the context of this first argument, he went on to consider what he saw as the underlying biblical texts for the practice of paedobaptism:

> The Minor is proved by examining the places that are brought for it, which are these: Genesis 17.7, etc. Acts 2.38, 39. 1 Cor. 7.14. Mark. 10.14. 16. Acts 16.15. 32. 1 Cor. 1.16. The Argument from Gen 17.7, etc. is almost the first and the last in this businesse; and therefore is the more accurately to be examined.[4]

Tombes often added color to the debate with maxims and Latin phrases. The first argument did not escape his cutting wit. Speaking of the argument for infant baptism from Genesis 17:7, etc., he added, "[B]ut it hath so many shapes, that I may here take up that Speech, *With what knot shall I hold shape-shifting Proteus?*[5] But in the issue, it falls into one or other of these forms."[6]

Tombes went on to build his foundation against the interest of

---

[4] John Tombes, *Two Treatises; and an Apendix to them Concerning Infant Baptisme. The Former Treatise being an Exercitation presented to the Chair-man of a Committee of the Assembly of Divines. The latter an Examen of the Sermon of Mr. Stephen Marshall, about Infant-Baptisme, in a letter sent to him* (London: 1645). The work includes an appendix to show that Col. 2:11-12 "proves not Infant-Baptisme," 1.

[5] Proteus is a striking analogy borrowed from mythology. As a shape-shifting being who possessed knowledge of the past, present and future, he would not answer questions from mortals unless bound and compelled to do so. Thomas Bulfinch, *Bulfinch's Mythology, The Age of Fable* (New York: Nelson Doubleday, 1968), italics mine.

[6] Tombes, *Exercitation*, 1. These interjections were typical in the debates Schoolmen would enter. They were utilized to express ideas and to evoke emotions within the argumentation of the day. They were verbal symbols. Here Tombes is using a written device to display his frustration in framing an argument that it might be understood and owned by its promoters. These interjections were taken as offensive by Stephen Marshall. Because of that offense, Tombes explains the use of these sayings in *Apology*, esp. 12-30 (first ¶).

believers' children in the promises of the Abrahamic covenant. He did not give multiple forms of the opposing argument but one form from which he drew four sub-arguments. He thus supported his refutation of the one argument from Genesis 17:7. This was an application of his overriding principle expressed in Argument One—that there is no Scripture to warrant the baptizing of infants. He continued with another syllogism as if arguing for paedobaptism:

> Major premise: To whom the Gospel-covenant agrees, to them the sign of the Gospel-covenant agrees also.
> Minor premise: But to Infants of Believers the Gospel-covenant agrees,
> Conclusion: [A]nd consequently Baptisme.[7]

Tombes added, "The Minor is proved from Gen. 17.7. where God promiseth to *Abraham, I will be a God to thee and to thy seed after thee*."[8]

Tombes proceeded to four sub-arguments that he believed exposed the basic assumptions of the greater argument presented. By way of introduction to his main point, they were: (1) the covenant with Abraham is not identical to the Gospel (new) covenant; (2) Abraham's seed has more than one meaning; (3) the promise of the gospel has always been the same irrespective of the age; and (4) some were circumcised who had no part in the promise made to Abraham. These four parts were intended to undermine the credibility of infant baptism by way of analogy from the Abrahamic covenant to the new, or in Tombes' favorite phraseology, the "Euangelicall [using the Greek alliteration]" or "Gospel-Covenant."[9] These also form the foundation of all of Tombes' arguments. They were points that were non-negotiable for him. It is important to see the detail in these sub-arguments in order to understand his inferences within other constructions. Tombes kept coming back to two foundational points: (1) the lack of positive instruction in special revelation for the practice of infant baptism and (2) an alternative (and creative) explanation of the biblical texts,

---

[7] Tombes, *Exercitation*, 1ff., argument structural components mine.

[8] Tombes, *Exercitation*, 1ff.

[9] Tombes, *Exercitation*, first appearance on 2, then throughout.

which became the foundation of his emerging covenantal and credobaptist theology.

On the first of these sub-arguments, Tombes declared:

1. The Covenant made with *Abraham*, is not a pure Gospel-covenant, but mixt, which I prove; The Covenant takes its denomination from the promises; but the promises are mixt, some Euangelicall, belonging to those to whom the Gospel belongeth, some are Domestique, or Civill promises, specially respecting the House of *Abraham*, and of *Israel*; *Ergo*.[10]

Explaining his distinction between evangelical and domestic or civil promises in the Abrahamic covenant, Tombes implied there were some spiritual promises and some physical or material promises that had to be distinguished. Tombes explained what he means by "Euangelicall promises":

That was Euangelicall which we read, *Gen 17.5. I have made thee a father of many nations;* and that which we find, *Gen 15.5. so shall thy seed be;* in which it is promised, that there shall be of all Nations innumerable that shall be *Abrahams* children by believing, Rom. 4.17,18. It was Euangelicall, which we find, *Gen 12.3. & Gen. 18.18.* and in thy seed shall all the kindreds of the earth be blessed; for in these is promised blessing to Believers, of whom *Abraham* is father, *Gal. 3.16. Acts 3.25.*[11]

Tombes then proceeded to the "Domestique" or "Civill" promises:

Domestique and Civill promises were many; of the multiplying the seed of *Abraham*, the birth of *Isaac'* of the coming of Christ out of *Isaac;* the bondage of the *Israelites* in

---

[10] Tombes, *Exercitation*, 2.

[11] Tombes, *Exercitation*, 2. Tombes assumes a high degree of biblical literacy on the part of his readers. He quotes only the essential parts of verses of Scripture as his authority when needed to make the case. In other cases, he just asserts the reference as his authority assuming one's familiarity with these texts.

Egypt, and deliverance thence; of possessing the Land of *Canaan, Gen. 15.13. 18. Gen. 17.7, 8. 15.16. Act. 7.4, 5, 6, 7, 8.* and many other places.[12]

The distinction is between the spiritual blessings (which are called evangelical) which accrue to believers as believers, and physical (or natural) consequences pertaining to Abraham's descendants as domestic (or civil). This distinction is also between a spiritual seed brought about by heavenly activity and a natural seed brought about by the earthly procreative act. Tombes continued to legitimize this distinction as he invoked a rigorous trinitarianism to clarify and balance the issues of continuity and discontinuity within the two aspects of the Abrahamic covenant (and the same issues as regards other covenants):

Yea, it is to be noted, that those promises which were Euangelicall, according to the more inward sense of the Holy Ghost, do point at the priviledges of *Abrahams* House, in the outward face [sense] of the words; whence it may be well doubted, whether this Covenant made with *Abraham,* may be called simply Euangelicall, and so pertain to Believers, as Believers. There were annexed to the Covenant on *Mount Sinai,* sacrifices pointing at the sacrifice of Christ, and yet we call not that Covenant simply Euangelicall, but in some respect.[13]

Based on the distinction that the Abrahamic covenant is not one and the same with the new or Gospel covenant, Tombes went on to answer the remaining three of his original four questions that paralleled the concerns already stated: "(2) Who is the seed? (3) What is the promise? (4) What of those who were circumcised who had no part in Abraham's covenant?"

Coming to his second question (Who is the seed?), Tombes says:

Secondly, The seed of *Abraham* is many wayes so called: First, Christ is called the seed of *Abraham,* by excellency, Gal

---

[12] Tombes, *Exercitation,* 2.
[13] Tombes, *Exercitation,* 2ff., clarification in brackets mine.

3.16. Secondly, all the Elect, Rom. 9.7. all believers, Rom. 4.11,12. 16.17, 18. are called the seed of *Abraham*, that is spiritual seed. Thirdly, there was a natural seed of *Abraham*, to whom the inheritance did accrue; this was *Isaac*. Gen. 21.12. Fourthly, a natural seed, whether lawfull, as the sons of *Keturah*, or base, as *Ishmael*, to whom the inheritance belonged not, Gen 15.5. But no where do I find, that the Infants of Believers of the Gentiles are called *Abrahams* seed, of the three former kinds of *Abrahams* seed, the promise recited, is meant, but in a different manner thus: that God promiseth, he will be a God to Christ, imparting in him blessing to all nations of the earth, to the spiritual seed of *Abraham* in Euangelicall benefits, to the natural seed inheriting, in domestick and politicall benefits.[14]

Tombes extended the blessings of the new covenant back upon the Abrahamic covenant in both aspects of the covenant—spiritual and civil. He saw this as part of the promise of the new covenant expressed in the time before Christ. He attempted to explain himself as he answered the third question (What is the promise?):

3. That the promise of the Gospel, or Gospel-covenant, was the same in all ages, in respect of the thing promised, and condition of the covenant, which we may call the substantiall and essentiall part of that covenant, to wit, *Christ, Faith, Sanctification, Remission of sins, Eternall life;* yet this Euangelicall covenant had divers forms in which these things were signified, and various sanctions, by which it was confirmed: To *Adam,* the promise was made under the name of the seed of the woman, bruising the head of the Serpent; to *Enoch, Noah,* in other forms; otherwise to *Abraham,* under the name of his seed, in whom all nations should be blessed; otherwise to *Moses,* under the obscure shadows of the Law; otherwise to *David,* under the name of a successor in the kingdome; otherwise in the New Testament, in plain words, *2 Cor. 3.6. Heb. 8.10.* It had likewise divers sanctions. The Promise of the Gospel was confirmed to *Abraham* by the sign

---

[14] Tombes, *Exercitation*, 3.

of circumcision, and by the birth of *Isaac*; to *Moses* by the Paschall Lamb, and the sprinkling of blood on the [door], the rain of Mannah, and other signs; to *David* by an oath; in the New Testament, by Christ's blood, 1 Cor. 11.25. Therefore circumcision signified and confirmed the promise of the Gospel, according to the form and sanction of the covenant with *Abraham*, Baptisme signifies and confirms the same promise according to the form, sanction and accomplishments of the new Testament.[15]

Tombes admitted that each of these covenants has a sign to confirm the promise made. However, he maintains a distinction between the specific sign of circumcision given in the Genesis 17 covenant (given to Abraham as part of that specific covenant) and the specific sign of baptism given in the new covenant. He went on to contrast other aspects of these covenants to demonstrate there was not a *quid pro quo* relationship between them. There was some continuity; there was also discontinuity. If they were identical in all things, they would be the same in essence, character, and name. Since there was at least one difference, the sign, it was, for Tombes' theological opponents, fallacious to impose a view of radical continuity between the covenant made with Abraham and the covenant brought about by Christ, the new covenant. Tombes continued by looking at the elements involved:

> . . . [N]ow these forms and sanctions differ many wayes, as much as concerns our present purpose in these: First, circumcision confirmed not Euangelicall promises, but also Politicall; and if we may believe *Mr. Cameron*, in his *Theses*, of the threefold Covenant of God, *Thesi. 78. Circumcision did primarily separate the seed of* Abraham *from other nations, sealed*

---

[15] Tombes, *Exercitation*, 3, brackets and 'door' inserted. The original has 'book.' Since this article makes no correction in the *errata*, and since this author knows of no narrative in the Pentateuch that deals with blood being sprinkled on a 'book,' the word has been changed. However, considering the context of Tombes' comments, the Passover, and having personally perused examples of his handwriting from which a printer or printer's apprentice (devil) would have copied, I believe it is no violence to the work in form or content to make this change.

unto them the earthly promise; Secondarily, it did signifie sanctification: But Baptisme signifies only Euangelicall benefits. Secondly, circumcision did confirm the promise concerning Christ to come out of *Isaac;* Baptisme assures Christ to be already come, to have been dead, and to have risen again. Thirdly, circumcision belonged to the Church, constituted in the House of *Abraham,* Baptisme to the Church gathered out of all nations; whence I gather, that there is not the same reason of circumcision and baptisme, in signing the Euangelicall covenant; nor may there be an argument drawn from the administration of the one to the like manner of the other.[16]

For Tombes, circumcision sealed an earthly promise and identified Abraham's seed as set apart to God for his purpose. A great part of that purpose was the incarnation of Christ from the line of Isaac. Tombes was not denying Israel's prized position as God's special ancient people; he was affirming it. However, for Tombes, it was important to understand the pre-incarnational covenants in the brighter light of the fulfillment in the new covenant. Salvific aspects of the new covenant were found in types and shadows within the older covenants (especially the Abrahamic), but their primary purpose was to anticipate the day when God would bring redemption. The new covenant, however, looked back to the reality of redemption accomplished and applied. It was through these new covenant glasses that Tombes saw the salvific aspects of all antecedent covenants. In Tombes' theological scheme, circumcision was the sign of the former, pointing to, among other things, the spiritual realities that will be the certain possession of Abraham's spiritual seed. Baptism is the sign of the latter, looking back at what has been done by the Mediator of the new covenant for his people.

Tombes demonstrated even more discontinuity between the Abrahamic and new covenants while anticipating the question as regards the subjects of circumcision:

4. That some there were circumcised, to whom no promise in the covenant made with *Abraham* did belong; of *Ishmael,* God

---

[16] Tombes, *Exercitation,* 3ff.

had said, that his covenant was not to be established with him, but with *Isaac;* and yet he was circumcised, *Gen. 17.29, 21. 25. Rom. 9.7, 8, 9. Gal. 4.29, 30.* the same may be said of *Esau:* All that were in *Abrahams* house, whether strangers, or born in his house, were circumcised, *Gen. 17.12, 13.* of whom nevertheless, it may be doubted, whether any promises of the covenant made with *Abraham,* did belong to them; there were other persons, to whom all, or most of the promises in the covenant pertained, that were not circumcised; this may be affirmed of the Females, coming from *Abraham,* the Infants dying before the eighth day, of just men, living out of *Abrahams* house, as *Melchisedech, Lot, Job.* If any say, that the females were circumcised in the circumcision of the Males, he saith it without proof; and by like, perhaps greater, reason it may be said, that the children of Believers are baptized in the persons of their own parents, and therefore are not to be baptized in their own persons. But it is manifest that the *Jewes* comprehended in the covenant made with *Abraham,* and circumcised, were neverthelesse not admitted to Baptisme by *John Baptist,* and Christs Disciples, till they professed repentance, and faith in Christ. Hence I gather, first, that the right to Euangelicall promises, was not the adequate reason of circumcising these or those, but God's precept, as is expressed, *Gen. 17.23. Gen. 21.4.* Secondly, that those terms are not convertible, *[federated and to be signed].*[17]

Tombes' conclusions were drawn from the positive, declarative use of circumcision and baptism in Scripture. His rigid adherence to the meaning of texts as God's words for his people and his governing principles for all matters of faith and practice compelled him to demand positive evidence for paedobaptism beyond mere theological constructions. Tombes demanded some evidence from "God's precept[s]" for the practice. He also saw more discontinuity between the Abrahamic and the new covenant through the assertion "those terms were not convertible." By "convertible," Tombes meant synonymous. There may be some similarities; yet great differences remained.

---

[17] Tombes, *Exercitation*, 4, italics and brackets in original.

Review and Conclusion

In review, Tombes' original, foundational argument was stated thus:

> Major premise: That which hath no testimony in Scripture for it, is doubtfull.
> Minor premise: But this Doctrine of Infant-Baptisme, hath no testimony of Scripture for it;
> Conclusion: *Ergo*, it is doubtfull.[18]

Applying this argument to baptism, he suggested a second:

> Major premise: To whom the Gospel-covenant agrees, to them the sign of the Gospel-covenant agrees also.
> Minor premise: But to Infants of Believers the Gospel-covenant agrees,
> Conclusion: [A]nd consequently Baptisme.[19]

After giving the four reasons above why this is not exegetically or theologically accurate, he concluded his first and most fundamental argument:

> Whereupon I answer to the Argument: First, either by denying the *Major*, if it be universally taken, otherwise it concludes nothing: or by granting it with this limitation; it is true of that sign of the covenant which agrees universally in respect of form and sanction, to them that receive the Gospel, but it is not true of that sign of the covenant, which is of a particular form or sanction, of which sort is circumcision.
> Secondly, I answer by denying the *Minor*, universally taken, the reason is, because those children only of believing *Gentiles*, are *Abrahams* children, who are his spiritual seed, according to the election of grace by faith, which are not known to us, but by profession, or speciall Revelation.[20]

---

[18] Tombes, *Exercitation*, 1.
[19] Tombes, *Exercitation*, 1ff.

Here, Tombes, in a summary, has given his refutation of the argument from Genesis 17:7. He denied the major premise to be universal. Circumcision was a particular part of a particular covenant made with Abraham. Circumcision fits within the structure of that narrow covenantal application to Abraham's descendants physically. It was a sanction or stipulation from God to Abraham for his house through procreation. Baptism, for Tombes, was a covenantal stipulation through the new covenant because of, and not antecedent to, regeneration.

However, within Tombes' conclusion there is this explanatory comment, "[T]he reason is, because those children only of believing *Gentiles,* are *Abrahams* children, who are his spiritual seed, according to the election of grace by faith."[21] The true children of Abraham are those who are brought into his family through an act of God. They are the professors of faith because they have known something of the work of God and, as much as man can tell from their fruit, they are possessors of faith. Based on these realities, the professors should receive the sign of the new covenant, baptism.

Baptism ought to be administered after the new birth has been given and a credible profession of faith, backed by a life transformed and being transformed by God's discipling grace. In that regard, perhaps, infants are the ones to be baptized—not infants by natural descent, but spiritual babes, who have been born again and now rest in the bosom of Christ. This fits the pattern of the early church, the testimony of Scripture, and a system of truth that honors the covenants God made within himself, with various men, families and nations, and his own unique people.

---

[20] Tombes, *Exercitation,* 5.

[21] Tombes, *Exercitation,* 5.

Chapter 3

John Owen, Baptism, and the Baptists

Crawford Gribben*

John Owen was, as Jim Renihan has put it, "the greatest English-speaking theologian," a commendation made all the more significant by the fact that Owen worked in a century of outstanding theological achievement and in extraordinarily diverse and sometimes dangerous circumstances.[1] Born in humble circumstances in the reign of James I, and ordained as an Anglican priest under Charles I, Owen became preacher to the Long Parliament (from 1646), preacher of the regicide (1649), chaplain to Oliver Cromwell on the invasions of Ireland and Scotland (1649-50), dean of Christ Church (1651-60) and vice-chancellor of the University of Oxford (1652-57), principal mover in the Cromwellian religious settlement, and active agent in the downfall of Richard Cromwell's administration (1659). The changing legal and cultural circumstances of the reign of Charles II forced Owen to withdraw from public life and facilitated the reenergizing of his already prolific publishing career in defense of high Calvinist theology and the toleration of Protestant dissenters. His complex and often difficult writing has been frequently reprinted in the centuries since his death, and now attracts more readers than ever before. Owen, who guided English Puritans through some of their darkest days,

* Crawford Gribben, Ph.D., is Professor of Early Modern Baptist History, Queen's University, Belfast, and author of *John Owen and English Puritanism: Experiences of Defeat* (Oxford: Oxford University Press, forthcoming). This chapter celebrates the extraordinary achievements of Jim Renihan, doyen of the historical and theological study of seventeenth-century Particular Baptists—and much else. The lecture on which this chapter is based was presented as the Annual Lecture of the Strict Baptist Historical Society, delivered at Kensington Particular Baptist chapel, London, on March 20, 2015, and is published simultaneously by the Society.

[1] James Renihan, "Foreword," Richard C. Barcellos, *The Lord's Supper as a Means of Grace: More than a Memory* (Fearn, Ross-shire, UK: Mentor, 2013), 14.

continues to guide a great deal of evangelical theological discussion.

In recent years, the significance of Owen's work has been debated by those who advocate the baptism of believers and those who argue instead for the baptism of believers and their children.[2] The debate is a complex one, for, as all participants in this debate recognize, Owen "wrote little about baptism," and what he did write is not always especially pertinent to these recent discussions.[3] Participants in this debate are not arguing about Owen's convictions as to the proper subjects of the sacrament: it seems clear, from his few references to the subject, that Owen consistently taught that the children of believers should be baptized, though there are times when he could have done so much more vigorously. Instead, the discussion addresses the issue of whether Owen's covenantal theology supported his practice of infant baptism, and good cases for his consistency, which have been made by Lee Gatiss, Mark Jones, and Stephen Westcott, among others, have recently been challenged.[4] It is also important to note that this debate echoes earlier discussions of the theme: some of Owen's contemporaries worried that his innovative covenant theology was giving too much away to "anti-peadobaptists," even as his Particular Baptist contemporaries rushed to appropriate his claims.[5] But it is also important to note that Owen's baptismal theology is so manifold in its long evolution that parties other than Particular Baptists and

---

[2] Richard C. Barcellos, ed., *Recovering a Covenantal Heritage: Essays in Baptist Covenant Theology* (Palmdale, CA: RBAP, 2014); Pascal Denault, *The Distinctiveness of Baptist Covenant Theology: A Comparison Between Seventeenth-Century Particular Baptist and Paedobaptist Federalism* (Birmingham, AL: Solid Ground Christian Books, 2013); Samuel Renihan, "'Dolphins in the woods': A critique of Mark Jones and Ted Van Raalte's presentation of Particular Baptist covenant theology," *Journal of the Institute of Reformed Baptist Studies* (2015): 63-90.

[3] Ryan M. McGraw, *A Heavenly Directory: Trinitarian Piety, Public Worship and a Reassessment of John Owen's Theology* (Bristol, CT: Vandenhoeck & Ruprecht, 2014), 111.

[4] Lee Gatiss, "From life's first cry: John Owen on infant baptism and infant salvation," in Kelly M. Kapic and Mark Jones, eds., *The Ashgate Research Companion to John Owen's Theology* (Farnham, UK: Ashgate, 2012), 271-82; Stephen P. Westcott, *By the Bible Alone! John Owen's Puritan Theology for Today's Church* (Fellsmere, FL: Reformation Media & Press, 2010), 546-57; Ronald D. Miller, James M. Renihan, and Francisco Orozco, eds., *Covenant Theology from Adam to Christ* (Palmdale, CA: Reformed Baptist Academic Press, 2005).

[5] McGraw, *A Heavenly Directory*, 174.

Reformed paedobaptists might legitimately lay claim to his legacy. Some of the positions taken in the recent debate about Owen's theology of covenants and baptism call attention to their own limitations even as they pay attention to some of the most important nuances in his argument.

The first erroneous assumption made by many participants in the debate is that Owen consistently defended the same ideas. It is not clear that this is the case.[6] Even within the locus of covenant theology, as Christopher Caughey has recently illustrated, Owen was able to argue both for and against the claim of the Westminster Confession of Faith that two dispensations existed within the covenant of grace—and this simultaneously. So, on the one hand, Owen could argue that his position on the Mosaic covenant was, as Caughey has put it, "only semantically and not substantially different [from] that of his peers who affirmed the Westminster formulation," a position which he had replicated in the Savoy Declaration. On the other hand, within the space of a few pages, he could also confirm that "Scripture doth plainly and expressly make mention of *two Testaments or Covenants,* and distinguish between them in such a way, as what is spoken can hardly be accommodated."[7] Owen did change his mind, but he was also capable of extraordinary nuance—sometimes verging on self-contradiction.

The second erroneous assumption made by some of the participants in this debate is that Owen's position on baptism did not change. This is partly right: it seems clear that Owen did continue to argue for the baptism of the children of believers. But this is also partly wrong: Owen changed, sometimes in foundational ways, the meaning he attached to the sacrament, and the identification of the grace of which it was a means. In this study, therefore, I will document Owen's changing theology of baptism, and describe corresponding changes in his attitude to the advocates of the baptism of believers, before reflecting upon the increasing

---

[6] See Crawford Gribben, *John Owen and English Puritanism: Experiences of Defeat* (Oxford: Oxford University Press, forthcoming), passim.

[7] Owen as quoted by Chistopher E. Caughey, "Puritan responses to antinomianism in the context of Reformed covenant theology, 1630-1696" (Ph.D. diss., Trinity College Dublin, 2013), 116.

disparity between his baptismal theology and practice.

I

Owen's early attitude to Baptists reflected the widespread suspicion of this new religious movement. Owen's earliest pastoral charge was in Essex, where Baptist preachers regularly itincratcd. His clerical neighbour, Ralph Josselin, recorded their impact in his journal, describing a "separatists sermon against learning, a more poore peice, men of ignorance and of very great and high conceits,"[8] and the suicide of an old man with "separatist" links.[9] In April 1645, Josselin was subject to the "reproaches" of an "Anabaptist,"[10] and exactly one year later he noted that "an Anabaptist, rebaptizing a mayde who dyed presently[,] was committed to prison."[11] (Josselin later recorded that he had publicly debated a Baptist, who would turn out to be the father of Titus Oates.[12]) Throughout this period, the Long Parliament, influenced by the Westminster Assembly, was working towards its Blasphemy Act (1648). This Act criminalized all dissent, including the public preaching of Baptist views—and it attached penalties of imprisonment to this crime of faith. Although the Act was never implemented, due to the army coup in December 1648, Owcn wao writing about baptiom in the context of a theologically conservative political culture which was turning Baptists into criminals. This was the social context in which Owen's earliest views of baptism, and Baptists, were developed.

Consequently, Owen's early views of Baptists were not positive, and his early writing developed a corresponding view of baptism. His earliest reference to the subject actually occurs in his first published work. *A Display of Arminianisme* (1643) is not Owen's most polished piece of polemic and makes sometimes confusing arguments against the theological party which had taken power in

---

[8] *The Diary of Ralph Josselin, 1616-1683*, ed. Alan Macfarlane (Oxford: Oxford University Press, 1976), 34.

[9] *The Diary of Ralph Josselin*, ed. Macfarlane, 27.

[10] *The Diary of Ralph Josselin*, ed. Macfarlane, 38.

[11] *The Diary of Ralph Josselin*, ed. Macfarlane, 58.

[12] *The Diary of Ralph Josselin*, ed. Macfarlane, 63.

the established church. But this defense of the Reformed doctrine of divine sovereignty also advocated the power of sacraments. This is a telling moment in the development of Owen's theological mind — for, even as he rejected the claims of the Laudian party, he expressed a theology of baptism to which many Laudians could subscribe, and from which many members of the Westminster Assembly would wish to dissent. Owen's earliest discussion of baptism rejected the *ex opere operato* sacramental theology which he associated (not unfairly) with the Laudian party, but also refused to move in a Calvinist or Zwinglian direction.[13] In one of the most complex passages in *A Display of Arminianisme*, Owen insisted that baptism does achieve something: it takes away "that which hinders our salvation; which is not the first sin of Adam imputed, but our own inherent lust and pollution."[14] Owen was arguing that baptism removes the inherent sin of those baptized — that is, the guilt associated with sins that individuals have themselves committed. But it does not remove the guilt of the sin they have inherited from Adam, which continues to be imputed to them, presumably until their regeneration, though this is not a point which Owen develops. Owen may well have been aware of the pastoral as well as theological difficulties he was creating: he immediately moved to argue that un-baptized children dying in infancy were not necessarily damned, for God could save them, either on the basis that "their immediate or remote parents" were "believers," or by "his grace of election, which is most free, and not tied to any conditions; by which I make no doubt but God taketh many unto him in Christ whose parents never knew, or had been despisers of, the gospel."[15] It was an unsatisfactory conclusion, which betrayed assumptions which Owen may not have been able to align with other elements of his thinking, and may suggest that he was publishing a doctrine he had not sufficiently considered. It is telling that his future work would never delineate a theology of baptism in

---

[13] For a general account of the doctrine and practice of baptism in the period, see Will Coster, *Baptism and Spiritual Kinship in Early Modern England* (Aldershot, UK: Ashgate, 2002).

[14] *The works of John Owen*, ed. W. H. Goold (London: Johnstone and Hunter, 1850-55), 10:80.

[15] Owen, *Works*, 10:81.

similar terms.

Nevertheless, Owen's defense of the saving power of baptism has eluded many of his students, and it suggests something of the complexity of his early theological thinking. His emphasis on the efficacy of baptism reflects that of Cornelius Burgess, whose *Baptismall regeneration of elect infants professed by the Church of England, according to the Scriptures, the primitive Church, the present reformed churches, and many particular divines apart* (1629) was published in Oxford around the same time that Owen began university studies in the city.[16] Burgess complained that he had been "peremptorily censured and condemned by many, as guilty not only of *Arminianisme*, but even of direct *Popery*, and of teaching a *Doctrine of divells*," although his book illustrated that a high view of the efficacy of baptism could be aligned with hostility to Arminian theology.[17] But for Burgess, and those who followed him, the conviction that regeneration was effected in the baptism of elect infants was a central tenet of the Church of England, which was supported by the arguments of the best of the Continental Protestant divines. Owen's argument did not immediately map onto Burgess', however it anticipated ideas later developed by Leonard Van Rijssen (1695).[18] But it indicates the existence of a party within the Church of England which was simultaneously hostile to Arminianism and supportive of the idea that regeneration, in certain circumstances, was effected by baptism.

Of course, Owen's argument about the efficacy of baptism created an important problem in his analysis. His admission that an un-baptized child which had died without hearing or responding to the gospel could be saved on the basis of the faith of her "immediate or remote parents," or merely by the "grace of election," raised the question of the destiny of other kinds of people who had a similar lack of access to the truth. The claim by Arminian and Socinian authors that the heathen could be saved by paying attention to

---

[16] *The Diary of Thomas Crosfield*, ed. F. S. Boas (London: Oxford University Press, 1935), 38.

[17] Cornelius Burgess, *Baptismall regeneration of elect infants professed by the Church of England, according to the Scriptures, the primitiue Church, the present reformed churches, and many particular divines apart* (1629), 4.

[18] Heinrich Heppe, *Reformed Dogmatics*, trans. G. T. Thomson (London: George Allen & Unwin, 1950), 619.

natural revelation cried out for qualification, for Owen was sure that salvation could not be attained by the "conduct of nature, without the knowledge of Christ."[19] If the heathen were to be saved, he concluded, it would be on the basis of special revelation rather than general revelation. And so, not wishing to "straighten the breast and shorten the arm of the Almighty," Owen found himself allowing the possibility that individuals could be recipients of extraordinary revelation, which they could believe and so be saved, outside the boundaries of the canon of Scripture and the visible church.[20] But he never explained how these individuals could be saved without their inherent sin being removed by baptism.

Owen's earliest discussion of baptism was fraught with tensions which he sought to avoid in his later work. Two years later, in 1645, Owen included in the shorter catechism which he drew up for the benefit of his congregation in Fordham, Essex, another reference to his high view of the sacramental efficacy of baptism. The catechism represented a modification of Owen's view that baptism removes inherent, but not imputed, sins, claiming instead that baptism is "an holy Ordinance, whereby being sprinkled with water according to Christ's institution, we are by his grace made children of God, and have the promises of the Covenant sealed unto us."[21] As before, Owen made no restriction as to those to whom baptism was thus effective—he did not limit this benefit of baptism to the elect, though presumably this is what he advocated as he searched for a usable sacramental theology.

So Owen may have found unsatisfactory his early attempts to define a theology of baptism. He began to withdraw from his robust sacramentalism, perhaps because of its divergence from the account of baptism offered in the new liturgical standard published with the authority of Parliament, the Westminster Assembly's Directory for Public Worship. The Directory allowed that baptism could be performed by "pouring or sprinkling," and not only, as Owen had insisted, by sprinkling; and it argued that the children of believers were already "Christians, and federally holy before Baptisme," and not, as Owen had insisted, turned into children of God by baptism.[22]

---

[19] Owen, *Works*, 10:14, 111.
[20] Owen, *Works*, 10:111.
[21] Owen, *Works*, 1:469.

It may be that Owen withdrew from his realist language because he found himself out of step with the thinking of the most important clerical assembly of the day, a body by which he would have been interviewed as part of his move from Fordham to his second pastoral charge at Coggeshall.[23] And this was not the only area in which Owen would have to revise his early thinking.

Owen expressed the ambiguity of these early years in the terms which he used to describe his theological position. In 1646, he dismissed the Anabaptists at Münster as seditious sectaries.[24] But he struggled to define his own position. Reflecting on the divisions of Christendom, the bifurcation of Protestants, and the parties within the English church, Owen admitted that his position could be described as that of a "Calvinistical, sacramentarian sectary."[25] Despite the neo-Ramist precision by which Owen had arrived at this descriptor, its key term was ambiguous. "Sacramentarian" had been introduced by Lutheran polemic in the mid-sixteenth century. By the early seventeenth century, it was being used in English to refer to those who opposed Luther's view of the real presence in the Lord's Supper, describing those who held a relatively low view of the sacrament: in 1624, for example, William Bedell referred to the "vehement speeches of Luther and some of his followers against those whom they call the Sacramentarians."[26] By the mid-seventeenth century, the term had developed new resonances, and could also describe those with a high view of the sacraments: in 1651, Noah Biggs dismissed those whom he called "papall Sacramentarians."[27] So Owen's recognition that his enemies could describe him as a "Calvinistical, sacramentarian sectary" reveals very little about his position on baptism or the Lord's Supper. For while "sacramentarian" could be used as a synonym for "Calvinist," its broader usage implied both a high and low view of sacramental efficacy.

---

[22] [Westminster Assembly,] *A directory for the publique worship of God in the three kingdomes* (1645), 20.

[23] Gribben, *John Owen and English Puritanism*, forthcoming.

[24] Owen, *Works*, 8:59.

[25] Owen, *Works*, 8:47.

[26] *OED*, s.v.

[27] Noah Biggs, *Matæotechnia medicinæ praxeos: The vanity of the craft of physic* (1651), 214; *OED*, s.v.

By the end of the 1640s, however, and as Owen's career took off, he grew less inclined to write about the meaning and effect of baptism. This may simply have reflected the pressure of new and often political responsibilities: as England was swept into the vortex of revolution, Owen became the favorite preacher of the army leaders, addressing Parliament on the day after the execution of Charles I; he was appointed as Cromwell's chaplain in the invasions of Ireland and Scotland, during which period he witnessed at first hand the horrors of early modern warfare; during the 1650s he settled down to become the dean of Christ Church, the vice-chancellor of the university of Oxford, and the chief architect of the republic's new religious settlement; and after the Restoration he became the pastor of a small and often discouraged community of dissenters. In fact, as we will see, Owen's responsibilities in planning the Cromwellian state church may have shaped the new view of baptism and the Baptists which he appears to have developed in 1652 and which he continued to defend thereafter. And the reason for his change of heart may be simple enough—for it is in 1652 that Owen may have met his first Baptists.

II

The occasion for Owen's meeting his first Baptists was prompted by England's first moral panic—a panic associated with the publication of the Racovian catechism (1651). This catechism, which appeared in Latin and in English translation, advocated Socinian views of the Godhead. Owen and a committee of leading Independents took advantage of the public furor to present a petition to Parliament which listed the catechism's serious errors—among them its defense of believer's baptism.[28] The committee appealed to Parliament to establish a new confession of faith and to more carefully monitor ministers and preachers. Parliament's response was to set up panels of "triers" and "ejectors," whose job it was to evaluate the orthodoxy and piety of ministers and preachers. And when Parliament established these panels in 1652, Owen found himself working for the first time alongside Baptists. The results must have

---

[28] Gribben, *John Owen and English Puritanism*, chapter five, forthcoming.

been satisfactory, for Parliament followed this by appointing Owen and several other Baptists, including Henry Jessey, to another committee charged with overseeing the production of accurate copies of Scripture.[29] Owen likely discovered that his new friends were much more orthodox than he had suspected—and that their position was far closer to his than was that of the Presbyterians with whom he had formerly been allied. Whatever the tone of these early encounters, Owen's sympathetic and supportive associations with Baptists were to continue throughout the rest of the decade, and far beyond.

Owen's return in his writing to the subject of baptism reflected this positive opinion of his new associates. After around eight years of silence on the issue of baptism, Owen's position had substantially moderated, and was now significantly to change. He was now clearly opposed to the theology of baptismal regeneration with which his earliest writing had toyed. In the *Doctrine of the Saints Perseverance* (1654), Owen explained that the theology of baptismal regeneration could not be supported by Titus 3:3-5.[30] He continued to regard the church as a baptized community, for the apostles and fathers considered "all baptized persons, continuing in the profession of the faith and communion of the church," to be "truly regenerate and justified, and spake so of them."[31] But, he continued, the apostles did not consider that this regeneration had been effected by or in baptism. Owen now associated baptism with a different kind of grace. In his discussion of the *Mortification of Sin* (1656; second ed. 1658), for example, Owen referred to baptism as a help in sanctification, while remaining curiously silent about the comparable status of the Lord's Supper or Christian fellowship. "We have in baptism an evidence of our implantation into Christ; we are baptized into him" in "his death," Owen explained.[32] Our being "baptized into the death of Christ" represents the mortification of our corruptions, with our total "conformity" to the experience of Christ, "so that as he was raised up to glory, we may be raised up to grace and newness of life."[33] Owen's discussion of

---

[29] *CSPD* 26:1-74.
[30] Owen, *Works*, 11:552.
[31] Owen, *Works*, 11:65.
[32] Owen, *Works*, 6:84.

the meaning of baptism emphasized its being a sign and a promise of the believer's status as being dead to sin. This re-appropriation of baptismal texts in discussions of sanctification continued in 1657, in Owen's discussion *Of Communion with God*. Owen discussed the opening section of Romans 6 in relation to sanctification, rather than baptism,[34] before going on to explain baptism as something which "signified" the "washing away of sin, and repentance from sin."[35] Turning again to Titus 3:3-5, Owen explained that the "washing of regeneration" related to "the grace of sanctification" in general, rather than to the new birth in particular.[36] In the mid 1650s, Owen's strategy seemed to be to read baptismal texts as bearing realistic language but in relation to progressive sanctification rather than to regeneration.

Owen was also considering whether baptism had any ecclesial significance. He had come to distinguish baptism not just from the application of salvation but also from the experience of joining a church. In *A Vindication of the Treatise on Schism* (1657), he argued that baptism "precedes admission into church membership, as to a particular church; the subjects of it are professing believers and their seed; as such they have right unto it, whether they be joined to any particular church or no." He insisted that "this judgment hath been my constant and uninterrupted practice" (though his claims to consistency should not always be taken at face value).[37] But Owen was also careful to defend those who denied the "rights" of the seed of believers. His *A Vindication of the Treatise on Schism* (1657) refused to admit that those individuals who renounced and repeated the baptism they had received as infants should be described as schismatic. In the face of widespread criticism, he defended Baptists from the charge of repeating the Donatist heresy, on the rather fine basis that the Baptists "do the same thing with them, but not on the same principles." Owen explained that the Donatists had claimed that they alone were the true church and consequently they alone could administer sacraments, and that the baptisms of candidates

---

33 Owen, *Works*, 6:84.
34 Owen, *Works*, 2:100.
35 Owen, *Works*, 2:161.
36 Owen, *Works*, 2:171.
37 Owen, *Works*, 13:259.

for membership had to be repeated. While Baptists also repeat the baptism of infants, Owen continued, they do so for different reasons, "that though baptism be, yet infant baptism is not, an institution of Christ, and so is null from the nature of the thing itself, not the way of its administration."[38] Owen continued to defend Baptists in his response to a work of Catholic apologetic, *Fiat lux* (1662).[39] Time and time again, when faced with an opportunity to critique the new religious movement which so many of his peers abominated, Owen refused to do so. Time and time again, he defended them from their critics.

Yet Owen continued to argue for the baptism of believers' children. The Savoy Declaration (1658), which he signed, argued that believers' children should be baptized while also arguing that these children were not thereby made members of a local church. Owen supported this statement while recognizing that the distinctions made in the Savoy Declaration were not reflected in the biblical and patristic evidence. In the *Discourse concerning Liturgies* (1662), for example, he recognized the metaphorical status of the baptismal texts he had formerly read in realist terms. Echoing his earlier argument, he insisted that the apostles and fathers regarded "all baptized, initiated persons, ingrafted into the church, as sanctified persons,"[40] even as he recognized that the early church required candidates to prepare for their baptism.[41] But Owen made this claim while also defending the proposition, in *A Brief Instruction in the Worship of God* (1667), that the "proper subjects of baptism" are "professing believers . . . and their infant seed," who, he was careful to argue, were not by baptism made members of the church.[42]

One of the longest of Owen's discussions of baptism may be found in his exposition of Psalm 130 (1668). Owen argued that baptism began as an ordinance of God with John, whose baptism was instituted "to declare the 'remissions of sins.'" Christ submitted to John's baptism for the same reason that he was circumcised, as being "under the law" and consequently required to "observe all

---

[38] Owen, *Works*, 13:184.
[39] Owen, *Works*, 14:82-83.
[40] Owen, *Works*, 10:367.
[41] Owen, *Works*, 15:23.
[42] Owen, *Works*, 15:512.

ordinances and institutions of the worship of God," though "not for any need he had in his own person of the especial ends and significations of some of them." For baptism was "a declaration of that forgiveness which is with God," Owen continued, and John was commanded to baptize those "who, confessing their sins, and professing repentance of them, should come to him to have a testimony of forgiveness." Thus, while continuing to link baptism with the promise of forgiveness, Owen backed away from his earlier realist language to describe the sacrament as working to

> represent the certainty and truth of his grace in pardon unto their senses by a visible pledge. [God] lets them know that he would take away their sin, wherein their spiritual defilement doth consist, even as water takes away the outward filth of the body.[43]

All of this Owen claimed for the baptism of John—he described John's baptism as a "visible pledge" and a representation of the promise that God will forgive sinners, a promise that was given to those sinners who came to John "confessing their sins" and seeking "a testimony of forgiveness." He, however, did not explain how this might permit or require the baptism of the children of these repenting sinners.

But Owen's discussion of the redemptive history of baptism continued as he explained how the sacrament gained dominical status. For after the ministry of John, Christ took baptism "into his own hand, and commands the observance of it unto all his disciples." Critically, Owen refuses at this point to "dispute . . . who are the proper immediate objects of [baptism]; whether they only who actually can make profession of their faith, or believers with their infant seed. For my part," he continued, "I believe that all whom Christ loves and pardons are to be made partakers of the pledge thereof."[44] Without further qualification, this was an extraordinary claim for Owen to make, but it is typical of the elliptical way in which he dealt with the subject throughout his published writings.

---

[43] Owen, *Works*, 6:465-66.
[44] Owen, *Works*, 6:466.

Owen's refusal to attack the theology of believer-baptism was followed by an admission that he understood the hesitations of those early Christians who refused to baptize their children:

> the sole reason why they of old insisted on why the infants of believing parents should not be baptized was, because they thought they had no sin; and therein we know their mistake. But I treat not now of these things. Only this I say is certain, that in the prescription of this ordinance unto his church, the great intention of the Lord Christ was to ascertain unto us forgiveness of sins. And sinners are invited to a participation of this ordinance for that end, that they may receive the pardon of their sins; that is, an infallible pledge and assurance of it, Acts ii. 38.[45]

Owen's overriding concern in discussing Baptists was not to critique their ideas, therefore, but to defend them from their antagonists. Sometime in the mid 1660s, for example, Owen wrote to a friend to advise him of the growth of a local Baptist community, commenting sympathetically on the opposition they were facing:

> A troop (viz. the county troop) came to Theobalds last Lords day thinking to catch the Anabaptists at their meeting, but you would not thinke how many came to warne them of it, so they dispersed and though the troopers stood gazing 3 or 4 hours on high ground to watch their rendezvous, yet they escaped their sight and met in a wood undiscovered.[46]

Later, in March 1669, Owen and other Independent clergy signed a letter to the Governor of Massachusetts, complaining of the colony's treatment of Baptists.[47] Later that year, Owen wrote to the Independent church in Hitchin, attempting to heal divisions which had been caused by the withdrawal of five members who had become convinced of believers' baptism, and advising the church

---

[45] Owen, *Works*, 6:466.

[46] *The Correspondence of John Owen*, ed. Peter Toon (Cambridge: James Clarke, 1970), 132-34.

[47] *The Correspondence of John Owen*, ed. Toon, 145-46.

members to respond to the secession of the Baptists with prayer and love, rather than with condemnation.[48] It may have been around this time that, according to an apocryphal story, Owen expressed his admiration for the preaching of Bunyan in a conversation with Charles II.

It is easy to see why seventeenth-century Baptists might have regarded Owen as a fellow-traveller. In his *Discourse concerning Christian Love and Peace* (1672), Owen explained that individuals could become disciples by "the preaching of the gospel and baptism,"[49] and that disciples could become members of local churches if they could evidence "baptism, with a voluntary credible profession of faith, repentance, and obedience unto the Lord Christ, in his commands and institutions."[50] Those who have been baptized into the catholic, visible church become "complete members of that church" upon their "personal avowment of that faith whereinto they were baptised."[51] Yet Owen does not appear to have been concerned that his arguments were supporting the cause of the Baptists.

But Owen did continue to be concerned by the possible appeal of theories of baptismal regeneration. In his treatise on justification (1677), he dismissed arguments that baptism washes away "any spiritual filth or stain of our nature" — which was, more or less, the position he had outlined in his first publication.[52] But this rejection of sacramental theory did not lead him to argue that baptism was unimportant. Reading Acts 2, Owen noted that baptism was "joined with faith no less than repentance."[53] Baptism was linked with spiritual privileges, but Owen could only explain why this was so by assuming the normative status of the baptism of believers. In *The Nature and Causes of Apostasy* (1676), he noted that

> baptism really was the beginning and foundation of a participation of all the other spiritual privileges that are

---

[48] *The Correspondence of John Owen*, ed. Toon, 146-48.

[49] Owen, *Works*, 15:144.

[50] Owen, *Works*, 15:154.

[51] Owen, *Works*, 15:95.

[52] Owen, *Works*, 5:21.

[53] Owen, *Works*, 5:105.

mentioned afterwards; for it was usual in those times, that, upon the baptizing of persons, the Holy Ghost came upon them, and endowed them with extraordinary gifts, peculiar to the days of the gospel.[54]

His focus on the normative status of the baptism of believers is striking. But he continued to defend the practice of infant baptism in vigorous terms.[55]

III

Owen's posthumous publications expanded upon his mature conclusions, but they also, in some senses, challenged them. *The True Nature of a Gospel Church and its Government* (1689) described baptism as the "symbol, the sign, the expression, and representation" of regeneration:

> unto those who are in a due manner partakers of it, it giveth all the external rights and privileges which belong unto them that are regenerate, until they come unto such seasons wherein the personal performance of those duties whereon the continuation of the estate of visible regeneration doth depend is required of them. Herein if they fail, they lose all privilege and benefit by their baptism.[56]

Baptism, Owen continued, effects a covenant between God and the baptized individual, "for it will give him a right unto all the outward privileges of a regenerate state," but, upon the individual's failure to maintain his obligations, "in the sight of God, his baptism is no baptism, as unto the real communication of grace and acceptance with him . . . So, in the sight of the church, it is no baptism, as unto a participation of the external rights and privileges

---

[54] Owen, *Works*, 7:18.

[55] John Owen, *An Exposition of the Epistle to the Hebrews*, ed. W. H. Goold, 7 vols. (Edinburgh: T&T Clark, 1862), 4:418. I owe this reference to Rev. Stephen Steele.

[56] Owen, *Works*, 16:12.

of a regenerate state."[57] Owen was clear that "conviction and confession of sin, with the way of deliverance by Jesus Christ, is that 'answer of a good conscience' that is required in the baptism of them that are adult," admitting that at least some of the New Testament descriptions of baptism could refer only to professing believers.[58] But here too Owen's theology was developing in unexpected ways, presupposing that the covenant reflected in baptism was a covenant of works, even as the covenant to which the sacrament pointed was a covenant of grace.

It is significant that the only one of Owen's texts which dealt exclusively with the subject of baptism was also posthumously published. Much of the recent debate on his view of baptism has centered upon a very short tract entitled *Of Infant Baptism and Dipping*, which was first published in a collection of Owen materials in 1721, in a volume edited by John Asty from manuscripts which had belonged to Sir John Hartropp. Asty does not explain when the text was written, whether it was intended to be a separately published item, nor why Owen did not publish it within his own lifetime. For Owen may not have been its author. Some of the texts within the edition were taken from manuscripts on Owen's hand, while others were "taken from his mouth by a Gentleman of honour and known integrity."[59] The tract's abbreviated form, and its lack of intellectual development, suggests that it may have its provenance in these auditor's notes. Despite this lack of information about the provenance of the tract, Gatiss has speculated that Owen may have completed its writing around 1657-8, on the basis that Asty's edition juxtaposes the tract with a response to Tombes' *Antipeadobaptism* (1657).[60] What is certain, however, is that Owen did not publish *Of Infant Baptism and Dipping* within his own lifetime, and that the text did not circulate as representing his thinking on this issue for almost 40 years after his death when it appeared in a volume alongside other texts reconstructed from auditor's notes. It is not clear what the text represents.

---

[57] Owen, *Works*, 16:13.

[58] Owen, *Works*, 16:16.

[59] *A Complete Collection of the Sermons of the Reverend and Learned John Owen*, ed. John Asty (1721), "Preface," n.p.

[60] Gatiss, "From life's first cry," 271, n. 4.

IV

As this survey suggests, therefore, Owen's theology of baptism and his attitude to Baptists does not lend itself to easy or unqualified appropriation by any of the parties involved in the current debate about his arguments. Owen developed his views on baptism—and his views of Baptists—in the changing contexts of the 1640s and 1650s. Owen did not substantially modify his views on baptism after the mid-1650s. His relationships with Baptists followed in parallel. And some of his posthumous publications qualify and complicate his earlier and clearer arguments.

Even in his own lifetime, Owen's view of baptism and associated subjects was the center of controversy. It is telling that some of Owen's Presbyterian contemporaries felt that he had given too much away to their sacramental antagonists, even as some of his Baptist contemporaries eagerly appropriated and identified themselves with his federal theological work. Modern Baptists may share aspects of his covenant theology, but they do not share his baptismal practice. Owen's modern paedobaptist defenders may share his practice, but do not regularly support his covenant theology, and rarely adhere to any of the meanings of baptism which Owen's early writings advanced. Owen employed several theologies of baptism to support a single baptismal practice over the course of his very long life. Owen's thought evolved in specific contexts—but there is little doubt about the direction it was taking.

Owen's changing baptismal theology was reflected in new attitudes of tolerance towards and protection of the advocates of the baptism of believers. He never attacked Baptists in print. He may have continued to baptize the children of believers—but his ongoing clarification of covenant theology and his enduring commitment to a visible saints ecclesiology meant that this was a practice which was increasingly out of step with his presuppositions, and increasingly lacking in theological rationale. Owen celebrated the catholic and visible church as being united in the "same Lord, faith, and baptism,"[61] but his own views on

---

[61] Owen, *Works*, 15:82-83.

baptism, as David Wright once put it, increasingly reflected "a practice in search of a theology."

Chapter 4

"Popery in new Dress"

Richard Baxter v. Benjamin Keach

on the Doctrine of Justification

Tom Hicks[*]

Dr. James M. Renihan's academic work has been a wonderful blessing to me over the years. I am deeply grateful for his faithful labors on behalf of the church, and I consider it an honor to contribute this chapter to his *festschrift*. I share Renihan's commitment to confessionally orthodox Reformed Baptist theology, and I have been greatly edified by his desire to see confessional orthodoxy practically and consistently applied in the context of local Baptist churches.[1] I am also thankful for his commitment to the orthodox doctrine of justification in a day when that glorious doctrine, which is at the heart of the gospel, has come under attack once again. One does not have to look very far to see remarkable affinity between historical errors on the doctrine of justification, such as that of Richard Baxter, and some of today's aberrant formulations.[2]

---

[*] Tom Hicks, Ph.D., is a pastor of Morningview Baptist Church, Montgomery, AL (www.morningview.org), author of "The Doctrine of Justification in the Theologies of Richard Baxter and Benjamin Keach" (Ph.D. diss, The Southern Baptist Theological Seminary) and of chapters in *Ministry by His Grace and For His Glory: Essays in Honor of Thomas J. Nettles*, *Recovering a Covenantal Heritage: Essays in Baptist Covenant Theology*, and *Whomever He Wills: A Surprising Display of God's Sovereign Mercy*.

[1] See Renihan's work on how historic Baptists applied confessional orthodoxy in Baptist churches: James M. Renihan, *Edification and Beauty: The Practical Ecclesiology of the English Particular Baptists, 1675-1705* (Eugene, OR: Wipf & Stock, 2008).

[2] The reader may notice certain affinities between Baxter's doctrine of justification and the doctrines of justification advocated by proponents of the New

In an article analyzing Richard Baxter's doctrine of justification and pastoral methodology, Renihan accurately stated, "Baxter's theology is at best heterodox and at worst heretical; his pastoral theology must therefore be treated with the greatest of caution."[3] I agree with Renihan that wise pastors should exercise caution with Baxter's practical works, such as *The Reformed Pastor*[4] and *A Christian Directory*[5] because Baxter's practical theology is rooted in and grows out of his deeply flawed understanding of the doctrine of justification and the gospel.[6] When theologians get the doctrine of justification wrong, they inevitably get the doctrine of the Christian life wrong as well. No one understood this better than Benjamin Keach, arguably the greatest theologian among Baptists of the second generation seventeenth-century Particular Baptists. As we will see in the following discussion, Keach believed that Baxter compromised the gospel and thus undermined the foundation of the whole Christian life.

This chapter will provide some historical background of the dispute between Baxter and Keach, and compare each man's respective doctrines, showing how Keach believed that Baxter not only departed from an orthodox formulation of justification, but also from the gospel of Jesus Christ itself.

Brief Historical Background

1. Richard Baxter's historical background relevant to the doctrine of justification

Richard Baxter was born in Rowton in Shropshire, England, on

Perspective, such as N. T. Wright, James Dunn, E. P. Sanders, etc., as well as proponents of the Federal Vision, such as Norman Shepherd, James Jordan, Peter Leithart, etc.

[3] James M. Renihan, "Reforming *The Reformed Pastor*: Baptism and Justification as the Basis for Richard Baxter's Pastoral Method," *The Reformed Baptist Theological Review* 2:1 (January 2005): 133.

[4] Richard Baxter, *The Reformed Pastor* (1656; reprint, Edinburgh; Carlisle, PA: Banner of Truth, 1994).

[5] Richard Baxter, *A Christian Directory* (1665; reprint, Morgan, PA: Soli Deo Gloria, 1996).

[6] See Renihan, "Reforming *The Reformed Pastor*," 111-34.

November 12, 1615. He was raised in an Anglican home in which his parents were devoted to Christ, loyal to the Church of England, and faithful to the Book of Common Prayer. In 1638, without any formal academic or theological training, Baxter was ordained in the Anglican Church by the Bishop of Worcester.

In 1642, the English Civil War broke out, and in 1644 Baxter left his position at Kidderminster to become an Army chaplain, until 1646. During his chaplaincy, Baxter preached once every Sunday to the soldiers and the townspeople. While Baxter served in the army, he was horrified by the open licentiousness of the soldiers. He was deeply disturbed by the way the soldiers excused their sinful lives by appealing to the imputed righteousness of Christ, and by claiming that they were justified by faith alone without any personal holiness. The soldiers boldly asserted that they had the right to sin with impunity because Christ had born all of their sins, past, present, and future.

As a result of his time as a chaplain in the army, Baxter became convinced that the Reformed doctrine of justification by faith alone on the ground of Christ's imputed righteousness alone necessarily leads to antinomianism. He did not believe that such a doctrine is the least bit compatible with holy living. He, therefore, set out to reformulate the doctrine in a way that necessarily involves human works.[7]

2. Benjamin Keach's historical background relevant to the doctrine of justification

Benjamin Keach was born to John and Fedora Keach on February 29, 1640, at Stoke Hammond, Buckinghamshire, England. He was converted when he was fifteen years old under the preaching of Matthew Mead, who was a warm evangelical Anglican Calvinist.

---

[7] For biographical information on Richard Baxter, see N. H. Keeble, *Richard Baxter: Puritan Man of Letters* (New York: Oxford, 1982); Marcus L. Loane, *Makers of Puritan History* (Grand Rapids: Baker Book House, 1980), 168-70; Geoffrey F. Nuttall, *Richard Baxter* (London: Thomas Nelson and Sons, 1965); Walter Wilson, *The History and Antiquities of the Dissenting Churches* (Paris, AR: Baptist Standard Bearer, 2004), 2:111-35.

When Keach was just eighteen years old, he demonstrated an aptitude for teaching and preaching; so, his home church ordained him for the preaching ministry, and he began to pastor a church in Winslow.

During his ministry, Keach was involved in a number of controversies, including baptism, hymn singing in public worship, the financial maintenance of ministers, Sunday Sabbath observance, and laying hands on baptized believers as an ordinance. Keach himself believed that his controversy with Baxter's neonomianism was one of the most important of all his polemical disputes because it was the most vital to the gospel itself. He initially decided to write against that error for pastoral reasons. Some people in his church had asked him to address the matter. When arguing against Baxter's doctrine, Keach understood that he was fighting against a "capital" error. Keach believed that neonomianism was nothing less than a full departure from the gospel. He wrote:

> We ought to keep clean from all errors, but especially such as are capital ones. I am afraid many good Christians are not sensible of the sad danger they are in. I cannot see but that the doctrine some men strive to promote, is but little better than popery in new dress. Nay one of the worst branches of it too, shall any who pretend to be true preachers of the gospel, go about to mix their own works or their sincere obedience with Christ's righteousness, nay, to put their obedience in the room and place of Christ's obedience, as that in which they trust and desire to be found? 2. Let me exhort you all to stand fast in that precious faith you have received; particularly about this great doctrine of justification, give your selves to prayer, and to the due and careful study of God's Word.[8]

Keach believed that Baxter's neonomianism was a reversion of the Roman Catholic doctrine of justification by faith and works and

---

[8] Benjamin Keach, *The Marrow of True Justification* (London: n.p., 1692), 17. All citations of Keach's works will modernize antiquated words and follow modern rules of capitalization.

a repudiation of the Reformed faith. Most of all, he believed it to be contrary to the Word of God.[9]

A New and Improved Law

1. Baxter's neonomian doctrine

Richard Baxter's system has been called "neonomianism," or "new-law-ism." His system might also be called "neocovenantalism" because, for Baxter, the words "law" and "covenant" are virtually interchangeable.

Baxter believed that when God created the world he made a covenant of works with Adam. That first covenant, or law, threatened death to any violation, and promised life to perfect, perpetual obedience. In his 1675 work, *Catholick Theologie*, Baxter said, "It pleased him first to make man perfect under a law of perfection, making innocency or perfection the only condition of life, and the contrary of death."[10]

Adam, however, sinned against this law of perfection, or covenant of works; therefore, according to Baxter, God graciously made a new law, or covenant of grace, that pardons sins against the first law, and provides terms easy enough for sinners to keep. This new law of grace is the gospel, according to Baxter. In his 1649 work, *Aphorisms of Justification*, Baxter wrote:

(1) Man having not only broken this first covenant, but disabled himself to perform its conditions for the future, and

---

[9] For biographical information on Benjamin Keach, see Thomas Crosby, *The History of the English Baptists* (London: n.p., 1739), 2:185-209; 3:143-47; 4:268-314; Michael A. G. Haykin, *Kiffin, Knollys, and Keach: Rediscovering Our English Baptist Heritage* (Leeds, UK: Reformation Today Trust, 1996), 82-103; Thomas J. Nettles, *The Baptists*, vol. 1, *Key People Involved in Forming a Baptist Identity* (Fearn, Ross-shire, Scotland: Mentor, 2005), 163-93; Austin Walker, *The Excellent Benjamin Keach* (Dundas, Ontario: Joshua Press, 2004); Walter Wilson, *The History and Antiquities of the Dissenting Churches* (London: n.p., 1808), 4:243-52.

[10] Richard Baxter, *Catholick Theologie*, vol. 1, Part 2, "Of God's Government and Moral Works" (London: n.p., 1675), 27. All citations of Baxter's works will modernize antiquated words and follow modern rules of capitalization.

so being out of all hope of attaining righteousness and life thereby, (2) it pleased the Father and the Mediator to prescribe unto him a new law, (3) and tender him a new covenant, (4) the conditions whereof should be more easy to the sinner and yet more abasing (5) and should more clearly manifest, and more highly honor the unconceivable love of the Father and Redeemer.[11]

The mild terms of the new law, or covenant of grace, include imperfect but sincere faith, love, and obedience. Baxter described the duties required under the covenant of grace in its new covenant administration:

It is plain in the Scripture, that when men are converted and baptized, the particular helps of grace are promised them upon further particular conditions: And that the continuance of pardon and right to life, is promised them upon the continuance of their faith, and use of means; and that actual glorification is promised them on condition of overcoming and persevering: And therefore that we must use and take all these as conditions.[12]

One, therefore, enters into the covenant of grace and a state of justification by means of faith and baptism, but he only retains his justification and continues in the covenant if he makes use of all the means, including the Word and sacrament, to persevere in faithful obedience to the end.

It is important to understand that while God added a new and easier law to the first law, he did not wholly abolish the first law of perfection. Believers who keep the new law are still subject to the guilt and penalties of the original law, or covenant of works. Baxter writes:

The commination of the said law [of perfection] is so far still in force, as to make punishment (even perpetual) to be our desert for every sin, and so far to oblige us to punishment,

---

[11] Richard Baxter, *Aphorisms of Justification* (London: n.p., 1649), 47-48.
[12] Baxter, *Catholick Theologie*, 1:2:73.

that if we are not pardoned, we shall not escape for it is natural for sin to deserve punishment.[13]

This means that when believers commit moral sins, they are guilty under the first law and bring themselves under its temporal punishments in this life. God only pardons the sins of believers if they repent and renew their faith and obedience under the terms of the new law. Therefore, believers are under two laws. They are under the first law, minus its rigor and its promise of eternal life.[14] God softened the first law by delaying and softening its penalties and adding some flexibility to it. But believers are also under a new law, which pardons sins against the first law and promises eternal life to their imperfect faithful obedience. The only way to sin against the new law of grace is to persist finally to the end of one's life in unbelief and impenitence, since Christ did not die for the sin of final unbelief. Baxter wrote, "the gospel threatens not death to any sin, but final unbelief and rebellion."[15] Therefore, when believers commit moral sins, they sin against the original law of works, and they incur its penalties, but because of the new law that they are also under, God will pardon the sins of believers, if they repent before the end of their lives.

To sum up, this new law doctrine is the key to understanding Baxter's doctrine of justification. According to Baxter, human beings are only justified when they conform to God's law. The first law required perfect obedience for justification. The second law pardons repentant sinners and requires their imperfect obedience for their justification. No sinful human being can keep the first law of works, but sinners can and do keep the second law of grace for justification.

2. Keach's response to Baxter's neonomianism

Keach argued that God could never justly relax or soften his own law. According to Keach, God does not stand above his law, so that he can issue or rescind laws by arbitrary fiat; rather, God's law is a

---

[13] Baxter, *Catholick Theologie*, 1:2:29.

[14] Baxter, *Catholick Theologie*, 1:2:29.

[15] Baxter, *Aphorisms*, 103.

reflection of his own glorious nature. His law is a necessary reflection of who he is. To say that God softens his law is to say that he compromises his own holiness, rectitude, and goodness. In 1692, Keach published two sermons, which he titled "The Marrow of True Justification." To Baxter's new law, he objected:

> Alas, sirs, the law of God is but as a transcript, or written impression of that holiness, and purity that is in his own nature, and serves to show us what a righteousness we must be found in, if we are ever justified in his sight. Nor can it be once supposed by any man, unless blinded, that God will ever loose or relax the sanction of his holy law, or abate a jot or tittle of that righteousness his holy nature and law requires in point of our being justified in his sight, it must be all fulfilled by us in our own persons, or by our surety for us, and imputed to us.
>
> The law did not only proceed from God, doubtless as an act of his sovereign will and prerogative, but as an act proceeding from his infinite justice and holiness.[16]

For Keach, Baxter's new law doctrine impugns God's holy character and darkens the radiance of his glory. Ironically, while Baxter was concerned about antinomianism among Christians, Keach believed that Baxter's theology made God out to be an antinomian. It appears that on Baxter's system, God refused to abide by his own law. He simply changed the law when it was convenient for him to do so.

Keach argued that not only is God's own glory diminished by Baxter's new law, but his glory is also diminished in believers who obey the new law. Keach said:

> For by this means says a learned author, God should lose much honor in making this second covenant, and granting such easy terms: for there is no comparison betwixt perfect obedience required by the law and due to God as our creator, and that imperfect obedience, which is accepted by the gospel, neither in quantity, quality, or duration. Here it

---

[16] Benjamin Keach, *The Marrow of True Justification* (London: n.p., 1692), 23.

is possible a man may be converted at the last hour and saved, though he have [*sic*] lived in rebellion against God many years. What little honor or service has God from such a man?[17]

Keach is demonstrating that a sinner's imperfect obedience to Baxter's new law is less pleasing and glorious than Christ's perfect obedience to the first law. Therefore, Keach says, God is less glorified by the obedience of believing sinners on Baxter's model. Keach believed that Christ's perfect obedience is imputed to believers; therefore, God is maximally glorified in every sinner who is joined to Christ.

Not only does Baxter's new law doctrine diminish the glory that God receives from believers, but Keach believed that it also gives them a ground of boasting. In his 1698 work, *The Display of Glorious Grace or The Covenant of Peace Opened*, Keach asserted:

They say, Christ has merited a new law, or easier terms and conditions, that our faith, obedience, and good works may justify, and save us; but what says Paul, 'All boasting is excluded;' not legal boasting only, but all boasting, but by their new law boasting is let in.[18]

Keach is arguing that on Baxter's model, the believer has a reason to boast because he is justified by his own gospel obedience to the new law. God accepts the believer and gives the believer a righteous status and a title to everlasting life, not because of the righteousness of another, but because of his own obedience to the terms of the new law.

To sum up, Keach finds Baxter's neonomianism objectionable for a number of reasons. First, if God were to soften his law, it would diminish his own glory, since his law is a reflection of his glory. Second, if God accepted the imperfect obedience of sinners to a soft law, then God would not receive great glory from their obedience. Third, if God gave sinners justification and life on the basis of a soft law that they could keep in their own persons, then sinners would have a ground for boasting.

---

[17] Keach, *The Marrow of True Justification*, 23.
[18] Benjamin Keach, *The Display of Glorious Grace* (London: n.p., 1698), 82.

The Non-Substitutionary Atonement of Jesus

1. Baxter's doctrine of Christ's atonement

Baxter's doctrine of the atonement denies the doctrine of penal substitution. He argued that Christ's atonement could not be strictly considered a substitution, since Christ did not actually pay the penalty of the law.

Baxter distinguished between "solution" and "satisfaction." To provide a "solution," according to Baxter, is to pay exactly what is owed, satisfying the debt itself, such that the payment cannot be refused. To provide a "satisfaction," on the other hand, is to give payment instead of the debt, satisfying the creditor. A satisfaction does not satisfy the debt, but only pays an equivalent value. A satisfaction may be justly refused, if it does not please the creditor. According to Baxter, Christ's atonement rendered "satisfaction" to the Lawgiver, but not "solution" to the law itself.[19]

Baxter provided a number of reasons that Christ could not provide a "solution" to the law. He argued, for example, that the law only threatened its penalty against the offender, but Christ was not the offender; therefore, Christ could not pay the law's penalty. The law threatened everlasting punishment, but Christ did not suffer an infinite duration. The law cursed mankind with a sinful nature, but Christ did not suffer the curse in his soul or experience any loss of the image of God. For all these reasons and more, Baxter taught that Christ could not have paid the exact penalty (solution) of the law.[20]

That is the theological basis on which Baxter opposed both the doctrine of substitution and imputed righteousness. He said:

> Most of our ordinary divines say, that Christ did as properly
> obey in our room and stead, as he did suffer in our stead;

---

[19] Baxter, *Aphorisms*, 17-18. In another place, Baxter speaks of this distinction in terms of "*idem*" and "*tantundem*." To pay the *idem* is to pay the same as what is due. To pay the *tantundem* is to pay the value or equivalent of what is due. See Baxter, *Aphorisms*, 32.

[20] Baxter, *Aphorisms*, 17-23.

and that in God's esteem and in point of law we were in Christ obeying and suffering, and so in him we did both perfectly fulfill the commands of the law by obedience, and the threatening of it by bearing the penalty; and thus (say they) is Christ's righteousness imputed to us.[21]

Baxter, however, believed this ordinary view of the orthodox divines to be false. He said that "the very core of the mistake, [is] to think that we have by delegation paid the proper debt of obedience to the whole law, or that in Christ we have perfectly obeyed."[22]

A question then arises. If Christ's work did not pay the exact penalty of the law to substitute for his people, so that his righteousness may be imputed to them, then why did Christ suffer and die? Baxter believed that God might have justly relaxed the law by kingly decree and spared his Son terrible sufferings. If God had done so, however, Baxter thought that he would have weakened the law's authority, undermined his reputation, and encouraged sin. Therefore, Baxter said, Christ's atonement was necessary. Baxter explained:

Therefore if God should relax his law, much more if he should wholly dispense with it by remission, the law would seem to lose much of its authority, and the Lawgiver be esteemed mutable.[23]

Later, he said:

It would have encouraged men to sin and condemn the law, if the very first breach and all other should be merely remitted; but when men see that God has punished his Son when he was our surety, they may easily gather that he will not spare them, if they continue [as] rebels.[24]

The atonement, then, shows sinners how seriously God takes

[21] Baxter, *Aphorisms*, 30-31.
[22] Baxter, *Aphorisms*, 32.
[23] Baxter, *Aphorisms*, 29.
[24] Baxter, *Aphorisms*, 29.

the law and encourages them not to think lightly of God's authority or of their sin. Since God sent his beloved Son to endure horrible sufferings for sins against the law, then no one should doubt the law's authority or God's willingness to punish lawbreakers.

Christ's work, according to Baxter, changes the law in two ways. First, it softens the original law of perfection, without completely canceling the curse. This means the law's curse is rightly applied, by degrees, to believers for their impenitent sins. Baxter claimed:

> It was not the intention either of the Father or the Son that by this satisfaction, the offenders should be immediately delivered from the whole curse of the law, and freed from the evil which they had brought upon themselves, but some part must be executed on soul and body, and the creatures themselves; and remain upon them at the pleasure of Christ.[25]

Second, it serves as the means by which God demonstrates his government and issues the new law of grace with its promise of pardon and life on the condition of easier obedience. Baxter explained:

> 52. The true reason of the satisfactoriness of Christ's sufferings was, that they were a most apt means for the demonstration of the government, justice, holiness, wisdom, and mercy of God, by which God could attain the ends of the law and government, better than by executing the law on the world in its destruction. . . . 53. The measure of the satisfaction made by Christ was that it was a full salvo to God's justice, and demonstration of it, that he might give pardon and life to sinners, upon the new terms of the covenant of grace, and give what he after gave.[26]

The preceding discussion shows that Baxter held to the "governmental theory of the atonement." This theory of atonement was championed by a number of theologians in Baxter's day, including Bradshaw and Grotius, two theologians who influenced

---

[25] Baxter, *Aphorisms*, 43.
[26] Baxter, *Catholick Theologie*, 1:2:40-41.

Baxter on this matter.[27] Louis Berkhof provides a helpful definition of the governmental theory of the atonement.

> The governmental theory was intended to be a mean between the doctrine of the atonement, as taught by the Reformers, and the Socinian view. It denies that the justice of God necessarily demands that all the requirements of the law be met. The law is merely the product of God's will, and He can alter or even abrogate it, just as He pleases. While in strict justice the sinner deserved eternal death, that sentence is not strictly executed, for believers are set free. For them the penalty is set aside, and that without strict satisfaction. Christ did indeed render a certain satisfaction, but this was only a nominal equivalent of the penalty due to man; something which God was pleased to accept as such. If the question is asked, why God did not remit the penalty outright, as He might have done, the answer is that He had to reveal in some way the inviolable nature of the law and His holy displeasure against sin, in order that He, the moral Ruler of the universe, might be able to maintain His moral government.[28]

Note that on the governmental theory of the atonement, Christ's work is not strictly necessary to fulfill the law. God might change the law or dispense with it according to his sovereign pleasure without any satisfaction or payment.

In sum, Richard Baxter's doctrine of the atonement can be understood in three parts. First, Christ didn't suffer the exact penalty of the law, only the equivalent; therefore, his work is not substitutionary. Second, Christ's work is the means by which God softens the original law of perfection, eliminating its rigor, and establishing a new law of grace that promises pardon and life on the

---

[27] Baxter, *Aphorisms*, 37.

[28] Louis Berkhof, *Systematic Theology*, new combined ed. (Grand Rapids: Eerdmans, 1996), 388. See also Louis Berkhof, *The History of Christian Doctrines* (Edinburgh; Carlisle, PA: Banner of Truth, 1997), 186-88. For a more recent discussion, see Robert Letham, *The Work of Christ*, Contours of Christian Theology, ed. Gerald Bray (Downers Grove, IL: InterVarsity Press, 1993), 167-69.

condition of imperfect obedience. Third, Christ's work was not strictly necessary, but it proves that God's law has authority and he will punish sinners.

Baxter's doctrine of the atonement ultimately allows for justification by works. Because Christ did not strictly pay the penalty of the law or meet the standard of divine justice, God may justly penalize believers for their sins and require good works of them for their justification.

2. Keach's doctrine of Christ's atonement

While Baxter denied penal substitution and the necessity of the atonement, Keach strongly affirmed both doctrines. According to Keach, Christ died to pay the law's penalty in the place of sinners. He substituted on behalf of his people in order to meet the demands of divine justice. Keach wrote:

> This notion . . . of Christ dying for us, must denote his dying in our stead; because it is so always generally taken, when one person is said to die for another, one is condemned, and another dies for him, that is, in his room, to save the guilty person from death. . . . Now it was so here, we were all criminals, guilty of the highest treason against the God of heaven; and were by the holy law of our offended Sovereign, condemned to die, and to bear eternal wrath; and our blessed Savior was chosen in our room, and given up as an act of the Father's infinite love and favor . . . to die for us, and to satisfy divine justice for us, or to bear the punishment we were to have born, and must (had he not born it for us) for ever.[29]

While in Baxter's theology Christ did not substitute for his people or guarantee their final salvation, in Keach's theology Christ's death substituted for the death of his people, guaranteeing their final salvation. In Baxter's theology Christ's death allegedly honors the law by paying an equivalent penalty, but in Keach's

---

[29] Benjamin Keach, *A Golden Mine Opened* (London: n.p., 1694), 237.

theology Christ's death actually honors the law by paying its identical penalty. While on Baxter's theology God may justly visit the penalties of the law on his people, since Christ did not substitute for them, on Keach's theology the law's penalty is wholly satisfied by Christ's substitutionary work; therefore, God's people are completely free from the law's curse. While on Baxter's model God changes the penalty of the law, on Keach's model God changes which person receives the penalty.

Keach also affirmed the necessity of the atonement. Because the law of God threatened the curse of death upon all who violate it, that curse must be carried out upon lawbreakers. The law is such that its threats may not be rescinded or modified by divine decree. If God failed to carry out the threats of the law, then he would violate his own judicial righteousness. Therefore, if sinners are to be saved, it was absolutely necessary for Christ to offer himself as a penal substitution for the sins of his people. Christ must pay the curse of the law and so satisfy God's justice or else justification is impossible. Keach wrote:

> The glory of his justice: God is just; He can as soon cease to be; as cease to be just. God declared, if man sinned he should die; therefore either he must destroy man to preserve his truth and justice, and see his law not violated and truth upside down, and so conceal his mercy; or else find out a way to satisfy his justice, and preserve his truth . . . therefore his wisdom found out a way to for the honor both of justice and mercy, by laying our sins upon his own Son as our surety, and to undergo that wrath and punishment, which we must otherwise have undergone for ever.

> Here is, brethren, no changing the sentence against sin, but of the person; our sins and punishment are transferred upon Jesus Christ; and since it was infinite justice our sins had wronged, an infinite punishment must be suffered, which none but one that was God could bear.[30]

On Baxter's view, if God's law is broken, then God has the

---

[30] Benjamin Keach, *Christ Alone the Way to Heaven* (London: n.p., 1698), 77.

sovereign right to soften or rescind the penalty according to what seems best to him. On Keach's view, however, if God's law is broken, then God's own justice as a judge necessarily requires him to levy the penalty. Either the sinner himself necessarily endures the law's penalties for his own sins or a suitable substitute necessarily endures them in his place.

To sum up, Keach's doctrine of the atonement is quite different from Baxter's. First, Christ paid the exact penalty of the law because that's what God's justice requires. Second, Christ offered himself as a penal substitutionary atonement for the sins of his people. Third, Christ's sufferings were absolutely necessary for sinners to be forgiven of their sins.

Justified by Faith and Works

1. Baxter's doctrine of justification

Baxter taught that believers are justified on the basis of a twofold righteousness. He said, "Therefore as there are two covenants, with their distinct conditions: so is there a twofold righteousness, and both of them absolutely necessary to salvation."[31] The righteousness of Christ satisfies the first law (or covenant) of works, but the righteousness of the believer satisfies the second law (or covenant) of grace. Both Christ's righteousness and our own righteousness are indispensable for justification and eternal life. Regarding the legal righteousness of the first covenant, Baxter said:

> Our legal righteousness, or righteousness of the first covenant is not personal, or consists not in any qualifications of our own persons, or actions performed by us, (For we never fulfilled nor personally satisfied the law:) but it is wholly without us in Christ. And in this sense it is that the Apostle (and every Christian) disclaims his own righteousness or works, as being no true legal righteousness.

---

[31] Baxter, *Aphorisms*, 66.

Phil. 3:7-8.[32]

So, Christ's obedience and death alone obtained legal righteousness, which we have already seen was the means by which God softened the first law and procured the second law. Legal righteousness is completely outside of the believer. Regarding gospel righteousness, however, Baxter wrote:

> Our evangelical righteousness is not without us in Christ, as our legal righteousness is: but consists in our own actions of faith and gospel obedience. Or thus: Though Christ performed the conditions of the law, and satisfied for our non-performance; yet it is our selves that must perform the conditions of the gospel.[33]

Baxter means that while Christ satisfies the law of the first covenant and so is justified by it, believers must keep the law of the second covenant and so be justified by that law. Nothing short of total conformity to the terms of the new law will suffice to justify the believer, though total conformity means imperfect faithful obedience to a soft law. That imperfect obedience is the believer's evangelical righteousness, which is the ground of his justification under the second law of grace.

Baxter understood that this was one of the main points at which his system differed from that of his opponents. While men like Owen and Keach believed that Christ's satisfaction of the law of works was a sufficient legal ground for the justification of all who belong to him, Baxter believed that a secondary righteousness, conforming to the terms of the gospel, was necessary for the believer's justification. He wrote:

> And this seems the very core of their error, that they think we must be justified in Christ by the law of innocency, which justified Christ himself; and that we are quit or washed simply from all guilt of fault, as well as obligation to punishment: which is a great untruth, contrary to all the

---

[32] Baxter, *Aphorisms*, 67.
[33] Baxter, *Aphorisms*, 70.

scope of the gospel, which assures us, that we are justified by the law of grace or faith, and not by the law of works.[34]

This provides a clear window into Baxter's theology of justification. All of those passages of Scripture that deny works any role in justification (e.g., Rom. 3:20, 28; 4:5, 6; 10:4; Gal. 2:15-16; 3:10, 21, etc.) are only denying that the believer is required to keep the first law for their justification. Those passages do not deny that the believer is required to perform good works under the second law for righteousness under that law. Good works are necessary to be justified under the law of grace. Baxter says, "The Apostle does professedly exclude the works of the law only from justification; but never at all the works of the gospel as they are the condition of the new covenant."[35]

The role of faith, then, is simply to meet the demands of the new law as part of the believer's evangelical righteousness. Faith is not merely the hand that grasps Christ's righteousness under the first law, which law alone satisfies God's justice. Rather, faith is itself the chief ground of the believer's righteousness before God under the second law. According to Baxter, faith implies all other acts of obedience that will inevitably flow from it. Faith is the seed of love and good works. Baxter said:

Faith therefore is the summary and chief of the conditions of the gospel, and not formally and strictly the whole: But as love is the fulfilling of the law, so faith is the fulfilling of the new law; or as taking the Lord for our only God, is the sum of the Decalogue, implying or inferring all the rest, and so is the great commandment, so taking Christ for our only Redeemer and Lord, is the sum of the conditions of the new covenant, including, implying or inferring all other parts of its conditions, and so is the great command of the gospel.[36]

Thus, when the Bible speaks of justification by faith, it always implies the love and good works that inevitably and increasingly

---

[34] Baxter, *Catholick Theologie*, 1:2:62.

[35] Baxter, *Aphorisms*, 187.

[36] Baxter, *Aphorisms*, 156.

accompany faith in believers who persevere. Faith is the root that must grow into the full fruit of evangelical righteousness, which is necessary for justification and life on the last day. Baxter explained:

> Though all our past sins are pardoned at our first faith or conversion (or as the ancients speak in baptism) yet is it most certain that pardon or justification is not perfect at first, no nor on this side of death: And the saying of many that justification is perfect at first and sanctification is only by degrees, is a palpable error, as I have elsewhere often shown.[37]

So for Baxter, faith and works combine to justify on the last day, and a person's justification by faith and works increases by degrees throughout his life and is only perfected on the last day. That having been said, Baxter also taught that faith alone, and not love and good works, is the primary ground of the believer's evangelical righteousness before God, though love and good works occupy a secondary ground. Baxter wrote:

> So that they [faith and works] both justify in the same kind of causality, viz. as *Causae sine quibus-non*, or mediate and improper causes; or as Dr Twisse *Causae dispositivae*: but with this difference: faith as the principal part; obedience as the less principal. The like may be said of love, which at least is a secondary part of the condition: and of others in the same station.[38]

Baxter thus reserves a unique and primary role for faith in justification, though works are equally required for justification, albeit in a secondary sense.

To sum up, Baxter's doctrine of justification has a number of features. First, he believed that a twofold righteousness is required for sinners to be justified. Christ's righteousness is required to satisfy the first law of the garden covenant, but the believer's own righteousness is required for justification under the second law of

---

[37] Baxter, *Catholick Theologie*, 1:2:85.
[38] Baxter, *Aphorisms*, 14-15.

"Popery in New Dress": Richard Baxter v. Benjamin Keach on the Doctrine of Justification

the covenant of grace. Second, when the Bible teaches that believers are justified by faith and not by works of the law, it only denies that believers are justified by keeping the terms of the first law; it does not deny that believers are justified by keeping the terms of the second law. Third, while faith and works both justify the sinner, works only justify in a secondary sense, though both are absolutely necessary for the fullness of justification. Highfill says that in Baxter's doctrine of justification, "the flood of works swells to threatening proportions, and he is not entirely successful in controlling it."[39]

2. Keach's response to Baxter's doctrine of justification

Keach strongly opposed Baxter's distinction between legal and evangelical righteousness. Keach believed that there is only one law of God, and therefore, only one righteousness necessary for justification. He argued:

> All works done by the creature are excluded in point of justification of a sinner in the sight of God, because we are justified by that righteousness by which the justice of God is satisfied, and his wrath appeased. That righteousness that delivers us alone from condemnation, and the curse of the law, does justify us and none else; and is not that the righteousness of Christ? Is not he that is acquitted from condemnation and death, put into a state of justification and life?

> What is it that these new doctors talk of? How is Christ's righteousness made our legal righteousness and not our evangelical righteousness? If the righteousness of Christ be imputed to us, as that which when applied by faith, delivers us from condemnation, wrath and death, certainly we need no other righteousness to justify us in God's sight unto

---

[39] W. Lawrence Highfill, "Faith and Works in the Ethical Theory of Richard Baxter" (Ph.D. diss., Duke University, 1954), 301.

eternal life.[40]

Keach's reaction to Baxter's position grows from his belief that God's law is one. This is the fundamental difference between Keach and Baxter. While Baxter believed that God stands above his law and has the right to change it, Keach believed that God's law is a reflection of his own holy nature, and therefore, God cannot justly change it. Since God's law is one, on Keach's theology only one righteousness can possibly be required to satisfy God's justice. Keach argued that Baxter's doctrine of two laws and a double righteousness destroys the law itself. Keach insisted, "Christ came not to destroy the law, but to fulfill it."[41] Keach believed that Baxter's doctrine of justification was flawed at a number of critical points.

First of all, and most fundamentally, Baxter failed to understand that only perfect obedience satisfies God's law and justifies the creature. God's justice requires that God only justify that which meets the standard of the law. Keach wrote:

> All works done by the creature are excluded in point of justification of a sinner in the sight of God, because we are justified by a perfect righteousness: if no man is in himself perfectly righteous, then no man can be justified by any works done by him.[42]

This is the essential difference between the two systems. Keach is clear that perfect obedience is required for justification. It may come from the believer, or it may come from Christ. But since no believer is capable of rendering perfect obedience to the law, and since a believer's faith lays hold of Christ's perfect righteousness, which fully satisfies the demands of the law, none of the believer's good works can possibly count for his justification.

---

[40] Keach, *The Marrow of True Justification*, 34.

[41] Keach, *The Marrow of True Justification*, 12. In Matthew 5:17, Jesus said, "Do not think that I have come to destroy the law or the prophets; I have not come to abolish them, but to fulfill them." Similarly, in Romans 3:31, the Apostle Paul wrote, "Do we then overthrow the law by this faith? By no means! On the contrary, we uphold the law."

[42] Keach, *The Marrow of True Justification*, 23.

Second, Baxter failed to grasp the relationship and distinction between the law and the gospel. Keach wrote:

> Moreover, pray wherein do the terms of the gospel differ from the terms of the law, "Do this and live;" or, 'The man that does these things shall live in them,' Gal. 3:12; Lev 18:5. These are the terms of the law. Thus runs the tenor of the law.

> But the terms of the gospel are quite different; 'Believe on the Lord Jesus and you will be saved,' Acts 16:31. . . .

> That doctrine which confounds the terms of the law and the gospel together in point of justification, is a false and corrupt doctrine. But the doctrine that mixes sincere obedience, or works of any kind done by us, with faith in point of justification, confounds the terms of the law and the gospel in point of justification; therefore that doctrine is false and a corrupt doctrine.[43]

Keach believed that the distinction between the law and the gospel at the point of justification is vital to the gospel itself. If the law and gospel are mixed at the point of justification, the gospel is lost. The true gospel calls sinners to renounce all works in the point of their justification and look to Christ alone by faith alone.

Third, Baxter rejected the doctrine of Christ's federal headship. Keach wrote that Jesus fulfilled the law "in our nature, and stead as our representative and surety, to do and perform the terms thereof; I mean the law of works, which we had broken."[44] Baxter, on the other hand, denied that Christ is the surety of his people, their representative head, who kept all the terms of the law as their substitute. This is the essential difference between Keach and Baxter on the nature of the gospel. Baxter believed that in the gospel a believer obeys the law for his justification. Keach believed that in the gospel Christ representatively obeys the law for the believer's justification.

Fourth, Baxter did not comprehend the biblical doctrine of

---

[43] Keach, *The Marrow of True Justification*, 21.
[44] Keach, *The Marrow of True Justification*, 12.

justification by faith alone. Keach said, "We affirm, as a worthy divine observes, that faith alone perfectly justifies, by trusting in the righteousness of Christ."[45] This critique flows from the first. Because Baxter failed to comprehend the federal headship of Christ, he had no space in his theology for justification by faith alone. According to Keach, because Christ is the representative head of his people, such that he completely satisfied the demands of the law in their stead, then Christ's people are justified simply by laying hold of their representative by faith alone. Riker rightly notes, "Keach wants to leave justification entirely dependent on monergistic free grace, through the mediation of human faith."[46] Keach insisted that faith is not part of the ground of justification as one of the conditions of the gospel. It is, rather, merely the means of grasping Christ and his righteousness, which is the sole and sufficient ground of justification.

Fifth, Baxter did not understand that the obedience that comes from faith is evidence of justification and not the ground of it. As we have already seen, Baxter believed that faith and works together form the ground of a believer's justification under the gospel. Keach responded, "We say obedience supposes a man justified; but these men say, that obedience concurs with faith to justify, or is part of our righteousness to justification."[47] On Keach's model, since Christ's righteousness has already fulfilled the law and satisfied God's justice, there is no room for the believer's personal obedience in justification.

Sixth, Baxter failed to grasp that faith's principal object is Christ himself. When Baxter speaks of justifying faith, he often speaks of trusting God and all that he has revealed in a comprehensive way. Keach believed Baxter placed far too little emphasis on trusting Christ's person and work for our salvation. Keach explained:

> Though I deny not, but that faith in God the Father, and in the Holy Ghost is, enjoined as well as faith in the Son; yet it

---

[45] Keach, *The Marrow of True Justification*, 12.

[46] D. B. Riker, *A Catholic Reformed Theologian: Federalism and Baptism in the Thought of Benjamin Keach, 1640-1704*, Studies in Baptist History and Thought (Eugene, OR: Wipf & Stock, 2009), 80.

[47] Keach, *The Marrow of True Justification*, 12.

is Christ who is the immediate object of our faith, and that too as he was crucified for us, and bore our sins, or was made sin for us, that we might be made the righteousness of God in him. And it is by him that we come to God, and believe in God, and are justified and accepted of God, other foundation (of these things) can no man lay. But Mr. Baxter speaks nothing of this, but of a faith in general in God the Father, Son and Holy Ghost, which faith he says is reputed truly to be the condition on our part on which Christ and life by that baptismal covenant is made ours.[48]

So Keach believed that Baxter fundamentally lacked a Christ-centered perspective on the gospel itself. The theological result is that Baxter emphasized law over Christ's person, and the practical result is that Baxter emphasized personal obedience over Christ's federal headship and imputed righteousness.

In sum, Keach believed a number of things about justification. First, justification is based on God's one law which is immutable and rooted in God's nature. Second, perfect obedience is required to satisfy God's law. Third, the law may either be satisfied by the creature for justification (law) or by Christ, the substitute and surety for sinners (gospel). Fourth, if a person believes in Christ for justification, then all of his own works are excluded from justification because Christ has satisfied the law in his place.

Loss of Justification

1. Baxter's doctrine of the loss of justification

Richard Baxter believed that justification increases or progresses by degrees and is only completed on the last day. Believers enter into the baptismal covenant and must persevere in gospel obedience, furthering their justification, until they are glorified in the end. The last thesis of Baxter's *Aphorisms of Justification* says:

To conclude: It is most clear in the Scripture, and beyond all

---

[48] Keach, *The Marrow of True Justification*, 13.

dispute, that our actual, most proper, complete justification, at the great judgment, will be according to our works, and to what we have done in flesh, whether good or evil: which can be no otherwise then as it was the condition of that justification. And so Christ, at that great assize, will not give his bare will of purpose, as the reason of his proceedings: but as he governed by a law; so he will judge by a law: and will then give the reason of his public sentence from mens keeping or breaking the conditions of his covenant; that so the mouths of all may be stopped, and the equity of his judgment may be manifest to all, and that he may there show forth his hatred to the sins, and not only to the persons of the condemned; and his love to the obedience, and not only to the persons justified.[49]

According to Baxter, the believer's past sins are pardoned at the initial verdict of justification, but then the believer must continue in the terms of the covenant, making right use of all the means of grace, in order to bring justification to completion on judgment day.

Since justification is not complete, prior to death and judgment, Baxter believed that it is possible for a believer to lose his justification. He wrote:

As to the question therefore whether justification be losable, and pardon reversible, I answer, that the grant of them in the covenant is unalterable; but man's will in it self is mutable, and if he should cease believing by apostasy, and the condition fail, he would lose his right and be unjustified and unpardoned, without any change in God. But that a man does not so de facto is to be ascribed to election and special grace, of which afterward.[50]

In other words, both the elect and non-elect enter into the baptismal covenant through baptism and faith. God eternally decreed that the elect would persevere to the end and receive final justification, and

---

[49] Baxter, *Aphorisms*, 203.
[50] Baxter, *Aphorisms*, 203.

he makes that certain by giving them preserving grace. The non-elect, however, eventually turn away from Christ, commit apostasy, lose their justification and go to hell, since God did not decree that they would endure. Therefore, believing in Christ, living faithfully before him as his child, and having a justified status is no proof of election and does not guarantee glorification. In another place, Baxter said:

> Men that are but thus conditionally pardoned and justified, may be unpardoned and unjustified again for their non-performance of the conditions, and all the debt so forgiven be required at their hands; and all this without any change in God, or in his law. See Ball of the Covenant, pag. 240.[51]

He then wrote:

> Yea, in case the justified by faith should cease believing, the Scripture would pronounce them unjust again, and yet without any change in God, or Scripture, but only in themselves. Because their justification does continue conditionally as long as they live here; the Scripture does justify no man by name, but all believers as such; therefore if they should cease to be believers, they would cease to be justified.[52]

Baxter is saying that God promises preservation in justification to no one. Justification is wholly conditioned upon a believer's obedience to the terms of the covenant of grace, and the covenant of grace does not contain in it any promise to preserve any of its members in a state of justification to the end. The grace of preservation comes only from the divine decree, which is hidden in God's secret counsels.

That having been said, Baxter recoiled a bit from his own conclusion. A few years after he wrote the *Aphorisms of Justification*, but before he wrote *Catholick Theologie*, Baxter said the following:

---

[51] Baxter, *Aphorisms*, 126.
[52] Baxter, *Aphorisms*, 127.

But yet I dare not say that I am certain of this, that all are elect to salvation, and shall never fall away totally and finally, who sincerely believe and are justified. It is my opinion, but I dare not put it into my creed among either the points of absolute necessity, or undoubted verity. . . . I know how many learned, godly men do differ from me, and deny the certainty of perseverance.[53]

Baxter apparently had pastoral reservations about the implications of his own theology. He said that in his opinion all who are justified and sincerely believe are elect, even though his own system provides absolutely no warrant for such a conclusion. In fact, Baxter's system infers the opposite of his opinion here. Of all those who are justified by God's revealed will in the baptismal covenant, certainly at least some of them would not be elect according to God's decree. Baxter provided no biblical or theological foundation for this statement, and he even seemed to hesitate in writing it down.

2. Keach on the loss of justification

Keach objected both theologically and practically to the notion that justification is by degrees and can be lost. Objecting theologically, Keach said:

[Those who teach] we are justified, or accepted, so far as our faith and obedience go, and no farther; and when they are perfect at judgment, we shall be perfectly justified; so that they render our justification to be as imperfect as our inherent personal holiness or sanctification is imperfect; or to give it in the words of a learned writer, they intimate, while we are imperfect our justification is imperfect also; and if our faith and obedience be interrupted or utterly lost, justification is interrupted or utterly lost likewise; nor is it

---

[53] Richard Baxter, *The Right Method For a settled Peace of Conscience* (London: n.p., 1653), 166.

any wonder our justification should be looked upon by them to be imperfect, while any imperfection remain in us, if the righteousness of Christ be not the matter of our justification, or that which does justify in God's sight; and on the other hand it is impossible, if we are justified and accepted as just persons, and graciously acquitted by the righteousness of Christ, there should be the least stain, imperfection, or spot in our justification; but that Christ must needs say of such, in respect of justification, as he does of his spouse, 'You are all fair, my love, and there is not spot in you,' Cant. 4:7.[54]

Keach's point is that because Baxter and those like him deny the imputation of Christ's righteousness as the ground of justification, they not only include good works at the foundation of the sentence, but also make it possible to lose justification altogether. If final justification is according to a believer's final perseverance in good works, and if those good works are lacking, then justification can be lost. If, however, justification is according to Christ's perfect obedience, since Christ was fully obedient, then justification cannot possibly be lost.

From a practical perspective, Keach believed that the Baxterian doctrine leads to the loss of assurance of salvation. He wrote:

Now if we are not perfectly justified, it follows then we are not perfectly delivered from condemnation, nor acquitted from the guilt of all sin, and so not in a state of life, nor made free indeed by the Son of God; and then also Christ's dove is not without spot, nor undefiled in respect to justification: And then also it follows (as the Papists say) there is no assurance can be had or attained in this life, or until death.[55]

Practically speaking, Keach's greatest concern with Baxter's theology, and others like it, was that it would rob the believer of his assurance of salvation. Instead of being powerfully motivated to gospel obedience by love, gratitude, and joy, the Baxterian doctrine could only "fill a poor Christian with terror, and slavish fear."[56]

---

[54] Keach, *The Marrow of Justification*, 12.
[55] Benjamin Keach, *A Medium Betwixt Two Extremes* (London: n.p., 1698), 38.

Keach said:

> The doctrine of justification by our own work of holiness or sincere obedience, holds a Christian down under slavish fear, by grounding his justification on his works of holiness and sincere obedience; therefore that doctrine is not of God. Christian take heed what books you read, if you would have a sound and steadfast ground of hope, peace, and comfort, nay not only have the joy of God's salvation, but salvation itself.[57]

Slavish fear does not produce the faithful, loving holiness without which none will see the Lord, but only a spirit of servitude by which men are forced to do their duties to save themselves from torment. Without assurance of final salvation based on Christ's righteousness alone, men are either crushed in despair or puffed up in pride, thinking that their own works of obedience will save them. Baxter's doctrine robs believers of the hope of heaven, the peace of God, the comfort of full assurance, and the joy and hope of eternal life.

Conclusion

Though they often used similar terminology, the doctrines of justification held by Baxter and Keach could scarcely have been more different. On Baxter's system God made an easy law by which men could justify themselves. But on Keach's system God sent his Son to keep the law in the place of sinners for their justification. On Baxter's system God substituted one law for another. But on Keach's system God substituted his own Son for sinners. On Baxter's system the righteousness of Christ and of men are required for justification. But on Keach's system Christ's righteousness alone justifies. On Baxter's system men must work to keep themselves in a state of justification and life. But on Keach's system God effectually works in Christ to keep men in a state of justification and life. On

---

[56] Keach, *A Medium Betwixt Two Extremes*, 52.
[57] Keach, *The Marrow of True Justification*, 29-30.

Baxter's system present assurance of salvation is possible through faith and baptism, but certain assurance of final salvation is impossible because one must endure to the end to be fully justified. But on Keach's system full assurance of final salvation is God's gift to all who lay hold of his Son.

The differences between Baxter and Keach are far from verbal. They are substantial and touch the very heart and essence of the gospel itself. According to Packer, Baxter "never got this streak of legalism out of his theological system," and "as a theologian he was, though brilliant, something of a disaster."[58] Keach believed that to affirm Baxter's doctrine is to deny the very gospel itself. In Keach's own words, "if you build on your own righteousness or obedience, and not on the righteousness of God, which is received by faith only, you will fall into hell."[59]

---

[58] J. I. Packer, *A Quest for Godliness: The Puritan Vision of the Christian Life* (Wheaton, IL: Crossway, 1990), 158-59.

[59] Keach, *The Marrow of True Justification*, 30.

Chapter 5

Separating God's Two Kingdoms

Two Kingdom Theology among New England Baptists in the Early Republic

Ronald S. Baines[*]

I first heard of Jim Renihan through Harry Maples, a Southern Baptist pastor and mutual acquaintance who had served near Jim in Herkimer, NY. Harry was now pastoring Heritage Baptist Church in Worcester, MA, and I was serving a small Southern Baptist mission in Westfield, MA. As Calvinists, Harry and I had become fast friends. When Jim returned with his family to Worcester in 1995 to finish his dissertation, they attended Heritage Baptist Church where I had the privilege to meet Jim face to face. From that meeting has grown a lasting friendship that began its third decade this year.

Meeting Jim was providential in that I had embraced the doctrines of grace sometime before but was just becoming acquainted with the Reformed Baptist movement. Along with befriending me, one of the first things Jim did was introduce me to the 1689 Confession, a rich doctrinal statement of which I was totally unfamiliar. I was immediately taken with its richness and its fullness. He further invited me to take a class in Baptist History he was asked to teach at an extension campus of Southern Seminary in nearby Northboro, MA. Being introduced for the first time to the rich heritage Baptists have in seventeenth-century England and early America was transformative. Additionally he invited me to

[*] Ronald S. Baines is pastor of Grace Reformed Baptist Church, Brunswick, ME. He received the M.A.R. from Reformed Theological Seminary and is a Ph.D. candidate at the University of Maine. This chapter first appeared in *Journal of the Institute of Reformed Baptist Studies* (2014): 27-69 and is used with permission.

attend a missions conference for Reformed Baptist Mission Services in Lafayette, NJ. In his words, "Ron, you should come and meet some of my friends!" I can still remember returning home and remarking to my wife that I had found a communion of brethren I could call home.

When ARBCA was formed, I was able to attend its constituting meeting in Mesa, AZ. Soon, the small mission church I pastored constituted and we were able to join ARBCA, establishing closer ties between Jim and me. When Jim was asked to consider taking the lead role as dean and instructor at the Institute of Reformed Baptist Studies in Escondido, CA, I can still remember sitting in his back yard on a summer afternoon suggesting that God had prepared him for just such a calling. Twenty years later I can see that this assessment was accurate.

Over the years I have come to recognize that my experience is not unique. Jim has befriended, educated, and encouraged so many. He has introduced the next generation of Reformed Baptists studying at the Institute to the theology of the Confession, our history as Baptists, and the distinctives of Reformed Baptist worship. He has also befriended numerous pastors at home and abroad in the same way he influenced me. It is a privilege and honor to be able to contribute to this volume an essay as a small token of my appreciation for one who has had greater influence in my personal and pastoral life that any other pastor, scholar, theologian, and historian I know.

Introduction

On September 21, 1808, Daniel Merrill, pastor of the Baptist Church in Sedgwick, Maine, ascended the pulpit of the Baptist Church of Ballstown, Maine, to give the "Introductory Sermon" at the Lincoln Baptist Association annual general assembly. His text was Ephesians 2:20 and his title, as it was later published, was *The Kingdom of Heaven Distinguished from Babylon.*

Not a lifelong Regular Baptist, Merrill, a Dartmouth educated paedobaptist Congregational cleric, had converted to Baptist principles three years earlier. Boston's Thomas Baldwin, pastor of the Second Baptist Church, made the arduous journey from Boston to Sedgwick to participate in the baptism and ordination of Daniel Merrill on May 15, 1805. It was, according to Baldwin, "a season to us uncommonly solemn and precious."[1] The ordination marked the final stage of Merrill's conversion from Congregationalism to Baptist principles. The path which led to these events was recounted by Merrill almost thirty years later and published in 1833, only days before he died at the age of sixty-two.[2]

Recording his pilgrimage, Merrill confessed that after some years in the ministry in Sedgwick members of his own congregation as well as some others challenged him to consider the subject of infant baptism more carefully. Intending to refute the "hurtful nature" of the Baptists' practice by writing a book confirming infant baptism, he took to "a careful and critical review of the oracles of God" expecting to find "the certain scripture evidence of their errors." To his "great disappointment and extreme regret" he found he could neither refute the Baptists nor confirm his own practice of infant baptism. The matter was exacerbated when eight children in the large Sedgwick congregation were presented to him for baptism. Confessing "distressing uncertainty and profound ignorance" he "administered no gospel ordinance for nine months." Struggling with what he described as "an unconquered antipathy against being a Baptist" and not being able to "bear the idea of being called one," he continued "from month to month, in Egyptian darkness." Finally, as he narrates, "by an unconditional submission to the will of God, I was enabled to roll my burden upon him, and found peace."[3]

The capstone of his conversion to Baptist doctrine came when, after preaching a series of seven sermons on the subject of baptism, he led the majority of his congregation to embrace Baptist principles.[4] His transition from standing order Congregationalism

---

[1] Thomas Baldwin, *A Sermon, Delivered at Sedgwick, May 15, 1805, at the Ordination of the Rev. Daniel Merrill to the Pastoral Charge of the Baptist Church of Christ in That Place* (Boston: Manning & Loring, printer, 1805), 29.

[2] Daniel Merrill, *Autobiography of Rev. Daniel Merrill* (Philadelphia: Baptist General Tract Society, 1833). The phrase "Regular Baptist" distinguished the Calvinisitic Baptists of New England from the Arminian or General Baptists during the colonial and early Republic periods.

[3] Merrill, *Autobiography*, 3-4.

to Baptist doctrine and practice, by his own admission, took the better part of two years, culminating in his May 15th submission to believer's baptism and re-ordination as a Baptist minister. The newly formed Sedgwick Baptist Church, once the largest Congregational Church in Maine, was now the largest Baptist church in the northeastern region.[5]

Merrill's story is one of a number of such Congregational clergy conversions in New England in the late eighteenth and early nineteenth centuries. C. C. Goen has shown decisively the movement in New England of many believers, clergy, and whole congregations converting to Baptist principles following the Great Awakening. Merrill's story, though significant, was not unique.[6]

While the proper administration of baptism was a critical dissimilarity between the Baptists and the standing order, it would be an unfortunate oversimplification to think that this was the sum and substance of their differences. As Merrill discovered in his pilgrimage from paedobaptism to believer's only baptism, the Baptists held to a cluster of beliefs that uniquely defined them and determined their interaction with other corporate and social entities at a number of levels. One of the most important doctrinal differences was with regard to the nature and subjects of the kingdom of God. The Baptist doctrinal formulation of the kingdom provided an overarching framework through which they not only identified themselves in ecclesiastically distinct ways from the standing order, but also defined their place in the social and civil world in which they lived day to day.[7]

The kingdom of God as a theological construct framed their

---

[4] The seven sermons were published prior to his May 15, 1805 ordination as *The Mode and Subjects of Baptism Examined, in Seven Sermons; to Which Is Added, a Brief History of the Baptists* (Salem: Printed by Joshua Cushing, 1804). It went through ten editions in eight years giving evidence of the popularity of the work.

[5] For the claim as to the work in Sedgwick being the largest in Maine, see Joshua Millet, *A History of the Baptists in Maine; Together with Brief Notices of Societies and Institutions* (Portland, ME: Printed by C. Day & co., 1845), 263.

[6] C. C. Goen, *Revivalism and Separatism in New England, 1740-1800: Strict Congregationalists and Separate Baptists in the Great Awakening* (Middletown, CT: Wesleyan University Press, 1987).

[7] The literature uses the phrases "the kingdom of God," "the kingdom of Christ," "the kingdom of Heaven," and the like interchangeably. Consequently there is no attempt to make the references uniform.

understanding of civil liberty and the limits of political power and, therefore, provided the paradigm through which the Baptists advocated what later became known as the separation of church and state. Likewise, it governed their understanding of the nature and character of the church, and so was the paradigm through which they viewed ecclesiastical communion and advocated separation from the state church. Separation for the Baptists was bi-directional. They were self-consciously active in separating God's two kingdoms, the civil and the ecclesiastical. Merrill came to realize that Baptists, though often "charged with a desire and purpose of dividing and breaking down all other churches," more basically desired

> . . . to preach the glad tidings of the kingdom of God, and so to preach them that they may have such an overcoming efficacy as to prevail with all the people of God, to leave the Pedobaptist church, and every other erroneous habitation, and be joined to this kingdom of God.[8]

Understanding the Baptist doctrine of the kingdom was foundational to Merrill's own conversion to the Baptist ranks and is therefore crucial to understanding their insistence on civil liberty, ecclesiastical independence, and a pure church ideal. Failing to distinguish the institutional limits of both church and state led to numerous abuses in Europe and America culminating in the magistrate's persecution of its citizens. Even during the Puritan era in America, Merrill noted, though the magistrate was apparently "seeking the well being of God's kingdom," citizens had been banished, whipped, and "some of the *friends* they *hanged, to keep the peace in God's kingdom.*"[9]

---

[8] Merrill, *Autobiography*, 6.

[9] *The Kingdom of God: A Discourse, Delivered at Concord, before His Excellency the Govenor [Sic], the Honorable Council, the Honorable Senate, and House of Representatives of the State of New-Hampshire, June 5, 1817, Being the Anniversary Election* (Concord, NH: Printed by Isaac Hill, 1817), 4. While Merrill does not name them, it is likely he is referring to famous dissenters such as the quasi-Baptist Roger Williams who was banished from the Bay Colony, the Baptist Obadiah Holmes who was whipped by the Massachusetts authorities, and Quakers such as Mary Dyer who were hanged on Boston Common.

Over the next twenty-seven years Merrill published some twenty different works that reflected the characteristic Baptist paradigm of the kingdom of God in distinction from the kingdoms of this world. Two of these works were direct expositions of kingdom theology while several of the others dealt with doctrinal subjects that directly derived from it such as believer's only baptism and closed communion.[10] In publishing on the kingdom of God, Merrill added his voice to a long transatlantic tradition of Baptist political and ecclesiastical thought that separated the Baptists from paedobaptists on the one side and Anabaptists on the other. This essay examines the two kingdom theology of the New England Baptists, especially, though not exclusively, Daniel Merrill and Isaac Backus, at this juncture in the early Republic.[11]

The Baptists and the Kingdom of God

The Baptist understanding of the kingdom of God reached back into the early seventeenth century in both Old and New England. In the late eighteenth century Isaac Backus (1724-1806), the most influential and prolific Baptist of his generation, wrote on the subject and the English Particular Baptist Abraham Booth's work on the kingdom went through at least four American editions between 1791 and 1811.[12] At the request of "many" who heard Merrill's

---

[10] The two works directly dealing with the kingdom of God are Daniel Merrill, *The Kingdom of Heaven, Distinguished from Babylon a Sermon Delivered at the Introduction of the Lincoln Association, Sept. 21-22, 1808* (Buckstown, ME: From the press of William W. Clapp, 1810) and *The Kingdom of God: A Discourse, Delivered at Concord*, cited above.

[11] Timothy George helpfully places the English Baptists' view of the civil magistrate between the poles of Anabaptist pacifism and, at times, antagonism and state church coercion, a *via media* the Baptists frequently advocated for themselves, though often with disappointing results. See Timothy George, "Between Pacifism and Coercion: The English Baptist Doctrine of Religious Toleration," *Mennonite Quarterly Review* 58, no. 1 (1984): 30-49. George covers the origin and early development of the Baptist pleas for religious toleration in the period from 1610-1625.

[12] Backus records in his *Diary* that Booth sent a copy of his 1788 work, *An Essay on the Kingdom of Christ*, to him in 1789. Backus' work, *The Kingdom of God Described by His Word*, followed in 1792. Isaac Backus and William Gerald McLoughlin, eds.,

introductory sermon, some with approval and some, in Merrill's words, "disgusted," the sermon was published in 1810. Addressing aspects such as the inauguration of the kingdom, the subjects of the kingdom, the relation of the church to the kingdom, the sword of the kingdom, the expansion of the kingdom, and the consummation of the kingdom, Merrill's sermon gives a useful framework for assessing the nature of the kingdom of God and its implications in Baptist life and thought and provides the basic foundation for what follows.[13]

1. The inauguration of the kingdom

Merrill began by asserting that the kingdom of heaven during the Jewish economy of the Old Testament was a "mystery . . . hid in God," and not inaugurated by its "divine Author" until the New Testament, when it was "revealed in His holy Apostles and prophets." The ecclesiastical and hermeneutical implications of this fact for Merrill and his Baptist brethren were crucial. If the Baptists were correct, then all other ecclesiastical communions who looked to circumcision in Old Testament Israel as somehow paradigmatic for baptism in the church were in error. In Merrill's mind this included all those within the fold of Rome and all Protestants who, though having left Rome and embraced the doctrines of the Reformation, yet still clung to Rome's practice of "*infant sprinkling, or infant baptism*; and thus build all their Churches after the model of the Jewish Synagogue."[14] According to Merrill, the ecclesiology of

---

The Diary of Isaac Backus, 3 vols. (Providence, RI: Brown University Press, 1979), 1280.

[13] Merrill, *The Kingdom of Heaven, Distinguished from Babylon a Sermon Delivered at the Introduction of the Lincoln Association, Sept. 21-22, 1808*. Merrill indicates that though "many" requested its publication, not all appreciated everything he said. While it is possible that some of Merrill's Baptist brethren were not in full agreement with the sentiments expressed in the sermon, it is hard to imagine that the members of the Association would request its publication if it failed to present a Baptist view of the kingdom. It is, therefore, more likely that Merrill's "disgusted" listeners were of the paedobaptist persuasion, whether clergy or laity cannot be determined definitively, but it is likely that both were present.

[14] Merrill, *The Kingdom of Heaven*, 3-4. Part of what possibly caused some of Merrill's hearers to be "disgusted" with his sermon was his designation of all

both Protestant and Catholic alike were defective.

Hermeneutically, Merrill was building on a long tradition of Baptist thinkers who saw a fundamental flaw in the typological paedobaptist practice of looking to Old Testament Israel as the foundation for infant baptism and church membership. This led them to see unwarranted typological connections between Israel and the church as well as between Israel and the civil magistrate. In other words, the hermeneutical error of the paedobaptists had both ecclesiastical and civil implications. The Baptists believed these implications provided long-standing justification for both civil and ecclesiastical tyranny in Old and New England.

Writing as one banished from the Massachusetts Bay Colony in the early seventeenth century for his dissenting religious views, Roger Williams challenged John Cotton and the New England standing order on this very point. Confronting John Cotton's typology, specifically with respect to the Old Testament Israelite king, Josiah, Williams noted, "*Josiah* was in the type, so are not now the severall Governours of Commonweals, *Kings* or *Governours* of the *Church* or *Israel*, whose state I have proved to be a *None-such*, and not to be parallel'd but in the *Antitype* the particular *Church of Christ*, where *Christ Jesus* alone sits *King* in his own most holy *Government*."[15] Williams was no stranger to typology. As Timothy Hall rightly notes, "In his hands, however, typology drove a deep wedge between Old Testament law and seventeenth-century society, pushing the Old Testament further away from Massachusetts rather than drawing it closer."[16]

Williams would be followed by New England Baptists like Isaac Backus and Daniel Merrill for more than a century before the fruits of their ecclesiastical and hermeneutical challenges to the standing order would bear lasting fruit. Backus' voluminous writings as an apologist for New England Baptists began with his conversion from

---

Protestant Churches as Jewish Synagogues, thus affirming that while they may have many true believers and even many good and godly brethren among them, they were not true churches. This understanding of the church would be important to Merrill's doctrine of closed communion to which we shall turn later.

[15] Roger Williams, *The Bloudy Tenent of Persecution* (Providence, RI: Narragansett Club, 1867), 401.

[16] Timothy L. Hall, *Separating Church and State: Roger Williams and Religious Liberty* (Urbana, IL: University of Illinois Press, 1998), 75.

the ranks of Separate Congregationalism in Connecticut in 1751 to closed communion Baptist in 1756. Like Williams before him and Merrill who would follow, Backus saw the hermeneutical issue of paedobaptist typology as foundational to the error of the standing order. Also like Williams, Backus felt the sting of standing order persecution for his convictions and wrote to defend his views and refute the errors of infant baptism.

Among his many writings stands his 1756 work, *A Short Description of the Difference Between the Bond-Woman and the Free.* McLoughlin affirms the purpose of this work was "to marshal all of the best arguments he could find to refute the Puritan claim that the covenant which God made with Abraham and the Jews in the Old Testament was carried over essentially unchanged in the covenant which God made with Christ and the Christians in the New Testament."[17] Turning to typology, Backus, using the language of the Apostle Paul in Galatians, conceived of the nation of Israel under the covenant made at Sinai, "commonly called the covenant of works," to be the bond-woman. Her children are "all that are *born after the* flesh . . . from which none can enter the kingdom of God."[18]

Backus defined the freewoman as "the glorious plan of salvation laid in the eternal mind from everlasting which in time has been made manifest, first by gradual discoveries thereof in the Old Testament, and then by Christ actually coming in the flesh." The children of the freewoman are, therefore, those born *"by promise."* Using this typological framework Backus distinguished Old Testament physical Israel, the bond-woman, from New Testament "spiritual" Israel, the church. Framed in this way, for Backus and the Baptists, "the Jewish church . . . and the Gospel-Church are set as wide apart as the old covenant and the new."[19]

By affirming that the kingdom of God did not commence with Israel in the Old Testament, Merrill, like Williams and Backus, was assigning to New Testament revelation the task of controlling

---

[17] Isaac Backus and William Gerald McLoughlin, *Isaac Backus on Church, State, and Calvinism; Pamphlets, 1754-1789,* The John Harvard Library (Cambridge, MA: Belknap Press of Harvard University Press, 1968), 130-31.

[18] Backus and McLoughlin, *Isaac Backus on Church, State, and Calvinism,* 136-38.

[19] Backus and McLoughlin, *Isaac Backus on Church, State, and Calvinism,* 140-41, 46.

typological interpretations respecting Old Testament Israel. If Israel was not the kingdom of God, though it could point to the church in a limited and typological way, it was not to be followed to any conclusion typological or otherwise that the New Testament did not warrant. Thus, the Baptists saw the need to interpret the Old Testament in light of the New Testament; failing to do so had and would continue to have drastic consequences.[20] As McLoughlin correctly notes, Backus (along with Williams and Merrill) left paedobaptism because he rejected the form of "covenant theology upon which the whole New England Standing Order was based."[21]

For the Baptists the new covenant community was a spiritual community, the church, and not the combined New England civil and religious institution typified by Old Testament Israel. Since the inauguration of the kingdom of heaven, the state and the church were no longer one, but separate divine institutions. In the words of McLoughlin, the Baptists separating the church and state constituted "not only an ecclesiastical revolution but a social one." Is it any wonder some found Merrill's 1808 sermon unsettling or even "disgusting?"[22]

2. The subjects of the kingdom

The kingdom of heaven, Merrill insisted, like any other kingdom has its subjects. Interpreting Moses' prophecy in Deuteronomy 18:15-19 of Christ, the future prophet, he concluded, "not one should have right to membership, but such as should *hear and be*

---

[20] One of the fullest expositions of typology from a Baptist perspective was that by Benjamin Keach. Keach, widely read by Baptists in both Old and New England, published a massive volume on typology, a portion of which was republished in Connecticut in 1817. While Keach saw a typological significance to Israelite circumcision, unlike the paedobaptists, it was not with respect to the subjects of baptism. Instead, Keach saw circumcision as typical of regeneration, thus typologically negating infant baptism. The hermeneutical differences between the two positions could not be more pronounced. Benjamin Keach, *Preaching from the Types and Metaphors of the Bible*, Kregel Reprint Library (Grand Rapids: Kregel Publications, 1972), 993.

[21] Backus and McLoughlin, *Isaac Backus on Church, State, and Calvinism*, 130.

[22] William McLoughlin, "Editor's Introduction," in Backus and McLoughlin, *Isaac Backus on Church, State, and Calvinism; Pamphlets, 1754-1789*, 169.

obedient to Jesus Christ." By describing the subjects of the kingdom in this way, Merrill was affirming *"the moral, or spiritual, character of the subjects of this kingdom."*[23] Since babies were not capable of savingly hearing Christ and only those who had professed faith in Christ could lay a credible claim to obedience, the subjects of the kingdom must be believers. As paedobaptists considered the baptized children of church members to be in the kingdom, the Baptists and the paedobaptists had differing conceptions of the subjects of the kingdom.

The important point at this juncture is that the difference between the Baptists, such as Merrill, and the standing order was greater than simply the sprinkling of children, the mode and subjects of baptism. The difference was the entire formulation of the nature of the kingdom. If the kingdom of God comprised the physical seed of believers, then the baptism of children, like circumcision in Israel, brought them into the kingdom. But if the kingdom was spiritual, as the Baptists insisted, no amount of water would suffice. In the words of Isaac Backus, "Christ by his death had disannulled the covenant of circumcision" and "gave the pure gospel commission to none but regenerate persons."[24] Only professed believers were subjects of the kingdom.[25]

This difference is underscored in Merrill's description of the standing order churches as Babylon. Merrill placed two biblical texts on the title page of his work reflecting the reference to the ancient Babylonians pretended desire to help ancient Israel rebuild their temple, a temple which had been destroyed by the Babylonians some seventy years previous. The Israelites saw this as an attempt to bring about the mingling of the religion of Israel with

---

[23] Merrill, *The Kingdom of Heaven, Distinguished from Babylon a Sermon Delivered at the Introduction of the Lincoln Association, Sept. 21-22, 1808,* 5.

[24] Isaac Backus, *The Kingdom of God, Described by His Word, with Its Infinite Benefits to Human Society* (Boston: Printed and sold by Samuel Hall, 1792), 9.

[25] A good example of the paedobaptist conceptualization of the kingdom to which Merrill and Backus seek a correction is Thomas James, *A Short Treatise on the Visible Kingdom of Christ.* James' intent was to prove the subjects of the kingdom were the same under the Old Testament and the New, *"viz.* Believers and their Infant-Seed," specifically targeting Baptists regarding the subjects of the kingdom. Thomas James, *A Short Treatise on the Visible Kingdom of Christ, and the Great Charter Privileges Granted by Him to His Subjects. . . . By Thomas James* (Philadelphia: Benjamin Franklin and David Hall, 1749), 2.

Separating God's Two Kingdoms: Two Kingdom Theology among New England Baptists...

that of the Babylonians, something expressly forbidden in the Old Testament. They understood it as mixing of the true religion and the false. Baptists such as Merrill saw the practice of bringing unregenerate infants into the churches, a practice instituted under the Church of Rome, as an attempt to introduce such true and false believers as subjects of the kingdom—hence, Merrill's title distinguishing mystical Babylon, the mixed church, with the true kingdom of God. As far as he was concerned, whether Protestant or Catholic, "the Paedobaptist Church is the visible Church of Babylon" also known as "mystical Babylon."[26] Merrill was not denying the regenerate status of some within the paedobaptist churches, but the presence of unregenerate members in these churches meant that the churches could not be a part of the kingdom of God. The subjects of the kingdom were foundational to his theology of the kingdom.

Backus, likewise, argued in a similar fashion in defending Baptist principles against the Congregational minister Reverend Joseph Fish of Stonington, Connecticut. Fish argued against the Baptists' insistence on the church being comprised of visible saints and advocated for the propriety of the church being of mixed communion. Backus knew Fish's position was contrary not just to Baptist theology but to the founding Congregational polity of New England. Late eighteenth-century Congregationalists, like Fish, had largely departed from their seventeenth-century roots.

One particular aspect of the Baptist practice that galled Fish and other Congregational ministers was their call for true believers in the mixed communion Congregational churches to come out from them and join the closed communion Baptists. Quoting the supposed Baptists, Fish noted, "They did not appear to grieve and mourn at the awful rent which they made, in the church and congregation: but seemed rather to glory in it; calling to others, that

---

[26] Merrill, *The Kingdom of Heaven, Distinguished from Babylon a Sermon Delivered at the Introduction of the Lincoln Association, Sept. 21-22, 1808*, 18, 19. The practice of calling the Roman Church by the name of mystical Babylon had a long history among the Baptists. For a seventeenth-century example among English Particular Baptists, see Hanserd Knollys, *Mystical Babylon Availed Wherein Is Proved, I. That Rome-Papal Is Mystical-Babylon, Ii. That the Pope of Rome Is the Beast, Iii. That the Church of Rome Is the Great Whore, Iv. That the Roman-Priests Are the False Prophet: Also a Call to the People of God to Come out of Babylon* ([London :: s.n.], 1679).

tarried behind, *Come out from among them, and be ye separate;* with this reflection, 'If they are christians, why don't they come away from the shades of Babylon!"[27]

Backus did not deny Fish's charge, but defended the practice noting the particular reference to Babylon.

> I suppose the use of the word *Babylon* here was thought as criminal as any of their language, but as its significance is *confusion* or *mixture*, are there not at least the *shades* of it where civil and ecclesiastical affairs, *church* and *world*, are *confounded* together, as we have proved they are in our land?[28]

As Backus and Merrill advocated, the Baptists were insistent that the kingdom of God was comprised of visible saints only. A credible profession of faith followed by baptism and a life that evidenced its fruit was requisite to entrance into the kingdom.

3.   The church and the kingdom

Narrowing the subjects of the kingdom of heaven to professed believers, or disciples, brought with it a re-assessment of the connection between it and the church. If the kingdom of heaven was not Old Testament Israel, being then a "mystery," inaugurated by Christ sometime "between the period in which he began his publick ministry, and that in which he suffered," and the subjects of the kingdom were only those who made a credible profession of saving faith, then the relationship of the kingdom of heaven to the church in Baptist theology clearly set them apart from the standing order.[29]

The Baptists held the state church system to be fundamentally at odds with the New Testament revelation of the kingdom of heaven

---

[27] Joseph Fish, *The Church of Christ a Firm and Durable House. Shown in a Number of Sermons on Matth. Xvi. 18. Upon This Rock I Will Build My Church, and the Gates of Hell Shall Not Prevail against It. The Substance of Which Was Delivered at Stonington, Anno Domini, 1765* (New London: Green, Timothy, 1767), 154.

[28] Isaac Backus, *A Fish Caught in His Own Net*, in Backus and McLoughlin, *Isaac Backus on Church, State, and Calvinism; Pamphlets, 1754-1789*, 216.

[29] Merrill, *The Kingdom of Heaven, Distinguished from Babylon a Sermon Delivered at the Introduction of the Lincoln Association, Sept. 21-22, 1808*, 8.

because of the necessary connection between the subjects of the kingdom and the members of the church. If the kingdom was spiritual rather than physical, then entrance into the kingdom and membership in the church must both be spiritual. Backus believed missing this point led to carrying over Old Testament elements of "the covenant of circumcision," where "regenerate and unregenerate were bound together in a national church," into the New Testament, leading to the theological justification for forming national churches. "But men . . . have generally held to the bringing of persons into the kingdom of God by blood, by their own wills, or by the wills of other men; and from thence have come all national churches."[30]

For Backus, Merrill, and the Baptists they represented, the church was to be the visible expression of the kingdom of heaven on earth. In other words, they are essentially the same; the Old Testament "mystery," seen only in shadows and types, became a visible reality with the commencement of Christ's earthly ministry.

> Our conclusion . . . we confined the setting up of the gospel Church, Christ's kingdom on earth, to the time between his saying, 'Repent for the kingdom of heaven is at hand;' and his declaration to the Pharisees, 'The kingdom of God has come.'[31]

The kingdom of heaven was the companion doctrine with which Baptists defined the theology and practice of the church, kingdom theology and ecclesiology mapped together. Equating the kingdom of heaven to the gospel church meant only those who were subjects of the kingdom could be admitted into the membership of the church; all others must be barred. Since the kingdom was a New Testament revelation, Old Testament circumcision held no import. In essence, the Baptists anchored the metaphorical doors of the church in a different place than their paedobaptist antagonists. Instead of the doors to the church being the communion table, as in

---

[30] Backus, *The Kingdom of God, Described by His Word, with Its Infinite Benefits to Human Society*, 9-10.

[31] Merrill, *The Kingdom of Heaven, Distinguished from Babylon a Sermon Delivered at the Introduction of the Lincoln Association, Sept. 21-22, 1808*, 8.

Congregationalism, the Baptists placed the doors to the church at the point of believer's baptism. Only then could the church determine if one was in the kingdom or not. As Merrill, describing the practice known as closed-communion, noted:

> We purposely exclude from our communion all Churches, which admit to their community any of the unbaptized: for all such pollute, if not destroy, the Church of God, and are not baptized Churches; but are Churches, or Societies, of spurious origin; or Churches bewitched . . . *the Paedobaptist Churches are NOT of the visible Church of Christ.*[32]

It is evident that in converting from paedobaptism to believer's baptism, Backus and Merrill had undergone a substantial paradigm shift.[33]

Isaac Backus experienced the move from paedobaptist to Baptist principles fifty years earlier than Merrill, but the connections at this point are unmistakable. Backus came to understand conversion as the prerequisite to baptism and baptism as the foundation of church membership in the 1750s. Subsequently, Backus held regeneration to be requisite to all other participation and blessing within the covenant community, the church. His pilgrimage is instructive.

Soon after being ordained to the gospel ministry, Backus became instrumental in forming the Separate Congregational Church in Titicut, Massachusetts and, as was customary, he drew up a Confession of Faith for the new congregation. Having rejected Solomon Stoddard's modifications to the Half-Way Covenant some years earlier, Backus was careful to formulate the new congregation's doctrinal foundation along evangelical paedobaptist lines consistent with the Savoy Declaration and Cambridge

---

[32] Merrill, *The Kingdom of Heaven, Distinguished from Babylon a Sermon Delivered at the Introduction of the Lincoln Association, Sept. 21-22, 1808,* 16.

[33] It is important to distinguish the different uses of the word "communion" in this debate. While the term often referred to the Lord's Supper, it also frequently meant "The fellowship or mutual relationship between members of one church, or between bodies which recognize each other fully as branches of the universal Christian Church; membership of a church," *Oxford English Dictionary,* "*Communion, N*" (Oxford University Press). The latter is how Merrill was using the term.

Platform.[34] Backus' 1748 article concerning baptism declared, "That true Believers and their infant seed and None but Such have a right to the ordinance of Baptism." However mixed the paedobaptist community might be, the article following baptism narrowed the field for church membership.

> That Whosoever Presumes to administer or Pertake of the Seals of the Covenant of Grace without Saveing faith are in Danger of Sealing their own damnation. Therefore The door of the Church should be Carefully Kept at all times against all Such as Canot Give Scriptural Evidence of their union to Christ by faith.[35]

In Titicut the doors to church communion were clearly set between the ordinances of baptism and the Lord's Supper. Unregenerate infants could receive the ordinance of baptism and by this enter the covenant community, but only those who subsequently were converted could participate in the Lord's Supper and entered into the full communion of the church.

After adopting believer's only baptism, Backus resigned his pastorate over the Separate Congregational Church in Titicut and in 1756 formed the Separate Baptist Church in Middleborough, Massachusetts, where he served the remainder of his life. In authoring a new confession to which all church members were to give their assent, Backus united the two ordinances of baptism and the Lord's Supper into one article and moved the doors of the church from between the two ordinances to precede the ordinance of baptism. The article reads:

That Baptism and the Lord's Supper are ordinances of Christ, to be continued until his second coming; and that the

---

[34] On the Half-Way Covenant, the Savoy Declaration, and the Cambridge Platform see Williston Walker, *The Creeds and Platforms of Congregationalism* (New York: Pilgrim Press, 1991). On Backus' rejecting the Half-Way Covenant and his care in preserving the older Congregationalism, see Alvah Hovey, *A Memoir of the Life and Times of the Rev. Isaac Backus, A. M.* (Boston: Gould and Lincoln, 1858; reprint, Harrisonburg, PA: Gano Books, 1991).

[35] Isaac Backus, "The Confession of Faith and Church Covenant, of the Church of Christ in the Joining Borders of Bridgwater and Middleborough," in Backus and McLoughlin, *The Diary of Isaac Backus*, 1530.

former is requisite to the latter, *that is to say*, that those are to be admitted into the communion of the Church, and to partake of all its ordinances, — who, upon profession of their faith, have been baptized by immersion in the name of the Father, and of the Son, and of the Holy Ghost.[36]

The importance of Backus' article on the ordinances for our study is evidenced by its verbatim incorporation into the "Summary Articles of Faith of the Lincoln Association" at their 1806 general assembly. Backus and Merrill were not only of one mind, they subscribed the same article of faith.[37] Both Backus and Merrill came to see the church, the visible expression of the kingdom of heaven on earth, as a restricted communion, placing the metaphorical doors of the church at the point of believer's only baptism and barring all unbaptized believers or baptized unbelievers from her membership.

The Baptists insisted that not only must the church be separate from the state, but it must be separated from all Christian communities which held to mixed communion. The Baptists not only envisioned tearing the church away from the state, but equally tearing the true church away from the state church.[38] This point is unmistakably made by Merrill, when he says, "In short, the Paedobaptist Church hath ever, by Ecclesiastical censure, or by fire and sword, been seeking the ruin of the visibility of the Baptist Church, and the Baptist have been, by the force of truth, always aiming at the destruction of the visibility of the Paedobaptist

---

[36] Isaac Backus, "THE CONFESSION OF FAITH AND COVENANT," in Hovey, *A Memoir of the Life and Times of the Rev. Isaac Backus, A. M*, 336-37.

[37] *Minutes of the Lincoln Association, Held . . . In Warren, September . . . 1806* (Wiscasset, MA: Babson & Rust, 1806), 2. This article is further evidence that Merrill's "disgusted" hearers were not his Baptist brethren as the entire Lincoln Association adopted closed communion principles two years before his *Kingdom* sermon of 1808.

[38] As a Congregationalist, Backus argued for a return to the concept of a "pure church" that had been largely abandoned by many New England Congregationalists. Some went so far as to argue that a pure church ideal was contrary to Scripture. Backus confronted this error on both theological and historical grounds in his pamphlet exchange with the Reverend Joseph Fish of Stonington Connecticut. See his, *A Fish Caught in His Own Net*, in Backus and McLoughlin, *Isaac Backus on Church, State, and Calvinism; Pamphlets, 1754-1789*, 185-87.

Church."[39]

Pursuing his desire to see the "destruction" of paedobaptist churches by seeking to convert them to Baptist churches, Merrill evidenced a theological priority that would have long range ramifications for the Baptists. Foundational to the doctrine of the subjects and mode of baptism was the larger framework of the kingdom of heaven and Baptist ecclesiology. They sought jealously to guard the purity of the church, the visible expression of the kingdom of heaven on earth. Because the paedobaptist churches were "*NOT of the visible Church of Christ*," the Baptists could have no communion with them. Because of paedobaptism, Protestant and Catholic churches were viewed together as disorderly and in need of removal. The kingdom would see to that.

> The Protestants are all such as have protested against the more gross abominations of Popery, but yet retain *that portion which is the peculiar shelter from the cross, either infant sprinkling, or infant baptism;* and thus build all their Churches after the model of the Jewish Synagogue. . . . This kingdom is to consume, and destroy all other kingdoms, and to bring to reproach, and everlasting contempt, all opposite schemes of religion, and all superstitious notions which both Papists and Protestants have imbibed of this.[40]

Merrill declined to view Baptist churches as Protestant because, in his mind, Baptists derived their ecclesiology from the primitive documents and practice of the New Testament church thereby, in his mind, historically preceding Protestantism. The Baptists had never submitted to the yoke of Rome and the practice of infant baptism which he believed derived historically and theologically from "Popery."[41] While Merrill admitted to desiring the

---

[39] Merrill, *The Kingdom of Heaven, Distinguished from Babylon a Sermon Delivered at the Introduction of the Lincoln Association, Sept. 21-22, 1808,* 18.

[40] Merrill, *The Kingdom of Heaven, Distinguished from Babylon a Sermon Delivered at the Introduction of the Lincoln Association, Sept. 21-22, 1808,* 3-4.

[41] Merrill's rejection of Protestantism as a historical foundation for the emergence of Baptists is chronicled in the Appendix to his first publication as a Baptist, *The Mode and Subjects of Baptism Examined, in Seven Sermons; to Which Is Added, a Brief History of the Baptists.* The popularity of his position among many

"destruction" of paedobaptist churches, he had no malice toward the paedobaptists. His desires were theologically driven, though rarely seen so by the paedobaptists.

> The Baptists are charged with a desire and purpose of dividing and breaking down all other churches, and this is said of them as though they had a mischievous purpose. Whereas all the Baptists desire in the case is, to preach the glad tidings of the kingdom of God, and so to preach them that they may have such an overcoming efficacy as to prevail with all the people of God, to leave the Pedobaptist church, and every other erroneous habitation, and be joined to this kingdom of God.[42]

The shift for Merrill was profound. Prior to converting to Baptist doctrine he sought union and communion with Baptists and included them in his Sedgwick Congregational Church. Now, as with many Baptists, the reassessment of the doctrine of the kingdom of God colored his view of the ecclesiological world in which he lived in life altering ways. The question that logically follows is the place the civil magistrate should play in the support and health of the church.

Baptists is proven by the republication of the Appendix as a stand-alone pamphlet in 1815. *A Miniature History of the Baptists* (New-Haven, CT: Printed by J. Barber, for Henry Lines, 1815). It is important to remember that Merrill is not denying the salvation of numerous paedobaptists, just the legitimacy of their churches.

Merrill expresses in this work the popular historiography of Baptists throughout much of the nineteenth century known as the Successionist theory of Baptist origins tracing their foundation back to the Apostles, Christ, or even John the Baptist. While this view is largely abandoned by Baptist scholars today, it is still held by many Baptists and is popularly represented in J. M. Carroll, *The Trail of Blood* (Lexington: American Baptist publishing co., 1931). For a scholarly refutation of the position see, James Edward McGoldrick, *Baptist Successionism: A Crucial Question in Baptist History*, Atla Monograph Series (Landham, MD: American Theological Library Association and The Scarecrow Press Inc, 1994). For a more full account of the theories of Baptist origins see Richard C. Weeks, "Forward," in Thomas A. Armitage, *A History of the Baptists*, Revised and Enlarged ed. (1890; reprint, Watertown, WI: Maranatha Baptist Press, 1976). I am indebted to James M. Renihan for this reference.

[42] Merrill, *Autobiography*, 6.

Separating God's Two Kingdoms: Two Kingdom Theology among New England Baptists...

4. The sword of the kingdom

One of the most important arenas of eighteenth- and early nineteenth-century Baptist public discourse was their contribution to the principles of civil and religious liberty, especially as it was articulated in discussions relating to what has come to be known as the separation of church and state. Happily, historians are recognizing the more central place religion played in the formulation of the U.S. Constitution's First Amendment protection of the religious freedom of its citizens. What needs further exploration in this process, however, is the formative role that the Baptist's doctrine of the kingdom of God played in the larger debate over the limits of civil authority.[43]

A pivotal New Testament passage that defined the Baptists' understanding of the separation of church and state was John 18:36, "Jesus answered, My kingdom is not of this world: if my kingdom were of this world, then would my servants fight, that I should not be delivered to the Jews: but now is my kingdom not from hence." Backus used this text against Stonington minister Rev. Joseph Fish who sought to justify the interrelation of church and state in Connecticut in the eighteenth century. Having suffered under the coercive power of the state as a Separate Connecticut Congregationalist and later advocating for Baptists under the yoke of religious tyranny in Massachusetts, Backus concluded from this passage, "Therefore the dignity of his [Christ's] government is

---

[43] For an example of a historian's recognition of the primacy of religion, especially the right of private judgment playing a formative role in the debate and adoption of the free exercise clause of the First Amendment, Mark Noll recommends Nicholas Patrick Miller, *The Religious Roots of the First Amendment: Dissenting Protestants and the Separation of Church and State* (New York: Oxford University Press, 2012). Miller centers on the Protestant Reformation's advocacy of the right of private judgment in interpreting Scripture as the most central religious doctrine historically culminating in the separation of church and state. My contention in what follows is that the right of private judgment relates to the spiritual nature of the kingdom of God. The illumination of Scripture to each and every subject of the kingdom by the reigning King Jesus through the indwelling Holy Spirit confirmed for the Baptists that the kingdom of God is the larger meta-theological framework from which this comes.

maintained not by *carnal* but by *spiritual* weapons."[44]

Backus envisioned a world in which the civil and religious spheres were not intertwined, but distinct. Two kingdoms, one "carnal" (physical) and one "spiritual;" one ruled by Christ as redeemer over those whom he had granted regeneration and who voluntarily gathered into visible churches and the other governed by God and ruled by morally responsible leaders gathered into nations. As he noted in his discussion of the kingdom of God, "his government of his church, hath ever been distinct from his general government of the world."[45]

Merrill also distinguished between the kingdom of God, "a kingdom of righteousness and governed by the Prince of Peace," and the kingdoms of this world, still governed by the sovereign God but separate from the church. In the eighteenth and early nineteenth centuries, many thought it would be better if the interests of true religion were encouraged, advocated, or even dictated by the civil magistrate. Should the magistrate not use all the coercive power it could wield to further the kingdom of God? According to Merrill, the problem with the logic behind such questions, a logic imbedded in the thinking and confessions of the standing order, was a fundamental misunderstanding of the very nature of the kingdom of God and the kingdoms of this world.[46] Merrill insisted:

---

[44] Backus and McLoughlin, *Isaac Backus on Church, State, and Calvinism; Pamphlets, 1754-1789*, 195.

[45] Backus, *The Kingdom of God, Described by His Word, with Its Infinite Benefits to Human Society*, 5.

[46] The *Westminster Confession of Faith,* to which many New England Congregationalists subscribed, accords the civil magistrate power over the churches to ensure their prosperity and purity. WCF 23, Of the Civil Magistrate "III. The civil magistrate . . . has authority, and it is his duty, to take order that unity and peace be preserved in the Church, that the truth of God be kept pure and entire, that all blasphemies and heresies be suppressed, all corruptions and abuses in worship and discipline prevented or reformed, and all the ordinances of God duly settled, administrated, and observed." *The Savoy Declaration*, the confession of Congregationalism more generally, in departing from WCF, softens its Erastianism but still accords the civil magistrate authority in church matters, warranting the abridging of liberty where error and perceived heresy was found. For a parallel edition of *The Westminster Confession, The Savoy Declaration,* and the Baptist confessions of 1644/46 and 1677/89 see James M. Renihan, *True Confessions: Baptist Documents in the Reformed Family* (Owensboro, KY: RBAP, 2004), 157-58.

... the kingdom, which the God of heaven hath set up, has never needed, so has never debased herself by soliciting, the secular arm to enforce the mandates of the Church. . . . Of the civil authority she asks no more, than to have it stand out of her sunshine. That Cesar, in agreement with the ordinance of heaven, would look well to the management of Cesar's kingdom, and leave it with the Lord to manage his.[47]

Merrill framed the discussion along the lines of legitimate yet different kingdoms which had been comingled by the theology and practice of the paedobaptists. What Merrill and the Baptists were attempting to do was to separate the two kingdoms of God, the civil and ecclesiastical, and so bring about a more consistent biblical model of church and state.

The Shaftsbury (Vermont) Baptist Association expressed similar sentiments in its 1796 circular letter. The "kingdom of heaven . . . is not defended by carnal weapons" and "forms no alliance with the kingdoms and states of this world, but is distinct from them." The Philadelphia Association likewise proclaimed, "Christ's kingdom needs no support from union with the governments of this world; that the more distinctly the line is drawn between them the better."[48] Merrill was simply adding his voice to the larger body of Baptists at this juncture.

Backus was quick to counter the implications some might make of removing the civil magistrate from using the sword to enforce religious affairs. It was not that the unbelief or recalcitrance of the citizenry was acceptable to God or the Baptists; rather God had ordained a different means for addressing the unbelief of those outside the church. "The question between us is not, whether it be

---

[47] Merrill, *The Kingdom of God: A Discourse, Delivered at Concord, before His Excellency the Govenor [Sic], the Honorable Council, the Honorable Senate, and House of Representatives of the State of New-Hampshire, June 5, 1817, Being the Anniversary Election*, 12, 38.

[48] *Minutes of the Shaftsbury Association; Holden at West-Stockbridge, June 1st & 2d, 1796. Together with Their Circular and Corresponding Letters* (Lansingburgh: Luther Pratt & Co., 1796), 17; A. D. Gillette, *Minutes of the Philadelphia Baptist Association, 1707 to 1807: Being the First One Hundred Years of Its Existence*, 1st tricentennial ed., Philadelphia Association Series (Springfield, MO: Particular Baptist Press, 2002), 362.

the duty . . . but it is, whether that duty ought to be enforced by the sword, or only by instruction, persuasion and good example?"[49] The Baptists argued for the latter, the paedobaptists for the former.

The Baptists were hopeful of being left alone and the proclamation of the truth would prevail to win the hearts where the sword could only coerce outward behavior. The kingdoms of this earth had their God-appointed means whereby they might exercise authority as did the kingdom of heaven, each requisite to its ordained sphere. To the civil magistrate was given the sword, to the church was given the proclamation of the truth; the sword was carnal, the proclaimed Word was spiritual. This provided Backus' counter to the Norwich, Connecticut, Congregational minister Benjamin Lord, "we . . . only desire peaceably to worship God according to our consciences, among ourselves; believing that Christ's church is founded in the *truth*, and supported by it, against all the powers of earth and hell."[50] As he remarked elsewhere, "TRUTH and MERCY shine with equal luster in the glorious kingdom of the Redeemer, and to his *works* of this nature he appeals as his greatest *witnesses* against the powers of darkness, *John* v, 36, 37. Their united influence convey the *golden oil* into the church to make her the *light of the world, Zech,* iv, 2-14,"[51]

Using military language, Backus again referenced John 18:36-37 in his 1773 advocacy for religious liberty for New England Baptists, *Appeal to the Public*, bringing to light the peculiar spheres of the two kingdoms and the primacy of the spiritual weapon of truth in the kingdom of heaven.

This is the nature of his kingdom, which he says, is not of

---

[49] Isaac Backus, *A History of New-England, with Particular Reference to the Denomination of Christians Called Baptists. Containing the First Principles and Settlements of the Country; the Rise and Increase of the Baptist Churches Therein; the Intrusion of Arbitrary Power under the Cloak of Religion; the Christian Testimonies of the Baptists and Others against the Same, with Their Sufferings under It, from the Begining [sic] to the Present Time. Collected from Most Authentic Records and Writings, Both Ancient and Modern*, 3 vols. (Boston: Edward Draper, 1777), 1:101.

[50] Isaac Backus, *A Letter to the Reverend Mr. Benjamin Lord, of Norwich; Occasioned by Some Harsh Things Which He Has Lately Published against Those Who Have Dissented from His Sentiments About the Ministry, the Church, and Baptism* (Providence: William Goddard, 1764), 37.

[51] Isaac Backus, *Truth Is Great, and Will Prevail* (Boston: Philip Freeman, 1781), 36.

this world: and gives that as the reason why his servants should not fight or defend him with the sword. John. 18. 36. 37. And it appears to us that the true difference and exact limits between ecclesiastical and civil government is this, That the church is armed with light and truth, to pull down the strong holds of iniquity, and to gain souls to Christ, and into his church, to be governed by his rules therein; and again to exclude such from their communion, who will not be so governed; while the state is armed with the sword to guard the peace, and the civil rights of all persons and societies, and to punish those who violate the same. And where these two kinds of government, and the weapons which belong to them, are well distinguished, and improved according to the true nature and end of their institution, the effects are happy, and they do not at all interfere with each other: but where they have been confounded together, no tongue nor pen can fully describe the mischiefs that have ensued; of which the Holy Ghost gave early and plain warnings.[52]

Since the civil and ecclesiastical spheres were different, in Backus' words "carnal" verses "spiritual," so their weapons were different.[53] The Baptists were building on a long tradition of seeing the civil magistrate's responsibility to govern outward moral behavior but having no ability or authority to control the consciences of men and women. So long as the subjects of the civil kingdom were obedient they were good citizens and should be left to worship according to their own consciences. The Baptist arguments followed those like Roger Williams who more than a century earlier established his arguments for religious liberty against John Cotton and the

---

[52] Isaac Backus, *An Appeal to the Public for Religious Liberty, against the Oppressions of the Present Day* (Boston: John Boyle, 1773), 13. McLoughlin notes that Backus wrote this work as the agent for the Baptists in New England, under commission from the Warren Baptist Association. This underscores the fact that the sentiments respecting the kingdom of God expressed in the work were those of the Baptists at large and not simply of Backus personally. Backus and McLoughlin, *Isaac Backus on Church, State, and Calvinism; Pamphlets, 1754-1789,* 304.

[53] Backus and McLoughlin, *Isaac Backus on Church, State, and Calvinism; Pamphlets, 1754-1789,* 195.

Massachusetts standing order upon twelve foundational premises, the sixth of which read:

> It is the will and command of God, that since the coming of his Son the Lord Jesus, a permission of the most paganish, Jewish, Turkish, or anti-Christian consciences and worships be granted to all men in all nations and countries, and they are only to be fought against with that sword which is only, in soul matters, able to conquer, to wit, the sword of God's Spirit, the word of God.[54]

One of the key features of the Baptists understanding of the kingdom of God was the need for men and women to be free to act according to their consciences. This could only be guaranteed by unraveling the two kingdoms into their respective spheres. As subjects of a civil magistrate the Baptists insisted on the necessity of obedience and cooperation, even to the point of serving within the sphere of civil government. In this manner they showed themselves to be quite different than the Anabaptists who advocated a more marked separation between the believer and the kingdoms of this world.[55]

---

[54] Roger Williams, *The Bloudy Tenent of Persecution for Cause of Conscience: Discussed in a Conference between Truth and Peace, Who, in All Tender Affection, Present to the High Court of Parliament, (as the Result of Their Discourse) These, (among Other Passages) of Highest Consideration*, 1st ed., Baptists (Macon, GA: Mercer University Press, 2001), 3. Backus would also allow for the free worship of those outside of Protestantism, quoting with approval Roger Williams' advocacy for "*impartial liberty* for the consciences of Papists with others, as to matters of worship." Backus, *Truth Is Great, and Will Prevail*, 33. However, I am not certain he would have been as open to some of the others listed by Williams.

[55] The Anabaptists were bitterly persecuted in Europe for their separatism and pacifism which were grounded in a view of the world and the civil magistrate quite disparate from those of the Particular Baptists. For polemical reasons the paedobaptists were constantly attempting to mark the Baptists as Anabaptists, a point to which they regularly objected, as can be seen in the title given to their first confession of faith; *The Confession of Faith, of Those Churches Which Are Commonly (Though Falsly) Called Anabaptists* (London: [s.n.], 1644). While polemically it may have been an effective *ad hominem* technique, it was in reality dishonest. Though there were similarities between Continental Anabaptists and English Particular Baptists, especially in limiting the subjects of baptism to disciples alone, there were substantive dissimilarities as well. The doctrine of the kingdom of God is

Where the Anabaptists saw serving within the civil government to be a compromise with the world, the Baptists saw no conflict. It was not a compromise with the forces of evil, but service to God in the civil kingdom; civil magistracy could be a God-honoring vocation. Backus, Merrill, and the Baptist Associations to which they belonged, owned the London Baptist *Confession of Faith* of 1677/89 which clearly spelled out their view of the civil magistrate.

God, the supream Lord, and King of all the World, hath ordained *Civil Magistrates* to be under him, over the people for his own glory, and the public good; and to this end hath armed them with the power of the Sword, for the defence and encouragement of them that do good, and for the punishment of evil doers. It is lawful for Christians to Accept, and Execute the Office of a *Magistrate*, when called thereunto . . .[56]

---

foundational to understanding those differences. Anabaptism viewed the kingdoms of this world to be inaugurated as a direct result and accommodation to the entrance of sin into the world. As Littell notes, "The attitude of restraint towards the magistrate's calling and various functions related to it was based upon the thought that there were two different worlds, and the things pertaining to life in one were not proper in the other." The point here is that Anabaptism viewed the civil magistrate as "given for [because of] the sins of the world" and the disciple was to have no part in it or risk being tainted by sin. In essence, as Littell further notes, the Anabaptists were guilty of an over-realized eschatology; for them the kingdoms of the world were totally separate from the kingdom of God and one could not be a willing participant in both. The Baptists, on the other hand, saw the kingdoms of this world as ordained by God and fundamentally for good. Thus one could be robustly a participant in both without mixing the authority of the one with the other. Franklin H. Littell, *The Anabaptist View of the Church; a Study in the Origins of Sectarian Protestantism*, 2nd ed. (Boston: Starr King Press, 1958), 103-05. Estep recognizes the importance of the "two world concept" of Anabaptism, acknowledging that it has been viewed as the defining characteristic of their theology by Anabaptist scholars. However, he plays down the importance of this distinction opting for "a distinctive view of the church" as the better entry point. It is instructive that in doing this he seems to rely heavily on the theology of Balthasar Hubmaier (1480-1528) whose Anabaptist views of the civil magistrate were, according to Stayer, "the least typical" of the continental Anabaptists. William Roscoe Estep, *The Anabaptist Story* (Grand Rapids: Eerdmans, 1975), 179-81; James M. Stayer, *Anabaptists and the Sword* (Lawrence, KS: Coronado Press, 1972), 336.

[56] *A Confession of Faith Put Forth by the Elders and Brethren of Many Congregations*

Unlike the Anabaptists, for the Baptists the two kingdoms were not antagonistic to each other but distinct, having different spheres, different governing rules, and different means for maintaining that rule. The Baptists did not seek to separate from the kingdoms of the world, but to see them operate within their God-ordained spheres. When this objective failed, when the physical sword was used in support of the spiritual sword, it spoke trouble for both kingdoms. Separating the two kingdoms, however, also required giving due attention to the ways God-ordained for the growth of his spiritual kingdom. If the kingdom was not to grow by the sword then there must be other means. It is to these we now turn.

5. The expansion of the kingdom

At the time of his conversion to Baptist principles, Merrill was overseeing the training and preaching of three candidates for ministry. One, William Allen, according to Henry Burrage, was already a Baptist. The other two soon followed suit. Phinehas Pillsbury, for some time a deacon in Merrill's Sedgwick Congregational Church, adopted Baptist principles and was immersed by Baptist itinerant Isaac Case at Isleborough, Maine, in 1804 and ordained in Fayette, Maine, in January of 1805, just five months before Merrill in Sedgwick. The second man, Henry Hale, received baptism on the island of Vinalhaven on October 28, 1804, again by Isaac Case, and was ordained as an evangelist at Sedgwick, April 22, 1807. Hale's ordination sermon was preached by Merrill and subsequently printed. In this sermon, Merrill outlined his thinking on the expansion of the kingdom of God. "As the kingdom of the Lord Jesus, or the kingdom which the God of heaven was to set up, was begun and increased, so it appears it must be augmented and completed."[57]

In bringing about the augmentation of this kingdom, Merrill

---

of Christians, (Baptized Upon Profession of Their Faith) in London and the Country with an Appendix Concerning Baptism (London: Printed for Benjamin Harris, 1677), 81.

[57] Daniel Merrill, *The Gospel Rangers; a Sermon Delivered at the Ordination of Elder Henry Hale by Daniel Merrill* (Buckstown: William W. Clapp, 1807), 6.

described the process of setting apart men to the gospel ministry using the analogy of army "rangers." The "gospel rangers" have four qualifying characteristics. First, they have experienced regeneration. Using the language of Ezekiel 36:26, Merrill described them as men whose "heart of stone is taken away, and an heart of flesh, a new heart is given." Second, Christ gives them a soldier's "courage" and a heart to engage in the spiritual battle for men's souls, a spiritual "holy war," wresting unbelievers from the domain of the enemy and winning them to Zion. Third, using language reminiscent of the military preparation that rangers might need, Merrill insists they are nourished by the "King" in ways that will sustain them for the "long" and "hard" journey which awaits them. Finally, the King gives them the knowledge requisite to the task to which they are fitted; "He gives them to understand the doctrines of the cross, and the mysteries of the grace of God."[58]

Merrill followed the discussion of their qualifications with their calling, that internal work of the Holy Spirit drawing them into the work of the kingdom, and their commissioning through the church's affirmation that the individual is both qualified and called.

> Hence, such as run to and fro should be commissioned as well as qualified and called. It is true, no commission, which can be given by men or angels, can of itself give authority to any of these runners; but, such as are qualified and called of God may have their commission by the instrumentality of men, or it may be in this way made visible.[59]

Merrill elucidated the Baptists' desire to avoid two errors evident in the all too often reality of unfit men in the ministry. History and experience had taught them that churches were plagued by men who lacked either the practical or spiritual qualifications necessary. Biblically uneducated or spiritually unregenerate men, though especially common in the frontier settlements, could not serve kingdom purposes. The function of the commissioning or ordaining process was to show that the church had examined both the qualifications and calling of the man put

---

[58] Merrill, *The Gospel Rangers*, 6-7.
[59] Merrill, *The Gospel Rangers*, 7-8.

forward and had good reason to believe that the candidate was properly fitted. The expectation was that the kingdom would be advanced by their faithful labors because they were owned by the King.

Backus dealt extensively with these same subjects in his debates with Congregational minster Rev. Joseph Fish. Like many paedobaptists, Fish questioned the legitimacy of the ministerial vocation of many of the Baptists and Separate Congregationalists. While the Baptists and Separate Congregationalists embraced important theological differences, especially respecting the proper subjects and mode of baptism, they agreed on a number of doctrinal tenants, the nature of the call to the gospel ministry being one of them.[60]

One practice of the "common ministers" that Backus sought to correct was the custom of accepting "an ordinary call" to the gospel ministry as sufficient to their being set apart thereto. By an ordinary call Backus meant they were "called only by men," or in Merrill's terms above, having a commission after a fashion but not the evident call of Zion's king. Backus believed this to be true of "a great part of the ministers in the land." His task then, was to defend the necessity of an internal call as a nonnegotiable prerequisite in the gospel ministry.[61]

Backus also had to counter the criticism of Rev. Fish and others to what was deemed an indefensible subjectivism. Apparently Fish suggested that Backus and the Baptists held to an internal call, but rejected the testing of the call by the church. Backus objected that Fish claimed "we hold to nothing external." Fish suggested further

---

[60] Proof of this in Backus' life alone is not hard to find. Backus' first published work was on the necessity of an internal call to the gospel ministry and was penned in 1754 while he was pastor of the Separate Congregational Church in Titicut, Massachusetts. Though Backus embraced Baptist principles three years earlier, he wrote as a Separatist who held to mixed-communion. He would not embrace closed-communion as a Baptist for two more years.

[61] Isaac Backus, *All True Ministers of the Gospel, Are Called into That Work by the Special Influences of the Holy Spirit. A Discourse Shewing the Nature and Necesity of an Internal Call to Preach the Everlasting Gospel. Also Marks by Which Christ's Ministers May Be Known from Others, and Answers to Sundry Objections: Together with Some Observations on the Principles and Practices of Many in the Present Day Concerning These Things. To Which Is Added, Some Short Account of the Experiences and Dying Testimony of Mr. Nathanael Shepherd* (Boston: Daniel Fowle, 1754), viii.

the Baptists exalted in the lack of education among their ministers claiming an inverse relationship between education and usefulness; suggesting a sort of Baptist motto—"*the less learning the more of faith.*"[62] Like Backus, Merrill lamented the misunderstanding of the place of education in the ministry in two directions. Those who held "a knowledge of Greek or Roman literature to be the principle qualifications of a Gospel minister" were as wrong as those who "ignorantly despise all scientific knowledge as being beneath the attention, and detrimental to the heralds of the Prince of Peace"[63] Backus's refutation of Fish mirrored Merrill's affirmation: "a person that is called to preach has not a right to act in those things which are peculiar to an officer in the church till he is publically set apart therein."[64]

First, Merrill argued for properly discerning and setting apart servants in the kingdom, for "Not all Christ's visible Church are to be his heralds. They are to be a picked company, called, chosen, faithful."[65] Second, Merrill dealt definitively with the arena of their labors. As the kingdom was spiritual rather than physical, the boundaries of each servant's labors defied geographical limitation. Since its inception, the standing order churches in New England mirrored almost exclusively the geography of the towns in which they were set. All those within the geographical boundaries of the township were considered the simultaneous subjects of both civil and ecclesiastical institutions. The Baptists recognized no such geographical or ecclesiastical limitations. They had no qualms about "trampl[ing] upon parish lines, and upon every hedge, erected by selfish ingenuity to prevent perishing souls from receiving divine knowledge."[66]

---

[62] Backus, *A Fish Caught in His Own Net*, 90-91.

[63] Merrill, *The Gospel Rangers*, 16.

[64] Backus and McLoughlin, *Isaac Backus on Church, State, and Calvinism; Pamphlets, 1754-1789*, 251.

[65] Merrill, *The Gospel Rangers*, 19.

[66] Merrill, *The Gospel Rangers*, 20. On the parish system in New England and its breakdown during the early republic as a direct result of Baptist and Methodist itinerancy, see especially Shelby M. Balik, "The Religious Frontier: Church, State, and Settlement in Northern New England, 1780-1830" (Ph.D. diss., Univ. of Wisconsin-Madison, 2006). For a similar study detailing the end of the parish system in Virginia, again due to effects of itinerant preachers making inroads for dissenting religion, especially Presbyterian, Baptist, and Methodist, see Rhys Isaac,

Merrill proclaimed the commissioned minister's field of labor in global terms. He said, "Christ's Rangers will penetrate the wilds of America, the burning sands of Africa, the vast regions of Asia, and make their way among the learned and rude of Europe. For their rout lies through every part and place under heaven." In addition to breaking the geographical boundary, there was not a person under the sun who was off limits for the itinerant's gospel ministrations. They were to go "wherever they can find a saint to comfort, or a sinner to teach."[67]

This understanding of the call to the gospel ministry meant that Baptist ministers were ready to travel wherever they saw an opportunity open to them. In fact, many, if not most, who took a settled pastorate over a specific congregation, made the freedom to pursue itinerant work a condition of their settlement. They were to be like Maine Elder Henry Kendall, who confessed, "Baptist ministers were few in this region. . . . In these days I was wont to devote one-half of my time to travelling and preaching lectures."[68]

As "rangers" of a world-wide spiritual kingdom, these men had a global vision commensurate with their global commission — to "*go into all the world, and preach the gospel to every creature.*"[69] The resulting outlook of the Baptists is noted by Shelby Balik:

> Under the itinerant system, religious ties among far-flung believers superseded the relationships between individual congregations and their towns. Rather than looking inward upon their own clustered communities, members of local churches looked outward to other, often faraway congregations with whom they shared common doctrines and rituals.[70]

The Transformation of Virginia, 1740-1790 (Chapel Hill, NC: Published for the Omohundro Institute of Early American History and Culture, Williamsburg, Virginia, by the University of North Carolina Press, 1982, 1999).

[67] Merrill, *The Gospel Rangers*, 13.

[68] Henry Kendall, *Autobiography of Elder Henry Kendall* (Portland, ME: Henry Kendall, 1853), 47.

[69] Merrill, *The Gospel Rangers*, 20.

[70] Shelby M. Balik, "Equal Right and Equal Privilege: Separating Church and State in Vermont," *Journal of Church & State* 50, no. 1 (2008): 28-29.

To this end they developed two vital structures intended to assist in this endeavor; regional associations and mission societies. The first, associationalism, was brought over to the colonies by English and Welsh Baptists in the seventeenth century and was expressed in the London Baptist Confession of 1677/89, Chapter 26, *Of the Church.*

> As each Church, and all the Members of it, are bound to pray continually, for the good and prosperity of all the Churches of Christ, in all places; and upon all occasions to further it (every one within the bounds of their places, and callings, in the Exercise of their Gifts and Graces) so the churches (when planted by the providence of God, so as they may enjoy opportunity and advantage for it) ought to hold communion amongst themselves for their peace, increase of love, and mutual edification.[71]

Among the confessional Particular Baptists, the first Baptist Association formed in the colonies of British North America was the Philadelphia Association founded in 1707. The first in New England was the Warren Association. Backus, representing his Middleborough Baptist Church, was present at the founding of the Warren Association in September 1767 and his church formally joined it in 1769. *The Sentiments,* outlining its value and purposes, was published that same year, saying:

> That such a combination of churches is not only prudent but useful, as has appeared even in America by the experience of upwards of 60 years, Some of its uses are — Union and communion among themselves — maintaining more effectually the order and faith once delivered to the saints — Having advice in cases of doubts, and help in distress, Being more able to promote the good of the cause.[72]

The Baptist Associations in Maine developed as a direct result of the work and cooperation of the Warren and Philadelphia Associations.[73]

---

[71] Renihan, *True Confessions,* 173-74.

[72] *The Sentiments and Plan of the Warren Association* (Germantown: Christopher Sower, 1769), 3.

The second structure, the mission society, was another English innovation established for the first time in the mid-seventeenth century during the *interregnum* to facilitate the separate English churches' material support of the work of John Eliot and Thomas Mayhew in New England. This missionary support structure would be adopted by the English Baptists in the late eighteenth century and would be replicated in the United States of America in the nineteenth century with stunning frequency as the push for foreign missions exploded. The differences between the association and the mission society would later become a point of contention and ultimately division among nineteenth-century Baptists, but for the present they were cooperative organizations among Baptists for the furtherance of the kingdom.[74]

While Baptist associations drew Baptist churches together to further the interests of the churches in a particular region, mission societies sought to draw Baptist attention to specific endeavors by raising support and sending missionaries to reach those currently outside of the Baptist fold in more remote areas. Thus, in 1802, the Massachusetts Baptist Missionary Society, which according to

---

[73] On Baptist associationalism in general, for seventeenth-century English Particular Baptists see, James M. Renihan, *Edification and Beauty: The Practical Ecclesiology of the English Particular Baptists, 1675-1705*, Studies in Baptist History and Thought (Colorado Springs: Paternoster, 2008). On American Baptist associationalism, see Walter B. Shurden, *Associationalism among Baptists in America, 1707-1814*, The Baptist Tradition (New York: Arno Press, 1980). Statistical data on Baptist Associations in America through the end of the eighteenth century can be found in Robert G. Gardner, *Baptists of Early America: A Statistical History, 1639-1790* (Atlanta: Georgia Baptist Historical Society, 1983), 137-48. The history of the Philadelphia Association is found in David Spencer, *The Early Baptists of Philadelphia* (Philadelphia: William Syckelmoore, 1877). On the formation of the Warren Association see Henry S. Burrage, *A History of the Baptists in New England* (Philadelphia: American Baptist Publication Society, 1894), 81-84 and Isaac Backus, "A History of the Baptist Warren Association in New England from the Year 1767, to the Year 1792," (MS in the Angus Library, Regent's Park College, Oxford.).

[74] For the history of the first English mission society see William Kellaway, *The New England Company, 1649-1776: Missionary Society to the American Indians* (Westport, CT: Greenwood Press, 1975). The well-known seventeenth-century Particular Baptist William Kiffin was a member of this society. The establishment of the English Baptist Missionary Society is detailed in F. A. Cox, *History of the English Baptist Missionary Society: From A.D. 1792 to A.D. 1842* (Boston: W. S. Damrell, 1845) and Michael A. G. Haykin, *One Heart and One Soul: John Sutcliff of Olney, His Friends and His Times* (Darlington, England: Evangelical Press, 1994).

Separating God's Two Kingdoms: Two Kingdom Theology among New England Baptists...

Albert L. Vail was the first Baptist missionary society in America, was formed in Boston with a view to "the enlargement of the Redeemer's Kingdom." To this end, the committee given oversight of the appointment of missionaries settled on three men, two to travel to the north and one to the west. Rev. Isaac Case, an itinerant who was sent by the Baptist Church in Dighton, Massachusetts, to serve in Maine in 1783, was one appointed to reach "the British Provinces, and the District of Maine."[75]

Because the missionaries were specifically appointed to the work of the Redeemer's kingdom, they were cautioned about the dangers of mingling the two kingdoms in their preaching endeavors and the special challenges political involvement could bring.

> The Committee most strenuously recommends that you solicitously avoid all interference and allusions to those political topics which divide the opinions and too much irritate the passions of our fellow citizens. Subjects of this description are not merely irrelevant to the spiritual purposes of missionary exertion, but manifestly subversive to all reasonable prospect of success . . .[76]

For missionaries traveling throughout the northern frontier and into the British provinces, encountering divergent political views was a certainty. Failing to exercise themselves in a politically peaceable fashion not only jeopardized the mission's purpose but it confused

---

[75] Albert L. Vail, *The Morning Hour of American Baptist Missions* (Philadelphia: American Baptist Publication Society, 1907), 96. W. H. Eaton, *Historical Sketch of the Massachusetts Baptist Missionary Society and Convention, 1802-1902* (Boston: Massachusetts Baptist Convention, 1903), 13-14. It is important to note that the Maine Baptist's interest in pursuing a "Gospel Mission" predated the formation of the Massachusetts Society by a few years. For instance the Bowdoinham Association began cooperatively raising money for missions at their 1799 annual General Assembly. See Association Bowdoinham, *Minutes of the Bowdoinham Association, Held at the Baptist Meeting-House in Livermore, August 28 and 29, 1799* (Portland, ME: Benjamin Titcomb, 1799), 6, and missionary Isaac Case's "very pleasing account, of the advancement of the Redeemer's Kingdom" the following year; *Minutes of the Bowdoinham Association, Held at the Baptist Meeting-House in Green, August 27 and 28, 1800* (Portland, ME: Eleazer Alley Jenks, 1800), 6.

[76] Eaton, *Historical Sketch of the Massachusetts Baptist Missionary Society and Convention, 1802-1902*, 14-15.

the nature of the kingdom of heaven with the kingdoms of this world.

Associations were meant to bring together churches of like faith and practice for mutual fellowship and support, including preaching in churches destitute of a settled minister. Evangelists like Henry Hale and Isaac Case and itinerant preachers such as Daniel Merrill would not only cross local boundaries but regional ones as well. Discerning the distinction between the kingdom of God and the kingdoms in which they itinerated was crucial to developing and expanding those interconnections within the kingdom of God that would eventuate in a global conquest by the Redeemer.

Case, Hale, and Merrill would travel frequently into the provinces of Nova Scotia and New Brunswick, influencing a number of Allinite converts and churches, many of whom adopted their closed-communion Baptist doctrines.[77] This gave rise to the Maritime Baptists establishing associations which formalized relations with a number of the Maine Baptist Associations. They would speak of each other in affectionate and familial terms. They were sister associations in the kingdom of God.

Beginning in the late eighteenth century, Maine and the Maritime provinces were under national governments headed in very different directions generating tensions on both sides of the

---

[77] On Henry Alline and the Allinite churches of Nova Scotia see J. M. Bumsted, *Henry Alline, 1748-1784*, Canadian Biographical Studies (Toronto: University of Toronto Press, 1971); Henry Alline, James Beverley, and Barry M. Moody, *The Life and Journal of the Rev. Mr. Henry Alline*, Baptist Heritage in Atlantic Canada (Hantsport, NS: Published by Lancelot Press for Acadia Divinity College and the Baptist Historical Committee of the United Baptist Convention of the Atlantic Provinces, 1982). For a scholarly examination of their interaction with General and Particular Baptists in Maine and beyond, see George A. Rawlyk, *Ravished by the Spirit: Religious Revivals, Baptists, and Henry Alline*, The 1983 Hayward Lectures (Kingston, Ontario: McGill-Queen's University Press, 1984); and Stephen A. Marini, *Radical Sects of Revolutionary New England* (Cambridge, MA: Harvard University Press, 1982). On the regionalism of the northeastern Baptists and the "special interest" New England Baptists expressed in their neighbor to the east, see Brackney, "The Planter Motif among Baptists from New England to Nova Scotia, 1760-1850," in William H. Brakney, Paul S. Fiddes, and John H. Y. Briggs, eds., *Pilgrim Pathways: Essays in Baptist History in Honour of B. R. White* (Macon, GA: Mercer University Press, 1999), 283-302.

Separating God's Two Kingdoms: Two Kingdom Theology among New England Baptists...

Atlantic. This would continue into the early nineteenth century as the War of 1812 unfolded. At the same time, spiritually, many churches in the northeastern region had been going through a process of drawing closer together. The Baptists recognized that an overemphasis on their political differences could well generate strained relations in the kingdom of God as that kingdom crossed their national boundaries. The War would test these bi-directional relationships as the two earthly kingdoms came to cross-purposes.[78]

Maine and Maritime Baptists would need to manage their complex spiritual and political relationships closely. One example of the Baptists' awareness of their two kingdoms theology giving a framework for managing their political and spiritual differences is reflected in the correspondence of Daniel Merrill of Maine and Edward Manning, one of the most prominent Baptist leaders in Nova Scotia. Merrill had come to develop a close relationship with Manning as a result of itinerant work in the region which both men engaged in regularly. The War eventuated in prohibiting their cross-border activity and illustrates the point at hand.[79]

Merrill was serving in the Massachusetts legislature representing Sedgwick as the prospect of war overshadowed that body politic. The civic responsibilities laid on him by the citizens of Sedgwick prohibited him from attending the Nova Scotia and New Brunswick Baptist Association held in Upper Granville, Nova Scotia, in June of 1812 as a representative of the Lincoln Association of Maine. He excused himself in a letter written to Manning from Boston in terms reflective of his two kingdoms perspective.

> My Dear Brother, I am for the present, very much

---

[78] For a brief and limited analysis of American Baptist views of the War of 1812, see Peirce S. Ellis, Jr., "Baptists and the War of 1812," *The Chronicle* 11, no. 11 (1948): 124-34. Ellis confirms that the Baptists in the United States were not uniform in their views of the War but that Baptists in the northeast were far more likely to reflect a form of neutrality over against those churches located in the south or west. There was considerable cross-border associationalism in Vermont that was interrupted by the War as well. See Stuart Ivison and Fred Rosser, *The Baptists in Upper and Lower Canada before 1820* (Toronto: University of Toronto Press, 1956).

[79] On Edward Manning see especially Daniel C. Goodwin, *Into Deep Waters: Evangelical Spirituality and Maritime Calvinistic Baptist Ministers, 1790-1855* (Montreal: McGill-Queen's University Press, 2010), 98-125.

occupied. The Legislature, of which I am a member, is now in session, and upon important business. They are about memorializing the general government, relative to the subject of peace or war. I wish the differences between your government and ours may be so accommodated, as to promote the good of both, and subserve Zion's best good. But I fear a contest is before us.

However the differences may be between the governments among men, be it our concern to be in obedience to the government of God.[80]

Merrill saw the two men as under two different governments respecting their national identities but under a single government respecting their spiritual identities.

Manning also struggled with the challenges he faced nationally and denominationally during the War. Cross-border fellowship quickly diminished after the declaration of war as the Associations suspended the practice of sending messengers to each other's assemblies and itinerants were required to stay within their own national borders. The effect was recorded by Manning in his private journal entry for January 9, 1813, only six months after the War began: "This day felt uneasy in the morning and [sic] unpleasant sensation. But in reading and meditation found my mind sweetly led after God and a sweet union to American brethren, notwithstanding the dreadful war that exists between the two powers." Manning powerfully reflects how the disunion between the "two [civil] powers" failed to curb his contemplation of the "sweet union" with Merrill and the other American Baptists to whom he had become attached. The distinction between the civil kingdom and the kingdom of God was clear enough for these men to maintain warm feelings for the other even though their governments were at arms.[81]

The attitudes of Merrill and Manning were also reflected

---

[80] Letter from Daniel Merrill to Edward Manning, June 2, 1812. In the Manning Collection, Esther Clark Wright Archives, Acadia University, Wolfville, NS. The transcription is my own.

[81] Journal of the Reverend Edward Manning of Cornwallis, Nova Scotia, Esther Clark Wright Special Collections, Acadia University, Wolfville, NS.

associationally as relations were restored after the War. This effect was most strikingly recorded by the Bowdoinham Association of Maine. In the corresponding letter for 1815 the Maine Baptists rejoiced at restored cordial relations with the Baptists of the Maritime Province:

> Through the blessing of returning peace, we once more are at liberty to communicate our friendship, and relate the state of our churches, not only to correspondents within the limits of our own territory, but also to our beloved brethren in the neighboring provinces of New Brunswick and Nova Scotia, with whom also, we have walked in company to the house of God, and there taken sweet council together.[82]

This was further exemplified by their receiving and seating the Maritime Association's messenger, David Harris, and by inviting him to preach to them the assembly's final sermon. The Bowdoinham Association reciprocated by appointing Isaac Case to be their messenger to the next annual assembly of the Nova Scotia and New Brunswick Association, an appointment he carried out. The Maritime Baptists' response to Case's postwar reappearance among them was recorded as "very pleasant to us."[83]

The itinerancy, associationalism, mission societies, and cross border connectionalism of the Baptists all reflected their desire to see the kingdom of God expand and demonstrated the ways in which parish boundaries, national borders, and frontier settlements or foreign lands were viewed through the lens of their two kingdoms theology. As they saw it, both their commission and their

---

[82] *Minutes of the Bowdoinham Association, Held in Bowdoin, September 27th & 28th, 1815* (Hallowell, ME: Nathaniel Cheever, 1815).

[83] "Minutes of the Nova Scotia and New Brunswick Association Held at the Baptist Meeting House, in Cornwallis, June 26th and 27th, 1815," (1815). At this same meeting the Nova Scotia and New Brunswick Baptists voted to establish a mission society replicating the model of the Massachusetts Baptist Missionary Society. Maritime Baptist Thomas Chipman wrote the Corresponding Letter for the Association that year and made specific reference to the New England Baptists' "spirited" efforts in "forming so many societies for the advancement of the Redeemer's Kingdom." Quoted in Brackney, "The Planter Motif among Baptists from New England to Nova Scotia, 1760-1850," 296.

task were global. The result was a shared identity that transcended local identities in important ways. These institutional, ecclesiastical activities were to continue unabated and, it was hoped, would flourish until the consummation of the kingdom of God.

6. The consummation of the kingdom

As Merrill looked to the future of the kingdom of heaven, he believed it would overcome obstacles from without and within and would "increase and roll along, till it shall have broken in pieces, and consumed all the mighty men, and mighty things which rise in opposition."[84] The kingdom, in its present earthly condition, was moving toward an ultimate goal — its consummation.

He saw the "extension" of the kingdom of God during his own lifetime as evidence that it would soon "fill the whole earth, as the waters do the seas."[85] Merrill spoke in eschatological terms using the imagery of the "beast" and "harlot" of the book of Revelation to describe what was presently taking place and what would ultimately come to pass as the kingdom expanded. He expected that following the Baptist's kingdom of God paradigm would bring global results reflected "in every clime, every nation, tribe, and language; *then* will the kingdom of God come."[86]

However much the kingdom would yet expand, its ultimate consummation was not earthly but the eternal, eschatological kingdom brought about by Christ's second coming. For Backus, the parable of the tares of Matthew 13 was instructive. Rev. Joseph Fish confusedly interpreted the parable of the wheat and tares with the

---

[84] Merrill, *The Kingdom of God: A Discourse, Delivered at Concord, before His Excellency the Govenor [sic], the Honorable Council, the Honorable Senate, and House of Representatives of the State of New-Hampshire, June 5, 1817, Being the Anniversary Election,* 4.

[85] Merrill, *The Kingdom of God: A Discourse, Delivered at Concord, before His Excellency the Govenor [sic], the Honorable Council, the Honorable Senate, and House of Representatives of the State of New-Hampshire, June 5, 1817, Being the Anniversary Election,* 8-9.

[86] Merrill, *The Kingdom of God: A Discourse, Delivered at Concord, before His Excellency the Govenor [sic], the Honorable Council, the Honorable Senate, and House of Representatives of the State of New-Hampshire, June 5, 1817, Being the Anniversary Election,* 44.

"field" as representative of the church; both regenerate and unregenerate would alike be in the church of Jesus Christ until the consummation. Backus found this almost laughable. Reminding his audience of their ability to judge for themselves, his readers could readily see that Christ taught the field was not the church, but the "world." This distinction brought into focus the differing eschatological visions of Backus and Fish. For Fish, there was really one kingdom marrying ecclesiastical and civil authority. For Backus, there would always be two kingdoms, that of the nations of the world, the tares, and those who were members of the kingdom of God, the wheat. For Backus and the Baptists, the separation of wheat and tares would be brought about by Christ himself at his second coming.[87]

The difference between Backus and Merrill was not one of kingdom theology but of eschatological emphasis. Merrill references the conditions in earth just prior to the dawn of the millennium while Backus pointed to the event of the second coming of Christ.[88] Both men saw the kingdoms of this world and the kingdom of God remaining separate institutions until the coming consummation. Merrill described the Baptist perspective of the expanded kingdom looking forward in its marked differences from what they had experienced looking backwards.

> *Then* would the rulers be nursing fathers to Zion. Not by enacting laws to compel belief, the practice, and the support of religion: but by countenancing each, by their example and exhortation. By discriminating clearly between this kingdom and those of men; between the religion from heaven and the superstitions of mortals. By so clearing the legal ground from the trappings of bigotry, that no more of the friends of God's kingdom shall be forced to prison, or their goods despoiled, for not voluntarily feeding blind guides, who

---

[87] Backus and McLoughlin, *Isaac Backus on Church, State, and Calvinism; Pamphlets, 1754-1789*, 187-88.

[88] Merrill, *The Kingdom of God: A Discourse, Delivered at Concord, before His Excellency the Govenor* [sic], *the Honorable Council, the Honorable Senate, and House of Representatives of the State of New-Hampshire, June 5, 1817, Being the Anniversary Election*, 16-17 and Backus, *The Kingdom of God, Described by His Word, with Its Infinite Benefits to Human Society*, 13.

cannot dig, and are ashamed to beg.[89]

Both men saw a free state as a state where the kingdom can flourish unhindered and realize the consummation of the kingdom.

Conclusion

The Regular Baptists in the early Republic were at the cross roads of a number of different currents. They were unfailing in their efforts to establish and expand God's kingdom wherever they went. The frontier settlements received special attention as associations and mission societies were constituted for this express purpose. The church must be wrested from the control of the government where it had not yet been freed and it must be wrested from the clutches of the state church where it was in danger of being eclipsed by the unregenerate. The marriage of church and state was rapidly being dismantled for the first time in millennia and the mixed communion paedobaptist churches were rapidly losing numbers and control. Separating God's two kingdoms, the civil and the ecclesiastical, was causing a stir.

As Baptist numbers increased rapidly they would tirelessly call

---

[89] Merrill, *The Kingdom of God: A Discourse, Delivered at Concord, before His Excellency the Govenor* [Sic], *the Honorable Council, the Honorable Senate, and House of Representatives of the State of New-Hampshire, June 5, 1817, Being the Anniversary Election,* 21. Merrill's reference to "nursing fathers" derives from Isa. 49:23 and draws on a long history among paedobaptists of using this text to justify their view of the civil magistrate's ecclesiastical responsibility. It was incorporated into the text of The Cambridge Platform of 1648, Chapter 9, "Of the maintenance of Church Officers"; "4 Not only members of churches, but all that are taught in the word, are to contribute unto him that teacheth, in all good things . . . and where church power, through the corruption of men, doth not, or cannot attain the end, the magistrate is to see the ministry be duly provided for . . . The magistrates are nursing-fathers, and nursing-mothers, and stand charged with the custody of both tables"; see Walker, *The Creeds and Platforms of Congregationalism,* 221. Though the American Presbyterians made modifications to the Westminster Confession of Faith in 1788 respecting the responsibilities of the Civil Magistrate, they incorporated the language of Isaiah into their revision referring to the magistrates as "nursing fathers." Merrill is surely adopting the language of the paedobaptists and turning it around on them. As far as he is concerned the magistrate is a true nursing father when he allows religious liberty to prevail.

Separating God's Two Kingdoms: Two Kingdom Theology among New England Baptists...

those regenerate in the paedobaptist churches to come out and join the redeemed communities as they challenged a one kingdom view and gave expression to the two kingdom theology that was foundational to their worldview. It was a rapidly changing world, one the Baptists envisioned, but one the paedobaptists feared and fought.

When Isaac Backus embraced Baptist beliefs in the mid-eighteenth century, the fruits of his two kingdom theology presaged hopes of a future vision. Fifty years later, as Backus was closing his life of ministry for the Baptist cause, men like Isaac Case, Daniel Merrill, Henry Hale, George Manning and others were taking up the mantle with vigor and energy in the northeastern borderland region. Their vision was global and the kingdom of God paradigm they saw explicitly defined in Scripture was the blueprint from which they worked. Its fruit would be evident in explosive growth during the religious fervor of the Second Great Awakening betokening a society nested with churches, but functioning in new and distinct ways: two kingdom ways. Christ as Lord of creation would rule the civil kingdom and Christ as Lord over his church would rule the spiritual kingdom — the kingdom of God.

Chapter 6

Robert Hall Jr. (1764-1831) and the Decline

of Historic Calvinism

among the English Particular Baptists

of the Early Nineteenth Century

Austin Walker[*]

Historians of English Dissent have recorded the remarkable expansion of evangelicalism during the late eighteenth and nineteenth centuries.[1] Baptists, Methodists, and Congregationalists mushroomed. For example, one historian indicates that "in the Baptist communion as a whole the numbers of churches grew from 652 in 1801 to 2,789 fifty years later."[2] Much of the impetus for this growth had come from the eighteenth-century Great Awakening and the Methodist movement associated with John Wesley. This expansion was reflected in Particular Baptist circles by the formation of the Northamptonshire Association, first organized in 1764, the year in which Robert Hall was born.[3] It was committed to evangelism both overseas and at home and the emergence of the Baptist Missionary Society in 1792 and then the Baptist Home

---

[*] Austin Walker is one of the pastors of Maidenbower Baptist Church, Crawley, Sussex, UK, and is the author of *The Excellent Benjamin Keach, God's Care for the Widow*, and co-author with Brian Croft of *Caring for Widows*.

[1] Ian Sellars, *Nineteenth-Century Nonconformity* (London: Edward Arnold Ltd., 1977); D. W. Bebbington, *Evangelicalism in Modern Britain: A History from the 1730s to the 1980s* (London: Unwin Hyman Ltd., 1989); Michael R. Watts, *The Dissenters II: The Expansion of Evangelical Nonconformity, 1791–1859* (Oxford: Clarendon Press, 1995).

[2] Sellars, *Nineteenth-Century Nonconformity*, 2.

[3] In this article, "Robert Hall" always refers to Robert Hall (1764-1831). His father was also known by the same name and will be referred to as Robert Hall, Sr.

Mission in 1797 owed much to the Association and its leaders. The Association was characterized by warm evangelical Calvinism, as opposed to the hyper-Calvinism that had marked some men and churches among the Particular Baptists. Furthermore, it was distinguished by a remarkable group of like-minded leaders. Robert Hall, Sr. (1728-1791) was one of those leaders, together with John Ryland (1753-1825), Andrew Fuller (1754-1815), John Sutcliffe (1752-1814), and William Carey (1761-1834).

Robert Hall, preaching in Bristol in 1820, testified:

During the latter part of the last century, and down to the present time, there has been a manifest increase and improvement of Christian instruction. Evangelical truth has been administered in a purity and abundance to which preceding ages bear no proportion.[4]

The growth of evangelicalism during this period is beyond dispute. However, there was a significant theological metamorphosis taking place at the same time. This change was not confined to Particular Baptists, though this grouping of Dissenters is our concern in this chapter. Hall mentioned "the purity" of evangelical truth. The "evangelical truth" that he believed and preached was not identical to the evangelical Calvinism of his father, or that of Andrew Fuller. As we shall demonstrate, there were significant differences in Hall's theology. Furthermore, this was not the same historic Calvinism that was formulated in the Puritan era and expressed in *The Second London Baptist Confession of Faith*, and prior to that in *The Westminster Confession of Faith* of the Presbyterians and *The Savoy Declaration* of the Congregationalists.

In a more recent Oxford University thesis Russell Campbell has maintained that the decline of Calvinism in England in the nineteenth century was the most significant theological change since the Reformation. He has traced some of those changes in the lives of three Baptists who succeeded Robert Hall — men who

---

[4] Robert Hall, "The Signs of the Times," in *The Works of Robert Hall, A.M. with a memoir of his life, and a critical estimate of his character and writings*, 6 vols., ed. Olinthus Gregory (London: Henry G. Bohn, 1851), 4:188. Subsequent references will be abbreviated thus: Hall, *Works*, with volume and page number.

moved even further away from historic Calvinism than Hall did.[5] He also maintained, at the time of writing in 2000, that there was no study on the decline of Calvinism in the nineteenth century.[6] Christians need to understand not only the great theologians but also the significant controversies of church history and be able to discern both the causes and the consequences of those controversies. The seeds of the Down-Grade Controversy that so profoundly affected Spurgeon and the Baptist Union in the late 1880s were sown in the early decades of the nineteenth century and Robert Hall had a marked influence among the Particular Baptists of his generation and succeeding generations of Baptists.[7]

Most interpreters of the early nineteenth-century Baptist history appear to suggest that Robert Hall and Andrew Fuller were exponents of a similar evangelical Calvinistic theology, sometimes called 'moderate Calvinism.' This study calls that conclusion into question. Ernest Payne suggested that 'Fullerism' should be seen as the bridge between Particular Baptists and the New Connexion of General Baptists.[8] On that basis Fuller would be seen as the man

---

[5] Russell S. Campbell, "The decline of Calvinism among British Baptists in the nineteenth century: a study of three ministers" (D.Phil. thesis, University of Oxford, 2000), referred to and quoted from with permission of the Modern History Faculty Board, University of Oxford. Campbell says very little about Robert Hall and concentrates on William Brock (1807-1875), Charles Stanford (1823-1886), and William Landels (1823-1899).

[6] Campbell, "The decline of Calvinism among British Baptists in the nineteenth century," 1. Since then there has been a significant study of the decline of Calvinism in the nineteenth century among the Scottish Presbyterians. See Ian Hamilton, *The erosion of Calvinistic Orthodoxy: Drifting from the Truth in Confessional Scottish Churches* (Fearn, Ross-shire, Scotland: Mentor Imprint by Christian Focus Publications, 2010). For a consideration of the atonement controversy in Wales see Owen Thomas, *The Atonement Controversy in Welsh Theological Literature & Debate 1707-1841*, trans. John Aaron (Edinburgh; Carlisle PA: The Banner of Truth Trust, 2002).

[7] Dr. Tom Nettles rightly attributes the long-term effects of Robert Hall's influence in forming "the climate for the energetic modernism of John Clifford." It was Clifford who stood opposed to Spurgeon in the Downgrade Controversy. Nettles says, "The ideas that Hall set in motion, both of open communion and diminished confessional consciousness, led to Clifford's powerful influence over the Baptist Union." See Tom Nettles, *The Baptists: Key People Involved in Forming the Baptist Identity, Volume Three, the Modern Era* (Fearn, Ross-shire, Scotland: Mentor Imprint for Christian Focus Publications, 2007), 58.

[8] Ernest A. Payne, *The Baptist Union: A Short History* (London: The Carey

who started the ball rolling, beginning a process that finally culminated in the formal union between General and Particular Baptists in 1891, a few years after the Down-Grade Controversy had erupted in 1887. That, to my mind, is an oversimplification of the matter.

Robert Oliver has rightly questioned whether Andrew Fuller should be understood as the catalyst for change. He suggests that Robert Hall should be seen as the catalyst given his rejection of particular redemption and his close association with General Baptists in the Leicester area during the years 1807-1826.[9] In addition, Hall's promotion of open communion and his opposition to confessions and creeds add weight to this conclusion. I intend to show that Hall's theology was not identical to that of his Particular Baptist forefathers, including Andrew Fuller, and that he made a significant contribution toward what Frank Rinaldi has called an "erosion of distinctives" between General and Particular Baptists.[10]

That erosion began long before the formal union in 1891. When the first Baptist Union was planned in 1812, and then formed the following year, some sixty men favored the plan for union. It was essentially a union of Particular Baptists with a Calvinistic doctrinal declaration. Interestingly, Hall was absent from the inaugural London meeting, yet he was invited to preach at the 1813 meeting to be held the following year.[11] Almost thirty years after the first meeting in London a new union of Baptist churches was created in 1832 (a year after the death of Hall). This time the "erosion of distinctives" was much easier to see. The basis for union was extremely vague: "the sentiments usually denominated evangelical."[12] It would be misleading and wrong to suggest that

---

Kingsgate Press Limited, 1959), 61.

[9] Robert W. Oliver, *History of the English Calvinistic Baptists, 1771-1892: From John Gill to C. H. Spurgeon* (Edinburgh; Carlisle, PA: The Banner of Truth Trust, 2006), 329-30. For his evidence Oliver refers to Angus Hamilton MacLeod, "The Life and Teaching of Robert Hall, 1764-1831," Master of Letters thesis, University of Durham, 1957. As far as I am aware this is the only substantial study of Hall's theological teaching.

[10] Frank W. Rinaldi, *The Tribe of Dan: The New Connexion of General Baptists 1770-1891: A Study in the Transition from Revival Movement to Established Denomination,* Studies in Baptist History and Thought, vol. 10 (Milton Keynes: Paternoster, 2008), 20.

[11] Payne, *The Baptist Union,* 21.

Robert Hall was the only catalyst for theological change among the Particular Baptists in the early nineteenth century but this study argues that he did play a leading role, albeit unconsciously perhaps, in that change. His theological views reflected not only the declining impact of Calvinism on his own thinking and ministry but also, and even more crucially, a less than biblical appreciation of the doctrine of justification by faith.

A Sketch of the Ministry of Robert Hall

The fame of Robert Hall rests largely on his gifts as a preacher. Among preachers he earned a reputation for being the greatest pulpit orator of his age. Some regarded him as the greatest orator of his day, superior even to William Pitt the Younger, the distinguished parliamentary orator, who at the age of twenty four became the youngest-ever Prime Minister of the British nation. By all accounts Hall was an electrifying preacher who gripped the hearts and minds of his hearers. Once into his stride his sermons were marked by clear thought and intellectual power, sincerity, intensity and vigour, earnestness, and, above all else, eloquence.[13] Spurgeon, commenting on Hall's sermons on Philippians recognized the limitations of his written sermons, "*Robert Hall* does not shine so much upon the printed page as he did when he blazed from the pulpit. . . . They are good as sermons, but not remarkable as expositions."[14] To a large extent the fame of Hall died with his own, and the succeeding, generation. There were numerous funeral eulogies spoken and subsequently published in newspapers and religious periodicals, together with memoirs and reminiscences published by his friends.[15] Since then—apart from one academic

---

[12] Payne, *The Baptist Union*, 61.

[13] For a sympathetic appreciation of Robert Hall as a preacher, see John Foster, "Observations on Mr. Hall's character as a preacher," in Hall, *Works*, 1:210-55.

[14] C. H. Spurgeon, Book IV "Commenting and Commentaries," in *Lectures to my Students* (Pasadena, TX: Pilgrim Publications, 1990), 180.

[15] The main biographies are Olinthus Gregory, "A brief memoir of the Rev. Robert Hall, A.M." in Hall, *Works*, 1:157; John Greene, *Reminiscences of the Rev. Robert Hall, A.M. Late of Bristol, and sketches of his sermons preached at Cambridge prior to 1806* (London: Frederick Westley, and A. H. Davis, 1832). This was subsequently

thesis—only two brief biographies have been written about Hall. Both of these biographies tend to focus only on his exceptional preaching abilities.[16]

Robert Hall was never based in London though he preached there on a number of occasions throughout his life. His ministry was focussed in three cities: Bristol from 1785 to 1791 and again in 1826 through 1831, Cambridge from 1791 to 1806, and Leicester (a few miles from his birth-place) from 1807 to 1826. All these were important centers of population at the turn of the eighteenth century. Cambridge was one of the hubs of intellectual life, dominated by the established church; Bristol was a major port and manufacturing center; Leicester was a textile manufacturing town.

Robert Hall was born in Arnesby, Leicestershire, in 1764, the fourteenth child of the Particular Baptist preacher Robert Hall, Sr. and his wife Jane. Only six children survived, and young Robert was one of those, yet he barely survived as an infant. He was a precocious child who, with the help of his nurse, learned to read from the graveyard inscriptions behind his father's chapel. Once at school in nearby Wigston, he was too bright for his teacher. He composed hymns, had his brothers and sisters hear him preach, knew Latin and Greek, and was reading Bishop Butler and Jonathan Edwards before he was ten years old. As part of his education he was sent to Northampton, to the school of John Collett Ryland (1723-1792). He professed faith in Christ and was baptized at the

---

published in the American edition of Hall's works, *The Works of the Rev. Robert Hall, A.M.*, 4 vols., ed. Olinthus Gregory and Joseph Belcher (New York: Harper and Brothers, 1849), 4:11-100, subsequently referred to as Hall, (eds. Gregory and Belcher), *Works*. A further biography was produced in 1833. This has recently been reprinted, John Webster Morris, *Biographical Recollections of Robert Hall A.M.* (New Delhi: Isha Books, 2013). A later and more restricted account of Hall is also found in Fred. Trestrail, *Reminiscences of College Life in Bristol during the Ministry of Rev Robert Hall, A.M.* (London: E. Malborough and Co., 1879). Gregory undertook the task of publishing the works of Hall. In 1831 he published the first of six volumes. Once completed, twelve editions of these works followed in the ensuing thirty-five years.

[16] See footnote 7 for details of MacLeod's thesis. The two biographies are E. Paxton Hood, *Robert Hall* (New York: A. C. Armstrong, 1881) and Graham W. Hughes, *Robert Hall* (London: The Carey Press, 1943). A briefer version subsequently appeared by the same author, *Robert Hall 1764-1831* (London: Independent Press Ltd., 1961).

age of fourteen and then at the tender age of sixteen he was set aside by the church to preach, studying at the Bristol Baptist Academy. As Oxford and Cambridge Universities were still closed to Dissenters, he then went to Aberdeen where he graduated M.A. in 1785. He was not fond of Aberdeen and in a letter to his father spoke against "frosty-spirited Calvinists" he heard preach there.[17]

Having graduated from Aberdeen he returned to Bristol Baptist Academy to assist the principal, Caleb Evans. Hall became the classics tutor and remained there until the middle of 1791. In the Broadmead church (the Academy was attached to the church) he was at first popular as a preacher but then suspicions arose as to his orthodoxy, a subject of which will be considered later. His friendship with Evans crumbled and a spirit of alienation set in. Hall resigned, writing a letter to the church to explain his views.

In July 1791 he moved to Cambridge, remaining there until March 1806. He replaced Robert Robinson in the Baptist church which was meeting in St. Andrew's Street. The church was in poor shape as Robinson had come to reject the Trinity and had also lost hold of the biblical doctrine of the atonement. While at Bristol, Robert Hall had been suspected of having Socinian sympathies but there was no questioning his orthodoxy on these matters.[18] From the beginning in Cambridge he preached positively on the divinity of the Lord Jesus Christ as well as substitutionary atonement.

After fifteen years in Cambridge, he had a valid and established reputation as a preacher and as a writer, as well as a defender of liberty and justice. In 1791 and 1793 he had argued for civil and religious freedom in two subsequently published sermons: first, *Christianity consistent with a love of freedom*, and then, *An apology for the freedom of the press*.[19] In these sermons he spoke and wrote as the

---

[17] R[obert] H[all] W[arren], *The Hall Family* (Bristol: J. W. Arrowsmith, 1910), 48.

[18] Hall, *Works*, 5:118-141. Gregory includes notes from twelve lectures Hall gave in 1823 in Leicester, in "Outline of the Argument of Twelve Lectures on the Socinian Controversy," and notes from two sermons, "On Christ's Divinity and Condescension," preached in London in 1813, and "On the Spirit and Tendency of Socinianism." No date is given for the latter sermon. There is no reason to doubt that these were substantially Hall's views when he first addressed the issue in Cambridge.

[19] Hall, *Works*, 4:1-146.

Robert Hall Jr. (1764-1831) and the Decline of Historic Calvinism...

defender of the Dissenters, still regarded by many in the established Church of England as the source of sedition and atheism. He pleaded for full toleration of religious opinion and protection for all parties in the way they worshipped. His popularity was increased with further published sermons. In November 1799 he preached on the phrase "without God in the world" from Ephesians 2:12, a sermon he called *Modern infidelity considered with respect to its influence on society.*[20] It was an unquestionable *tour de force*, attacking atheism. It served to catch the mood of the nation after the French Revolution. Two other sermons were to arrest the public ear and eye. Hard on the heels of the French Revolution, Napoleon Bonaparte arrived as a force on the European political and military landscape. On June 1, 1802, appointed as a day of thanksgiving for general peace established by the Treaty of Amiens, Hall preached from Psalm 46:8-9, *Reflections on War.*[21] Within a year Britain had declared war on France as the peace treaty crumbled. In Bristol on October 19, 1803, a day of national fasting, Hall preached this time on *The sentiments proper to the present crisis*, calling the nation to repentance.[22]

These sermons were important because they were widely received in Britain. It seems that he had an aptitude for saying the right thing at the right time and in the right way. The sad events that led to his departure from Bristol in 1791 were far behind him. Now he had risen to prominence: he was recognized as an eloquent and passionate gospel preacher who commanded a wide hearing even though he was a Baptist Dissenter. The fact that he accomplished this in Cambridge, a stronghold of the Established Church of England, is testimony to his powerful intellect and his outstanding gift of oratory. However, his ministry in Cambridge was to end in another sad event, but of a quite different character. In November 1804 Hall experienced the first of two mental breakdowns. We shall assess the significance of these breakdowns later when we consider Hall's health and the effects it had on his life and ministry.

In 1807, once he had recovered from his affliction, he accepted

---

[20] Hall, *Works*, 2:1-60.
[21] Hall, *Works*, 2:61-94.
[22] Hall, *Works*, 2:95-144.

an invitation to become the pastor of Harvey Lane Church in Leicester, William Carey's former congregation. Within a year he had married Eliza Smith (his doctor had advised marriage following his breakdown). They had three daughters, and two sons, one of whom died in infancy. Only eighteen months after his arrival the chapel in Harvey Lane had to be enlarged. This meant it had a capacity for 800 people. By 1817 it was enlarged again, this time to seat 1,000 people.

While in Leicester he became involved in a number of different ways in life outside of the congregation at Harvey Lane. He was eager to progress the work of the Leicester Auxiliary Bible Society; he wrote appeals for the new Baptist Academy in Stepney, East London; he preached and wrote on behalf of the Baptist Missionary Society, and preached a sermon in 1814 when Eustace Carey was designated as a missionary to India.[23] Hall was an arch-advocate of open communion and entered into a lengthy public debate with Joseph Kinghorn about terms of communion. The editor of his works, Olinthus Gregory, devoted one complete volume to this issue.[24]

Again in 1817 Hall caught the attention and mood of the nation when he preached an apt and moving funeral sermon on the death of Princess Charlotte following childbirth.[25] He was also involved in education and supported parliamentary and penal reform. In 1819 he came to the defense of the framework knitters in the Leicester hosiery industry who were victims of a boom and bust economy. Hall wrote anonymously on their behalf, appealing to the public for help in establishing a friendly relief society.[26] He also added his voice to the anti-slavery lobby in 1823, speaking on behalf of the Leicester Auxiliary Anti-Slavery Society.[27]

On June 5, 1825, he preached a funeral sermon following the death of Dr. John Ryland, the pastor at Broadmead Chapel in Bristol and principal of the Baptist College.[28] The passing of Ryland

---

[23] Hall, *Works*, 2:202-34.

[24] Hall, *Works*, vol. 3.

[25] Hall, *Works*, 5:1-38.

[26] Hall, *Works*, 4:167-214.

[27] "An Address on the State of Slavery in the West India Islands," in Hall, *Works*, 4:215-36.

[28] Hall, *Works*, 5:39-71.

provided the church in Bristol with an opportunity to invite the aging sixty-two year old Robert Hall to return to Bristol. The previous events in Bristol had been forgotten. Hall was now regarded by many as "the champion of evangelical truth, both in the pulpit and the press."[29] There had been some disagreements over the discipline of some church members in Leicester and Hall decided to leave, beginning his ministry in Bristol in 1826. Here he became the pastor of both the Baptist and the Congregational congregations associated with Broadmead.[30] He continued to support causes he had supported most of his life such as Bible societies, education, parliamentary reform, and he remained keenly anti-slavery. He remained a popular preacher and was heard by such men as Thomas Chalmers, William Sprague, and William Wilberforce. However, ill-health was rapidly overtaking him in his old age. In addition to his continued intense pains as a result of renal calculus (kidney stones), his eyesight deteriorated and there were clear signs of heart failure. The last service in which he played any part was the church meeting on February 9, 1831. Shortly afterward, realizing that he would never again minister among his people, he said, "But I am in God's hands, and I rejoice that I am. I am God's creature, at his disposal for life and death; and that is a great mercy."[31] He died twelve days later on February 21 at the age of sixty-seven and was buried first in the vault at Broadmead and later in Arnos Vale cemetery in Bristol.

Hall's Health and Conversion

In his *Memoir of Robert Hall*, Gregory records his first impressions of

---

[29] James Bennett, *The History of Dissenters during the Last Thirty Years, 1808-1838* (London: Hamilton, Adams and Co., 1839), 488.

[30] The Congregational church was comprised of paedobaptists. They received communion separately from the Baptist church members. This was a fairly common practice in Baptist churches until open communion principles came to prevail. It had been the case at Cambridge. See John Greene, "Reminiscences of the Rev. Robert Hall, A.M. Late of Bristol, and sketches of his sermons preached at Cambridge prior to 1806," in Hall, (ed. Gregory and Belcher), *Works*, 4:14-15.

[31] Hall, *Works*, 1:152.

him:

> I was struck with his well-proportioned athletic figure, the
> unassuming dignity of his deportment, the winning
> frankness which marked all that he uttered, and the
> peculiarities of the most speaking countenance I ever
> contemplated, animated by eyes radiating with the brilliancy
> imparted to them by benevolence, wit and intellectual
> energy.[32]

Such a figure was completely unrecognisable for several months
first in late 1804 and again in November 1805, when Hall became
temporarily insane.

Robert Hall was born into a family which had experienced
mental breakdowns. His mother Jane had undergone a period of
insanity from which she did partially recover, but not before she
had made several attempts to commit suicide. Her sufferings were
almost certainly responsible for her premature death in 1776 when
her youngest son was a mere twelve years old.[33] His mother's
sufferings and death made a deep impression on him. As a result of
the encouragement of friends his father published a detailed
account of her experiences.[34]

Writing thirty years after the events of 1804 and 1805, neither
Gregory nor Greene (two of his main biographers) gave their
readers a full account of events surrounding these two periods of
Hall's own mental breakdown. Recently, drawing on an unknown
eyewitness' account of events between October 31 and November
11, 1804, which he found in the Angus Library, Oxford, Timothy
Whelan has provided a fuller and very helpful picture of what
actually happened.[35] Whelan suggests that his early biographers did

---

[32] Hall, *Works*, 1:47. Cf. Gregory's estimate of Hall with Foster, in Hall, *Works*,
1:204-05.

[33] At least one writer has suggested that the Calvinism of his upbringing was
responsible for his doubts, depression, and breakdown but they do not take into
account the family history. See Angus Hamilton MacLeod, "The Life and Teaching
of Robert Hall, 1764-1831" (Master of Letters thesis, University of Durham, 1957),
197.

[34] Robert Hall, *Mercy manifested: a letter to a friend, relating the dying consolations
of Mrs. Jane Hall* (London, 1777).

not reveal all the details of what took place because they wished to preserve Hall's reputation.

Hall's condition was brought on by a bout of fever, by solitude and excessive hours of reading, invariably a minimum of twelve hours a day. Hall felt this amount of reading was necessary to keep ahead of the reading men in Cambridge. But such labour unhinged him: he became severely depressed, displayed manic feelings, felt a great sense of unworthiness and sinfulness, and also experienced delusions of grandeur. In one evening of intense derangement he "deliver'd a kind of prophecy, and declared his commission which was that he was the Greatest Prophet the world ever saw."[36] When Mr. William Hollick, the senior deacon from the church in Cambridge, arrived to see Hall

> he was no sooner seated than in the utmost grandeur of voice he said *'I am the son of God'* talked about his supernatural birth, said he was born with only half a head, which was always too small for his brains, but that he had a new head given him.[37]

When Mr. Hollick dared to disagree, an enraged Hall drove him out, "leaping out of bed, ran after him downstairs, through the passage & round the garden—declaring he would send him to Hell &c—."[38] Hall was restrained by a straitjacket but he broke free and refused all medication. Some days later in a calmer spirit he asked that Psalm 51 be read to him. This was done and the eyewitness recorded that Hall "turned every verse into prayer applying it to his own case in a most sublime manner the most sublime language as he thinks was ever uttered by mortal—After this he became happy & comfortable."[39]

Hall spent some time recovering in a private asylum in Leicester under the care of Dr. Thomas Arnold. By April 1805 he was able to

---

[35] Timothy Whelan, "'I am the greatest of the prophets": a new look at Robert Hall's mental breakdown,' November 1804, *Baptist Quarterly*, Vol.42 (April 2007): 114-26.

[36] Whelan, "'I am the greatest of the prophets,'" 118.

[37] Whelan, "'I am the greatest of the prophets,'" 118.

[38] Whelan, "'I am the greatest of the prophets,'" 118.

[39] Whelan, "'I am the greatest of the prophets,'" 119.

return to Cambridge and his ministry, only to suffer a second breakdown in the following November. This time his brother-in-law in Bristol took the initiative for his care and upon Hall's recovery he returned to relatives and friends in Leicestershire, including visits to his former home in Arnesby, but not to the place of his labours in Cambridge. There were fears that such periods of insanity would return and doubts were expressed about the counsel given to him to get married. However, he did marry and he was never afflicted in the way again.

Hall had professed faith in Christ and was baptized at the age of fourteen. As Hall reflected on his experiences of 1804 and 1805, it appears that he called into question the genuineness of his professed conversion. Letters Hall wrote to William Hollick and James Phillips during his period of recovery in Leicestershire record the deep impression his afflictions had left on him, but these letters contain no specific evidence that he thought of himself as being unconverted before 1805. Writing to Phillips, he records, "I am a monument of the goodness and severity of God."[40] Likewise he records, "with the sincerest gratitude I would acknowledge the goodness of God in restoring me," adding a few sentences later:

> during my affliction I have not been entirely forsaken of God, nor left destitute of that calm trust in his providence which was requisite to support me; yet I have not been favoured with that intimate communion and that delightful sense of his love which I have enjoyed on former occasions.[41]

Those letters are not conclusive, however, for they provide only some of Hall's own testimony. On the basis of personal conversations with Hall, Gregory records:

> His [Hall's] own decided persuasion was that, however vivid his convictions of religious truth, and of the necessity of a consistent course of evangelical obedience had formerly been, and however correct his doctrinal sentiments during

---

[40] Hall, *Works*, 1:94.
[41] Hall, *Works*, 1:290.

Robert Hall Jr. (1764-1831) and the Decline of Historic Calvinism...

the past four or five years, yet he did not undergo a thorough transformation of character, a complete renewal of heart and affections until the first of these seizures.[42]

Gregory continued by noting that some of his friends who had heard his penitent confession when Psalm 51 was being read to him were "rather inclined to concur with him as to the correctness of his opinion."[43] David Bennett, a contemporary of Hall and, who with David Bogue, wrote a history of Dissent, observed that Hall's "religious character was so much improved by his afflictions, that he deemed them the means of his *first* acquaintance with the genuine religion of the heart."[44]

In similar fashion to Bennett, Robert Oliver is also persuaded by Hall's own testimony that he was not converted until 1805.[45] Hall's close friend and biographer remained undecided. Gregory said that "the wonderful revelations of "the great day" can alone remove the doubt."[46] However, what is clear is that Hall was a changed man as a result of his experience — more dependent on God, more devotional in his habits, and more fervent and elevated in his spiritual exercises.[47] Largely as a result of these changes, Hall was to make a solemn dedication of himself to God, which he renewed each year on May 2, his birthday. The first time he did this was in May 1809, by which time he was a pastor in Leicester. In this document he undertook a "solemn engagement of myself to thy service." He acknowledged his sinfulness, the mercy of God in willing to pardon and accept penitent sinners on the grounds of the blood and righteousness of Jesus Christ, and spoke of Christ as his Priest, Prophet and King, saying, "I dedicate myself to him, to serve, love, and trust in him as my life and my salvation and my life's end."[48] His solemn dedication shows him to be a man of sincerity

---

[42] Hall, *Works*, 1:93.

[43] Hall, *Works*, 1:93.

[44] James Bennett, D. D., *The History of Dissenters during the Last Thirty Years, 1808-1838* (London: Hamilton, Adams and Co., 1839), 488.

[45] Oliver, *History of the English Calvinistic Baptists, 1771-1892: From John Gill to C. H. Spurgeon*, 236.

[46] Hall, *Works*, 1:93.

[47] Hall, *Works*, 1:93.

[48] Hall, *Works*, 1:94-96.

and earnestness, devoted to serving God. Whatever other conclusions we draw, such characteristics are a standing rebuke to any half-heartedness on our part in serving God.

However, an intriguing and crucial question remains. Most of Hall's theological convictions were in place by the time he began his ministry in Leicester. There is very little evidence to suggest that he modified any of his views once he left Cambridge. If that is the case, then we are left asking whether he formulated most of his life-long views and convictions as a converted or an unconverted man.

One further comment must be made about Hall's health. For much of his life he was plagued with intense back pain due to renal calculus. In order to alleviate this pain he took large doses of laudanum, the prescribed painkiller of the day. Hall's habit of taking laudanum was life-long as it was with other well-known figures among his friends—William Wilberforce and Sir James Mackintosh.[49] The medicine prescribed was a tincture of alcohol and opium. As well as relieving pain, it invariably had a powerful narcotic effect capable of producing hallucinations and deep sleep. Several drops were the recommended dose. Hall was taking very large doses of laudanum and taking it with an additional half glass of brandy! Greene records how one day he found Hall (then in his late fifties) in intense pain and highly dependent on laudanum (which he was now taking in the form of opium tablets). On taking a further dose, Hall said he had now taken the equivalent of 1,500 drops that day and was resolved to take another 250 if he got no relief. Greene managed to restrain him, urging a cup of warm tea instead to aid diffusion of the opium. When a medical friend joined them Hall remarked to him:

> What a merciful provision laudanum is, sir! I could not exist without it. It seems as if Providence has designed it as a specific for me. Most persons complain that it affects the head, and stupefies them; I always feel more lively after taking it. How do you account for this, sir?[50]

---

[49] Robert Hall became a close friend of Mackintosh when they were students in Aberdeen. Mackintosh spent his life in law and politics. Gregory gives an account of their friendship in Hall, *Works*, 1:17-19.

[50] Hall, (ed. Gregory and Belcher), *Works*, 4:90-91.

Robert Hall Jr. (1764-1831) and the Decline of Historic Calvinism…

The gentleman confessed his inability to account for it, and stated that Mr. Hall's was a solitary instance.[51]

It is hard to imagine that the amounts of opium had no detrimental effects on Hall. It seems extremely likely that he was addicted to the opium, even if he did not realize it. However, he did not die a premature death. Furthermore, there is no evidence from Hall himself, his congregations, or his close friends that he suffered any debilitating effects despite the huge amounts that he took in order to ease his intense pain. John Foster was of the opinion that Hall only experienced diminished energy in the last few years of his life, "the period when an increased, but reluctant use of opiates became absolutely necessary, to enable him to endure the pain which he suffered throughout his life," and when the heart disease that led to his death set in.[52] One witness recorded in a letter to Gregory "the only instance in which I have ever seen him at all overcome by the soporific quality of the medicine."[53] That occasion was a few days before his death when Hall took no less than 125 grains of solid opium, which is more than 3,000 drops, and equivalent to four ounces of laudanum! Neither is there any evidence that he wrote and preached under the stimulating but potentially wild effects of laudanum. Samuel Taylor Coleridge wrote the well-known poem *Kubla Khan* as a result of the hallucinatory effects of the drug. He was one of several contemporary poets and authors, especially among the Romantics, who used laudanum to stimulate creativity in their writing. Although Hall said he felt "more lively after taking it," it would be reading too much into that statement to suggest that he was deliberately using it in order to provide himself with a stimulant. However, that statement may reflect the unintended effects of such doses as he imbibed.

Hall's Theological Views — an Overall Picture

When Hall was asked during his Cambridge ministry whether he was an Arminian or a Calvinist, he replied:

---

[51] Hall, (ed. Gregory and Belcher), *Works*, 4:90-91.
[52] Hall, *Works*, 1:204.
[53] Hall, *Works*, 1:150-51.

Neither, Sir: but I believe I recede farther from Arminianism than from Calvinism. If a man profess himself a decided Arminian, I infer from it that he is not a good logician; but, Sir, it does not interfere with his personal piety; look at good Mr Benson, for example. I regard the question more as metaphysical than religious.[54]

Some years later while they were engaged in conversation together in Leicester, Greene recorded a comment Hall made on his father's theology: "My father, sir, was very doctrinal in his preaching, and more attached to Calvinism than I am. If there are any sentiments to which I could subscribe, they are Baxter's."[55]

These two quotations provide us with some insights into Hall's priorities. By these comments, Hall was saying that he was less inclined to Arminianism than he was to Calvinism but that he regarded the question as being one that was, in effect, irrelevant speculation. He wanted to emphasize that such questions have very little bearing on a man's heart and life, on his personal piety. Personal piety was an important factor for Hall, something which was reflected in his warm friendships with men whose piety he found attractive. A number of them were not Particular Baptists in their sympathies, a point that Robert Oliver made when he suggested that Hall rather than Fuller was the catalyst for theological change.

For example, while he was in Leicester he enjoyed a very real friendship with Joseph Goadby, who was a New Connexion Baptist in Ashby, and Joseph Freeston, pastor of a General Baptist congregation in Hinckley. He was in the habit of exchanging pulpits with Goadby. In addition Hall's family would go and stay there for two weeks and Hall would join them during their stay to take his tea and smoke his pipe.[56]

His appreciation of Joseph Freeston is reflected in the following tribute he made to him in 1821.

---

[54] Hall, *Works*, 1:60.

[55] Hall, (ed. Gregory and Belcher), *Works*, 4:75.

[56] Bertha Goadby and Lilian Goadby, *Not Saints but Men: Or the Story of the Goadby Ministers* (London: Kingsgate Press, n.d.), 63.

Though he exercised his ministry through the whole of his life among the General Baptists, his sentiment approached nearer to those of Mr. Baxter than the system of Arminius, nor could his statement of christian doctrine have given the slightest offence to a congregation of moderate calvinists. But to polemical theology he was not attached; his religion was entirely of a practical and experimental character; nor did he attach the smallest importance to correct views of christian doctrine, any further than they tended to influence the heart.[57]

It would appear to me that the last sentence also accurately reflects Hall's own particular disposition and sympathies.

Hall's priorities reflected in his sympathies and friendships were different from those of his father and Andrew Fuller. Fuller and Hall, Sr. represented the previous generation of Particular Baptists. Hall wrote a preface to the 1814 edition of his father's book *Help to Zion's Travellers*. Like Fuller, Hall, Sr. had come to reject the hyper-Calvinism that denied the duty of repentance and faith. He believed that the inability of the unregenerate was of a moral nature, due to the will's corruption, and therefore provided no basis for excuse.

Hall spoke positively of the effects that his father's book and Fuller's *The Gospel Worthy of all Acceptation* had had on the sentiments of the denomination to which he belonged. He spoke of

> emancipating them from the fetters of prejudice, and giving free scope to the publication of the gospel, [and went on,] "the excresences of calvinism have been cut off;—the points of defence have been diminished in number, and better fortified;—truth has shone forth with brighter lustre;—and the ministry of the gospel has been rendered more simple, more practical and more efficacious.[58]

However, having said that his father's views were "decidedly

---

[57] 'Preface to the Memoirs of the Rev Joseph Freeston,' in Hall, *Works*, 4:324.
[58] Hall, *Works*, 4:375.

Calvinistic," he stressed once again his own convictions that the questions at issue between Calvinists and Arminians were not about fundamentals.

> I beg leave . . . to express my explicit dissent; being fully satisfied that upon either system the foundations of human hope remain unshaken, and that there is nothing, in the contrariety of views entertained in these subjects, which ought to obstruct the most cordial affection and harmony among christians.[59]

Given such statements, it is not surprising to find Hall critical of the attitude of some men of his father's generation, in particular Andrew Fuller. Writing in 1821 and comparing Fuller to the Independent minister Thomas Toller, also of Kettering, he offered the following observation.

> The secretary of the Baptist Mission attached, in my opinion, too much importance to a speculative accuracy of sentiment; while the subject of this Memoir [Toller] leaned to the more contrary extreme. Mr. Fuller was too prone to infer the character of men from their creed; Mr Toller to lose sight of their creed in their character.[60]

Did this mean that Hall minimized the importance of all doctrinal truth? That would be a wrong assessment. He was vigorously opposed not only to hyper-Calvinism but also to Socinianism and antinomianism. He defended the need for controversy in religion on the grounds that despite the way controversies have been handled they assist each generation to discover and state the truth. He opposed hyper-Calvinism, Socinianism, and antinomianism because they attacked the fundamentals of the Christian religion, but as has been seen he did not believe the differences between Calvinists and Arminians to be about fundamentals.

Did Hall elevate the need for personal piety above the need for

---

[59] Hall, *Works*, 4:370.
[60] Hall, *Works*, 4:313-14.

accurate doctrine, or to unnecessarily oppose these two things? He seemed to lean in that direction, judging by his tribute to Freeston. Yet Hall believed that there were fundamentals of the faith such as the deity of the Son of God, the substitutionary atonement provided by Christ's death on the cross, the necessity of regeneration and sanctification as a result of the work of the Holy Spirit. Hall had no sympathy with denials of these doctrines. Fuller and the older Hall would have been more balanced in their assessment of the relationship between personal piety and accurate doctrine, emphasizing the importance and inter-relationship of both.

So far we have taken a bird's eye view and used as our evidence Hall's own words, but we need to probe further. Another of Hall's biographers, John Webster Morris, provides additional information about Hall's early views during the period 1781-1787, when he was a student first at Bristol Academy and then at Aberdeen, before going to Broadmead and the Bristol Academy as a tutor. Morris confirms that almost from the very beginning Hall had doubts about the Calvinism of his Particular Baptist fathers and that he was charting his own theological course while at the same time concerned about holiness of life. Perhaps he was over-reacting to the hyper-Calvinism which had been so prevalent in some of the Particular Baptist churches, although it was certainly not characteristic of Caleb Evans and the Bristol Baptist Academy.

Morris stated that Hall had sympathies with certain aspects of Arminianism during the period 1781-1787. He wrote:

> In the early part of his ministry . . . he was strongly inclined to Arminianism, on account, as he said, of its practical tendency; admitting withal, that the Calvinistic system, in a speculative point of view, was in some respects more satisfactory and consistent with itself. . . . the Arminianism of Mr. Hall, however, was never complete; it was chiefly confined to two or three points, confessedly of some importance, but did not extend to an entire adoption of the system. He demurred to the doctrine of original sin and invincible depravity; to the final perseverance of all the regenerate; while, with Baxter, he admitted the perseverance of all the elect. Though not an advocate of universal grace,

he maintained that the influence of the Holy Spirit was indefinitely promised, and might be obtained in answer to the prayers of the unregenerate, if offered up with fervour and sincerity.[61]

A theological change was definitely taking place among Particular Baptists. It gathered momentum in the latter years of Hall and even more so after his death. Rinaldi appears to follow Payne and other Baptist historians who have suggested that it was Andrew Fuller who provided the bridge between Particular Baptists and the Baptists of the New Connexion, leading ultimately to their formal merger. He says, "The day of rigid Calvinism began to wane among Particular Baptists."[62] If by "rigid Calvinism" he means hyper-Calvinism we would be inclined to agree. However Robert Hall and Andrew Fuller did *not* share the same theological convictions. In Robert Hall we see that it is not so much "rigid Calvinism" that was in decline but Calvinism itself. Hall was well aware of the differences between himself and his father and other men who belonged to his father's generation and held his father's convictions.

How 'Particular' was Hall?

Robert Hall had been raised in a home, in a church, and under a ministry which were Particular Baptist in their tenor. He had been under the influence of the elder Ryland. He had studied at Bristol Academy, which was a Particular Baptist Academy under the leadership of Caleb Evans. He had become a tutor in the Academy and a pastor at the historic Broadmead church, a long-standing Particular Baptist church. Subsequently he became a pastor first at St Andrew's Street Baptist Church in Cambridge and then Harvey Lane Baptist Church in Leicester (formerly the church where

---

[61] John Webster Morris, *Biographical reflections of the Rev. Robert Hall* (London: Houlston and Stoneman, 1846), 36-37.

[62] Frank W. Rinaldi, *The Tribe of Dan: The New Connexion of General Baptists 1770-1891: A Study in the Transition from Revival Movement to Established Denomination*, Studies in Baptist History and Thought, vol. 10 (Milton Keynes: Paternoster, 2008), 21.

William Carey ministered). Both of these congregations were listed among the Particular Baptists in 1811.[63]

While Hall believed firmly in the *necessity* of the atonement, he did not, however, believe in *particular* or *limited* atonement. In one of his most famous sermons, preached in 1822 from Isaiah 53:8, he affirmed:

> that the sufferings of the Redeemer were vicarious and piacular [i.e., expiatory or atoning], that he appeared in the character of a substitute for sinners, in distinction from a mere example, teacher, or martyr, is so unquestionably the doctrine of the inspired writers, that to deny it, is not so properly to mistake, as to contradict, their testimony; it must be ascribed, not to any obscurity in revelation itself, but to a want of submission to its authority.[64]

However, he had long believed that Jesus Christ died for all men. Morris indicated that Hall held these views as far back as his early Bristol days.[65] Hall believed that the universality of the atonement was the only ground for the free offer of the gospel, that the obligations of faith were co-extensive with the preaching of the gospel, and that men, whatever their moral condition, were to pray and not faint.

Confirmation and clarification of Hall's views comes from correspondence Hall held with Rev. Robert Balmer of Berwick-upon-Tweed between the years 1819 and 1823.[66] Balmer was then a

---

[63] "A List of the Particular Baptist Churches and Ministers in England, corrected to October, 1811," *Baptist Magazine* (1811): 458-63, 496-97.

[64] "On the Substitution of the Innocent for the Guilty," in Hall, *Works*, 5:78.

[65] John Webster Morris, *Biographical Recollections of Robert Hall A.M.* (New Delhi: Isha Books, 2013), 37.

[66] Robert Balmer (1787-1844) was a member of the United Secession Church and had become the minister in Berwick-upon-Tweed in 1814. He was in correspondence with Hall and also visited him in Leicester when he travelled to London. See http://www.electricscotland.com/history/other/balmer_robert.htm. It would appear that he was questioning the extent of the atonement and wrote to Hall for counsel. Balmer was to play a significant role in the atonement controversy in Scotland that erupted in the years 1841-1845, a decade after Hall's death. Balmer was one of two professors (the other was John Brown) who believed that there was a divinely-intended universal reference to Christ's atonement, "teaching which

young Presbyterian minister in the United Secession Church in Scotland. He had consulted Hall about the extent of the atonement but he remained unconvinced by the replies he received from Hall. Hall had told him "I believe firmly in 'general redemption:' I often preach it, and I consider the fact that 'Christ died for all men' as the only basis that can support the universal offer of the Gospel." Asked then about election, Hall continued:

> I believe firmly in election, but I do not think it involves particular redemption; I consider the sacrifice of Christ as a remedy, not only adapted, but intended, for all, and as placing all in a salvable state; as removing all barriers to their salvation, except such as arise from their own perversity and depravity. But God knew that none would accept the remedy, merely of themselves, and therefore, by what may be regarded as a separate arrangement, he resolved to glorify his mercy, by effectually applying salvation to a certain number of our race, through the agency of the Holy Spirit. I apprehend, then, that the limiting clause implied in election refers, not to the purchase, but to the application of redemption.[67]

In further conversation with Balmer, Hall recommended his enquirer to read Joseph Bellamy's *True Religion Delineated* for further light.[68] The Connecticut Congregationalist, Joseph Bellamy (1719-1790), was part of the New Divinity school of thinking, men who had been influenced by Jonathan Edwards (1703-1758) but who developed views that were different from those of Edwards himself.

---

went beyond the traditional Lombardian sufficiency-efficiency commonplace," Hamilton, *The erosion of Calvinistic Orthodoxy*, 45. Balmer eventually reached conclusions that appear very similar to those held by Hall.

[67] "Miscellaneous Gleanings from Mr. Hall's Conversational Remarks," in Hall, *Works*, 1:60.

[68] Bellamy's *True Religion Delineated* was first published in America in 1750 and then in England in 1806. Other men in the New Divinity school of thinking included Samuel Hopkins (1721-1803), Jonathan Edwards Jr. (1745-1801), and Stephen West (1735-1819). They claimed to stand in the Puritan tradition and to be Calvinists. However they were revisers of that tradition, though they claimed they were facing the intellectual challenges of the day and re-contextualising Calvinism.

In dealing with John 3:16 in the second part of *True Religion Delineated*, Bellamy taught that Jesus Christ died for the world, by which he meant all mankind, all the posterity of Adam.[69] B. B. Warfield has described Bellamy as a 'partial forerunner' of the governmental theory of the atonement, over against the satisfaction doctrine.[70] Bellamy's commitment to the governmental view of the atonement was prominent in his book but that same prominence was not reflected in Hall's writings. The governmental theory of the atonement states that the death of Christ was accepted by God as the moral governor of the world but not as a creditor or offended party. The death of Christ served to show the punishment which sin brings and acts primarily as a deterrent. Consequently Christ did not actually atone for anyone's sin but he was punished in order to show that God's rule was just.[71] This being so it is possible to see why advocates of the governmental theory of atonement have often adopted the view that Christ died for all men.

On this basis of this theory it is also possible to see why Christ's death is not a penal substitution for particular sinners. The theory led to the rejection of the doctrine of substitutionary atonement, a doctrine that Hall, however, consistently affirmed. Nevertheless, despite Hall's affirmation of substitutionary atonement, he was drifting away from and diluting historic Calvinism. The seeds were sown, although it was only after Hall's death that the bitter fruits became evident. Some subsequently adopted the New Haven Theology of Nathaniel William Taylor (1786-1858) and the theology of Charles Grandison Finney (1792-1875).

Hall held to general redemption from his early days. It may be that Hall had already been influenced by Baxter, and that Bellamy's writings simply confirmed Hall in some of his own opinions. There is no conclusive evidence about this fact from Hall's own writings

---

[69] Joseph Bellamy, *True Religion Delineated* (Boston: Applewood Books), 365ff., http://books.google.co.uk/books. Accessed September 2010.

[70] "Edwards and the New England Theology," in Benjamin Breckenridge Warfield, *Studies in Theology*, vol. IX, *The Works of Benjamin B. Warfield* (Grand Rapids: Baker Book House, 1981), 535.

[71] Andrew Fuller had also been influenced by reading about the governmental theory of the atonement and sometimes used governmental theory language to describe the atonement. However, he did not imbibe the developments in New Divinity theology.

and letters. However, it is clear that Hall's views on the extent of the atonement placed him closer to the Baptists of the New Connexion than it did to Fuller and his peers among the Particular Baptists. In simple terms the New Connexion General Baptists believed that God loved all men, that Christ died for all men, and that the Spirit strove with all men. Hall was almost certainly reacting strongly to what he regarded as the pernicious effects of hyper-Calvinism, but he moved several steps further away from the 'moderate Calvinism' of his father and Andrew Fuller.[72] Fuller maintained particular redemption *and* the free offer of the gospel. The younger Hall's views on the extent of the atonement, on election, and on the basis for the free offer of the gospel, were a significant departure from the teaching of the 2LCF.[73]

Hall, Open Communion, and the Universal Church

Between 1814 and 1820 Robert Hall was engaged in a written debate with Joseph Kinghorn, pastor of the Baptist church in Norwich (who had been a student in Bristol when Hall was a tutor there), over the validity of closed communion. The practice of open communion had become an issue again around 1770 and different opinions emerged among Particular Baptists.[74] Men like Abraham Booth and Andrew Fuller believed firmly in maintaining a closed table. The Lord's Supper was for those who had been baptized as believers. William Carey, John Sutclif, John Ryland, and Caleb Evans favored the practice of open communion. Robert Hall argued stridently against Abraham Booth's position, stating no one had the right to make the terms of communion any different from those of

---

[72] 'Moderate Calvinism' was the term Robert Hall used to describe the system of divinity adhered to by men like Fuller, Carey, and Ryland. He correctly identified Jonathan Edwards as being the predominant influence on them. See "A sermon occasioned by the death of Rev. John Ryland, D.D.," in Hall, *Works*, 5:61.

[73] See in particular chapters 3, 8, and 20.

[74] In the seventeenth century the matter had been debated by William Kiffin and John Bunyan. In the eighteenth century Abraham Booth had been opposed by Robert Robinson, Hall's predecessor in Cambridge. For a full discussion of the issues and persons involved see Oliver, *History of the English Calvinistic Baptists, 1771-1892*, 58-88, 231-59.

salvation. Baptism, he asserted, was not essential to salvation and Christian love and unity demanded an open table.

His arguments eventually prevailed with many Particular Baptist churches which had once practiced closed communion. Disagreement with open communion practice led to the formation of Strict Baptist congregations, although open communion was not the only issue. 'Fullerism' was also seen as a problem by some who still embraced hyper-Calvinism.[75]

The practice of open communion as advocated by Hall tended to minimize doctrinal differences. Hall had urged open communion with all who agreed with the fundamentals of the Christian faith. This approach was largely the result of the evangelical revival of the previous century which led to the breaking down of denominational boundaries, in itself not necessarily a bad thing. For Hall the unity of the universal church was paramount. Men like Joseph Kinghorn were much more cautious. Kinghorn argued that the practice of open communion contravened the positive commands of the Lord Jesus Christ and apostolic practice. He insisted on the importance of the local church but also saw the adoption of an open table as a misguided attempt to create Christian unity at a price that he and other Particular Baptists were not willing to pay. Kinghorn was right to see the danger. Once the table was open to non-Baptists and evangelical Arminians, the chief support to Calvinism—the local church—was pulled away. This was but another step in "the erosion of distinctives."[76]

Evaluation of the Theology of Robert Hall and its Consequences

Robert Hall was very impatient with John Gill and in conversation famously but unjustly dismissed Gill's writings as "a continent of mud."[77] Yet, as a number of people have pointed out, Gill firmly

---

[75] See Oliver, *History of the English Calvinistic Baptists, 1771-1892*, 260-87.

[76] For further consideration of the significance of this issue see Nettles, *The Baptists: Key people involved in forming the Baptist identity*, 3:59-61.

[77] Hall, *Works*, 1:175. His comments were made in a conversation with Christmas Evans (1766-1838), the Welsh Baptist preacher, who happened to say that he wished Dr. Gill's works had been written in Welsh. Hall replied, "I wish

defended trinitarian theology against Socinianism and also firmly resisted antinomianism. English Particular Baptists would have been the weaker but for John Gill, and might well have followed many of the General Baptists and Presbyterians into Unitarianism. Similarly, Robert Hall, despite the fact that he diluted historic Calvinism, firmly resisted Socinianism, hyper-Calvinism, and antinomianism. Furthermore, he was a man characterized by a humble devotional spirit, a man of prayer, a zealous evangelist and a popular and passionate preacher. He did a great amount of good during his life. For example, he was bold in his stand for freedom of the press, and provided relief for Leicester framework knitters. He was resolute in defending the cause of Protestant Dissenters and promoted the work of Carey and the Baptist Missionary Society.

Once he was established in Cambridge, and even more so in Leicester, Robert Hall became regarded by many among the Baptists as a correct and eloquent champion of evangelical truth. That fact in itself reflects a change in the theological climate among English Particular Baptists. 1805 was a crisis year for Hall, leading to a transformation of his character, but it did not lead on his part to any significant return to historic Calvinism. By the time he began his ministry in Leicester the die had been cast. Genuine doubts about his orthodoxy had been raised while he was a tutor in Bristol. His father had pleaded with him, in vain at the time, to forsake his own speculative theology. Andrew Fuller and John Ryland were apprehensive and prayerful about Hall during the same period—"O may God keep this young man in the way of truth and holiness" was Fuller's plea.[78]

Robert Hall was without doubt a catalyst for theological change. He was not a Calvinist in the mold of his father, nor those like Andrew Fuller who belonged to his father's generation. There are other aspects of Hall's theology that need to be carefully examined, especially his understanding of justification by faith.[79] However, the fact remains—he rejected federal theology, original sin, and the imputation of Adam's sin. He did not interpret election in the same

---

they had, Sir; I wish they had with all my heart; for then I should never have read them. They are a continent of mud, Sir."

[78] Hall, *Works*, 1:22-23.

[79] This is beyond the scope of this study.

Robert Hall Jr. (1764-1831) and the Decline of Historic Calvinism...

way as historic Calvinism, and he held firmly to a universal atonement. In these ways, then, Robert Hall departed from the full-orbed Calvinistic theology that had been expressed in the 2LCF by his Particular Baptist forefathers.

There were others in Britain who were thinking along similar lines as Hall. For example, Daniel Turner (1710-1798), Particular Baptist pastor in Abingdon, had embraced general redemption, although he had also expressed dissatisfaction with the Athanasian Creed.[80] Robert Robinson (1735-1790), Hall's predecessor in Cambridge, had grown impatient with Calvinistic teaching and even with the doctrine of the Trinity.[81] Hall was eventually firmly committed to trinitarianism (once he had overcome his problem with the person of the Holy Spirit) and to the two natures of Christ, and to the doctrine of penal, substitutionary atonement.

After Hall's death, Calvinism among those still designated as Particular Baptists continued to be eclipsed by a broader-based evangelicalism. Other voices were heard but they raised no cry of lament over the loss of Calvinism. John Howard Hinton (1791-1873), pastor of the historic Devonshire Square Church in London, who became the secretary of the newly-formed Baptist Union for twenty-five years, admitted that if predestination and election were abandoned and Arminianism were to triumph, "I confess it would not be to me the heavy calamity which some people perceive it to be."[82] Dr. Russell Campbell has traced the decline and loss of Calvinism in the lives and ministries of three Baptist pastors, William Brock (1807-1875), Charles Stanford (1823-1886), and William Landels (1823-1899).[83] He maintained that these men together with other Baptists were driven by a spirit of pragmatism. Brock remained more Calvinistic but promoted an open table and open membership as he was more concerned with evangelical unity than church purity. Campbell described Stanford as an evangelical ecumenist, but demonstrated how this cost him his Calvinism by

---

[80] Oliver, *History of the English Calvinistic Baptists, 1771-1892*, 62.

[81] Oliver, *History of the English Calvinistic Baptists, 1771-1892*, 79.

[82] Quoted in J. H. Y. Briggs, *The English Baptists of the Nineteenth Century* (Didcot: The Baptist Historical Society, 1994), 163.

[83] Russell S. Campbell, "The decline of Calvinism among British Baptists in the nineteenth century: a study of three ministers" (D.Phil. thesis, University of Oxford, 2000).

the 1870s. Landels embraced a great deal of Finney's theology and his version of revivalism. Given the prevailing winds of opinion, the union of the two groups of Baptists in 1891 was little more than a formality. Historic Calvinism did not survive within the Baptist Union. To survive it put down new roots in different soil outside of the Baptist Union.

Chapter 7

The Life and Vision of Abraham Kuyper

Joel R. Beeke[*]

In 1898 Benjamin B. Warfield introduced Abraham Kuyper to American readers, saying, "Dr. Kuyper is probably today the most considerable figure in both political and ecclesiastical Holland." Abraham Kuyper was a scholar, theologian, preacher, reformer, educator, journalist, writer, orator, politician, and statesman. He was also a devout Christian, a passionate family man, a prodigious worker, a patriot, and the leading exponent of Calvinism's world and life view.

According to Kuyper, the dominating principle of Calvinism was "the sovereignty of the triune God over the whole cosmos, in all its spheres and kingdoms, visible and invisible." He spent most of his life working out the implications of that principle. He wrote, "There is not a square inch in the whole domain of our human experience over which Christ, who is Sovereign over *all*, does not cry, 'Mine!'"

Here is a brief look at Kuyper's remarkable life and some highlights of his Calvinistic worldview.[1]

Childhood and Education

Abraham Kuyper was born October 29, 1837, in the small fishing village of Maasluis. He was the eldest son of Henriette Huber, a teacher of Swiss descent, and Jan Frederick Kuyper, a minister in

---

[*] Joel R. Beeke, Ph.D., is president and professor of Systematic Theology and Homiletics at Puritan Reformed Theological Seminary, pastor of the Heritage Netherlands Reformed Congregation of Grand Rapids, MI, and editor of *Banner of Sovereign Grace Truth.*

[1] A bibliography of sources is provided at the end of this chapter.

the *Hervormde Kerk* or Dutch state church. By that date, liberal modernists who had abandoned Reformed confessional theology occupied most of the pulpits in the Netherlands and held significant posts in the universities and seminaries. Orthodox Reformed ministers and people were a minority within the state church. Abraham's father took a middle position between liberal modernism and the orthodox Reformed.

In 1841 the Kuyper family moved to Middleburg, provincial capital of Zeeland. In this historic seaport, young "Bram" developed a strong love for the sea and yearned to be a sailor. He was home-schooled, chiefly by his mother, who taught him French. His father taught him German. Bram showed an aptitude for languages and was able to master nearly any subject.

In 1849 Bram's father took a call to Leiden. For six years Bram attended the Leiden Gymnasium, a school that prepared students for university. He delivered the valedictory address in German titled "Ulfilas, the Bishop of the Visigoths, and his Gothic Translation of the Bible."

In 1855 Kuyper entered the renowned University of Leiden. The school was infested with modernism. Kuyper was most influenced there by Matthias DeVries, professor of literary studies, who taught the beauty and power of good writing. Kuyper graduated in 1858, *summa cum laude.*

Following in his father's footsteps, Kuyper prepared for the ministry at Leiden in the years 1858 to 1861. The theological faculty was uniformly liberal. Church history professor L. W. Rauwenhoff embraced an evolutionary view of history. Abraham Keunen, a higher critic, taught biblical studies. Joannes Henricus Scholten, who taught systematic theology, denied the bodily resurrection of Christ. Kuyper was deeply influenced by the modernist theology of his professors. At one time, he even joined other students in applauding a professor who openly denied the bodily resurrection of Jesus Christ.

In addition, two schools of thought in the Netherlands molded Kuyper's thinking. The Groningen School, which dominated the state church until about 1860, promoted Christian humanism based on the thinking of Erasmus, the most famous Reformation era humanist. P. Hofstede de Groot (1801-1866), foremost Groningen theologian and author of *Natural Theology,* promoted a religion of feelings. He said Christ was to be venerated as the leader of humanity, a supreme religious teacher, and an excellent moral example. But he denied the deity of Christ and the Trinity of Persons in the Godhead. He and his colleagues at Groningen published *Truth in Love,* a journal aimed at "cultured Christians to promote reasonable faith."

The other influence was the Ethical School, which promoted a religion of tolerance based on the inner, ethical life of man. Ethical Theology was championed by Daniel Chantepie de la Saussaye (1818-1874), a pastor in Leiden. He published *Ernst en Vrede* ("Sincerity and Peace"), a magazine that said that "ethical" conveyed the personal kind of faith missing in orthodox Calvinism. Ethical theologians denied the doctrine of human depravity and embraced theories of the day about the origin, composition, and unreliability of the Bible. By God's grace, Kuyper never fully succumbed to modernism. But Kuyper's flirtation with liberal theology helps explain why he became such an ardent foe of modernistic thinking after his conversion to orthodox Calvinism.

Kuyper earned a doctorate in theology on September 20, 1862, after completing a dissertation comparing the ecclesiology of the Polish reformer John à Lasco with that of John Calvin. Kuyper's dissertation was significant in two ways. The first was the extraordinary way in which Kuyper located a treasury of à Lasco's writings after a fruitless search of the holdings of major European university libraries. While Kuyper was at Leiden, the theological faculty at Groningen offered a prize for the best essay comparing the ecclesiologies of à Lasco and Calvin. The problem with this project, as Kuyper discovered, was that the majority of à Lasco's writings seemed to have disappeared. Matthias DeVries, the Leiden professor who encouraged Kuyper to write for the prize, suggested that he check some private libraries, beginning with that of De Vries's father, a clergyman in Haarlem. Kuyper was astonished to discover a treasury of à Lasco's writings. Twelve years later Kuyper described that find as "a miracle of God" (*een wonder Gods*) given by the "finger of God" (*vinger Gods*). Kuyper wrote the essay in Latin and obtained the prize, then developed it later for his doctoral dissertation. The other effect of this study was that it acquainted

Kuyper with the writings of John Calvin, which served him well in later years. It also raised questions in his mind about ecclesiology and church reform. Kuyper's later work as a reformer in the Dutch State Reformed Church was deeply influenced by the ecclesiology of à Lasco.

Conversion and Early Ministry

Kuyper's conversion from liberal modernism to Reformed orthodoxy and his subsequent passion for church reform were influenced by three factors. The first was God's providential leading in the discovery of the à Lasco collection.

Second was Charlotte Yonge's novel, *The Heir of Redcliffe*, which Kuyper read during a time of nervous exhaustion due to overwork. The story of a proud successful man, Philip de Morville, who is humbled, convicted Kuyper of his own sin. He later wrote: "What I lived through in my soul in that moment I fully understood only later, yet from that hour, after that moment, I scorned what I formerly esteemed, I sought what I once dared to despise." Nevertheless, Kuyper did not yet understand or embrace the gospel.

Third was Kuyper's experience of conversion, which happened during his contact with church members in his first pastoral charge at Beesd from 1863 to 1867. The summer after graduation, Kuyper married Johanna Schaay and moved to Beesd. The church consisted of simple villagers, some of whom had embraced modernism, as well as others who were committed Calvinists and would concede nothing to liberalism. Pietronella Baltus, a peasant woman in her thirties, confronted Kuyper about his modernistic thinking, lack of Reformed experiential preaching, and lack of saving faith in Christ. She even refused to shake the pastor's hand. In successive conversations, this young woman told Kuyper that he was preaching false doctrine and that his soul was in danger of eternal hell. Such biblical forthrightness wedded to the spiritual practice of such parishioners convinced Kuyper that they possessed a faith in Christ that he lacked. Eventually, God used those humble, yet determined, parishioners to lead their pastor back to Calvin and the

Reformed fathers, to the Scriptures, and to personal faith in Jesus Christ.

Preacher and Pastorates

Kuyper's preaching dramatically changed after his conversion. His sermons combined head and heart knowledge. He began attracting attention both for his oratorical skills and for how his teaching satisfied the hunger of the spiritually-minded *kleine luyden* ("little people," or common folk) such as Pietronella Baltus. "My life's goal was now the restoration of a church that could be our mother," Kuyper said.

In 1867 Kuyper accepted a call to Utrecht, a church with eleven ministers and 35,000 members. During his three years in Utrecht, Kuyper became a very popular preacher. He met Groen VanPrinsterer during that time and took up the cause of the Anti-Revolutionary Party.

In 1870 Kuyper accepted a call to the Reformed Church at Amsterdam, the most influential and prestigious church in the country, consisting of 140,000 members, 136 office-bearers, 28 ministers, and 14 sanctuaries and chapels. Here Kuyper reached the height of his power as a preacher. He was able to reach both the intellectuals and the common folk, whom he loved. Children were also fascinated with his teaching. His prayers were eloquent and humble; his reading of Scripture, heartfelt. A fellow professor, Frederik L. Rutgers, said that just hearing Kuyper read Psalm 148 from the pulpit was a clearer exposition than most sermons preached on that Psalm.

But Kuyper's preaching also evoked opposition. When he preached a sermon on "The Assurance of Election," for example, a modernist colleague preached the following Sabbath: "Let Anyone Who Comes with Another Gospel than that Christ Died for All Men be Accursed." After prolonged struggle and bitter infighting, the majority of ministers and elders in Amsterdam sided with Kuyper. That did not mean that the liberals were expelled, however, for the state church was a comprehensive church, embracing all shades of belief and practice as a matter of policy.

Church Reformer

The battle lines drawn between Kuyper and the modernists in the Dutch Reformed Church eventually led to a major secession of conservatives from the state church in 1886. The breach was called the *Doleantie,* from the French word *doleance,* meaning "grievance" or "complaint." Kuyper and his followers were dubbed the *Dolerenden,* "the aggrieved ones." In many ways the *Doleantie* was a continuation of the long-standing protest against modernism in the Dutch Reformed Church that had led to the *Afscheiding* ("Secession") of 1834. The *Dolerenden* were protesting the doctrinal tolerance and laxity (*leervrijheid,* "liberty of doctrine") of the state church. Like the leaders of the Secession of 1834, Kuyper and others called for a return to the theology of the Reformed confessions (Belgic Confession of Faith, Heidelberg Catechism, and Canons of Dort), and the Church Order of Dort.

The Church Order of Dort, which stressed the autonomy and authority of the local congregation and its consistory or council, had been struck down by the royal decree of 1816. A change in the form of subscription, which office-bearers in the church had to sign to indicate their agreement with the Reformed confessions, raised questions about their binding character. The debate raged furiously in the nineteenth century and centered on whether the confessions were binding *because (quia)* they agree with the Word of God, or *insofar as (quatenus)* they agree with the Word of God. Liberalism was making its influence felt. By 1854 candidates for the ministry were only required to acknowledge and promise to defend "the spirit and main points of doctrine" contained in the confessions. From 1878 on, consistories were not permitted to refuse church membership to anyone for doctrinal reasons.

The matter of church membership and the authority of local consistories to exercise church discipline had been the main impetus for the *Doleantie* of 1886. The insistence of the majority of the Amsterdam consistory on maintaining strict standards for church membership resulted in the suspension of Kuyper and four other ministers, forty-two elders, and thirty-three deacons. Two hundred congregations, with about 150,000 people, chose to leave the state church. This exodus resulted in the formation of the *Nederduits*

Gereformeerde Kerk (Dolerende).

The Secession of 1834 and the Reformation movement of 1886 proceeded from similar principles. Both were committed to the doctrine set forth in the Reformed confessions and the polity of the Church Order of Dort. Both strove for a church free from the domination of the state and deviations from Reformed doctrine. Like the Secession of 1834, the *Doleantie* was strongly supported by the common people. This tie was not only a matter of political expediency but of principle. For Kuyper, Calvinism would always be a democratic movement of the common people.

The Secession and the *Doleantie* were also alike in stressing personal piety. The Reformed experiential emphasis of the Secession is most evident in Kuyper's meditations that appeared weekly in the journal *De Heraut* ("The Herald") and later collected in volumes such as *Falling Asleep in Jesus, To be Near Unto God, As You Sit in Your House,* and *Honey from the Rock.* Many of Kuyper's followers later departed from this experiential emphasis, but that didn't negate Kuyper's evident commitment to it in his meditations.

Even so, the Kuyper-led *Doleantie* was also different from the Secession of 1834. Doctrinal differences centered on the covenant of grace. The Secession churches stressed the need for covenant children to be born again and to experience saving grace, whereas most of the *Doleantie* churches embraced Kuyper's notion of presumptive or presupposed regeneration and treated covenant children as possessors of saving grace in Christ from infancy. That naturally led to downplaying the experimental emphasis prevalent in Secession churches.

Then too, the Secession had been strictly a church-reform movement. The *Doleantie* wanted more, because of Kuyper's expanded interpretation of Calvinism, sometimes called "neo-Calvinism." For Kuyper, Calvinism stood for a total world and life view (Dutch: *wereldbeschouwing;* German: *Weltanschauung*), not merely an ecclesiastical, confessional, or theological system. As such it was opposed to the world and life views presented by other belief systems such as paganism, Islam, Romanism, and modernism. Kuyper's goal was not only church reform but also a spiritual victory in all areas of life over the atheistic worldview of modernism.

Despite these differences, Kuyper was instrumental in merging the *Doleantie* churches with the majority of the 1834 Secession churches in 1892, giving birth to the *Gereformerde Kerken in Nederland* ("Reformed Churches in the Netherlands"). The new denomination consisted of 400 Secession churches, 300 *Doleantie* churches, and 300,000 members. Similarly in North America, the Christian Reformed Church, founded in 1857 by Secession immigrants, welcomed large numbers of *Doleantie* immigrants who crossed the Atlantic in the 1890s and later.

The merger was a tenuous one, however. Eventually people referred to the churches of the Secession as the "A-Stream" churches, and the churches of the *Doleantie* as the "B-Stream" churches. Frequently, ministers or people of one group refused to preach or worship in the churches of the other.

As a leader of the Anti-Revolutionary Party, Kuyper insisted that Christians draw clear battle lines against life systems of contemporary European culture, which he traced back to the French Revolution. He wrote:

> If this battle is to be fought with honour and with a hope of victory, then *principle* must be arrayed against *principle*; then it must be felt that in Modernism the vast energy of an all-embracing *life-system* assails us, then also it must be understood that we have to take our stand in a life-system of equally comprehensive and far-reaching power. And this powerful life-system is not to be invented nor formulated by ourselves, but is to be taken and applied as it presents itself in history. When thus taken, I found and confessed, and I still hold, that this manifestation of the Christian principle is given us in *Calvinism*. In Calvinism my heart has found rest. From Calvinism have I drawn inspiration firmly and resolutely to take my stand in the thick of this great conflict of principles. . . . Calvinism [is] the only decisive, lawful, and consistent defense for Protestant nations against encroaching and overwhelming Modernism.

So Kuyper taught that modernism in all of its socio-cultural manifestations must be fought in idea and principle. It was a spiritual struggle for the heart and soul of the nation, Kuyper believed, and pivotal for the very future of Western civilization. According to Kuyper, the finest fruits of European civilization in art, science, commerce, and industry were due to the influence of Calvinism. Calvinism was the origin and safeguard of constitutional political liberty. Only by forsaking the ideals of the French Revolution and returning to a pre-Enlightenment theonomous (but not theocratic) ideal could Western civilization hope to survive. That was Kuyper's lifelong pursuit as a journalist, as the founder of a Calvinistic university, as the leader of a Calvinistic political party, as a member of parliament, and as prime minister of the Netherlands.

Theologian

For Kuyper, the "dominating principle" of Calvinism, he noted, "was not, soteriologically, justification by faith, but in the widest sense cosmologically, *the Sovereignty of the Triune God over the whole Cosmos* in all its spheres and kingdoms, visible and invisible." This idea of the "Sovereignty of the Triune God over the whole Cosmos" led Kuyper to three important doctrines.

1. Common grace

This doctrine is based on Kuyper's conviction that prior to and independent of the *particular grace* (Dutch: *genade*) of God expressed in redemption, there is a *universal grace* (Dutch: *gunst*) of God at work in creation and providence. This universal or common grace, which restrains sin and mitigates its consequences in human society, is the basis of Kuyper's call for Christian involvement in the general cultural, socio-political life of humanity.

The doctrine of common grace enabled Kuyper to stand against wrong views of culture held by many Christians. On the one hand, Kuyper opposed Anabaptists and pietists who shrank from cultural involvement, fearful of contamination or "worldliness." On the other hand, Kuyper rejected the ecclesiasticizing of cultural life practiced by the pre-Reformation papal church, seeking to bring all of life under the control of the institutional church. Cultural life, rooted in creation and common grace, has a life and a goal of its own, apart from the sphere of redemption and particular grace, Kuyper believed.

Kuyper's explanation of common grace in *Gemeene Gratie* wasn't always consistent. He was less concerned with a systematic definition of common grace than he was with its value in overcoming the cultural alienation of many orthodox Dutch Reformed people. According to S. V. Zuidema, Kuyper used the doctrine of common grace

> to stimulate, as well as to justify, truly Christian action by God's people from out of the particular grace of regeneration by the light of Holy Scripture. Common grace supplies the believer with the material for fulfilling his calling to be culturally formative and to fight the battle of the Lord in the world of culture.

2. Antithesis

Kuyper's view on common grace was linked with his insistence upon a radical *antithesis* between general human cultural activity and Christian cultural activity. Kuyper's doctrine of common grace is misunderstood if it is regarded simply as a call for Christians to join with all men in a human cultural project. As Kuyper wrote, "Two *life-systems* are wrestling with one another, in mortal combat."

Regeneration by the Holy Spirit is the theological foundation for the doctrine of the antithesis. According to Kuyper, Christianity speaks of regeneration "which changes man in his very being, and that indeed by a change or transformation which is effected by a supernatural cause." So, just as two kinds of people will develop two kinds of science because their conflict is not between faith (or religion) and science, but between *"two scientific systems . . . each having its own faith,"* so Christians and humanists promote different types of cultural activity.

Kuyper therefore devoted his life to the establishment of Calvinistic cultural institutions of many kinds, including a

Calvinistic university, a Calvinistic political party, a Calvinistic labor union, and numerous associations and organizations.

3. Sphere sovereignty

Kuyper was not satisfied with opposing the spirit of modernism with general Christian principles but with specifically Calvinistic principles (*gereformeerde beginselen*). Chief among these principles was the doctrine of sphere sovereignty. This theme was formulated to counter the notion of statism or state sovereignty in various areas of life. As Kuyper explained:

> In a Calvinistic sense we understand hereby, that the family, business, science, art and so forth are all social spheres which do not owe their existence to the state, and which do not derive the law of their life from the superiority of the state, but obey a high authority within their own bosom; an authority which rules, by the grace of God, just as sovereignty of the state does.

The various spheres are autonomous in their own right. This autonomy was God-given in creation and it is to God alone that they are ultimately responsible. As Kuyper wrote:

> In this independent character a special *higher authority* is of necessity involved and this highest authority we intentionally call *sovereignty in the individual social spheres,* in order that it may be sharply and decidedly expressed that these different developments of social life have *nothing above themselves but God,* and that the State cannot intrude here, and has nothing to command in their domain.

The doctrine of sphere sovereignty roots all authority in divine sovereignty, thus safeguarding the public order from all forms of state absolutism and providing the guarantee for civil liberty. The state has certain responsibilities to the various spheres, however. As Kuyper says:

It possesses the threefold right and duty: 1. Whenever different spheres clash, to compel mutual regard for the boundary lines of each; 2. To defend individuals and the weak ones, in those spheres against the abuse of power of the rest, and 3. To coerce all together to bear *personal* and *financial* burdens for the maintenance of the natural unity of the State.

Only constitutional government and constitutional law can properly guarantee civil liberties and the proper autonomy of the various spheres.

The doctrine of sphere sovereignty also countered the medieval Roman Catholic notion of church sovereignty in society. God's rule over the spheres of human society is not mediated by the church but is direct and immediate, Kuyper said. Prior to and quite apart from his relation to men as redeemer, God is directly and universally related to men as their Creator, and his law is the law of their life. Kuyper distinguished between the church as *organism* (the people of God in the world) and the church as *institute*, gathered into congregations, governed by office-bearers and assemblies (consistories, classes, and synods), bound by the confessions, and regulated by the church order. Accordingly, Kuyper called for organized Christian activity in areas other than the work of the institutional church. Christians were expected to respond to the needs of society, not as church members but as Christians in society, by forming Christian labor unions, Christian political parties, Christian social organizations, and institutions of Christian education.

Politician

In 1869 Kuyper got to know the secretary of the king's cabinet, Groen VanPrinsterer (1801-1876). It turned out to be a career-changing experience. VanPrinsterer, who had a doctorate in law and in literature and was a gifted lawyer and historian, had been converted through the influence of the Reformation historian J. H. Merle d'Aubigne (1794-1872). He was also greatly influenced by men associated with religious revivals in various parts of Europe, beginning in French-speaking Switzerland after the defeat of Napoleon. That movement, known as the *Réveil* (French for "Awakening"), countered the rationalism of the German Enlightenment (*Aufklärung*). When the *Réveil* reached the Netherlands, Willem Bilderdijk (1756-1831), a Calvinist poet, started a study group aspiring to restore the Reformed faith in the churches. One of his converts, fellow poet Isaak da Costa (1798-1860), assailed rationalists within the Dutch Reformed Church and opposed the spirit of modernity.

The Dutch *Réveil* greatly influenced Hendrik de Cock (1801-1842) and other pioneers of the 1834 Secession as well as VanPrinsterer, though they responded to the influence in different ways. VanPrinsterer described his own worldview as "anti-revolutionary" and "Christian historical." VanPrinsterer was the mastermind of what would evolve into the Anti-Revolutionary Party (ARP) in the Netherlands. This party would assert Christ's lordship over public affairs and oppose the principles expressed by the French Revolution and political liberalism in general.

Kuyper cast in his lot with the ARP. In 1874, he was elected to the Second Chamber of Parliament. Since Dutch law excluded ministers of churches from membership in the Parliament, Kuyper resigned his office as pastor. Many people questioned the wisdom of Kuyper's choice. The following year Kuyper was reelected, but his term was interrupted by another nervous breakdown. He was incapacitated for fifteen months, most of which were spent in Switzerland and Italy.

When he returned to work, Kuyper thoroughly reorganized the ARP with a constitution, a statement of principles, and a well-formulated platform. Under his leadership, the ARP became the first properly organized Dutch political party, complete with a national committee, headquarters, treasury, newspapers, and an annual national convention. In 1878 Kuyper published *Ons Program* ("Our Program"), the party's political manifesto.

In time, Kuyper concluded that the only way to break the hold of the two main liberal parties in Parliament was to form a coalition with the Roman Catholics. Though the two groups were theologically opposed to each other, they did have mutual concerns about education. Their coalition defeated the liberals in the election of 1888, but lost again in 1891 and didn't regain power until 1901, when Kuyper was asked to head the new government as prime minister.

Kuyper's five-year stint as prime minister was only partially successful. A school bill was passed that gave Christian schools legal parity with government schools. Kuyper was also instrumental in ending the railway strike of 1903. Most of the ARP goals, however, were not achieved.

Kuyper's coalition was defeated in the election of 1905. Kuyper briefly served Parliament two more times but achieved little because of medical problems. In his last years Kuyper became increasingly critical of his own party. Some viewed him as a bitter old man who could not surrender his autocratic leadership nor tolerate the leadership of any who disagreed with him.

The ARP abandoned most of its principles in the twentieth century. By 1980 it merged with the Catholic People's Party to form the Christian Democratic Appeal.

Journalist and Writer

Kuyper's influence continued through five decades because of his prolific writing. That career began in 1866 with the preparation of à Lasco's works for the press. Kuyper wrote a lengthy introduction for those works. Later, he edited selected writings of Franciscus Junius (1545-1602) and Gisbertus Voetius (1589-1676), leading Dutch Reformed theologians.

In 1869, Kuyper became editor of the weekly *De Heraut*, calling "For a Free Church and a Free School in a Free Land." In 1872 Kuyper became editor of *De Standaard* ("The Standard"), a Christian daily newspaper and official organ of the ARP. He continued to edit both papers until he was eighty-two years old. He wrote thousands of articles, many of which were later published as books.

Kuyper was a multifaceted writer. He wrote about theology, history, philosophy, politics, and aesthetics. Some of his books were warmly devotional, such as *Nabij God te Zijn (To Be Near Unto God)*. He wrote hundreds of meditations and scores of articles on practical Christianity, and allowed his *Dictaten Dogmatiek* ("Notes on

Systematic Theology") to go to press unedited. He published an exposition of the Heidelberg Catechism, *E Voto Dordraceno* ("According to the Wish of Dort"), so named because the Synod of Dort had recommended the Catechism as a form of instruction for use in the churches and schools of the nation. Kuyper's greatest work was probably his *Encyclopedia of Sacred Theology* (3 vols). He also wrote three volumes on common grace *(Gemeene Gratie)*, a massive volume on the Holy Spirit, and a book on Revelation. He published four volumes on eschatology, *Van de Voleinding* ("Of the Consummation") and three volumes of *Pro Rege* ("For the King").

In 1898, Kuyper delivered the Stone Lectures at Princeton University and received an honorary doctorate. The lectures set forth his Calvinistic worldview, and have often been reprinted as *Calvinism*. He wrote two large volumes on the geography, history, and cultural life of the people of the Mediterranean basin. Four volumes of his political speeches were published from 1908 to 1910. Other significant volumes include *Dat de Genade Particulier is* (newly published in English as *That Grace Is Particular*), *De Leer der Verbonden* ("The Doctrine of the Covenants"), *De Hedendaagsche Schrift Kritiek* ("Today's Criticism of the Bible"), and *De Engelen Gods* ("The Angels of God").

Kuyper's writings influenced thousands throughout the twentieth century. His books and articles generated praise as well as criticism. Men such as Herman Bavinck and Herman Dooyeweerd, though not uncritical of Kuyper's thinking, were greatly influenced by him. Professors Lucas Lindeboom and Maarten Noordtzij, representing the "A-Stream" churches, felt that Kuyper's theology was not sufficiently scriptural. They believed it was too speculative and deductive, particularly his views on baptism, on justification from eternity, and on the scientific character of theology. G. C. Berkouwer wrote, "There was doubt about his doctrine of common grace, doubts about his view of the antithesis between Christianity and other life-views, and doubts about the polemics that those views had aroused." Many people feared that Kuyper's ideas would secularize Christianity. They said such "Neo-Calvinism" was "a deceptive synthesis" and that his use of secular worldviews weakened his case for the distinctiveness of the Calvinistic worldview.

Cornelius Van Til advanced Kuyper's ideas in the United States, particularly in the area of presuppositional apologetics. Francis Schaeffer also helped popularize some of Kuyper's ideas. Various Dutch Reformed denominations in North America have been greatly impacted by Kuyperianism. South Africa's Potchefstroom University for Christian Higher Education was modeled after the Free University of Amsterdam and has greatly impacted Christian education and scholarship in Africa. Today Kuyper's influence may be stronger in North America and South Africa than in the Netherlands.

In the twentieth century, Kuyper's doctrines of common grace and presumptive regeneration spun off views and practices that carried the movement well beyond what he would have approved. Though Kuyper made common grace a doctrine of importance far beyond traditional Calvinism, he would not have endorsed his successors using his doctrine of common grace to elevate social responsibilities above evangelism or to justify their conformity to worldly ideas and practices.

Kuyper's notion of presumptive regeneration led some to conclude that baptism assures salvation, or at least that covenant children should not be told that they need to be born again. Many children grew up thinking that sound doctrinal knowledge and biblical ethical conduct are sufficient for salvation without experiencing conviction of sin and conversion, or any need for self-examination with regard to the marks of grace. The net result was that, over time, Reformed experiential religion became deemed largely superfluous.

Educator

Dissatisfied with government schools and universities, Kuyper established a Christian university free from state control or influence. The Free University of Amsterdam, designed to affirm a biblical and Reformed worldview throughout its curriculum, was established on October 20, 1880. Kuyper organized it as a school operated by Christian parents and supported by the prayers and gifts of Reformed Christians. The university began with five professors and only five students, but continued to grow, training ministers and school teachers for the *Gereformeerde Kerken*. Kuyper served as rector and professor at the Free University from 1880 to 1901.

As prime minister, Kuyper helped pass a law granting full legal standing for private universities and technical schools that were preparing students for higher education. The Free University then received state recognition of its awarded degrees.

The Free University strayed from Kuyper's teachings in the twentieth century. By 1960, many of its 12,000 students expressed little or no allegiance to the Christian faith. The institution even declared in 1971 that it had abandoned its commitment to Calvinism, though it would retain the gospel for its basis of teaching.

As a Man

Kuyper lived out his Calvinistic faith as a believer. He reveled in the life of his family with his wife, five sons, and two daughters. He faithfully conducted family worship after the evening meal, reading and explaining the Scriptures to his family and servants.

Like other believers, he struggled with losses. His 9-year-old son passed away in 1892 and his beloved wife in 1899 at the age of 58. Kuyper never remarried. He continued his heavy workload—except for periods of nervous exhaustion—to the end of his life.

Though short of stature, Kuyper's appearance was commanding. He held audiences spellbound with his uncompromising convictions and compelling oratory. Spiritually, communion with Christ sustained him throughout his long career.

Perhaps Kuyper's greatest personal flaw was his intolerance of those who disagreed with him. His tendency to act like a dictator in ecclesiastical and political matters seemed to grow with age. The last years of his life were neither happy nor fruitful.

Abraham Kuyper died on November 8, 1920, at the age of 83, after a public career of 57 years. The funeral was simple, at Kuyper's request, but thousands attended, including so many deputies from Parliament that no business could be conducted that day due to a lack of a quorum. It concluded with the singing of Kuyper's favorite — Psalm 89:7-8:

> How blessed, Lord are they who know the joyful sound,
> Who, when they hear Thy voice, in happiness abound!
> With stedfast step they walk, their countenances beaming
> With brightness of the light that from Thy face is streaming;
> Exalted by Thy might from depths of desolation,
> They praise fore'er Thy Name, Thy justice and salvation.
>
> Thou art, O God, our boast, the glory of our power;
> Thy sovereign grace is e'er our fortress and our tower;
> We lift our heads aloft, for God, our shield is o'er us;
> Through Him, through Him alone, whose presence goes before us,
> We'll wear the victor's crown, no more by foes assaulted,
> We'll triumph through our King, by Israel's God exalted.

On his tombstone were engraved the words:

> Dr. A. Kuyper
> Born October 29, 1837
> And fallen asleep in his Savior
> November 8, 1920

Kuyper's influence remains powerful today. Many throughout the international Reformed community continue to wrestle with the implications of Kuyper's declaration:

> God's majesty and sovereignty require that we believe God's Word, not because of what it says, but because *it is His Word*, not because we think it beautiful and true, but because *He has spoken it*.

Select Bibliography

For a thorough bibliography of Abraham Kuyper's own writings, see Tjitze Kuipers, *Abraham Kuyper: An Annotated Bibliography 1857-2010*. Leiden: Brill, 2011.

For secondary sources on Kuyper, see:

Augustijn, Cornelis, and Jasper Vree, eds. *Abraham Kuyper: Vast En Veranderlijk: De Ontwikkeling van Zijn Denken*. Zoetermeer: Meinema, 1998.

Bacote, Vincent E. *The Spirit in Public Theology: Appropriating the Legacy of Abraham Kuyper*. Grand Rapids: Baker Academic, 2005.

Bolt, John. *A Free Church, a Holy Nation: Abraham Kuyper's American Public Theology*. Grand Rapids: Eerdmans, 2000.

Bratt, James. *Abraham Kuyper: Modern Calvinist, Christian Democrat*. Grand Rapids: Eerdmans, 2013.

De Bruijn, Jan. *Abraham Kuyper: A Pictorial Biography*. Grand Rapids: Eerdmans, 2014.

Kobes, Wayne A. "Sphere Sovereignty and the University: Theological Foundations of Abraham Kuyper's View of the University and Its Role in Society." Ph.D. diss., Florida State University, 1993.

Langman, H. J. *Kuyper en de Volkskerk: Een Dogmatisch-Ecclesiologische Studie*. Kampen: Kok, 1950.

Lugo, Luis E., ed. *Religion, Pluralism, and Public Life: Abraham Kuyper's Legacy for the Twenty-First Century*. Grand Rapids: Eerdmans, 2000.

McGoldrick, James E. *Abraham Kuyper: God's Renaissance Man*. Darlington, England: Evangelical Press, 2000.

Mouw, Richard J. *Abraham Kuyper: A Short and Personal Introduction*. Grand Rapids: Eerdmans, 2011.

Praamsma, Louis. *Let Christ Be King: Reflections on the Life and Times of Abraham Kuyper*. Jordan Station, Ontario: Paideia Press, 1985.

Puchinger, George. *Abraham Kuyper: His Early Journey of Faith*. Translated by Simone Kennedy. Edited by George Harinck. Amsterdam: VU Press, 1998.

Rullmann, J. C. *Kuyper-Bibliographie*. 3 vols. 's-Gravenhage: Js.

Bootsma, 1923-1940.

Schaeffer, J. C. *De Plaats van Abraham Kuyper in "De Vrije Kerk."* Amsterdam: Buijten & Schipperheijn, 1997.

Stellingwerff, Johannes. *Dr. Abraham Kuyper En De Vrije Universiteit.* Kampen: Kok, 1987.

Van Leeuwen, Petrus Antonius. *Het Kerkbegrip in de Theologie van Abraham Kuyper.* Franeker: Wever, 1946.

VandenBerg, Frank. *Abraham Kuyper.* Grand Rapids: Eerdmans, 1960.

Velema, Willem H. *De Leer Van De Heilige Geest bij Abraham Kuyper.* 's-Gravenhage: Van Keulen, 1957.

Vree, Jasper. *Kuyper in de Kiem: De Precalvinistische Periode van Abraham Kuyper, 1848-1874.* Hilversum: Uitgeverij Verloren, 2006.

Van der Kooi, Cornelis and Jan de Bruijn, eds. *Kuyper Reconsidered: Aspects of His Life and Work.* Amsterdam: VU Uitgeverij, 1999.

Wood, John Halsey, Jr. *Going Dutch in the Modern Age: Abraham Kuyper's Struggle for a Free Church in the Nineteenth-Century Netherlands.* New York: Oxford University Press, 2013.

Young, William. "Historic Calvinism and Neo-Calvinism." *Westminster Theological Journal* 36 (1974): 48-64, 156-173.

Chapter 8

Getting the Garden Right

From Hermeneutics to the Covenant of Works

Richard C. Barcellos[*]

In this study, I want to focus on the hermeneutical principles that guided the Reformed theologians of the seventeenth century in their formulation of the doctrine of the covenant of works. Many in our day deny this doctrine. Some deny it because they think it derives from a theology that produces a hermeneutic that is then imposed upon the text of Scripture. Others deny it because they view all of God's covenantal relationships with man as gracious and not works- or merit-based. I will not deal with all the various types of denials related to the covenant of works. My focus will be upon hermeneutics. More specifically, I want to show you some of the hermeneutical principles that led to the formulation of this doctrine and then apply those principles to the text of Scripture in an attempt to justify the doctrine. In so doing, I will argue that the covenant of works is a conclusion based on the exegesis of texts and the theological synthesis of that exegetical work. In other words, the formulation of the covenant of works is based on exegesis and is the result of reducing the exegetical fruit to a doctrinal formulation which reflects that fruit.

It is only proper in a book like this to acknowledge that Dr. James M. Renihan is to be thanked for his friendship, example, influence, and encouragement toward me over the years. It is due to

[*] Richard C. Barcellos, Ph.D., is pastor of Grace Reformed Baptist Church, Palmdale, CA. He is author of *The Lord's Supper as a Means of Grace: More than a Memory, Better than the Beginning: Creation in Biblical Perspective*, and *The Family Tree of Reformed Biblical Theology: Geerhardus Vos and John Owen — Their Methods of and Contributions to the Articulation of Redemptive History*. English Bible references are taken from the New American Standard Updated, 1995.

Jim recommending books and articles about ten years ago that the foundation was laid for me to be able to work through a subject like hermeneutics and the covenant of works (and many other subjects). Jim, thank you.

The Importance of Getting the Garden and the Covenant of Works Right

In a conversation with Dr. Vern Poythress several years ago, I asked him something like, "Dr. Poythress, is it true that if you get the Garden wrong you get eschatology wrong?" He said something like, "Well, if you get the Garden wrong, you get everything wrong!"

C. H. Spurgeon said:

The doctrine of the covenant lies at the root of all true theology. It has been said that he who well understands the distinction between the covenant of works and the covenant of grace, is a master of divinity. I am persuaded that most of the mistakes which men make concerning the doctrines of Scripture are based upon fundamental errors with regard to the covenants of law and grace.[1]

The Dutch Reformed theologian, Wilhelmus a' Brakel, in his discussion of the covenant of works, said:

Acquaintance with this covenant is of the greatest importance, for whoever errs here or denies the existence of the covenant of works, will not understand the covenant of grace, and will readily err concerning the mediatorship of the Lord Jesus. Such a person will very readily deny that Christ by His active obedience has merited a right to eternal

---

[1] This comes from C. H. Spurgeon, "Sermon XL, the Covenant," *The Sermons of Rev. C. H. Spurgeon of London*, 9th Series (New York: Robert Cater & Brothers, 1883), 172, as quoted in Pascal Denault, *The Distinctiveness of Baptist Covenant Theology: A Comparison Between Seventeenth-Century Particular Baptist and Paedobaptist Federalism* (Birmingham, AL: Solid Ground Christian Books, 2013), 6, n. 4.

life for the elect. This is to be observed with several parties who, because they err concerning the covenant of grace, also deny the covenant of works. Conversely, whoever denies the covenant of works, must rightly be suspected to be in error concerning the covenant of grace as well.[2]

And the seventeenth-century Particular Baptist, Nehemiah Coxe, while discussing God's transactions with Adam said, "If a man misses the right account of this, he is certainly bewildered in all further searching for that truth which most concerns him to know."[3]

I agree with these men about the importance of getting the covenant of works right. I think there are very dangerous ramifications of its rejection, though this is outside of our particular focus.

Working Definition of the Covenant of Works

1.   A brief definition of covenant when it relates to God and man

A divine covenant with man can be defined very briefly as follows: a divinely sanctioned commitment or relationship. In this sense, covenants come from God to man. They are not contracts between equal business partners. They are not up for negotiation. They are imposed by God upon man and, as Coxe says, "[for] the advancing and bettering of his state."[4] The divine covenants are not intended to merely sustain man in the condition he was in prior to those covenants being revealed to him. They are, in some sense, intended for the "bettering of his state." Coxe also says this, while defining covenants between God and man, "[They involve a] declaration of his sovereign pleasure concerning the benefits he will bestow on

---

[2] Wilhelmus a' Brakel, *The Christian's Reasonable Service*, 4 vols. (Grand Rapids: Reformation Heritage Books, 1992, Third printing 1999), 1:355.

[3] Nehemiah Coxe and John Owen, *Covenant Theology From Adam to Christ*, ed. Ronald D. Miller, James M. Renihan, and Francisco Orozco (Palmdale, CA: Reformed Baptist Academic Press, 2005), 42.

[4] Coxe and Owen, *Covenant Theology*, 36.

them, the communion they will have with him, and the way and means by which this will be enjoyed by them."[5] Note well that Coxe says covenants are imposed on man by God "[for] the advancing and bettering of his state." Improvement and betterment, in some sense, are built into all covenants that God makes with man, and the covenant of works is no exception. As we will see below, the improvement that the covenant of works proffered was eschatological in nature.[6]

2. The definition of the phrase "covenant of works"

Our working definition of the covenant of works is as follows: that covenant (or that divinely sanctioned commitment or relationship) God imposed upon Adam, who was a sinless representative of mankind (or a public person), an image-bearing son of God, conditioned upon his obedience, with a penalty for disobedience, all for the bettering of man's state. Here we have: 1) sovereign, divine imposition, 2) representation by Adam, a sinless image-bearing son of God[7] (i.e., federal headship), 3) a conditional element (i.e., obedience), 4) a penalty for disobedience (i.e., death), and 5) a promise of reward (i.e., eschatological potential). It is important to keep this definition in mind as we work our way through this study.

How the Doctrine of the Covenant of Works was Formulated

In this section, I will concentrate on how the doctrine of the covenant of works was formulated in the seventeenth century. I believe the doctrine predates the seventeenth century, going all the

---

[5] Coxe and Owen, *Covenant Theology*, 36.

[6] I am indebted to Samuel Renihan for helping me state my thoughts more clearly in these two sentences.

[7] It is important to recognize that the covenant of works was made with a representative sinless image-bearing son of God. It could only be fulfilled by a sinless image-bearing son of God since disobedience violates its terms, which happened with Adam and all in him.

way back to Moses. For the purposes of this chapter, however, I will concentrate on the method of the seventeenth-century federal theologians and how they got from the Garden to the covenant of works.

We will now consider how this doctrine was not formulated.

1. Negatively or how the doctrine of the covenant of works was not formulated

How was the doctrine of the covenant of works formulated? It was not formulated because the Westminster divines came up with a theory then tried to find it in the Bible, forcing biblical texts into a pre-conceived theological system. The same goes for the Savoy and the London Particular Baptist divines. This is essentially what I was told during my seminary days in the late 1980s. The theology of the seventeenth-century divines, so I was told, stood over the Bible as its interpretive lord.

Some think that a theology of the Garden was constructed in the minds of men, which included the covenant of works, then a hermeneutic was invented to get there. In other words, an extra-biblical theology led to an extra-biblical hermeneutic, which led to an extra-biblical confessional formulation. Again, in this view, their theology and hermeneutical principles stood over the Bible as its interpretive lord.

Let me say at this point that I do believe that the covenant theologians presupposed a hermeneutic that led to their covenant theology. If we take theology here to mean what the seventeenth-century federalists said the Bible teaches, and hermeneutics to mean the interpretive principles they *took to the Bible to determine its meaning*, then it is not the case that they presupposed a hermeneutic that led to their theology. It is the case, however, that their theology and their hermeneutical principles, though in part distinguishable, were not separate, unrelated categories, one derived from special revelation (i.e., Scripture) and the other from general revelation (i.e., hermeneutics). In other words, part of their theology (i.e., what they said the Bible taught) was hermeneutics (i.e., the principles they utilized to determine what the Bible taught). To be more specific, their interpretive principles came, in part, from what they believed the Bible said about itself and how the Bible interpreted itself. They saw texts interacting with texts and further explaining them. They saw texts within Scripture interpreting texts within Scripture, and sometimes using words to describe concepts that are not contained in the text being referenced. For example, in Acts 2:31 Peter says that David "spoke of the resurrection of the Christ" in Psalm 16. The Psalm, however, has neither the word "resurrection" nor the word "Christ" in it. Peter is describing *concepts* from Psalm 16 in *words* not used by Psalm 16. Later texts can, and do, describe earlier *concepts* with different *words*. In our day, we would say they saw inner-biblical exegesis occurring in the Bible, that is, they saw later texts interpreting and applying earlier texts, and they accounted for it in the way they understood other texts. In other words, they did not impose an extra-biblical theory of hermeneutics upon the Bible that produced their federal theology. We will discuss this in more detail below. This leads to my next question: How was the doctrine of the covenant of works formulated or upon what principles was it based?

2. Positively or how the doctrine of the covenant of works was formulated

How did the older covenant theologians go from the Garden to the covenant of works? The answer is that they utilized long-standing hermeneutical principles somewhat typical of the entire Christian theological tradition from the early centuries to the post-Reformation era.[8] In other words, they utilized a pre-critical or pre-Enlightenment method of interpreting Scripture.[9] They did not believe the Bible was to be interpreted like any other book. They believed the Bible was the written Word of God and that it was its only infallible interpreter. They not only believed the writers of Scripture to be God's penmen, they also believed that they were

---

[8] A good case can be made that the principles they used predate post-apostolic reflection and are imbedded in the text of Scripture (Old and New Testament) itself. Proving this is beyond the scope of this chapter.

[9] See David C. Steinmetz, "The Superiority of Pre-Critical Exegesis," *Theology Today* (April 1980): 27-38, for an introduction to pre-critical hermeneutics. Thanks to Jim Renihan for pointing me to this article many years ago.

infallible theologians as they wrote. They believed that the Bible often interpreted itself and that later texts often used earlier texts in a way that gave the divine, and therefore infallible, interpretation of those earlier texts.

Let's explore some of the hermeneutical principles of the covenant theologians of the seventeenth century. These are inter-related principles with some overlap between them. I think you will see how important it is to understand their hermeneutical principles in order to see how they came to their doctrinal formulations.

Some Hermeneutical Principles of Seventeenth-Century Federal Theology

We will now identify and discuss four principles utilized by the federal theologians.

1. The Holy Spirit is the only infallible interpreter of Holy Scripture.

As an example of this principle, John Owen says, "The only unique, public, authentic, and infallible interpreter of Scripture is none other than the Author of Scripture Himself . . . that is, God the Holy Spirit."[10] Nehemiah Coxe says, ". . . the best interpreter of the Old Testament is the Holy Spirit speaking to us in the new."[11] This meant that they saw the Bible's interpretation and use of itself as infallible and with interpretive principles embedded in it. When the Bible comments upon or utilizes itself in any fashion (e.g., direct quotation, fulfillment [prophetic or typological], allusion, or echo in the OT or NT), it is God's interpretation and God's understanding of how texts should be understood. This often means that later texts shed interpretive light on earlier texts. Or, we could put it this way: Subsequent revelation often makes explicit what is implicit in antecedent revelation. The Holy Spirit as the only infallible interpreter of Scripture led to three more related concepts.

---

[10] John Owen, *Biblical Theology or The Nature, Origin, Development, and Study of Theological Truth in Six Books* (Pittsburgh: Soli Deo Gloria Publications, 1994), 797.

[11] Coxe and Owen, *Covenant Theology*, 36.

2. The analogy of Scripture (*analogia Scripturae*)

Here is Richard A. Muller's definition of *analogia Scripturae*: "the interpretation of unclear, difficult, or ambiguous passages of Scripture by comparison with clear and unambiguous passages *that refer to the same teaching or event.*"[12] An example of this would be utilizing a passage in Matthew to help understand a passage dealing with the same subject in Mark. This principle obviously presupposes the divine inspiration of Scripture.

The principle of *analogia Scripturae* gained confessional status as follows: "The infallible rule of interpretation of Scripture is the Scripture itself . . ." (2LCF 1.9).

3. The analogy of faith (*analogia fidei*)

Muller defines *analogia fidei* as follows:

> the use of a general sense of the meaning of Scripture, constructed from the clear or unambiguous *loci* . . ., as the basis for interpreting unclear or ambiguous texts. As distinct from the more basic *analogia Scripturae* . . ., the *analogia fidei* presupposes a sense of the theological meaning of Scripture.[13]

---

[12] Richard A. Muller, *Dictionary of Latin and Greek Theological Terms* (Grand Rapids: Baker Book House, 1985, Second printing, September 1986), 33, emphasis added, hereafter *Dictionary*.

[13] Muller, *Dictionary*, 33. Cf. Walter C. Kaiser, Jr., *Toward An Exegetical Theology* (1981; reprint, Grand Rapids: Baker Book House, Sixth printing, January 1987), 134ff., where Kaiser fails to distinguish properly between *analogia Scripturae* and *analogia fidei* and advocates what he calls "The Analogy of (Antecedent) Scripture." In the conclusion to his discussion (140), he says, "However, in no case must that *later* teaching be used exegetically (or in any other way) to unpack the meaning or to enhance the usability of the individual text which is the object of our study" (emphasis Kaiser's). This is, at worst, a denial of the historic understanding of *analogia fidei* and, at best, a very unhelpful and dangerous modification of the principle. It seems to me that this would mean, for example, that we cannot utilize anything in the Bible outside of Genesis 1-3 to help us interpret it. Since there is nothing in the Bible antecedent to Genesis 1-3, interpreters are left with no subsequent divine use, no subsequent divine explanation of how to understand those chapters. This method ends up defeating itself when we consider that Genesis (and all other books of the Bible) was never intended to stand on its own

An example of this would be interpreting texts that speak of the humanity of Christ in the wider textual-theological context of the incarnation of the eternal Son of God. For example, in Acts 20:28, God is said to have purchased the church "with His own blood." "Be on guard for yourselves and for all the flock, among which the Holy Spirit has made you overseers, to shepherd the church of God which He purchased with His own blood." From other texts of Scripture, according to the principle of *analogia fidei*, we learn that Christ, according to his divine nature, is invisible (John 1:1, 18). So according to the analogy of faith, we can affirm that God has blood, in so far as the person of the Mediator has blood, according to his human nature.

The inspired and infallible rule of faith is the whole of Scripture whose textual parts must be understood in light of the theological whole. This insures that the theological forest is not lost for the textual trees.

The principle of *analogia fidei* gained confessional status as follows: "The infallible rule of interpretation of Scripture is the Scripture itself . . ." (2LCF 1.9).

4. The scope of Scripture (*scopus Scripturae*)

Terms such as Christ-centered and Christocentric are used often in our day. But what do they mean? The older way of describing the concept these terms point to, the target or end to which the entirety

---

and that the Bible itself comments on antecedent texts, helping its readers understand the divine intention of those texts. Kaiser's method seems to imply that the exegesis of a given biblical text is to be conducted as if no subsequent biblical texts exist. We must realize that, in one sense, we have an advantage that the biblical writers did not have—we have a completed canon. But we must also realize that the Bible's use of itself (whenever and wherever this occurs) is infallible. If this is so, then the exegete, using tools outside of the biblical text under consideration, ought to consult *all* possible tools, which includes how the Bible comments upon itself no matter where or when it does so. If the Holy Spirit is the only infallible interpreter of Holy Scripture, then certainly exegetes ought to utilize biblical texts outside of Genesis to aid in the understanding of Genesis. Kaiser's proposal would give warrant for exegetes to consult fallible commentaries on Genesis to aid in its interpretation, but deny the use of the Bible itself (which contains inspired and infallible commentary) to that same end.

of the Bible tends, is encapsulated by the Latin phrase *scopus Scripturae* (i.e., the scope of the Scriptures). This concept gained confessional status in the Westminster Confession of Faith, the Savoy Declaration, and the Second London Confession of Faith in 1.5, which, speaking of Holy Scripture, says, ". . . the scope of the whole (which is to give all glory to God) . . ."

Reformation and post-Reformation Reformed theologians understood scope in two senses. It had a narrow sense—i.e., the scope of a given text or passage, its basic thrust—but it also had a wider sense—i.e., the target or bull's eye to which all of Scripture tends.[14] It is to this second sense that we will give our attention.

Scope, in the sense intended here, refers to the center or target of the entire canonical revelation; it is that to which the entire Bible points. And whatever that is, it must condition our interpretation of any and every part of Scripture. For the covenant theologians of the seventeenth century, the scope of Scripture was the glory of God in the redemptive work of the incarnate Son of God.[15] Their view of the scope of Scripture was itself a conclusion from Scripture, not a presupposition brought to Scripture, and it conditioned all subsequent interpretation.

William Ames said, "The Old and New Testaments are reducible to these two primary heads. The Old promises Christ to come and the New testifies that he has come."[16] Likewise, John Owen said, "Christ is . . . the principal end of the whole of Scripture . . ."[17] He continues elsewhere:

This principle is always to be retained in our minds in

---

[14] See the discussion in Richard A. Muller, *Post-Reformation Reformed Dogmatics*, 4 vols. (Grand Rapids: Baker Academic, 2003), 2:206-23, hereafter *PRRD*, where he discusses these distinctions.

[15] See my forthcoming *The Doxological Trajectory of Scripture: God Getting Glory for Himself through what He does in His Son—An Exegetical and Theological Case Study*, chapter 5, "Christ as *Scopus Scripturae*—John Owen and Nehemiah Coxe on Christ as the Scope of Scripture for the Glory of God."

[16] William Ames, *The Marrow of Theology* (Durham, NC: The Labyrinth Press, 1983), 202 (XXXVIII:5).

[17] John Owen, *The Works of John Owen*, 23 vols., ed. William H. Goold (Edinburgh: The Banner of Truth Trust, 1987 edition), 1:74.

reading of the Scripture,—namely, that the revelation and doctrine of the person of Christ and his office, is the foundation whereon all other instructions of the prophets and apostles for the edification of the church are built, and whereunto they are resolved . . . So our Lord Jesus Christ himself at large makes it manifest, Luke xxiv. 26, 27, 45, 46. Lay aside the consideration hereof, and the Scriptures are no such thing as they pretend unto,—namely, a revelation of the glory of God in the salvation of the church . . .[18]

Nehemiah Coxe said, ". . . in all our search after the mind of God in the Holy Scriptures we are to manage our inquiries with reference to Christ."[19]

Their Christocentric interpretation of the Bible was a principle derived from the Bible itself and an application of *sola Scripturae* to the issue of hermeneutics. In other words, they viewed the Bible's authority as extending to how we interpret the Bible. They saw the authority of Scripture applicable to the interpretation of Scripture.

Having considered some of the hermeneutical principles utilized while formulating the doctrine of the covenant of works, let's consider a common object to this doctrine.

A Typical Objection to the Covenant of Works

Many have denied the covenant of works for various reasons. For the sake of space, I want to deal with one typical objection.

1. The objection stated

Probably the most obvious objection, and a very common one, is that the word "covenant" is nowhere to be found in the first two chapters of Genesis. In fact, the Hebrew word for covenant, *berith*, does not occur in the book of Genesis until chapter 6. These observations lead to the conclusion, so goes the objection, that there

---

[18] Owen, *Works*, 1:314-15.
[19] Coxe and Owen, *Covenant Theology*, 33.

is no covenant in the Bible until Genesis 6. A covenant of works in the Garden, then, lacks biblical evidence and is, in fact, unbiblical.[20] It is an extra-biblical, human construct imposed on the Bible to justify one's theological system, which obviously needs re-casting. The covenant of works has human origins, not divine origins, so it is said. It is man's theology, not God's. Put in the form of a question, this objection can be stated as follows: How can there be a covenant in Genesis 2 if Moses does not say so? My short answer to this legitimate question would be because God says so. But to be fair to any objectors, I will answer this objection under three points of consideration.

2. The objection answered

First, this objection assumes that if a word is not in a text its concept cannot be there either. This is the word-concept fallacy. The Bible itself sees concepts in texts and then uses words that do not occur in the text being referenced to describe those concepts. For example, consider Acts 2:22-31 again. Here Peter references Psalm 16:8-11. Then notice what he does in 2:31.

> "Men of Israel, listen to these words: Jesus the Nazarene, a man attested to you by God with miracles and wonders and signs which God performed through Him in your midst, just as you yourselves know — [23] this *Man*, delivered over by the predetermined plan and foreknowledge of God, you nailed to a cross by the hands of godless men and put *Him* to death. [24] "But God raised Him up again, putting an end to the agony of death, since it was impossible for Him to be held in its power. [25] "For David says of Him, 'I SAW THE LORD ALWAYS IN MY PRESENCE; FOR HE IS AT MY RIGHT HAND, SO THAT I WILL NOT BE SHAKEN. [26] 'THEREFORE MY HEART WAS GLAD AND MY TONGUE EXULTED; MOREOVER MY FLESH ALSO WILL LIVE IN HOPE; [27] BECAUSE YOU WILL NOT ABANDON MY

---

[20] Cf. Richard L. Mayhue, "New Covenant Theology and Futuristic Premillennialism," *The Master's Seminary Journal,* 18.2 (Fall 2007): 221 and 225 for this kind of argumentation.

SOUL TO HADES, NOR ALLOW YOUR HOLY ONE TO
UNDERGO DECAY. [28] 'YOU HAVE MADE KNOWN TO
ME THE WAYS OF LIFE; YOU WILL MAKE ME FULL OF
GLADNESS WITH YOUR PRESENCE.' [29] "Brethren, I may
confidently say to you regarding the patriarch David that he
both died and was buried, and his tomb is with us to this
day. [30] "And so, because he was a prophet and knew that
GOD HAD SWORN TO HIM WITH AN OATH TO SEAT
one OF HIS DESCENDANTS ON HIS THRONE, [31] he looked
ahead and spoke of the resurrection of the Christ, that HE
WAS NEITHER ABANDONED TO HADES, NOR DID His
flesh SUFFER DECAY. (Acts 2:22-31)

Peter uses *words* that are not in the Psalm to describe *concepts* from
the Psalm. He says that David "spoke of the resurrection of the
Christ." The words "resurrection" and "Christ" do not occur in the
Psalm. Peter uses these words to describe concepts implicit in the
Psalm though not used explicitly by the psalmist. The point is that
concepts can be present without the words we normally use to
describe them. If I said, "Base hit, home run, strike three, and walk-
off single," you would, most likely, reduce those phrases and the
concepts indicated by them to a single word — baseball — yet I did
not use the word baseball.

Second, there are words used outside of the Garden narrative to
describe Adam and his Edenic vocation which are not contained in
the narrative of Genesis 1-3. For example, in Luke 3:38, Adam is
called "the son of God." However, Moses does not call Adam the
son of God in Genesis and, in fact, the word "son" first occurs in
Genesis 4:17 with reference to Enoch's son. If God tells me Adam
was a son of God, it does not matter where he tells me. The case is
settled, even if he tells me in Luke 3. Also, Adam did not first
become a son of God when Luke penned his Gospel. He was
constituted as such long before. Therefore, the concept of Adam as a
son of God is implicit in the Genesis 1-2 narrative, even though the
word "son" is nowhere to be found there. How do we know this?
God tells us in subsequent, written revelation, the only infallible
interpretation of Scripture we possess.

In Romans 5:14, Adam is called "a type of Him who was to

come." However, Moses does not call Adam a type of Christ in Genesis and, in fact, the word "type" first occurs in the Bible in Romans 5:14. If God tells me Adam was a type of Christ, it does not matter where he tells me. The case is settled, even if he tells me in Romans 5. Also, Adam did not first become a type of Christ when Paul penned Romans. Therefore, the concept of Adam as a type of Christ is implicit in the Genesis narrative, even though the word "type" is nowhere to be found there. How do we know this? God tells us in subsequent, written revelation, the only infallible interpretation of Scripture we possess.

In 1 Corinthians 15:22, Paul says, "For as in Adam all die . . ." However, Moses does not tell us that Adam was the representative of men in the Genesis narrative. The phrase "in Adam" is not in the book of Genesis or anywhere else in the Old Testament. As a matter of fact, the phrase "in Adam" occurs only in 1 Corinthians 15:22. If God tells me "in Adam all die," it does not matter where he tells me. The case is settled, even if he tells me in 1 Corinthians 15. Also, all did not die in Adam when Paul penned 1 Corinthians 15. Therefore, the concept of Adam as the representative man in the Garden is implicit in the Genesis narrative, even though the words "in Adam" are nowhere to be found there. How do we know this? God tells us in subsequent, written revelation, the only infallible interpretation of Scripture we possess.

Third, the Bible itself, looking back upon Adam in the Garden, uses the explicit language of covenant. Since this is an important link in the argument for the doctrine of the covenant of works, we will explore this in our next major heading in more detail. But for now, let me draw a conclusion to this typical objection.

3. Conclusion

I think the objection is cleared, though I could give more counter-arguments. The account of Genesis 1-3 contains more than meets the eye. It is a narrative, not an exhaustive theological essay drawing out all the implications embedded or assumed in its terms. It is one of those texts that ends up being referenced many times in subsequent, written revelation. Other texts assume it and draw out of it what is implied in it. What is implicit in it becomes explicit by the subsequent, written Word of God. The biblical writers were theologians after all. They articulated the meaning of ancient texts in their own words. As stated above, subsequent revelation often makes explicit what is implicit in antecedent revelation. In other words, the Bible often comments upon and explains itself. And, in the case of Adam in the Garden, this is exactly what happens.

From Hermeneutics to the Covenant of Works

In this section, I will not offer all the arguments that could be marshaled in formulating a biblical doctrine of the covenant of works. I simply want to illustrate the hermeneutical principles discussed above and how these led and, I think, lead to the doctrine of the covenant of works. Remember our working definition of the covenant of works. It is that divinely sanctioned commitment or relationship imposed upon Adam, who was a sinless representative of mankind (or a public person), an image-bearing son of God, conditioned upon his obedience, with a penalty for disobedience, all for the bettering of man's state. I will offer seven considerations which, taken together, are an attempt to display the biblical basis for the formulation of the covenant of works and to suggest that the seventeenth-century Reformed theologians were right in going from the Garden to the covenant of works.

1. **Consider Moses' subsequent and inspired, and therefore infallible, reflection upon the acts of God at creation as recorded for us in Genesis 2:4ff.**

It is important to understand the relationship between God's acts and the Holy Scripture. In large part, Holy Scripture is the recording, interpretation, and application of God's previous acts. In other words, the Scripture writers don't simply record God's acts. They interpret them and apply them in their own words—i.e., they do theology. For example, our Lord Jesus Christ lived and died before the divine interpretation of his sufferings and glory were given to us in the form and unique words of the New Testament.

Likewise, the creating act of God occurred prior to Moses' writing about it (as did all the events subsequent to creation recorded in the Pentateuch). What's the point? In Genesis 2:4, Moses goes from the term *Elohim* for God to the phrase *Yahweh Elohim*, *Yahweh* being the covenantal name of God (cp. Gen. 1:1, 2, 3, 4, 5, 6, 7, 8, 9, 10, 11, 12, 14, 16, 17, 18, 20, 21, 22, 24, 25, 26, 27, 28, 29, 31; 2:2, 3 with Gen. 2:4, 5, 7, 8, 9, 15, 16, 18, 19, 21, 22). Many believe that at 2:4 Moses goes from creation in general to the apex of creation, man in God's image, and his covenantal responsibility to God. The use of *Yahweh* here could indicate a covenantal act of God toward Adam. This suggests that covenant and Adam's vocation or calling go together. Moses, reflecting upon God's act of creation and its immediate aftermath, uses the covenantal name of God in the context of discussing Adam and his Edenic vocation. For us that might not seem to be an issue worth noting. However, for ancient readers/hearers of this passage, they most likely would have noticed the shift in language, a shift with theological and covenantal implications, whether they recognized it or not.[21]

2. Consider the words of the prophet Isaiah.

> The earth is also polluted by its inhabitants, for they transgressed laws, violated statutes, broke the everlasting covenant. [6] Therefore, a curse devours the earth, and those who live in it are held guilty. Therefore, the inhabitants of the earth are burned, and few men are left. (Isa. 24:5-6)

The curse which extends to the entire earth came about due to transgressed laws, violated statutes, and a broken covenant. Since the earth was cursed due to Adam's sin as our representative, Adam broke covenant with God in the Garden of Eden and the effects of his covenant-breaking affects "those who live on the

---

[21] I added "whether they recognized it or not" because the text meant and means what it does irrespective of the understanding of its original recipients. See the discussion on Moses' use of the covenantal name of God in Michael G. Brown and Zach Keele, *Sacred Bond: Covenant Theology Explored* (Grandville, MI: Reformed Fellowship, Inc., 2012), 47-48.

earth," that is, everyone. As Michael Brown and Zack Keele say:

> For all mankind to be under such a covenant, it must be the same covenant God made with Adam as the father of all humanity. Isaiah, then, assumes the covenant of works in order to apply it to all fallen humanity.[22]

Here is a prophet, writing long after Adam was created and long after Moses wrote, utilizing principles that first started with Adam to explain the universal guilt of man. In this sense, Isaiah was very Pauline; or better yet, Paul was very Isaianic.

3.   Consider the words of the prophet Hosea.

I realize this text is disputed as far as its translation goes. I think the NASB's translation is the preferred one. You can read B. B. Warfield's study of the history of this text in his *Selected Shorter Writings* for details, as well as the chapter in *The Law is not of Faith* on this passage.[23] Witsius cited this text in support of the covenant of works, as did Brakel and others.[24] In fact, Muller goes so far as to say, "The text indicated, as virtually all of the patristic and medieval commentators concluded, a prelapsarian covenant made by God with Adam and broken in the fall."[25]

In Hosea 6:7, Israel is likened unto Adam. "But like Adam they

---

[22] Brown and Keele, *Sacred Bond*, 53.

[23] Cf. Benjamin B. Warfield, "Hosea VI.7: Adam or Man," in *Selected Shorter Writings: Benjamin B. Warfield*, I, ed. John E. Meeter (Phillipsburg, NJ: P&R Publishing, Fourth Printing, January 2001), 116-29 and Bryon G. Curtis, "Hosea 6:7 and Covenant-Breaking like/at Adam," in *The Law is not of Faith: Essays in Works and Grace in the Mosaic Covenant*, ed. Bryan D. Estelle, J. V. Fesko, and David VanDrunen (Phillipsburg, NJ: P&R Publishing, 2009), 170-209.

[24] Cf. Herman Witsius, *The Economy of the Covenants Between God and Man: Comprehending A Complete Body of Divinity*, 2 vols. (Escondido, CA: The den Dulk Christian Foundation, re. 1990), 1:135; Brakel, *The Christian's Reasonable Service*, 1:365-67; and Rowland S. Ward, *God & Adam: Reformed Theology and the Creation Covenant—An Introduction to the Biblical Covenants/A close examination of the Covenant of Works* (Wantirna, Australia: New Melbourne Press, 2003). Ward's book is highly recommended.

[25] Muller, *PRRD*, 2:437.

have transgressed the covenant . . ." (Hos. 6:7). Both Adam and Israel broke a covenant imposed upon them by God. They both disobeyed. They sinned and violated a covenant. Both covenants were conditional, requiring the obedience of those in the covenant to enjoy the benefits of the covenant. As Moses says, ". . . in the day that you eat from it you will surely die" (Gen. 2:17; cf. Exod. 19:5-6 for the conditional nature of the Mosaic covenant).

Here is yet another prophet, looking back at previous written revelation, making explicit what was implicit in it. Remember, subsequent revelation often makes explicit what was only implicit in antecedent revelation. The inspired prophet gives us God's infallible understanding of one of the similarities between ancient Israel and Adam. Both had a covenant imposed on them by God and both transgressed their covenants.[26] Also, as with Isaiah above, the inspired prophet uses words (e.g., in the case of Hosea, "transgressed" and "covenant") to describe concepts first revealed by Moses though in different words than Moses. As Brown and Keele say, "Once more, the prophet's interpretation of Genesis 2-3 peeks through his prophecy, and it reveals that Adam was in covenant with God."[27]

4. Consider why it is denominated the covenant of works.

It is called the covenant of works due to the fact that it was conditioned on Adam's obedience or his works. The term "works," in the phrase "covenant of works," is a synonym for "obedience." It is a term that reflects subsequent biblical, and therefore infallible, reflection upon Adam's Edenic vocation (cf. Rom. 5:12-21). Romans 5:19 justifies this term when it says, "For as through the one man's *disobedience* the many were made sinners, even so through the *obedience* of the One the many will be made righteous" (emphases added). The opposite of "disobedience" is "obedience." A legitimate synonym for "obedience" is "works."

The term "works" is also a good choice of words because it

---

[26] For a biblical example where a covenant is first revealed without the word covenant being used then explicitly identified as a covenant by subsequent revelation, cp. 2 Sam. 7:8-17 w. Psalm 89, esp. v. 3.

[27] Brown and Keele, *Sacred Bond*, 54.

contrasts with "grace" and gift" in Romans 5:17. Paul says there:

> For if by the transgression of the one, death reigned through the one, much more those who receive the abundance of *grace* and of the *gift* of righteousness will reign in life through the One, Jesus Christ. (Rom. 5:17; emphases added).

Adam's disobedience brought death. Christ's obedience brings life, a quality of life Adam did not have, i.e., eternal life (John 17:3; Rom. 5:21).

5. Consider the fact that Adam was "a type of Him who was to come" (Rom. 5:14).

Let me first give some brief thoughts on typology. *First*, a type is an historical person, place, institution, or event designed by God to point to a future historical person, place, institution, or event. An example of this would be the sacrificial system revealed to us in the Old Testament. That institution was designed by God to point to Christ's once for all sacrifice. *Second*, that to which types point is always greater than the type itself. For example, "the blood of bulls and goats" could point to Christ but could not and did not do what Christ's sacrifice did — take away sins. *Third*, types are both like and unlike their anti-types. The blood of animals was shed; the blood of Christ was shed. The blood of animals did not take away sins; the blood of Christ takes away sins. *Fourth*, anti-types tell us more about how their typical antecedents function as types. The blood of Christ takes away sins; the blood of animals pointed to that.

It is important to note some specific considerations in light of Adam as a type of Christ. Adam was a type of Christ in his prelapsarian state (Rom. 5:14). Adam was a type of Christ as a public person (1 Cor. 15:22). Adam's failure is seen in the fact that he disobeyed or he failed to obey (Rom. 5:12ff.). He did not obey so did not attain to the better state of existence to which the covenant of works pointed. But what if he had obeyed? Would he have stayed in the state in which he was created — able to sin and able not to sin? I don't think so and, I think, for good reason. And let me add that this is not an impractical, speculative, or abstract question, the answer of which cannot be known. It is a question related to the fact that Adam was a type of Christ.

In Romans 5:21, God says, "even so grace would reign through righteousness to eternal life through Jesus Christ." The righteousness that is "to eternal life" comes as a gift to sinners and is based on Christ's obedience. The life-unto-death obedience of Christ constitutes a righteousness "*to* eternal life." In other words, according to his sinless human nature as the anti-type of prelapsarian Adam, Christ, our Mediator, earned eternal life for us. His righteousness was "*to* eternal life." Guy Waters comments:

> The fact that Christ purchased eternal "life" for his own, and that he did so for those who were eternally "dead" in Adam means that Christ's work was intended to remedy what Adam had wrought (death), and to accomplish what Adam had failed to do (life). Paul emphasizes disparity in his argument precisely in order to underscore the breathtaking achievement of what Christ has accomplished in relation to what Adam has wrought. This means that if Adam by his disobedience brought eternal death, then his obedience would have brought eternal life. In other words, Christ's "obedience" and its consequence ("eternal life") parallel what Adam ought to have done but did not do. The life that Adam ought to have attained would have been consequent upon Adam's continuing, during the period of his testing, in obedience to all the commands set before him, whether moral or positive. This life, it stands to reason, could be aptly described "eternal."[28]

Eternal life was earned by Christ, the anti-type of Adam, for us and given by Christ to us. The quality of life Christ attains for us and gives to us is not what Adam had and lost but what Adam failed to attain. Adam did not possess "eternal life" via creation. Robert Shaw, commenting on the covenant of works, says:

> There is a *condition* expressly stated, in the positive precept

---

[28] Guy P. Waters, "Romans 10:5 and the Covenant of Works," in *The Law is not of Faith*, 230.

respecting the tree of knowledge of good and evil, which God was pleased to make the test of man's obedience. There was a *penalty* subjoined: 'In the day thou eatest thereof, thou shalt surely die.' There is also a *promise*, not distinctly expressed, but implied in the threatening; for if death was to be the consequence of disobedience, it clearly follows that life was to be the reward of obedience. That a promise of life was annexed to man's obedience, may also be inferred from . . . our Lord's answer to the young man who inquired what he should do to inherit eternal life: 'If thou wilt enter into life, keep the commandments' (Matthew 19:17); and from the declaration of the apostle, that 'the commandment was ordained to life' (Romans 7:10).[29]

Just as Adam's disobedience brought upon him a status not his by virtue of creation (cp. Gen. 2:17 w. Gen. 3:8ff.; Rom. 5:12ff.; and 1 Cor. 15:22), so his obedience would have brought upon him a status not his by virtue of creation. Christ, as anti-typical Adam, the last Adam, takes his seed where Adam failed to take his. As will be argued below, Christ takes his seed to glory (Heb. 2:10), something to which Adam fell short.

6. Consider the fact that Adam sinned and fell short of something he did not possess via creation (Rom. 3:23).

In Paul's writings, it is clear that Adam was the first man who sinned. The first man sinned and fell "short of the glory of God" (Rom. 3:23), something of which he did not possess or experience via his created status. He was not created in a state that could be called "glory" and he fell short of that state by sinning. He failed to attain to that state because he sinned. In other words, Adam was created in a state that could have been improved, God being the efficient cause and Adam's obedience the instrumental cause of the improvement. He was created in a mutable state, a changeable condition. He was righteous but he could sin. His obedience would

---

[29] Robert Shaw, *An Exposition of the Westminster Confession of Faith* (Fearn, Ross-shire, Scotland: Christian Focus Publications/Christian Heritage, 1998), 124-25.

have brought him to a higher state, an immutable state, conferred upon him by God due to his voluntary, condescending kindness expressed in the covenant of works (cf. 2LCF 7.1). Adam was not created with eternal life. Adam's obedience could have attained something he was not created with, "the reward of life," according to our Confession. In other words, Adam had an eschatology before the need of soteriology. The soteriological strand of revelation comes because the eschatology of the Garden was never attained by Adam. Or in the words of Geerhardus Vos, "The eschatological is an older strand in revelation than the soteric."[30] The soteriological strand of Scripture takes us to the eschatological that was imbedded in the protological.

Because the subject of Edenic eschatology might be new to some, and is a debated issue in Reformed thought, let me take a brief excursus to show you that what I am asserting is not new in the history of Reformed theology. Take for example Nehemiah Coxe. According to Coxe, Adam had "the promise of an eternal reward on condition of his perfect obedience to these laws."[31] The tree of life functioned sacramentally as "a sign and pledge of that eternal life which Adam would have obtained by his own personal and perfect obedience to the law of God if he had continued in it."[32] Remember, according to Coxe, God sovereignly proposes covenants with men in order to bring them to an advanced or better state than they are currently in and ultimately "to bring them into a blessed state in the eternal enjoyment of himself."[33] Adam, Coxe says, "was

---

[30] Geerhardus Vos, *Biblical Theology: Old and New Testaments* (1948; reprint, Grand Rapids: Wm. B. Eerdmans Publishing Company, 1988), 140.

[31] Coxe and Owen, *Covenant Theology*, 44, 51. Coxe gives three proofs with discussion for the promise of an eternal reward on pages 45-46.

[32] Coxe and Owen, *Covenant Theology*, 45. Coxe justifies this function of the tree of life as follows: "The allusion that Christ makes to it in the New Testament (Revelation 2:7). . . . The method of God's dealing with Adam in reference to this tree after he had sinned against him and the reason assigned for it by God himself [i.e., Genesis 3:22ff.]. . . . This also must not be forgotten: that as Moses' law in some way included the covenant of creation and served for a memorial of it (on which account all mankind was involved in its curse), it had not only the sanction of a curse awfully denounced against the disobedient, but also a promise of the reward of life to the obedient." Here Coxe is articulating Owen's (and others') view of the relation of the covenant of works to the Mosaic covenant.

[33] Coxe and Owen, *Covenant Theology*, 36.

capable of and made for a greater degree of happiness than he immediately enjoyed [which] was set before him as the reward of his obedience by that covenant in which he was to walk with God."[34]

According to Witsius, the covenant of works or nature or of the law (as it functioned in the Garden), ". . . promised eternal life and happiness if [Adam] yielded obedience."[35] Witsius sees Adam in a probationary state and capable of arriving at a higher, more blessed state of existence. He says:

> That man was not yet arrived at the utmost pitch of happiness, but [was] to expect a still greater good, after his course of obedience was over. This was hinted by the prohibition of the most delightful tree, whose fruit was, of any other, greatly to be desired; and this argued some degree of imperfection in that state, in which man was forbid the enjoyment of some good.[36]

The more blessed state of existence was "eternal life, that is the most perfect fruition of himself [i.e., God; this echoes the WCF 7.1], and that forever, after finishing his course of obedience . . ."[37] This promise of life flowed out of God's goodness and bounty and not out of any strict necessity.[38] God voluntarily condescended in the revelation of the covenant of works, offering a reward to Adam for his obedience. The Garden of Eden, according to Witsius, was a pledge, a type, a symbol, both temporary and anticipatory of a better state yet to be enjoyed.[39] In other words, protology is eschatological or the eschatological is embedded in the protological. Adam had an eschatology that he failed to attain.

Now let's get back to Romans 3:23. Listen to John Owen. Notice that he references Romans 3:23 in this quotation:

---

[34] Coxe and Owen, *Covenant Theology*, 47.

[35] Witsius, *Economy of the Covenants*, 1:150. The covenant of works has been termed the covenant of creation, nature, and the law by various older authors. They all refer to the same doctrinal formulation.

[36] Witsius, *Economy of the Covenants*, 1:69; cf. also 1:123-24.

[37] Witsius, *Economy of the Covenants*, 1:73.

[38] Witsius, *Economy of the Covenants*, 1:76ff.

[39] Witsius, *Economy of the Covenants*, 1:106ff., esp. 1:109.

Man, especially, was utterly lost, and came short of the glory of God, *for which he was created*, Rom. iii. 23. Here, now, doth the depth of the riches of the wisdom and knowledge of God open itself. A design in Christ shines out from his bosom, that was lodged there from eternity, to recover things to such an estate as shall be exceedingly to the advantage of his glory, infinitely above what at first appeared, and for the putting of sinners into inconceivably a better condition than they were in before the entrance of sin.[40]

For Owen, "the glory of God" here does not refer exclusively to what God *possesses*, but also to what God *confers*. The eschatological state, glory, is that "for which . . . [man] was created." The state of existence, to which Christ takes elect sinners, is "inconceivably a better condition than they were in before the entrance of sin."

Now listen to Paul in Romans 5:1-2, "Therefore, having been justified by faith, we have peace with God . . . and we exult in hope of the glory of God." Charles Hodge says:

It is a[n] . . . exultation, in view of the exaltation and blessedness which Christ has *secured for us*. . . . The glory of God may mean that glory which God gives, or that which he possesses. In either case, it refers to the exaltation and blessedness *secured to the believer*, who is to share the glory of his divine Redeemer.[41]

We get glory, a state of existence, because it is conferred upon us, having been secured for us by Christ. This is why we can "exult in hope of the glory of God." Since justified, therefore glory awaits. This "glory" is that to which Adam fell short.

7. **Consider the fact that Christ, upon his resurrection, entered into glory.**

---

[40] John Owen, *The Works of John Owen* (Edinburgh; Carlisle, PA: The Banner of Truth Trust, Reprinted 1990), 2:89, emphasis added.

[41] Charles Hodge, *The Epistle to the Romans* (1835; reprint, Edinburgh; Carlisle, PA: The Banner of Truth Trust, Reprinted 1983), 133, emphases added.

The Old Testament spoke about the Messiah who would come, suffer (due to Adam's sin and us in him), and enter into glory. Consider these inspired and infallible theological reflections on the Old Testament.

Was it not necessary for the Christ to suffer these things and to enter into His glory? (Luke 24:26)

and He said to them, "Thus it is written, that the Christ would suffer and rise again from the dead the third day, (Luke 24:46)

"So, King Agrippa, I did not prove disobedient to the heavenly vision, [20] but *kept* declaring both to those of Damascus first, and *also* at Jerusalem and *then* throughout all the region of Judea, and *even* to the Gentiles, that they should repent and turn to God, performing deeds appropriate to repentance. [21] "For this reason *some* Jews seized me in the temple and tried to put me to death. [22] "So, having obtained help from God, I stand to this day testifying both to small and great, stating nothing but what the Prophets and Moses said was going to take place; [23] that the Christ was to suffer, *and* that by reason of *His* resurrection from the dead He would be the first to proclaim light both to the *Jewish* people and to the Gentiles." (Acts 26:19-23)

As to this salvation, the prophets who prophesied of the grace that *would come* to you made careful searches and inquiries, [11] seeking to know what person or time the Spirit of Christ within them was indicating as He predicted the sufferings of Christ and the glories to follow. [12] It was revealed to them that they were not serving themselves, but you, in these things which now have been announced to you through those who preached the gospel to you by the Holy Spirit sent from heaven—things into which angels long to look. (1 Pet. 1:10-12)

The Son of God incarnate both suffered and entered into glory, a glorified state according to his human nature after his sufferings via his resurrection and as a reward for his righteousness, which, according to Paul, was "to eternal life." In other words, Christ, according to his human nature, became what he was not at the resurrection.

Suffering and glory is another way of saying humiliation and exaltation. Paul speaks of the incarnate Son's humiliation and exaltation in Romans 1:1-4 and Philippians 2:6-9.

> Paul, a bond-servant of Christ Jesus, called *as* an apostle, set apart for the gospel of God, 2 which He promised beforehand through His prophets in the holy Scriptures, 3 concerning His Son, who was born of a descendant of David according to the flesh, 4 who was declared the Son of God with power by the resurrection from the dead, according to the Spirit of holiness, Jesus Christ our Lord (Rom. 1:1-4)

> who, although He existed in the form of God, did not regard equality with God a thing to be grasped, 7 but emptied Himself, taking the form of a bond-servant, *and* being made in the likeness of men. 8 Being found in appearance as a man, He humbled Himself by becoming obedient to the point of death, even death on a cross. 9 For this reason also, God highly exalted Him, and bestowed on Him the name which is above every name (Phil. 2:6-9)

Christ's representation in the state of humiliation started at his conception and ended at his death. Upon his death, because of his obedience to the point of death, God "highly exalted him . . ." The incarnate Son of God according to his human nature obeyed and suffered due to our sin. He entered into glory as a result of or reward for his obedience and he did both as the sinless last Adam, representing those given to him by the Father before the world began (Eph. 1:4).

Adam failed to comply with the condition of the covenant God imposed upon him and brought with that the ruin of the human race. He fell short of the glory of God, a permenant state of existence in God's special presence he did not possess via creation. But here is the good news—another came, the last Adam, our Lord Jesus Christ, who suffered, then entered into glory at his resurrection, and will bring many sons to glory (Heb. 2:10) who will also "gain the glory of our Lord Jesus Christ" (2 Thess. 2:14). Owen says on 2 Thessalonians 2:14, "The glory of our Lord Jesus Christ," or the obtaining a portion in that glory which Christ *purchased* and *procured* for them . . ."[42] Christ *purchased* glory for all he came to save. He did so as the last Adam. He suffered to satisfy the justice of God and his obedience unto death resulted in his exaltation, an entrance into glory, and all those who are his will enter into that same glory as well. The last Adam takes his seed where the first Adam failed to take his. Adam sinned, he violated the covenant of works, and he fell short of the glory of God. Christ did not sin, he perfectly upheld the stipulations of the covenant of works (precepts and penalties) and entered into glory as our fore-runner.

This is the covenant of works and this is how our theological forefathers got from the Garden to the covenant of works.

Conclusion

Moses, writing after the historical account of creation, utilizes the covenantal name of God, *Yahweh*, while discussing Adam's Edenic vocation (Gen. 2:4ff.). Isaiah utilizes concepts that started with Adam to explain the universal guilt of man, while using the word "covenant" (Isa. 25:5-6). Hosea, looking back upon previous written revelation, makes explicit what was implicit in it. The inspired prophet gives us God's infallible understanding of one of the similarities between ancient Israel and Adam. Both had a covenant imposed on them by God and both transgressed their covenants (Hos. 6:7). Paul, while reflecting on Adam's Edenic vocation, contrasts the disobedience of Adam and its results with the obedience of Christ and its results (Rom. 5:19). The term "works" in the phrase "covenant of works" contrasts with "grace" and "gift" in Romans 5:17. Paul asserts that Adam was a type of Christ (Rom. 5:14). Adam sinned and fell short of the glory of God (Rom. 3:23). Christ did not sin (Heb. 4:15) and, upon his resurrection, entered into glory (Luke 24:46; Acts 26:19-23; 1 Pet. 1:10-12), a quality of life conferred upon him due to his obedience (Rom. 5:21).

---

[42] Owen, *Works*, 11:203, emphases added.

These biblical realities, understood by the utilization of the hermeneutical principles of the Holy Spirit as the only infallible interpreter of Holy Scripture, *analogia Scripturae, analogia fidei,* and *scopus Scripturae,* led to the formulation of the doctrine of the covenant of works. One might disagree with the exegetical conclusions that led to the formulation of the doctrine, but no one can claim the seventeenth-century men came to their theological conclusions prior to the exegesis of the biblical text. Anyone who does so either misunderstood what they read when they studied the seventeenth-century men or they did not study the seventeenth-century men.

Chapter 9

A Little Cabinet Richly Stored

Robert Purnell*

In the ensuing Treatise,[1] and for the accomplishment of this great work, which is of highest concernment, let us first endeavor to unravel, unmask and unbowel the Covenant of Grace, and for our more orderly proceeding therein, let us enquire into these particulars.

The Sum and Substance of the Covenant of Grace or New Covenant

Question 1. What is the sum and substance of this Covenant of Grace, or New Covenant? *Answer:* The Covenant of Grace is called a testament or will: indeed the will of the Father, revealed to the Son, and by the Son revealed to the world, to manifest the Father's love unto the sons and daughters of men, and testified to the world, that what he declared was the mind of God, and so sealed it with his blood, *Heb.* 10:29. So that his blood that he shed, is called the blood of the Covenant; yea of the everlasting Covenant, *Heb.* 13:20. Or,

The Covenant of grace is full of sure mercies, and sweet promises, that God will give a new heart, a heart to know him, and that he will write his Law within us, put his fear into us, cause us to walk in his statutes, forgive our iniquities, cleanse us from our filthiness, be our God, and make us his people, *Ezek.* 36. and *Jer.* 31.

This Covenant doth fall into these six parts, *viz.*

---

* Robert Purnell (d. 1666) was a pastor at the Broadmead Baptist Church, Broadmead, Bristol, England. Edited by Samuel Renihan.

[1] Robert Purnell, *A Little Cabinet Richly Stored with All Sorts of Heavenly Varieties and Soul-Reviving Influences* (London: R.W., 1657), 19-28, 47-50, 53-55. Some minor changes were made to assist the reader.

1. It is a free Covenant.
2. It is a full and complete Covenant.
3. It is a well ordered Covenant.
4. It is a sure and firm Covenant.
5. It is a peaceable Covenant.
6. It is an everlasting Covenant.

1. It is a free Covenant.

    1. Because the foundation of it is free.
    2. Because it is freely given to those that do partake of it, *Isa.* 42:6, *Isa.* 49:8.
    3. Because there is no active condition required on our part, *Jer.* 31:33, 34.
    4. It is free in respect of his entering into Covenant with us, *Isa.* 65:1.
    5. It is free in respect of his performances of it, *Mich.* 7:20.

2. It is a full and complete Covenant, richly and plentifully stored with all suitable promises, both for this life, and that which is to come, for soul and body, being and well being, there is some remedy in it for every malady.

3. It is a well ordered Covenant.

    1. In respect of the persons with whom it is made, and that is first with Christ, then with his seed.
    2. In respect of the promises, and parts of the Covenant.
    First God becomes our God, then we become his people, *Jer.* 32:38.
    3. In respect of manifestations, he first reveals it, and then seals it by his Spirit, *Ezek.* 16:8, 9; 2 *Tim.* 1:10.
    4. In respect of the ends of it, which is God the Father, and the Son's glory, in the riches and freeness of his Grace; which should caution us not to darken the Glory of free Grace.

4. It is a sure and firm Covenant, founded upon that Rock Jesus

Christ, *Isa.* 26:4; *Rom.* 4:16, *Our salvation is by Grace, to the end that the promises might be sure to all the seed*, Isa. 55:3, *I will make an everlasting Covenant with you, even the sure mercies of David.* Now it is sure and firm:

1. Because it is made by an immutable God.
2. He hath confirmed this Covenant with an oath, *Heb.* 6:17, 18.
3. He hath sealed it with the blood of his Son, *Heb.* 13:20.

5. It is a peaceable Covenant, in this Covenant he doth freely give peace to the soul, and so keeps the soul in peace, the heart being stayed on him, *Isa.* 26:3.

In this Covenant there is a three-fold peace conveyed to the soul, *Eph.* 2:14, He is our peace who hath made both one.

1. He is our peace with the Father.
2. He gives peace of conscience, he stills and quiets that.
3. He is the Author and cause of our peace with men.

6. It is an everlasting Covenant, *Jer.* 32:40, *And I will make an everlasting Covenant with them, that I will not turn away from them, to do them good, but I will put my fear into their hearts, that they shall not depart from me.* The motives that did move God to make this Covenant, was his everlasting love; the righteousness upon which it is grounded, is everlasting righteousness. In this Covenant is presented to us everlasting pardon, everlasting kindness, everlasting mercy, everlasting joy and consolation, and everlasting life and salvation, all these are fully proved, by these and the like Scriptures, *Psal.* 105:8; *Isa.* 40:18; *Heb.* 8:12; *Isa.* 54:8. & 35:10; 2 *Thes.* 2:16.

What shall I say more to the nature of this Covenant; it is sometimes called a New Covenant, sometimes it is called a better Covenant, as appears by *Heb.* 12:24. Compared with *Heb.* 8:6. Sometimes it is called a Covenant of grace, now by a New Covenant, a better Covenant, a Covenant of grace. All serious Christians do understand the engagements which God hath laid upon himself: to bestow on them for whom Christ died, all good temporal, spiritual and eternal blessings, so that by this God doth make himself debtor to his people, in Covenant with him, and is bound in justice to perform his word and promise.

Now this Covenant is sometimes called a New Covenant, because it succeeds in the place of the other Covenant of works; and it is called a Covenant of grace, because all the effects thereof do flow down to us, merely of free grace and favor of God, and the merits of Christ, *Zach.* 9:11.

In the Covenant of Grace we may find the mouth of the law stopped, and all the accusations of Satan answered, and the justice of God fully satisfied.

God will have all blessings and happiness to flow to us, through and by the Covenant of Grace.

1. That the worst of sinners may have strong ground of hope.
2. For the praise of his own glory.
3. That vain man may not boast.
4. That our mercies and blessings may be sure to us, our salvation is by grace, saith *Paul, Rom.* 4:16, that the promises might be sure to us; for if it in any sense depended upon works, we could not be sure thereof. Reader, understand these four choice things, *viz.*

1. That Christ by the will of God gave himself a ransom and sacrifice of a sweet smelling savor unto God, in behalf of the elect, *John* 6:27. *Heb.* 5:10. *&* 10:9, 10; *Eph.* 5:2.

2. That this ransom was alone, and by itself a perfect satisfaction to Divine Justice for all their sin, *Heb.* 1:3, When he had by himself purged our sins, sat down on the right hand of the Majesty on high, *Heb.* 10:10, By the which will we are sanctified, by the offering of the body of Jesus Christ once for all, *verse* 14, *For by an offering he hath perfected, forever, them that are sanctified,* 1 *John* 1:7, *The blood of Christ cleanses us from all sin.*

3. That God accepted it, and declared himself well pleased, and fully satisfied therewith, *Mat.* 3:17, *And lo a voice from heaven, saying, this is my beloved Son in whom I am well pleased, Isa.* 42:1, 4, 6, *I will give thee for a Covenant of the people, for a light of the Gentiles,* &c. God was so well pleased in him, that he hath covenanted and sworn that he will never remember their sins, nor be wroth with them

anymore, *Isa.* 43:25.

4. That by this ransom of his we are delivered from the curse of the law: *Gal.* 3:13, *Christ hath redeemed us from the curse of the law, being made a curse for us.*

To close up all as to the nature of this Covenant. Let me tell thee the main substance of the Covenant is in these words, *I will be their God, and they shall be my people,* but sprinkling with clean water, taking away the stony heart, and giving a heart of flesh, all these are nothing but the fruits of the Covenant. So Christ is given for a Covenant to the people: that is the Covenant of Grace takes its being from Christ to us: *Adam* was all mankind, as all mankind was in *Adam,* in the loins of *Adam;* so Christ is the Covenant, and all the Covenant is as it were in the loins of Christ, and springs to us out of him; in this sense he is the Covenant-maker, he is the Covenant-undertaker, he is the Covenant-manager, he is the Covenant-dispenser, he doth everything in the Covenant, he makes the articles, he draws God the Father to an agreement unto the articles, *Psal.* 110:3, *thy people shall be a willing people in the day of thy power,* and God is in Christ, reconciling the world unto himself: 2 *Cor.* 5:19. Hence Christ is also called the Mediator of the Covenant, that is, he is one that hath the managing of it on both sides, and he alone is able to bring both sides together, and make up a conclusion, and thus Christ is the Covenant, and the Mediator of the Covenant, *&c.*

With Whom was this Covenant First Made?

Question 2. The second thing to be enquired into, is with whom this Covenant was first made? *Answer:* This Covenant was not made with us, but with Christ for us; God did not immediately make this Covenant with us, we were children of disobedience and of wrath, who were not capable of any such Covenant and conditions, but it was made with Christ for us, that upon the making of his soul an offering for sin, he would give unto his seed eternal life, *Zech.* 9:11, *As for thee also by the blood of thy Covenant, I have sent forth thy prisoners out of the pit wherein is no water.* Adam lost his righteousness, the foundation of the first Covenant: But the righteousness of Christ the second *Adam,* can never be lost, it being grounded upon better promises, *Heb.* 8:6.

The Covenant made with Christ, hath these promises, *Gen.* 12:3, *In thee shall all families of the earth be blessed,* 2 *Cor.* 1:20, *All the promises of God, are Yea and Amen in him;* so then this Covenant was made with him actively, as a person that performed all the conditions upon which the promises were grounded; but with us passively, as the persons to whom the benefits of these promises do belong. If Christ merited nothing for himself, but wholly for the elect of God, then all the promises made to him do belong to them; or the Covenant which was made with him as Mediator, doth belong to us, for whom he doth mediate. Now the parties concerned in this Covenant, are first God the Father, and Jesus Christ the Mediator, and the Church or body of Christ, for whom he was to mediate. Now this Covenant being made with Christ, he as a Surety is bound to perform and see performed, all the duties that God requires of believers; so he was arrested, and brought to the bar of God's justice, where he is convicted, adjudged, and arraigned as a sinful transgressor, so he suffered the uttermost rigor of the law, and not one grain of justice abated him, nor a farthing of the debt forgiven him, no nor so much as one sin unaccounted for or blotted out, till satisfaction was first made and given. But after the full account and perfect payment, this Surety Christ Jesus pleaded for a dismission, and discharge, and so got a general discharge, acquittance, and releasement, under the King of heaven's hand and seal for us, *&c.*

If any man desire further satisfaction, whether this Covenant was first made with Christ for us, yea or no, let him consult with these precious Scriptures, *Psalm* 89:24, 27, 28; *Hebr.* 13:20; *Isaiah* 42:6; *Isa.* 55:3; *Zach.* 6:13; *Isa.* 50:5–6; *Zach.* 9:11; *Isa.* 53:10.

Now if any one ask, what were the conditions between the Father and the Son, when this Covenant was made, they are as followeth. First see what God the Father promised unto Christ on his part.

1. That he would anoint him, and fill him with the Spirit above all others, *Heb.* 1:9; *Isa.* 11:2.
2. That he would prepare him a body to sacrifice for sins, *Heb.*

10:5, 10.

3. That he would uphold him, and strengthen him, that he should not be ashamed by the things he should suffer, *Isa.* 42:6. *&* 50:5, 7.

4. That he would justify and glorify all his seed, *Isa.* 50:8; *Joh.* 17:22, 24, *Isa.* 53:11.

5. That he should see and enjoy the travail of his soul, and the purchases of his blood, *Isa.* 53:10; *Heb.* 2:7.

6. That he should have all power in heaven and in earth given him, *till all his enemies were made his footstool, Ephes.* 5:25, 27, *Matthew* 28:18; 1 *Cor.* 15:28.

Next let us examine what Christ did perform or promise to perform on his part,

1. To become a Mediator, Surety and Savior for all those that his Father should give him, *Heb.* 8:6; *Heb.* 7:22; *Act.* 13:23; *Joh.* 17:11, 12; *Ephes.* 1:10; *Col.* 1:20; 1 *John* 2:1.

2. To take upon him the nature of man, and so to become flesh, in his Father's appointed time, *Gal.* 4:4; *Mat.* 11:27; *John* 17:4.

3. That he would glorify his Father, by keeping, revealing, and doing his will, *John* 15:10; *John* 6:39.

4. That he would suffer and satisfy personally and perfectly for the sins of men, *Luke* 24:46; *Hos.* 13:14; 1 *Pet.* 2:24.

5. That he would bring himself, and all those given him by his Father, unto glory, *Heb.* 10:14; *Joh.* 14:4, 9; *John* 10:18.

The word of God doth contain the articles of this Covenant; those that desire further satisfaction, search the Scriptures, wherein you shall find that Christ did willingly undertake this work, *Heb.* 10:7, 9, and did faithfully discharge it, *Heb.* 10:5, 6, 7, *&c.* so our reconciliation was wrought by the Son, *Isa.* 61:1; *John* 1:3; *John* 5:36, 37; *Col.* 1:16, 17; *Hebr.* 1:3; *John* 5:17. *&* 3:17, and sealed by the Holy Ghost, *Ephes.* 1:13. *&* 4:30.

The Difference Between
the Covenants of Grace and Works

Questions 3. The [third] thing to be considered of, is this, wherein doth the Covenant of grace, and the Covenant of works differ? *Answer*: For answer hereunto, consider the vast difference between the law and the gospel, *viz.* the law affords not a drop of grace, it bestows nothing freely: the language of the law is, do thou and live; if not die; no work no wages; but in the gospel, the yoke of personal obedience is translated from believers to their surety; there is nothing for them to pay; all that they have to do, is to hunger and feed; their happiness is free, in respect of themselves, though costly to Christ, who by his merits hath purchased for them whatsoever they would obtain, and by his Spirit worketh in them whatsoever he requires.

The first Covenant of works is old, the Covenant of grace is new: the first is the law of the letter, the second is the law of the Spirit; the first is a law of death, the second is a law of life: the first was wounding, the second is healing; the first a natural law, the second a spiritual law; the first a law of types, the second a law of substance: the first was to be done away, the second is to continue; the first a Covenant of earthly blessings, the second a Covenant of spiritual blessings: the first was to stand for a time, the second was to stand for ever.

Again, this Covenant of grace doth differ from the Covenant of works in the universality and large extent of it: the first Covenant requires a righteousness in us, the second doth give and accept of a righteousness which is another's, and imputed to us.

It is true, that religion for the substance thereof, was ever one and the same, and unchangeable, as appears, *Heb.* 13:8; *Ephes.* 4:5; *Jude* 3; *Acts* 26:22; *Tit.* 1:1, 2. And so the word of God written by *Moses* and the Prophets, did contain whatsoever was needful for the salvation of the Israelites, *Deut.* 4:2. & 12:32; *Psal.* 1:2; *Mal.* 4:4; *Hos.* 8:12; *Luk.* 10:26. But the New Testament our Savior made known unto his disciples, the last and full will or Covenant of his heavenly Father, *John* 14:26. & 15:15. & 16:13. & 1:18. And what they received of him, they faithfully preached unto the world, *Acts* 20:27; 1 *Cor.* 15:1, 2:3; *Gal.* 1:8; 1 *John* 1:3. And the sum of what they preached is committed to writing, and left upon record for our learning, *Act.* 1:1, 2; *Joh.* 20:31; 1 *Joh.* 5:13; *Act.* 8:5; 1 *Cor.* 2:2; *Rom.* 10:8, 9, 10.

The difference between the Covenant of works, and the Covenant of grace, may be reduced to these three heads.

> 1. The first was a ministration of the letter, a naked commandment, carrying with it no aptness, disposition, or ability to keep it.
> 2. It breeds enmity and fear; looking on God as a hard taskmaster, and so fills the soul full of terrors.
> 3. It is a ministration of death, namely by the curse, to them that keep it not.

But the Covenant of grace is a ministration of the Spirit, requiring no more than what it promiseth to give. In a word, it is a ministration of the Spirit, of love, freedom, and righteousness, and of life; for that it shews the guilty a righteousness to satisfy the law, and the way to obtain a pardon.

The first Covenant was made altogether upon condition on both sides; the condition on God's part was, they should live; the condition on man's part was, he must do this: but in this Covenant there is not any condition, I mean in the Covenant of grace.

True it is, could we justify the law by keeping it; the law would justify us, in and by that obedience to it. But now the law is become weak and unable to justify any man, though powerful and strong enough to condemn every man.

In the Covenant of works a man is left to stand by his own strength; but in the Covenant of grace, God undertakes to keep us through faith to salvation.

In the Covenant of works, God's highest end is the glorifying of his justice; and in the Covenant of grace, it is to glorify his grace. The voice of the Covenant of works, is like the first speech of *Nathan* to *David, Thou art the man;* the voice of the Covenant of grace is like his after-speech, *The Lord hath put away thy sin:* the voice of the Covenant of works, is, the soul that sinneth shall die, *Ezek.* 18.

In the Covenant of grace, he saith, *Ezek.* 33:11. *As I live saith the Lord, I desire not the death of a sinner.*

There is help for such as break the Covenant of works, but no help for such as make void the Covenant of grace.

A Little Cabinet Richly Stored

God's Order and Method
of Bringing People into the Covenant of Grace

Question 4. The [fourth] thing to be enquired into is this, what is God's order and method, that he generally makes use of, to bring his people into the bond of the Covenant, and to bestow the blessings of the Covenant upon them. *Answer*: First, in the making up of the Covenant between God and us: God is the first with us, he is the first mover, he begins with us, before we begin with him: we should never seek to be in Covenant with him, if he did not first allure us, and draw us, invite us, and entreat us, *Ezek.* 20:37, *I will bring them (saith the Lord) into the bond of the Covenant:* it is the Lord that brings them, they do not first offer themselves.

God prepares his own way for entering into Covenant with us, and then he finisheth the work, and in this preparation he doth these three things.

1. He breaks us of our Covenant with hell and death, and makes us sensible of our undone estates, & makes us to see that we are without God, without Christ, without hope, that we are not under mercy, that we are not as yet of his people, *Eph.* 2. *& 1 Pet.* 2.

2. He opens to us his mind and will, shewing himself willing to receive us to grace, and to enter into a new Covenant with us, yet again to take us to be his people, and he to be our God: and so he goes into the streets, and open places as it is in *Prov.* 1:20, 21. And there makes public proclamation: ho, every one that will, come ye to me, and I will make an everlasting Covenant with you, *Isa.* 55:3; *Isa.* 65:1. And if we come not at this first invitation, then he comes and beseecheth us to be reconciled to him, *2 Cor.* 5:20. And speaks to us as pitying us, *Jer.* 3:12, and lamenting over us, *Ezek.* 33:11. And all this he doth to persuade us to come and strike a Covenant with him.

3. By the hearing of these promises and offers of grace, the Lord usually scattereth some little seeds of faith in the hearts of those that he will bring unto himself; which seeds being sown, do quickly put forth, and act towards the Covenant, before by the Father tendered, and lays hold of it, as we see in *Lydia*, the Jailor, *Zacheus, &c.* So by an act of faith, we come to close with the Covenant, revealed and offered freely unto us, by accepting the grace offered, resting upon

God for all the mercy which he hath promised; and then taking God to be a God over us, submitting to his government and authority, to command us, and to rule us in all things according to his own will; these two things faith doth, and so takes hold of the Covenant more firmly, in the same way and order as God offers it. First God makes himself known to us as a God of mercy, gracious, long suffering, pardoning iniquity, transgression and sin, and so offers himself to be reconciled to us, though we have rebelled against him, promising to be a Father unto us, and to accept of us in his beloved, as his sons and daughters: and thus is the Covenant made up between God and us; and the soul now begins to say in itself, I that was an enemy, he hath now reconciled unto himself; I that was in times past, without God, without Christ, without promise, without Covenant, without hope, and none of God's people—Yet now I have God for my God, Christ is my peace, and I am now become one of God's people, the Covenant of his peace now belongeth to me, and the Lord is become my salvation, saying as *Jacob*, *Gen.* 33:11, *The Lord hath had mercy on me, therefore I have enough, I have all that my heart hath desired.* The Lord doth acquaint the soul with those absolute promises, which shew unto us the only cause of our salvation, even free grace and no other thing. Secondly, they are a foundation for the faith of adherence or dependence to stay upon, they yield a singular encouragement to a poor dejected soul, that finds nothing in itself but sin and misery, with hope to cast itself upon the free grace of God, seeing he looks at nothing in us, for which he should save us. There be two acts of faith, one of adherence or dependency, another of assurance; there be also two kinds of promises, absolute, and conditional. Mark now how these do fit and answer one to the other, the absolute promises to the faith of adherence, the conditional to the faith of assurance. Now faith helps us to close with the Covenant, and enables us to walk with God according to the Covenant which we have made. There is a keeping of Covenant required of us, as well as a making a Covenant with God, *Gen.* 17:7, 9; *Psal.* 50:5. The Saints are said to make a Covenant with God, but in *Psal.* 103:18. they are said to keep his Covenant; so there is a making and a keeping of Covenant, and both by faith.

The Blessings and Benefits of the Covenant of Grace

Question 5. The [fifth] thing to be enquired into is, what are the blessings and benefits of this Covenant to us-ward. *Answer:* We can never know the things which are given to us of God, but by knowing of the Covenant, which conveys all the blessings from God to us. O let us lift up our hearts, to look for great things, great blessings, such as the great God hath promised. The blessings are suitable to our wants; the things of the Covenant are great things, *Hos.* 8:12.

The Covenant is as full of blessings as of letters, or syllables, and more; it is a rich storehouse, replenished with all manner of gifts and graces, spiritual and temporal; it is as a tree of life to those that feed upon it, they shall live forever; it is a well of salvation, it is a fountain of good things, to satisfy every thirsty soul, *Zach.* 13:1; it is a treasure full of goods, as *Deut.* 28:12. Here is unsearchable riches, unspeakable mercy, which can never be fathomed, or emptied: all these blessings of the Covenant are wrapped up in the promises of it, every promise of grace containing a blessing; as every threatening of the law contains a curse. Now the promises and blessings of the Covenant are of two sorts: First, of things spiritual and eternal. Secondly, of things temporal; the spiritual blessings of the Covenant are chiefly comprehended in these places of Scripture, *Jer.* 31:31, 33; *Ezek.* 36:25, 26, 27, 28; *Jer.* 32:38, 39, 40; *Gen.* 17:7. God in Trinity enters into Covenant with us.

1. The Father enters into Covenant with us, and promiseth to be a Father to us; hence saith the Lord, *Exod.* 4:22, *Israel is my son, my first born,* and Jer. 31:9, 20, *is Ephraim my dear son, is he my pleasant child?* So the Lord hath a care to provide both heavenly and earthly inheritance for his children: he hath also a care to nurture and instruct them in his ways, *Deut.* 32:10.

2. Christ the Son enters into Covenant with us, and speaks to us, as in *Isa.* 43:1, *Thou art mine* and Hosea 13:14, *I will redeem them, I will ransom them. Oh death, I will be thy death; thou hast destroyed my people, but I will destroy thee.* So he undertakes to take up all controversies, which may fall between God and us, he promiseth to restore us to the adoption of sons, and to the inheritance of sons, that we might be where he is, *Joh.* 17:24.

3. The Holy Ghost makes a Covenant with us, as *Heb.* 10:15, 16, *whereof the Holy-Ghost also is a witness to us,* testifying of this Covenant, which he makes with us, although the Father be employed in it, yet here is the power and work of the Holy-Ghost; what the Father hath purposed from all eternity, and the Son hath purchased for them in time, that the Holy-Ghost effects in them, and applies to them, *viz.* he enables them to apply the blood of Christ for the remission of sins, he writes the law in our hearts, he teacheth us, he washeth us from our filthiness, and comforteth us in our sadness, supports us in our faintings, and guides us in our wanderings, &c. I may say as *Moses* to the people, *Deut.* 33:29, *Happy art thou O Israel, who is like unto thee, O people saved by the Lord?* and as David, Psal. 33:12, *Blessed is that Nation whose God is the Lord.*

By faith we look at Christ, as having all fullness of grace in himself, *John* 1:16. & *Col.* 1:19. All other angels and saints have but their measure, some more, some less, according to the measure of the gift of Christ, *Eph.* 4:7, but Christ hath received the Spirit, not by measure, but in the fullness of it, *Joh.* 3:34.

Now whatsoever fullness of grace there is in Christ, he hath received not for himself, but for us, that he might communicate unto us, and we might receive from him, *Psal.* 68:18. It is said he received gifts for men; not for himself, but for men, that we might receive from him; and thence it is, that in *Joh.* 1:16, of his fullness we receive grace for grace, his wisdom is to make us wise, his meekness and patience, is to make us meek and patient, and Christ is faithful to distribute to us all such graces that he hath received for us, he is faithful in all his house. What shall I say more in this Covenant, God unbosoms himself unto us, and shines forth upon us, and there is now and then a sweet intercourse of love between him and thy soul. In the blessing of this Covenant there is remedy for every malady, promises suitable to every condition, for being and wellbeing, for this life, and that which is to come. I omit here to mention such blessings of the Covenant as I might, and the nature of the same, having spoken something to it in the former part of this treatise, &c.

Chapter 10

Reformed Baptist Covenant Theology

and Biblical Theology

Micah and Samuel Renihan*

This material was originally presented by the authors to students of Westminster Seminary California during a lunch hour on campus in response to inquiries about how Reformed Baptists view covenant theology. Given the time constraints of a one-hour presentation, the focus of the material was on areas of positive argument for the credobaptist position where it differs from paedobaptism. Key points of covenant theology are absent from this presentation, not because they do not form a part of Reformed Baptist covenant theology, but because there is no disagreement between our position and that of the paedobaptists. For example, there is no discussion of the covenant of works, fully affirmed by the Second London and Westminster Confessions, and there is no discussion of the definition of a covenant since we agree with the basic definition formulated by Meredith G. Kline: a commitment with divine sanctions between a lord and a servant. Other arguments and significant points were omitted for the sake of time, such as the relation between kingdom and covenant or exegetical discussions of specific key passages around which this dialogue normally revolves. What follows are foundational assertions

---

* Micah Renihan (M.Div., Westminster Seminary California) is a pastor at Grace Reformed Baptist Church in Brunswick, ME. Samuel Renihan (M.Div., Westminster Seminary California) is a pastor at Trinity Reformed Baptist Church in La Mirada, CA. Sam is currently working on his Ph.D. through the Free University of Amsterdam. He edited *God without Passions: a Reader* and authored *God without Passions: a Primer*. Scripture references are taken from the ESV. This chapter first appeared in *Recovering a Covenantal Heritage: Essays in Baptist Covenant Theology* (Palmdale, CA: RBAP, 2014) and is used with permission.

arguing for a Reformed Baptist view of covenant theology and biblical theology, applied specifically to credobaptism.

Foundations of Reformed Baptist Covenant Theology

1. The covenant of redemption informs and unites all of redemptive history.

The *pactum salutis*[1] establishes the redemption of the elect through Christ's incarnation, life, death, resurrection, and ascension as that which is the driving purpose of history. God's decree is that from fallen humanity, the Son, empowered by the Spirit, should redeem a specific number of his own people to be granted to him as a reward for the completion of his work on their behalf.

2. The new covenant is the final and full accomplishment of the covenant of redemption in history.

Where do we see the accomplishment of the redemption of the elect in history through the incarnation and death of Christ? It is in the new covenant, made in the blood of Christ.[2] What is it that Christ claims that he has come to do? He claims that he has come to redeem those whom the Father has given to him.[3] His purpose is to accomplish the *pactum salutis* in time and history. The new covenant goes no further than the *pactum salutis*, not only because Christ specifically said that his mission was purely to redeem the elect, but also because the new covenant is made in Christ's blood, redeeming blood, the salvific benefits of which have never been and will never be applied to any but the elect. This means that the parties of the

---

[1] "**pactum salutis**: *covenant of redemption;* in Reformed federalism, the pretemporal, intratrinitarian agreement of the Father and the Son concerning the covenant of grace and its ramifications in and through the work of the Son incarnate." Cf. Richard A. Muller, *Dictionary of Latin and Greek Theological Terms* (Grand Rapids: Baker, 1985, Second printing, September 1986), 217.

[2] Cf. Heb. 7:20-22.

[3] Cf. John 6:38-40; 10:14-16, 26-28; 17:6-11, 17-21.

new covenant are no other than God and Christ, and the elect in him.

Although the *pactum salutis* has been finally and fully accomplished in history through Christ's work, what remains is entrance into the consummated blessings and rewards of Christ's kingdom. That will not occur until every last elect person for whom Christ died has been gathered in by Christ himself through the preaching of the gospel to all nations.

3. **The covenant of grace is the in-breaking of the covenant of redemption into history through the progressive revelation and retro-active application of the new covenant.**

Herman Bavinck says, "The covenant of grace was not first established in time, but has its foundation in eternity, is grounded in the pact of salvation, and is in the first place a covenant among the three persons of the divine being itself."[4]

Geerhardus Vos says:

> The covenant of redemption is the pattern for the covenant of grace. However, it is more than that. It is also the effective cause for carrying out the latter. As far as its offer and application are concerned, the covenant of grace lies enclosed in the counsel of peace, so that with respect to the latter it appears completely as a gift, as a covenantal benefit.[5]

There is one uniting and driving force in redemptive history, and that is the covenant of redemption. Although it is not accomplished in history until Christ comes, we see the gathering in of the elect who believe in Christ from the fall onward. Where we see that in-gathering of the elect who believe in the gospel as it is revealed progressively in promises, types, and shadows, there we see the retro-active new covenant, and that is the covenant of grace. What has been required of all men at all times in all places is to

---

[4] Herman Bavinck, *Reformed Dogmatics*, vol. 3 (Grand Rapids: Baker, 2006), 405.

[5] Geerhardus Vos, *Redemptive History and Biblical Interpretation* (Phillipsburg, NJ: P&R Publishing, 2001), 252.

believe the gospel however it has been revealed in a particular moment of redemptive history.[6] Because the covenant of grace is the retro-active new covenant, ultimately being founded in the covenant of redemption, its parties are the same as the new covenant: God, Christ, and the elect in him. Vos says:

> In other words, the bond that links the Old and New Covenants together is not a purely evolutionary one, inasmuch as the one has grown out of the other; it is, if we may so call it, a transcendental bond: the New Covenant in its preexistent, heavenly state reaches back and stretches its wings over the Old, and the Old Testament people of God were one with us in religious dignity and privilege; they were, to speak in a Pauline figure, sons of the Jerusalem above, which is the mother of all.[7]

Bavinck says:

> This pact of salvation, however, further forms the link between the eternal work of God toward salvation and what he does to that end in time. The covenant of grace revealed in time does not hang in the air but rests on an eternal, unchanging foundation. It is firmly grounded in the counsel and covenant of the triune God and is the application and execution of it that infallibly follows . . . It is a false perception that God first made his covenant with Adam and Noah, with Abraham and Israel, and only finally with Christ; the covenant of grace was ready-made from all eternity in the pact of salvation of the three persons and was realized by Christ from the moment the fall occurred . . . For though God communicates his revelation successively and historically makes it progressively richer and fuller, and humankind therefore advances in the knowledge, possession, and enjoyment of that revelation, God is and remains the same. . . . Although Christ completed his work on earth only in the midst of history and although the Holy

---

[6] Cf. Heb. 4:2; Gal. 3:8-9; 1 Pet. 1:10-11; Eph. 3:4-6, 8-12.
[7] Vos, *Redemptive History*, 199.

Spirit was not poured out till the day of Pentecost, God nevertheless was able, already in the days of the Old Testament, to fully distribute the benefits to be acquired and applied by the Son and the Spirit. Old Testament believers were saved in no other way than we. There is one faith, one Mediator, one way of salvation, and one covenant of grace.[8]

4. The old covenant is theocratic Israel, defined by the Abrahamic, conditioned by the Mosaic, and focused by the Davidic covenants. The old covenant, and thus each of these three covenants, differs from the new covenant not merely in administration, but also in substance.

The Abrahamic covenant, called the covenant of circumcision by Stephen in Acts 7:8, promised Abraham three things primarily. It promised him a land, a people, and a kingship. In other words, Abraham's physical descendants would inherit the land and grow into an innumerable people ruled by their own kings. This was called the covenant of circumcision because circumcision was the sign of these blessings and separated Abraham's offspring from the rest of the world as the heirs of these promises.[9]

Abraham was the federal head of this covenant because the promises were made to him and to his physical seed. All those who were of Abraham, or in Abraham we might say, were heirs of the national promises. This defined the membership of the covenant.

One of the most distinctive features of this covenant was that God immutably promised to bring about these blessings apart from any merit on Abraham's part, and for that reason the covenant of circumcision can rightly be called *a* covenant of grace. But can it rightly be called an administration of *the* covenant of grace? If the covenant of grace is the accomplishing of the covenant of redemption in history, the retro-active application of the new covenant, then what do national promises have to do with Christ's redeeming and gathering of the elect? It must be noted that

---

[8] Bavinck, *Reformed Dogmatics*, 3:215-16.

[9] This is not to say that circumcision had no further significance, but that the national promises were its primary referent.

although all the Abrahamic promises typologically reveal the new covenant, in their substance and essence they are distinct from it. Abraham knew that Canaan was not heaven.

The Mosaic covenant was added and attached to the Abrahamic covenant in such a way that it conditioned the enjoyment of the Abrahamic blessings. God immutably promised Abraham that the covenant blessings would be realized. The extent to which those blessings would be enjoyed, however, depended upon the obedience of the people of Israel. To put it simply, in the Abrahamic covenant, God promised Abraham a land, nation, and kingship, and in the Mosaic covenant God said "If you're going to be My people, this is how you must live." These conditions were strong enough that although God would inevitably bring the promises to realization, they could be lost through disobedience. That the Mosaic covenant conditions the Abrahamic covenant is evident not only by virtue of the fact that its obedience is directly tied to the enjoyment of the Abrahamic promises, but also by virtue of the fact that it was made specifically with the Abrahamic people.

That the Mosaic covenant is not one in essence and substance with the covenant of grace is further recognized by the fact that, as the book of Hebrews tells us, the sacrifices had no power to remove sin. "The law has but a shadow of the good things to come instead of the true form of these realities" (Heb. 10:1). Hebrews 8:5 calls the Mosaic system a "copy and shadow of the heavenly things." Paul, speaking in Colossians of Mosaic rites such as new moons, festivals, and Sabbaths, says that "These are a shadow of the things to come, but the substance belongs to Christ" (Col. 2:17). Using the same question that was applied to the Abrahamic, is the conditioning of national promises by law the accomplishing of the redemption of the elect in history? No, the Mosaic covenant is separate from the covenant of grace in its substance. However, every single element of the Mosaic economy typologically revealed and set before the eyes of the Jews the covenant of grace wherein true righteousness, true forgiveness of sins, and true holiness could be found. Since tenure in the land was what was in view in the Mosaic law, offenses against that covenant could be addressed within that covenant and sacrificial system. But concerning true spiritual realities, concerning offenses committed against a holy God, the sacrifices could do nothing but point ahead to that one true sacrifice, Jesus Christ.

Even until today, many have wrestled with how it could be that the covenant of grace was being administered by a strict works principle. This difficulty is simply and rightly avoided when one recognizes that the Mosaic covenant is not an administration of *the* covenant of grace, but rather typologically reveals it in its law and worship. The Mosaic covenant is then free to be affirmed as a graciously administered works principle, controlling the extent to which the Abrahamic blessings are enjoyed. "The one who does them shall live by them" (Gal. 3:12).

The Mosaic covenant lacked a federal head until the kingship was established. The Abrahamic people as a whole were judged on different levels, sometimes the individual, sometimes the family, sometimes the tribe, and sometimes the nation. Everyone did what was right in his own eyes, and there was no king in Israel.

The Davidic covenant brings all of the Abrahamic promises to final completion and focuses the Mosaic covenant into one person. It was under the line of David, specifically Solomon, that at last the nation of Israel reached the fulfillment of being the Abrahamic people ruling all of the Abrahamic land, under Abrahamic, specifically Judean, kings. The biblical authors are careful to record when these promises are fulfilled (Josh. 21:43-45 and 1 Kings 4:20). Under David and his line, the national people of Abraham enjoyed the blessings and benefits of the promised-land to the extent to which the Davidic king obeyed the Mosaic law. This is the concern of the records of the kings. They did what was right in the eyes of the Lord, or they did what was evil. Israel was blessed or cursed accordingly.

Because the Mosaic covenant controls both the Abrahamic and the Davidic covenants, it is the primary referent of the New Testament when speaking about the old covenant. However, the Mosaic covenant cannot be divided or disconnected from the Abrahamic and Davidic covenants, and thus all three combine to form the old covenant, in every aspect typological of the covenant of grace, yet in every aspect different in substance from the covenant of grace.

5. The old covenant is related to the new covenant historically and typologically.

Is the old covenant entirely unrelated to the covenant of grace? Have we utterly divested the old covenant of its theological richness and significance? No, we are merely making careful distinctions. There is historical and typological unity between the old and the new covenants. There is historical unity in that Abraham was also promised that the nations would be blessed through him. Israel was designated the mother of the Messiah, the guardian of the gospel in its promissory and shadowy forms. The birth of Christ was a fulfillment of the Abrahamic covenant.[10] Israel's disobedience to the law of Moses could not prevent this immutable promise of God from coming to pass. There is typological unity in that every single part of the old covenant, that is, every single part of the Abrahamic, Mosaic, and Davidic covenants, typologically revealed the new covenant, whether through what was lacking or what was being commended. This allows us to affirm heartily every single aspect of a redemptive-historical hermeneutic and approach to preaching. Christ is everywhere, the gospel is everywhere, the covenant of grace is everywhere, because it is God's driving and uniting purpose to gather the elect in history. The Abrahamic people in Canaan were not a realization of the promises of the covenant of grace. The Abrahamic covenant revealed the promises of the covenant of grace, drove history towards its realization, and thereby provided sufficient revelation for the participation of elect believers in its promises. But the type is not the anti-type. The new covenant *fulfills* the old; it does not *replace* the old.

Therefore, the Abrahamic, Mosaic, and Davidic covenants were national, temporary, and typological covenants that placed Israel in an external relationship with God and in which the new covenant was revealed through promises, types, and shadows. On the one hand they are, in their substance and essence, distinct from the covenant of grace, and on the other hand they are related to it through rich typology and historical progression.

Meredith G. Kline says:

---

[10] Luke 1:55, 73.

When Paul, in Romans 9-11, defends God's covenantal faithfulness in the face of Israel's fall, he bases his case on the identification of the promised seed as the individual election, a remnant-fullness of Jews and Gentiles, spiritual children of Abraham, all like him justified by faith. The apostle finds within the Lord's revelation of the promises to Abraham explicit warrant for distinguishing this spiritual seed of Abraham from the physical offspring. What is remarkable is how he bypasses the more literal first level significance of Abraham's seed and takes for granted the second, spiritual level of meaning as *the* meaning of the promise.[11]

What are these two levels? They are the physical offspring and the spiritual offspring of Abraham, the first being a "provisional and prototypal" people, and the other being a "messianic and eternal" people.[12] From where do they come? The two circles of the internal and external distinction are the result of two different covenants. As was shown by Vos previously, the paradigm for the covenant of grace is not the Abrahamic covenant, but the covenant of redemption. We are not arguing that the unregenerate have never been or can never be in a covenantal relationship with God. Rather, we are arguing that the covenant of grace has always been an internal covenantal relationship with God through Christ, while the national covenants were an external covenantal relationship with God through Abraham. In Galatians 4, Paul distinguishes between two covenants, Jerusalem above and Jerusalem below, contrasting them as being born according to the flesh and according to the Spirit. One is clearly a physical covenant, the other is clearly spiritual. Paul is contrasting the difference between old covenant Israel and new covenant Israel. The difference is the Spirit and the flesh, the external and the internal, and they are two different covenants. Furthermore, Paul's distinction is not purely between the Abrahamic and Mosaic covenants, because as Kline has pointed out,

---

[11] Meredith G. Kline, *Kingdom Prologue: Genesis Foundations for a Covenantal Worldview* (Overland Park, KS: Two Ages Press, 2000), 335, emphasis his. Kline makes the same point with regard to Gal. 3:16.

[12] Kline, *Kingdom Prologue*, 334.

246 | BY COMMON CONFESSION

when Paul speaks of the Abrahamic promises he is deliberately ignoring the national Abrahamic promises and looking at the Messianic promises. We are asserting that those Messianic promises point to the Messianic covenant, that is the new covenant, the covenant of grace, and that as such they point to a covenant distinct from the covenant of circumcision with Abraham and his natural offspring. This means that not only has that typical, external covenantal relationship been abrogated and passed away, but also that the Messianic and eternal relationship was always active, embedded within that external covenant. The internal and external circles, visible in the Old Testament, are not the result of two levels of covenantal membership, but are the result of two different covenants, the covenant of circumcision and the covenant of grace.

With the triangular shape of typology in mind,[13] using the type (Abrahamic, old covenant Israel) to shape the anti-type (covenant of grace, new covenant Israel), not only reverses the progress of redemptive history, but also fails to understand the new covenant antitype as it is founded in the arch-type (i.e., the covenant of redemption).

Covenant of Redemption (Arch-type)

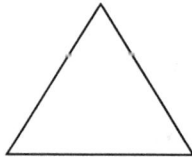

Old Covenant (Type)   **New Covenant (Anti-type)**

6. **To be in a covenant, you must be united to the federal head of that covenant. Federal headship is immediate in every covenant.**

Nehemiah Coxe says:

> This is also worthy to be noted by us: that when God has made covenants, in which either mankind in general or

---

[13] See Vos, *The Teaching of the Epistle to the Hebrews* (Grand Rapids: Eerdmans, 1965), 55-65.

some elect number of men in particular have been involved, it has pleased him first to transact with some public person, head, or representative for all others that should be involved in them.[14]

He adds:

The right of the remotest generation was as much derived from Abraham and the covenant made with him, as was that of his immediate seed, and did not at all depend on the faithfulness of their immediate parents. Thus, the immediate seed of those Israelites that fell in the wilderness under the displeasure of God were made to inherit the land of Canaan by virtue of this covenant with Abraham. They never could have enjoyed it by virtue of their immediate parent's steadfastness in the covenant.[15]

Because covenant membership and covenant blessings depend on the federal head, immediately, every member of every covenant, according to the terms of a given covenant, is entitled to every blessing or curse incurred by the federal head. Every human being stands on equal ground in the covenant of works because they are Adam's offspring, no matter how far removed. Each human being is directly and immediately federally united to Adam. We are in Adam, not because of our parents, but because of our direct federal relation to Adam. The same principle applies with Christ as federal head of the covenant of grace.

7. **Jesus Christ has been and always will be the federal head of the covenant of grace/new covenant. To be federally united to him you must be 1) promised to him outside of time in the covenant of redemption and 2) brought into union with him in time by the Holy Spirit.**

The Son was the one elected by the Father to win the redemption of

---

[14] Nehemiah Coxe, "A Discourse of the Covenants," in *Covenant Theology: From Adam to Christ*, eds. Ronald D. Miller, James M. Renihan, and Francisco Orozco (Palmdale, CA: RBAP, 2005), 39.

[15] Coxe, "A Discourse of the Covenants," 97.

the elect. All of this is accomplished in the new covenant, which is the historical climax of the covenant of grace. To be in the covenant of grace/new covenant, you must be united to Christ, its federal head.[16]

Since the covenant of grace is the retro-active application of the new covenant, if we posit that Christ is the mediator of the covenant of grace, we can only understand the terms of his role as mediator, and our relation to him as such, through the way that he is presented in the new covenant. That Christ is the mediator of the covenant of grace, the new covenant, no Reformed theologian denies. Thus, in line with New Testament doctrine, the only way to be under Christ's federal headship is to be united to him by the Holy Spirit. This union finds its roots outside of time as we are chosen in Christ in the covenant of redemption and is applied to the elect in time by the Spirit, begun in effectual calling and consummated in the faith of the believer. Apart from saving faith there can be no union with Christ, because the Spirit does not indwell any except the elect, those who have been justified by faith.[17] Christ is the one and only federal head of the covenant of grace, the new covenant. Federal headship is never mediate, thus none can enter the covenant other than those who are directly or immediately under his federal headship by the Holy Spirit.[18]

Vos says, "However narrowly or widely the boundary of the covenant of grace be drawn, in any case it involves a relationship with Christ, whether external or internal, by which it is tied to the covenant of redemption."[19] He adds:

One is first united to Christ, the Mediator of the covenant, by a mystical union, which finds its conscious recognition in faith. By this union with Christ all that is in Christ is simultaneously given. Faith embraces all this too; it not only grasps the instantaneous justification, but lays hold of Christ as Prophet, Priest, and King, as his rich and full Messiah.[20]

---

[16] Cf. WLC 31 and 57-59.

[17] Cf. Acts 2:38, Eph. 1:13.

[18] Cf. WLC 65-69.

[19] Vos, *Redemptive History*, 252.

[20] Vos, *Redemptive History*, 256.

Bavinck says:

> On the Christian position there can be no doubt that all the benefits of grace have been completely and solely acquired by Christ; hence, they are included in his person and lie prepared for his church in him . . . And since these benefits are all covenant benefits, were acquired in the way of the covenant, and are distributed in the same covenantal way, *there is no participation in those benefits except by communion with the person of Christ*, who acquired and applies them as the mediator of the covenant.[21]

Fairbairn says:

> Here, precisely as in the rending of the veil for the ceremonials of Judaism, the exclusive bond for the people was broken at the center: Christ's very mother and brothers were to have no precedence over others, nor any distinctive position in His kingdom; spiritual relations alone should prevail there, and the one bond of connection with it for all alike, was to be the believing reception of the gospel and obedience to it . . . So far, therefore, as regards Israel's typical character, their removed and isolated position is plainly at an end: all tribes and nations are on a footing as to the kingdom of God — members and fellow-citizens if they are believers in Christ, aliens if they are not.[22]

Fairbairn adds, "And wherever there is found a soul linked in vital union with Christ, there also are found the essential characteristics of Abraham's seed, and title to Abraham's inheritance."[23]

> Anyone who does not have the Spirit of Christ does not belong to him. (Rom. 8:9)

---

[21] Bavinck, *Reformed Dogmatics*, 3:591, emphasis added.

[22] Patrick Fairbairn, *The Interpretation of Prophecy* (London: The Banner of Truth, 1964), 261-62.

[23] Fairbairn, *Interpretation of Prophecy*, 270.

For the Scripture says, "Everyone who believes in him will not be put to shame." [12] For there is no distinction between Jew and Greek; for the same Lord is Lord of all, bestowing his riches on all who call on him. [13] For "everyone who calls on the name of the Lord will be saved." (Rom. 10:11-13)

All these are empowered by one and the same Spirit, who apportions to each one individually as he wills. [12] For just as the body is one and has many members, and all the members of the body, though many, are one body, so it is with Christ. [13] For in one Spirit we were all baptized into one body — Jews or Greeks, slaves or free — and all were made to drink of one Spirit. (1 Cor. 12:11-13)

for in Christ Jesus you are all sons of God, through faith. [27] For as many of you as were baptized into Christ have put on Christ. [28] There is neither Jew nor Greek, there is neither slave nor free, there is no male and female, for you are all one in Christ Jesus. (Gal. 3:26-28)

And he put all things under his feet and gave him as head over all things to the church, [23] which is his body, the fullness of him who fills all in all. (Eph. 1:22-23)

There is one body and one Spirit — just as you were called to the one hope that belongs to your call — [5] one Lord, one faith, one baptism, [6] one God and Father of all, who is over all and through all and in all. (Eph. 4:4-6)

The covenant of grace is so called because its blessings are freely given to its members. Those blessings are free because they have been won solely by Christ's obedience in fulfillment of his commission in the covenant of redemption. Thus understood, the covenant of grace arises in history in contradistinction to the covenant of works. That covenant having been broken, all mankind is born immediately federally united to Adam, under the curse of the law. When man is liberated from this condemnation, his liberation comes through the propitiatory satisfaction of Christ on his behalf and the gracious imputation of Christ's righteousness to his account, appropriated by faith. In other words, as Genesis 3 shows, the covenant of grace is the solution to the curses of the covenant of works.

The fact that we see this redemption promised and typified from the fall onward has led Reformed theologians to see God's grace extending into history prior to the incarnation and death of Christ. Where God's grace extended into the past, it came by way of covenant, wherein Christ's blood of the new covenant was retroactively applied to those who believed in the promise, and that retroactivity of the new covenant was and remains essentially distinct from the old covenant, which was established on worse (and thus distinct) promises than the new covenant (Heb. 8:6). Thus, Christ's people have always been those who were promised to him by the Father, and it is those people for whom he spilled his blood.

Scripture teaches that Christ brings his own to himself through the work of the Spirit, and that he dwells in his own by the Spirit. Therefore, without the Spirit, none belong to Christ. If you belong to Christ, you are in the covenant of grace. If you do not belong to Christ, you are in the covenant of works. You cannot be in both.[24] If it is possible to be born into the covenant of grace through the mediated federal headship of a parent, then, unless regeneration is presumed, one is both in Adam and in Christ at the same time. However, this is impossible. One man sinned and brought death to all mankind; another obeyed and brought life to his people. You are either in Adam or in Christ.

To bring this to a conclusion, a right understanding of the membership of the covenant of grace is founded on the covenant of redemption and the new covenant. Those who are in the covenant of grace are those who were promised to the Son by the Father in the covenant of redemption, won by the Son's life, death, and resurrection, and sealed by the Holy Spirit, uniting them to their federal head, Jesus Christ. Laying claim to Christ and his benefits is a serious matter, and as Scripture shows, only those who have saving faith can truly make that claim. There is no external federal relation to Jesus Christ. In terms of membership or qualification, there are no distinctions in the body of Christ, that is, the church.

---

[24] Cf. Rom. 7:4-6.

All are sons of God through faith, under one head, indwelt by one Spirit. "Anyone who does not have the Spirit of Christ does not belong to him" (Rom. 8:9). In spite of the false professions, unbelief, and lies of apostates, God knows his own, Christ knows his sheep, and the Spirit of adoption knows the children of God.[25] The covenant people of God are "a chosen race, a royal priesthood, a holy nation, a people for his own possession" (1 Pet. 2:9). The glorious new covenant does not look to the old for its pattern and people but stands on the eternal foundation of the covenant of redemption and comes to the elect as a covenant of grace, purchased, mediated, and eternally kept by "our great God and savior Jesus Christ who gave himself for us to redeem us from all lawlessness and to purify for himself a people" (Titus 2:14).

The Biblical-Theological Basis for Credobaptism

1. Redemptive history moves forward progressively, giving rise to new revelation.

Geerhardus Vos famously argued that we must view revelation as a progressive unfolding coinciding with the progressive unfolding of redemptive history itself. In other words, this progressive unfolding of redemptive history gives rise to new revelation. One of the primary applications of that point is that we must look at the various parts of Scripture in the specific context of their period of redemptive history. Thus the New Testament believer must be careful about how the Old Testament is read and even how the Gospels are read since they refer to a redemptive historical era prior to the one in which we now live.

2. The different epochs of redemptive history are governed by their own covenantal canons.

Meredith Kline continued this idea by relating it more specifically to

---

[25] Cf. 2 Tim. 2:19, John 10:27, Matt. 7:15-23, Rom. 8:16.

covenant documents. He argued that the Old Testament itself made up the covenant document of the old covenant. Likewise, the New Testament is the covenant document of the new covenant. Kline says:

> The Old and New Testaments, which respectively define and establish these two structures, will be clearly seen as two separate and distinct architectural models for the house of God in two quite separate and distinct stages of its history. The distinctiveness of the two community organizations brings out the individual integrity of the two Testaments which serve as community rules for the two orders. The Old and New Testaments are two discrete covenant polities, and since biblical canon is covenantal polity-canon, they are two discrete canons in series.[26]

Kline draws out some of the implications of this idea.

> The old covenant is not the new covenant. The form of government appointed in the old covenant is not the community polity for the church of the new covenant, its ritual legislation is not a directory for the church's cultic practice.[27]

Kline is not saying that the Old Testament is of no use for New Testament Christians. Instead, he is saying that as a defining covenant document that includes all of the pertinent sanctions and stipulations for the covenant, the new covenant people of God must look to the New Testament and not the Old Testament.[28]

As we will mention in a moment, this has obvious implications

---

[26] Meredith G. Kline, *The Structure of Biblical Authority* (Eugene, OR: Wipf & Stock, 1997), 98-99.

[27] Kline, *Structure*, 99.

[28] Michael Horton says essentially the same thing. "The new covenant is constituted by its own canon . . . the New Testament. . . . It has its own stipulations (both doctrines and commands) and sanctions (life and death)." Cf. Horton's *The Christian Faith* (Grand Rapids: Zondervan, 2011), 153. He goes on to say, "There can be no covenant without a canon or canon without a covenant. In fact, the covenant *is* the canon and vice versa" (155, emphasis his).

for baptism. Baptism is the sign of the new covenant. It is not a sign of the old covenant. To understand the correct administration of the sign of the new covenant, we must look to its own covenant document—the New Testament.

3. Positive law elements of different covenant-canons are restricted to their particular covenant-canons.

Richard Muller defines natural/moral law in this way: "the universal moral law either impressed by God upon the mind of all people or immediately discerned by the reason in its encounter with the order of nature."[29] Moral law endures throughout all of the covenants, but positive laws do not. A positive law may be generally defined as "something that is dependent on direct revelation for its obligation."[30] In other words, without some form of special revelation, we would not know of these positive laws and we would not be required to obey them. For example, the civil and ceremonial laws of the Old Testament are positive laws. There was no requirement placed on other nations to follow the same civil laws as Israel. These are not laws that are morally binding on all people in all places at all times. They are binding only for a particular people and for a particular time. This is because they are positive laws.[31]

---

[29] Muller, *Dictionary*, 174.

[30] From IRBS PT 600 lecture by Dr. James M. Renihan.

[31] This can be seen in the Sabbath command. The 4th commandment has both a moral and positive aspect to it. This was affirmed by the Synod of Dordt in their resolutions regarding the Sabbath:

1. "In the fourth Commandment of the divine law, part was ceremonial, part is moral."

2. "The rest of the seventh day after creation was ceremonial and its rigid observation peculiarly prescribed to the Jewish people."

3. "Moral in fact, because the fixed and enduring day of the worship of God is appointed, for as much rest as is necessary for the worship of God and holy meditation of him." (translation by R. Scott Clark, http://clark.wscal.edu/dortsabbath.php).

These theologians at the Synod of Dordt affirmed that the observance of a Sabbath rest, a one day in seven ceasing from all work and worshiping God was required by moral law. However, they also affirmed that the particular day upon which God is to be worshipped is a matter of positive (or ceremonial) law. In the

When it comes to positive laws we should not assume they are in effect unless rescinded. Positive laws, instead, end with the termination of the covenant in which they were given. Positive laws are given in a particular redemptive-historical setting and in a particular covenant document. Positive laws only apply to the covenantal context in which they are given. This is why we no longer are obligated to follow the ceremonial laws of the Old Testament.[32]

4. In order to understand a particular covenantal-canon's stipulations and sanctions we can look only to that particular covenant.

It follows that if different covenants have their own covenant canons and those covenant canons contain positive laws, then we should only look to those particular covenant-canon documents to understand their corresponding sanctions and stipulations. As Kline says, "The treaty canon that governs the church of the new covenant as a formal community is the New Testament alone."[33]

This point has the potential to be misunderstood. It does not say that the Old Testament has no bearing on the New Testament. We certainly do not want to suggest that. The Old and New Testaments do have a very intimate connection, but it is one of promise and fulfillment. Nevertheless, while there is unity between the Old and New Testaments, the fact remains that they are separate and distinct periods of redemptive history with separate and distinct covenant-canons. For this reason, when we want to understand the particular requirements of a particular covenant, we must look at that covenant's particular covenant document.

Patrick Fairbairn says:

It is implied that the revelations by prophecy, respecting the

---

Old Testament it was the seventh day of the week, but in the New Testament it is the first day of the week.

[32] Col. 2:16-17, "Therefore let no one pass judgment on you in questions of food and drink, or with regard to a festival or a new moon or a Sabbath. [17] These are a shadow of the things to come, but the substance belongs to Christ."

[33] Kline, *Structure,* 100.

gospel age and its realities, were necessarily defective as to clearness and precision, and are not capable of bearing so exact an interpretation, or yielding so explicit a meaning, in respect to the affairs of Christ's kingdom, as is conveyed by the writings of the New Testament. But such, precisely, is the result that was to be expected, from the place and calling of the Old Testament prophets . . . There cannot be a surer canon of interpretation, than that *everything which affects the constitution and destiny of the New Testament Church has its clearest determination in New Testament Scripture.*[34]

To summarize, our understanding of redemptive history, as articulated by men such as Vos, Owen, and Ridderbos, tells us that the redemptive-historical context in which Scripture is written *must* be taken into account when understanding that passage of Scripture. Kline and others have combined this with the idea of covenant and canon, showing that the Old Testament and New Testament are separate covenantal documents governing separate covenants. When understanding essential elements of a particular covenant, we must look to that covenant's own document to properly understand those essential covenantal elements.

5. **Circumcision is a positive law from the old covenant canon and thus applies only to that covenant except insofar as it acts as a type.**

Circumcision must be a positive law since it is neither commanded in the New Testament nor was it commanded prior to Abraham.[35]

6. **Baptism is a new covenant ordinance established by Christ through positive law. Our understanding for the carrying out of this requirement, therefore, is restricted to the covenantal-canon under which it was given.**

Baptism is a positive law since it is not commanded in the Old

---

[34] Fairbairn, *Interpretation of Prophecy*, 157-58, emphasis his.
[35] Cf. Gal. 5:6; Acts 7:8; 1 Cor. 7:19; Rom. 2:25-27.

Testament. The 2LCF 28.1 says "Baptism and the Lord's Supper are ordinances of positive and sovereign institution, appointed by the Lord Jesus, the only Lawgiver, to be continued in His church to the end of the world."

We should remind ourselves here that baptism is a key component of the covenant. As one of the two sacraments of the new covenant, it is not a minor point. It is precisely the type of thing for which you would want to look to the new covenant document. The new covenant document, the New Testament, ought to dictate how its own sacraments are administered.[36]

Furthermore, the regulative principle of worship necessitates that we look only to the explicitly prescribed way of administering baptism. The 2LCF (22.1), in almost identical language to the Westminster Confession of Faith (21.1) articulates this principle, "The acceptable way of worshipping the true God is instituted by himself, and so limited by his own revealed will, that he may not be worshipped according to . . . any other way not prescribed in the Holy Scriptures." Since the sacraments of baptism and the Lord's Supper are elements of worship, they too must fall under this criteria of the regulative principle. The administration of baptism must be limited by God's own revealed will according to the way prescribed in Scripture.[37] Since the baptism of infants is not prescribed in Scripture, it ought not to be done.

Compare this to what B. B. Warfield said:

It is true that there is no expressed command to baptize infants in the New Testament, no express record of the baptism of infants, and no passages so stringently implying it that we must infer from them that infants were baptized. If such warrant as this were necessary to justify the usage we should have to leave it incompletely justified. But the lack of this express warrant is something so far short of forbidding

---

[36] This is the same principle as is exercised with the Lord's Supper. While we acknowledge a typological connection between Passover and the Lord's Supper, our understanding of the observance of the Supper comes from the New Testament, not from the Old Testament observance of Passover.

[37] Cf. Fred A. Malone, *The Baptism of Disciples Alone* (Cape Coral, FL: Founders Press, 2003), xv.

the rite; and if the continuity of the church through all ages can be made good, the warrant for infant baptism is not to be sought in the New Testament but in the Old Testament when the church was instituted, and nothing short of an actual forbidding of it in the New Testament would warrant our omitting it now.[38]

While we certainly disagree with Warfield's conclusions that infant baptism may still be justified, we appreciate his admission that the New Testament itself does not adequately justify the practice of infant baptism. Warfield admits that it is necessary to rely on the teaching of the Old Testament to arrive at the practice of infant baptism. However, as we have shown, the nature of redemptive history, as well as the covenantal character of the New and Old Testament canons, shows that we need to look to the New Testament canon to understand this practice.

7. Proper weight must be given to the newness of the new covenant.

Speaking of the old and new covenants, Kline says:

They are of course, indissolubly bound to one another in organic spiritual-historic relationship. They both unfold the same principle of redemptive grace, moving forward to a common eternal goal in the city of God. The blessings of old and new orders derive from the very same works of satisfaction accomplished by the Christ of God, and where spiritual life is found in either order it is attributable to the creative action of the one and selfsame Spirit of Christ. According to the divine design the old is *provisional* and *preparatory* for the new, and by divine predisclosure the new is prophetically anticipated in the old. External event and institution in the old order were divinely fashioned to afford a systematic representation of the realities of the coming new order, so producing a type-antitype correlativity

---

[38] B. B Warfield, *Studies in Theology* (Grand Rapids: Baker, 2003), 399-400.

between the two covenants in which their unity is instructively articulated.[39]

When dealing with types we must acknowledge a basic and fundamental unity, yet not such as to ignore the typological and thus different character of the type. The Old Testament covenants do indeed reveal the new covenant, but in a progressive, typological way. The new covenant is further revealed by various steps throughout the Old Testament era, first in the *protevangelium*, and then throughout all of the Old Testament covenants. Just as the gospel was revealed step by step, so also is the new covenant because it is in essence the gospel.

This is basically what the 2LCF says in 7.3:

This covenant is revealed in the gospel; first of all to Adam in the promise of salvation by the seed of the woman, and afterwards by farther steps, until the full discovery thereof was completed in the New Testament.

This is also not far from what Vos says:

The successive stages of God's redemptive and revealing work in the pre-Christian era are measured by successive covenants, each introducing new forces and principles and each imparting to the ensuing period a distinctive character of its own. Thus the covenant-idea is an eminently historical idea, most intimately associated with the gradual unfolding of God's self-disclosure to His people.[40]

So, there is a basic unity which begins at the fall, well before Abraham ever appeared on the scene, as the various covenants in the Old Testament progressively and typologically reveal the new covenant which is made when Christ's blood is shed on the cross. But because the Old Testament covenants are types of the new covenant, we must recognize the discontinuity that also exists between them. This explains the language of Jeremiah 31 or Joel

---

[39] Kline, *Structure*, 98, emphasis added.
[40] Vos, *Redemptive History*, 192.

2:28-29.

> And it shall come to pass afterward, that I will pour out my
> Spirit on all flesh; your sons and your daughters shall
> prophesy, your old men shall dream dreams, and your
> young men shall see visions. [29] Even on the male and female
> servants in those days I will pour out my Spirit. (Joel 2:28-29)[41]

Proper weight must be given to the *newness* of the *new* covenant by
seeing it as something that has not yet come about from the
perspective of the Old Testament. This is not merely a scale in
which the new covenant is "more of the same." It is not merely
quantitatively different from the old covenant. It is something
qualitatively different. There will be terms that are present in the
new covenant that are not present when any Old Testament author
writes. Similarly, there are terms that will no longer be present in
the new covenant that are present in the old covenant.

When the Old Testament speaks of the new covenant, it speaks
of it as something future and as something truly different from
what is currently in place. The language of both Joel and Jeremiah
clearly indicates that things will be different in this future new
covenant from how they were in their day.

Again, Vos says this very well, "The revelation of the New
Covenant is not only better comparatively speaking; it is final and
eternal because delivered in a Son, than whom God could send no
higher revealer."[42] The most essential difference between the new
covenant and all the covenants of the Old Testament is that it is
made and sealed in the blood of Christ and it is revealed in Christ
(Heb. 9:15-16). For this reason, the new covenant is different in
substance from all the Old Testament covenants.

As Vos goes on to say, the new covenant is necessarily

---

[41] Jeremiah 31:33-34, "But this is the covenant that I will make with the house
of Israel after those days, declares the LORD: I will put my law within them, and I
will write it on their hearts. And I will be their God, and they shall be my
people. [34]And no longer shall each one teach his neighbor and each his brother,
saying, 'Know the LORD,' for they shall all know me, from the least of them to the
greatest, declares the LORD. For I will forgive their iniquity, and I will remember
their sin no more."

[42] Vos, *Redemptive History*, 194.

connected to the new age, the consummation. With the inauguration of the new covenant, the new age breaks forth into this current age. Vos says, "The New Covenant, then, coincides with the age to come; it brings the good things to come; it is incorporated into the eschatological scheme of thought."[43] If the new covenant truly coincides with the new age, we should not look back at the old covenant to understand this new covenant. Instead we should look forward to the consummation. True, we live in the "not yet." But it is just as true that we live in the "already." For these reasons, we must conclude that theologies that rely too heavily on the old covenant for their description and articulation of the new covenant demonstrate an under-realized eschatology. They do not give enough weight to the "already."

Thus the discipline of biblical theology, the study of redemptive history, and the nature of revelation teach us that we ought to treat the new covenant as different in substance from the Old Testament covenants.

8. **Furthermore, the New Testament treatment of the Old Testament Scripture as mystery, shadows, and types indicates that the New Testament must be the lens through which we view the Old Testament and not vice versa.**

Any Reformed theologian speaking of hermeneutics will agree that the New Testament is the lens through which we must interpret the Old Testament. Usually the famous saying attributed to Augustine is quoted, "The New is in the Old concealed; the Old is in the New revealed." So trying to understand the anti-type by looking at the type causes difficulties. It is difficult to know which aspects of the type are carried over into the anti-type and which aspects are to be cast aside.

The New Testament affirms the difficulty of understanding the Old Testament types. Paul has a well-developed theology of mystery.[44]

---

[43] Vos, *Redemptive History*, 195.

[44] Cf. Herman Ridderbos *Paul: An Outline of His Theology* (Grand Rapids: Eerdmans, 1977), 44-49.

the mystery hidden for ages and generations but now revealed to his saints. [27] To them God chose to make known how great among the Gentiles are the riches of the glory of this mystery, which is Christ in you, the hope of glory. (Col. 1:26-27)

making known to us the mystery of his will, according to his purpose, which he set forth in Christ [10] as a plan for the fullness of time, to unite all things in him, things in heaven and things on earth. (Eph. 1:9-10)

because of his own purpose and grace, which he gave us in Christ Jesus before the ages began, [10] and which now has been manifested through the appearing of our Savior Christ Jesus, who abolished death and brought life and immortality to light through the gospel. (2 Tim. 1:9-10)[45]

Ridderbos points out that this mystery now revealed has both "a noetic and a historical connotation."[46] So, there is both a greater understanding and new revelation (especially in the form of new redemptive historical events). If we follow Warfield in looking at the Old Testament as our basis for how we administer baptism, we violate this fundamental principle of hermeneutics.

Promise and Fulfillment

For our last point, we want to notice a couple of the elements of promise and fulfillment, of type and anti-type, that we find in the Old and New Testaments.

Ridderbos says:

God's people are those for whom Christ sheds his blood of

---

[45] Cf. Tit. 1:2-3, "in hope of eternal life, which God, who never lies, promised before the ages began [3]and at the proper time manifested in his word through the preaching with which I have been entrusted by the command of God our Savior."

[46] Ridderbos *Paul*, 46.

the covenant. They share in the remission of sins brought about by him and in the unbreakable communion with God in the new covenant that he has made possible . . . The rejection of Israel as God's people does not annihilate the idea of covenant, but imparts to it a *new*, or at least a *more definite content*. The particular character of grace and of communion with God is fully maintained. But the circle in which it is granted and where God's people are found, is no longer that of the empirical Israel, but it is that of those who are given remission of sins in Christ's death, and whose hearts have been renewed by the Holy Spirit.[47]

The point Ridderbos makes here is that a fundamental change has taken place from the old covenant to the new covenant. The people of God in the Old Testament were made up of an empirical people. Ridderbos explicitly speaks of a "new formation of God's people."[48] He recognizes that there is something very different about the people of God in the new covenant from the people of God in the old covenant. The people of God in the new covenant are characterized by faith, by remission of sins, and by regeneration. Ridderbos continues:

The special relation between God and Israel as his people is one of the foundations of the gospel . . . At the same time we have noticed a transition in this basic idea, in the sense that, by the side of and in the place of empirical Israel, those who believe the gospel are considered as the flock of the Lord, the seed of Abraham, and the children of the kingdom.[49]

Fairbairn says it this way:

The seed of Israel, as an elect people, placed under covenant with God, represented the company of an elect church, redeemed from the curse of sin, that they might live forever

---

[47] Herman Ridderbos, *The Coming of the Kingdom* (Philadelphia: P&R Publishing, 1976), 202, emphasis added.

[48] Ridderbos, *Kingdom*, 351.

[49] Ridderbos, *Kingdom*, 351-52.

in the favour and blessing of Heaven: and when the redemption came, the representation passed into reality.[50]

Ridderbos continues his argument by saying:

This result is of the greatest importance for the question under discussion. For this rejection of Israel and this new formation of God's people is not simply something of the eschatological future, but has already begun to be realized with the coming of Jesus.[51]

He goes on to say:

The *ekklesia* in all this is the people who in this great drama have been placed on the side of God in Christ by virtue of the divine election and covenant. They have been given the divine promise, have been brought to manifestation and gathered together by the preaching of the gospel, and will inherit the redemption of the kingdom now and in the great future . . . So there is no question of *basileia* and *ekklesia* as being identical.[52]

Let's pull together some of these strands. In the Old Testament, the old covenant was a type and shadow of the fullness to come. That fullness was shrouded in mystery and types waiting for its revelation in Christ. With the coming of Christ we now have that fullness. The external, typological elements of the old covenant are cast off. The mystery and shadows are gone. With the new covenant comes the in-breaking of the eschatological age in its "already-not yet" form. The old covenant people were naturally generated and marked by circumcision of the flesh. The new covenant people are Spiritually generated, thus circumcised in heart, the anti-type of circumcision. Thus, baptism should only be administered to those who are Spiritually born into the covenant. The only way prescribed in Scripture to evaluate if someone is in the covenant is by a

---

[50] Fairbairn, *Interpretation of Prophecy*, 267.
[51] Ridderbos, *Kingdom*, 352.
[52] Ridderbos, *Kingdom*, 354-55.

profession of faith. Upon profession of faith baptism is administered. This is precisely the pattern we see in the New Testament — baptism follows a profession of faith.[53]

This fits exactly with our understanding of covenant theology. All of those who are in the covenant have Christ as their federal head. The only way to be "in Christ" is to have the Holy Spirit (Rom. 8:9), and those who have the Spirit are those who have faith. All of this is rooted and grounded in the great covenant of redemption, the *pactum salutis*, where the Father covenanted with the Son to give him an elect people. Thus baptism as a sign of the covenant is administered only to those who make a profession of faith. It is an effectual means of grace for those who receive it in faith. Apart from faith it does nothing.

Conclusion

In closing we want to consider a quotation from Charles Hodge.

> The difficulty on this subject is that baptism from its very nature involves a profession of faith; it is the way in which by the ordinance of Christ, He is to be confessed before men; but infants are incapable of making such confession; therefore they are not the proper subjects of baptism. Or, to state the matter in another form: the sacraments belong to the members of the Church; but the Church is the company of believers; infants cannot exercise faith, therefore they are not members of the Church, and consequently ought not to be baptized. In order to justify the baptism of infants, we must attain and authenticate such an idea of Church as that it shall include the children of believing parents.[54]

Hodge recognizes that the doctrine of baptism itself excludes the

---

[53] Louis Berkhof says that the New Testament "points to faith as a prerequisite for baptism," *Systematic Theology* (East Peoria, IL: Versa Press Inc., 2005), 637. Cf. Acts 2:41; 10:44-48; 18:8.

[54] Charles Hodge, *Systematic Theology*, vol. 3 (Peabody, MA: Hendrickson, 2003), 546-47.

idea of baptizing infants, and so he resorts to defining the church in such a way that it may allow for this practice. However, as we have shown, the movement of redemptive history, the full revelation in Christ, the in-breaking of the eschatological age, the regulative principle, the nature of covenant, the nature of positive law, and the basic principles of biblical hermeneutics all show that this move by Hodge simply cannot be made. Instead we must recognize the newness of the new covenant in its fulfillment of the types and shadows of the Old Testament as well as in its connection to the consummation.

Chapter 11

The Belgic Confession and the True Church

W. Robert Godfrey[*]

Dr. James M. Renihan has been a distinguished servant of Christ as a minister, teacher, and scholar as well as a Christian husband and father. It has been a privilege for me to be his friend and colleague over many years and I am very pleased to join in this project to honor him. My choice of topics may seem a strange one: Does the Belgic Confession, as some claim, require its subscribers to confess that all Baptist churches are false churches? As one who subscribes the Belgic Confession, I want to understand the meaning of the Confession for my work and cooperation with others. Dr. Renihan, as a strong confessionalist himself, will also appreciate the value of this topic (even as it may cause him to smile). This question is important to our cooperation across confessional differences without compromise in our common commitment to Christ's truth and to our Reformation heritage.

The Belgic Confession (1561) has been the confession of faithful Dutch Reformed churches for over 450 years. The confession was written by the minister and missionary Guido De Bres during a time of great persecution of Reformed churches in the Netherlands. De Bres himself died a martyr at the hands of the Roman Catholic civil authorities in 1567. He wrote the Belgic Confession to distinguish clearly the teaching of the Reformed churches in the Netherlands both from the Roman Catholic Church and from the Anabaptist churches there.

The Belgic Confession has a strong and detailed doctrine of the church which reflects the Reformed conviction that the church was a central doctrinal concern and that the reform of the church according to the Bible was a key work of the Reformation. The

---

[*] W. Robert Godfrey, Ph.D., is President and Professor of Church History, Westminster Seminary California, Escondido, CA.

Roman Church had long insisted that it was the only true church and that membership in that church was necessary for salvation. The Reformers strongly rejected these claims of the Roman Church and indeed concluded that Rome was in fact a false church, not a true church.

John Calvin had developed a strong doctrine of the church in several of his writings, most notably the fourth book of his *Institutes of the Christian Religion* and in his treatise on "The Necessity of Reforming the Church." Calvin is also believed to have been the principal author of the Confession of the French Reformed Churches of 1559. In that Confession nine articles out of forty (namely Articles 25-33) are devoted to the doctrine of the church.

The French Confession of 1559 is an important source which De Bres used in writing the Belgic Confession. He followed closely the order and teaching of Calvin's Confession. While De Bres has six articles on the church in his confession (Articles 27-32), his teaching is more specific and detailed on some points, particularly on the marks of the true church. Calvin characteristically taught two marks (preaching and sacraments), whereas De Bres added the third mark of discipline.

De Bres' strong doctrine of the church at least in part reflected the particular ecclesiastical situation that he faced in the Netherlands. He wanted to make clear the differences between Rome and Reformed Christianity on the church. He wanted to show that the Reformed doctrine of the church was biblical and the Roman doctrine was of human invention.

De Bres also wanted to distinguish clearly between the Reformed and Dutch Anabaptists, who also claimed that their churches were the only true churches. The Dutch Anabaptist movement rejected infant baptism in the interests of a pure church composed of those who individually believed and were committed to living a righteous life separated from the world. These Anabaptists departed from the gospel of the Bible and the Reformation by making works foundational to justification. Among the Dutch Anabaptists some believed that the righteous standards of the law required a church to withdraw from the wicked world as much as possible, becoming pacifists and refusing any involvement with ordinary civil governments. Others wanted violently to overthrow the civil government to establish a kingdom of righteousness now on earth. (Hence the language of Belgic Confession, Article 36, "Wherefore we detest the error of the Anabaptists and other seditious people . . .") Today the violent wing of Anabaptism has disappeared, but in the sixteenth century it was the wing that non-Anabaptists saw as the dominant and most characteristic group. Lutherans and Reformed wanted strongly to dissociate themselves from this violent and dangerous movement.

The character of Dutch Anabaptism as understood by De Bres becomes clear in the three explicit references to it in the Confession. The first is in Article 18 on "The Incarnation of Jesus Christ," where De Bres wrote: ". . . we confess (in opposition to the heresy of the Anabaptists, who deny that Christ assumed human flesh of His mother) . . ." Menno Simons' novel doctrine of the celestial flesh of Christ is here sharply rejected as a heresy against catholic Christology. The second reference is in Article 34 on "Holy Baptism": "we detest the error of the Anabaptists, who are not content with the one only baptism they have once received, and moreover condemn the baptism of the infants of believers . . ." This error (not heresy!) leads to the terrible conclusion that most Christians are not baptized at all. The third reference is in Article 36, "The Magistracy":

> we detest the error of the Anabaptists and other seditious people, and in general all those who reject the higher powers and magistrates and would subvert justice, introduce community of goods, and confound that decency and good order which God has established among men.

Here De Bres rejects the doctrine and practice of all those who undermine proper social order through their sedition. This picture of Anabaptism shows how far removed that movement is from the character of confessional Baptist churches which embrace historic catholic Christology and eschew sedition.

The Belgic Confession begins its discussion of the church with an examination of the basic character of the church: Article 27, "Of the Catholic Church."[1] This article focuses on the essence of what the church is. The church is an "assembly of true Christian believers, expecting all their salvation in Jesus Christ, being washed by his blood, sanctified and sealed by the Holy Ghost." The heart of this definition is that the church is the gathering of those who are truly saved in Christ.

We should also note that here and throughout the Confession the focus is on the church in terms of local congregations. The assembly of believers, the offices of minister, elder, and deacon (Article 30), and the marks of preaching, sacraments, and discipline (Article 29) are all elements in the first place of the local church, as established by God in his Word. The church is not a church of popes, bishops, and priests as Rome taught or a church of prophets as some Dutch Anabaptists taught. Rather, it is preeminently a congregation of the faithful.

Article 28, "Of the Communion of the Saints with the True Church," addresses the vital and necessary relationship of Christians to the church. Christians are not to live in isolation from one another, but must be part of the life of a true church of Christ. Confessional Reformed Baptists would heartily agree with the understanding of the church stated in Articles 27 and 28 of the Belgic Confession.

Since connection with the true church is so important, Article 29, "On the Marks of the Church," tells Christians how they may recognize the true church among the many groups that claim that name. Article 30, "On the Government of the Church," states how according to the Word of God the church is to be governed through ministers, elders, and deacons. Article 31, "On the Calling of Ministers," shows how ministers, elders, and deacons are to be chosen by election and honored in the church. Finally Article 32, "On the Power of the Church in Establishing Ecclesiastical Laws and in Administering Discipline," shows the extent and limits of the power of the church in directing its own life under the Word of God.

The discussion of the true church and how to recognize it is most fully addressed in Article 29. This article, which is at the center of the concern of this study, makes several points. The first is that

---

[1] The titles of the articles cited in this essay are not the standard English ones, but are my translation of the Latin titles in Philip Schaff's *Creeds of Christendom*.

the true church must be discerned from the teaching of the Word of God because many claim the title of church which are not faithful to the Scriptures. Here the claims of popes and Anabaptist prophets are implicitly rejected. Second, while the true church will have hypocrites in it, it remains distinct from all sects. By sects here the Confession seems to reject groups that have excessive, non-biblical claims of moral purity for their adherents. Third, the article lists three marks by which Christians can identify the true church: "if the pure doctrine of the gospel is preached therein; if she maintains the pure administration of the sacraments as instituted by Christ; if church discipline is exercised in punishing sin . . ." Fourth, the article summarizes the three marks in terms of adherence to the teaching of the Word of God alone and recognition that Jesus is the only head of the church: "in short, if all things are managed according to the pure Word of God, all things contrary thereto rejected, and Jesus Christ acknowledged as the only Head of the Church." Fifth, to aid Christians in identifying the true church, Article 29 notes the marks of Christians who will be found in the true church. Christians are those who believe in Christ as their savior, pursue righteousness, repent of the infirmity that clings to them, and seek refuge in Jesus. Sixth, the three marks of the false church are presented in contrast to the three marks of the true church:

> she ascribes more power and authority to herself and her ordinances than to the Word of God, and will not submit to the yoke of Christ. Neither does she administer the Sacraments, as appointed by Christ in his Word, but adds to and takes from them as she thinks proper; she relieth more upon men than upon Christ; and persecutes those who live holily according to the Word of God, and rebuke her for her errors, covetousness, and idolatry.

And finally, this article assures us that the true church and the false church are easily distinguished from one another.

Some in reading Article 29 have suggested that the article means to distinguish sects from false churches. I believe that this reading of the article is wrong. The terms are used largely synonymously. The true church is contrasted with "all sects" which claim the name church and Christians are called upon to distinguish the true church from the sects. This same word, distinguish, is used at the end of the article when Christians are told that it is easy to distinguish the true church from the false church. No distinct definition or characteristic of a sect over against a false church is given in the article. Clearly sect and false church are simply used interchangeably.

In reflecting on the Confession's teaching on the marks of the true church some Christians have understandably asked if the Belgic Confession intends to label all Baptist churches as false churches since they deny the sacrament of baptism to the children of believers. Clearly at least some Baptist churches preach the gospel faithfully and practice biblical discipline. If "the pure administration of the sacraments" is a mark of the true church, however, must it not follow that Baptist churches are not true churches? In its most pointed form, the question, as we noted at the beginning of this essay, is this: Does the Belgic Confession require its subscribers to confess that all Baptist churches are not true churches?

This is an important question. It is important for Reformed Christians and churches that want to be fully confessional. And it is important as Reformed Christians seek to communicate honestly and lovingly with Baptist friends. To answer this question we must examine the historical setting and doctrinal teaching of the Belgic Confession very carefully. Although the conclusion that all Baptist churches are false churches may seem inevitable and unavoidable, in fact it is not. Indeed, reflection on the doctrinal teaching and historical setting of the Belgic Confession leads to quite a different conclusion.

Let us look more carefully at the marks. First, we can notice that three times the word "pure" is used in Article 29. The French word in the original text of the Confession [*pure*] means pure, unmingled, unalloyed or unadulterated. It does not mean absolutely perfect, but rather genuine. The preaching of the gospel, the administration of the sacraments, and the practice of discipline in the true church are not always perfect.

If we focus on the mark of the sacraments, history shows us that the confessionally Reformed did not believe that the Lutheran doctrine of the Lord's Supper was perfect, but they did believe that the Lutheran churches were true churches. Indeed, the Zwinglian doctrine of the eucharist is not perfect (and probably cannot be conformed to the high Calvinist eucharistic theology in the Belgic Confession), but the Reformed always acknowledged that the Reformed church of Zurich was a true church. The Dutch Reformed invited that true Reformed church to the Synod of Dort in 1618. Also, the great Reformed scholastic theologian of seventeenth-century Geneva, Francis Turretin, indicated clearly that he regarded Lutheran and Zwinglian churches as true churches in his *Institutes of Elenctic Theology*, Eighteenth Topic, "The Church," specifically in the Tenth Question, "Where was our church before Luther and Zwingli, and how was it preserved?"[2]

We can make a similar point in looking at the discussion of the government of the church in Article 30. That article states:

> We believe that this true Church must be governed by the spiritual policy which our Lord has taught us in his Word — namely, that there must be Ministers or Pastors to preach the Word of God, and to administer the Sacraments; also elders and deacons, who, together, with the pastors, form the council of the Church . . .

But Lutheran and Anglican churches did not follow this polity, the Lutherans neglecting the office of elder and the Anglicans adding the office of bishop. Yet they were recognized as true churches. Anglican church leaders served as members of the Synod of Dort as representatives of a true Reformed church and one Anglican bishop was a very influential member of the Synod. And at the Synod of Dort the Anglican church approved the Belgic Confession, except what it taught about church government!

Are we being unfair to Baptists to suggest that they are not true churches, when we recognize Lutheran, Anglican, and Zwinglian churches as true churches? Or are we being inconsistent and in the name of confessional consistency should label them all false churches? If we choose the latter option, we must recognize that we

---

[2] Francis Turretin, *Institutes of Elenctic Theology*, ed. James T. Dennison Jr., trans. George Musgrave Giger, vol. 3 (Phillipsburg, NJ: P&R Publishing, 1997), XVIII.9.10.

The Belgic Confession and the True Church

are going against the interpretation of the Belgic Confession that the Dutch Reformed churches have always held. The historical evidence should encourage us to consider being as inclusive of the Baptists as of others.

Some may wonder, however, whether the Confession's explicit rejection of Anabaptist views does not mean that it regards the Baptist churches as false churches. Such a conclusion would be entirely a-historical. The Baptist churches today are not descended from the Anabaptist churches of the sixteenth century. Rather, they are largely churches that developed out of Reformed churches in the seventeenth century from a conviction that believer's baptism was more faithful to the Bible. Baptists are not Anabaptists historically and it is anachronistic to believe that the Confession speaks explicitly about Baptists.

In rejecting the idea that the confession teaches that Baptist churches are not true churches, we do not rely only on historical evidence, however. The theology of the marks of the true church in the Belgic Confession itself also makes that point doctrinally.

The three marks of the true church are not expressed simply in abstract terms. These marks are not only presented positively in Article 29, but are also contrasted with the three marks of the false church. We understand the meaning of the marks of the true church fully only when we see them contrasted with the marks of the false church. The first mark of the true church is that "the pure doctrine of the gospel is preached therein . . ." That mark is contrasted and explained in relation to the first mark of the false church: "she ascribes more power and authority to herself and her ordinances than to the Word of God, and will not submit herself to the yoke of Christ." The false church adds her own ordinances to the gospel by her authority and therefore does not accept the pure gospel of Christ given in the Scriptures.

The third mark of the true church is this: "church discipline is exercised in punishing sin . . ." By contrast, the false church's third mark is that it "relieth more upon men than upon Christ; and persecutes those who live holily according to the Word of God, and rebuke her for her errors, covetousness, and idolatry." The false church, far from punishing sin, persecutes those who live holy lives and critique sin.

Also on the second mark the marks of the true and false churches illumine one another. The true church "maintains the pure administration of the sacraments as instituted by Christ . . ." The false church, by contrast, does not "administer the Sacraments, as appointed by Christ in his Word, but adds to and takes from them as she thinks proper . . ." Failure to rightly administer the sacraments is especially where the Word of God is violated in increasing or decreasing the biblical number of sacraments. Twice in Article 29, in both the marks of the true church and the marks of the false church, reference is made to the sacraments instituted [*ordonnes*] by Christ. In Article 33, "Of the Sacraments," we read: "Moreoever, we are satisfied with the number of Sacraments which Christ our Lord hath instituted [*ordonnes*], which are two only . . ." A primary concern about the pure administration of the sacraments is that only the two instituted by Christ be used in the church. Rome had seven sacraments and many Anabaptist churches had three (including footwashing). Baptist churches do maintain the two sacraments instituted by Christ, seek to understand them only according to the Word of God, and therefore do meet the most stressed elements of the second mark of the true church.

Both the history of Dutch Reformed thought and practice as well as the doctrinal statements of the Belgic Confession themselves then lead to the conclusion that the Confession does not require its adherents to declare that all Baptist churches are false churches. Indeed the best reading of the Confession leads to the opposite conclusion.

The Belgic Confession is indeed sharply critical of Anabaptists for rejecting infant baptism. As cited above, Article 34 declared, "Therefore we detest the error of the Anabaptists, who are not content with the one only baptism they have once received, and moreover condemn the baptism of infants of believers . . ." But this sharp language shows that the Confession regards the rejection of infant baptism as a serious error, not as a heresy. Certainly the Confession does not state that a church which denies infant baptism is a false church.

If we conclude that at least some Baptist churches are true churches, does that mean that they are perfect churches or that we may not criticize anything in their doctrine or practice? Not at all.

We do not claim that true churches are perfect churches in doctrine or life. Churches in the Reformed and Presbyterian family of churches do not agree on all points and have been known to criticize one another. For example, some Reformed churches have only sung psalms while others have sung psalms and hymns. This difference has been serious and intensely debated. Each side in the debate has believed that its practice was more biblical than that of the other side, but has not led to the conclusion that either side was no longer a part of the true church.

In recognition of these realities the Westminster Confession of Faith (25.4) states that visible true churches

> are more or less pure, according as the doctrine of the gospel is taught and embraced, ordinances administered, and public worship performed more or less purely in them.

The distinction between more pure and less pure true churches is not a distinction found in the Belgic Confession. But it is not a distinction rejected by the Belgic Confession, or incompatible with it. Not all truths are stated explicitly in the Confession.

Indeed, this distinction between more pure and less pure true churches is necessary for sound theology. If this distinction is rejected, we must say either that only one denomination and its practices manifest the true church or that all differences among true churches are matters of indifference. The former position is sectarian and the latter is latitudinarian. Neither is taught by any of the Reformed confessions or has ever been held by sound Reformed churches.

If the language of the Confession were pressed in such a radical way as to suggest that all Baptist churches are false churches, one would logically be forced by the language of the Confession to conclude that no Baptists are Christians. The Belgic Confession, Article 28, declares that "out of it [the true church] there is no salvation." Does the Confession then force us to the conclusion that no Baptists are saved? Such a conclusion is absurd, unbiblical, and contrary to the explicit teaching of the Confession. Certainly there are Baptists that exhibit the marks of true Christians described in Article 29.

In any case, the statement about no salvation outside the church was originally made by Cyprian in the ancient church period, and is cited by De Bres to demonstrate the importance of the church for the Reformed and the continuity of Reformed thought with the ancient church. This statement was certainly not meant absolutely. Christians had always recognized that the thief on the cross, although not baptized or a member of the church, had been saved. Also the Reformers believed that there were true Christians in the Roman church. We must not press the language of the Confession to theological conclusions not made or intended by the Confession itself.

In our eagerness to exalt and defend the truths and glories of Reformed Christianity we must avoid an arrogant or triumphalist confessionalism. We need to communicate clearly and charitably. We ought to seek to attract people to our biblical convictions and to give them time to grow into those convictions. To say that all Baptist churches are false churches is not consistent with our confession and is unnecessarily offensive. It is contrary to Christian charity and doctrinal consistency. Let us uphold the importance of the true church and of true Christianity without impugning the churches and Christianity of those Baptists with whom we recognize a common faith in so many ways.

Personally, I look forward to continuing to work with Dr. Renihan to advance the cause of Christ, and from time to time looking into the Scriptures with him to study the doctrine of baptism. Both of us want to reject all human inventions on the matter of baptism and both of us want to submit to the Bible's teaching alone. Only turning again and again to study the Bible on these matters will lead us to greater clarity and unity. And only in this return to his Word do we together honor our Christ.

Chapter 12

A Practical Scholasticism?

Edward Leigh's Theological Method

James E. Dolezal[*]

Can scholastic theology be practical? Debate over this issue has persisted for centuries and has not been an insignificant question within recent Reformation and post-Reformation historiography. Some historians assert that the first two generations of Protestant Reformers were primarily concerned with the religion of the heart whereas the post-Reformation theologians (beginning roughly in the 1560s) shifted the focus of divinity away from the heart and toward the intellect.[1] The post-Reformation appropriation of scholasticism is said to be in conflict with the humanism seen in the Reformers. Hence, Brian Armstrong, a proponent of this thesis, asserts that by 1660

> the major part of international Calvinism had replaced with a quite different theological expression and spirit the humanistic orientation which characterized most of the early reform movements. The phenomenon many have called Protestant scholasticism had set in.[2]

Clearly humanism and scholasticism have been assumed to be fundamentally at odds in this perspective.

---

[*] James E. Dolezal, Ph.D., is Assistant Professor of Theology, Cairn University and author of *God without Parts: Divine Simplicity and the Metaphysics of God's Absoluteness*. This essay originally appeared in *Westminster Theolgical Journal* vol. 71, no. 2 (Fall 2009): 337-54, and is used with permission.

[1] Representatives of this perspective include R. T. Kendall, Alister McGrath, and Brian Armstrong.

[2] Brian G. Armstrong, *Calvinism and the Amyraut Heresy: Protestant Scholasticism and Humanism in Seventeenth-Century France* (Madison, WI: The University of Wisconsin Press, 1969), 31.

Armstrong, while acknowledging the difficulty of precisely defining Protestant scholasticism, suggests that it has four identifiable tendencies. First, it tends to assert religious truth on the basis of deductive ratiocination from assumed principles. It relates to medieval scholasticism in that it shares the same commitment to Aristotelian philosophy. Second, it elevates reason in religious matters to at least an equal standing with faith, and so subverts the authority of revelation. Third, it embraces the notion that Scripture contains a unified and rationally understandable system of doctrine that can be formed into a statement so definitive as to be the measure of orthodoxy. Fourth, it manifests a "pronounced interest in metaphysical matters, in abstract, speculative thought, particularly with reference to the doctrine of God."[3] Indeed, this "rationalistic" approach is thought to represent "a profound divergence from the humanistically oriented religion of John Calvin and most of the early reformers."[4]

This carving up of the Reformed tradition that reads Calvin as a humanist fundamentally opposed to the seventeenth-century scholastic Calvinists has not gone unchallenged.[5] This article aims to nuance one dimension of the challenge by asking if the scholastic method of theology, as developed among the seventeenth-century Reformed orthodox, was inherently impractical and opposed to the religion of the heart. Inasmuch as a full answer to that question would demand extensive interaction with a host of international theologians and sources, a case study of a particular work seems to be an appropriate starting point. Thus, this study will examine the theoretico-practica construction of Edward Leigh's theology as contained in his *A Systeme or Body of Divinity* (1662), with a particular focus on his treatment of God's simplicity. Protestant

---

[3] Armstrong, *Calvinism*, 32.

[4] Armstrong, *Calvinism*, 32.

[5] It is beyond the scope of this article to go into a detailed critique of the humanism-versus-scholasticism approach to the history of the Reformed tradition. For a historiographical critique of this tendency to oppose Calvin and the Calvinists see Richard A. Muller, *After Calvin: Studies in the Development of a Theological Tradition* (Oxford: Oxford University Press, 2003); Carl R. Trueman, "Calvin and Calvinism," in *The Cambridge Companion to John Calvin*, ed. Donald K. McKim (Cambridge: Cambridge University Press, 2004), 225-44; Paul Helm, *Calvin and the Calvinists* (Edinburgh: Banner of Truth Trust, 1998).

scholastics, such as Leigh, have often been accused of being especially speculative and non-practical in their handling of theology proper. Before examining Leigh's theological method and treatment of divine simplicity, a brief biographical sketch is in order.

Edward Leigh's Education, Career, and Writings

Edward Leigh (1603-1671) was born into a wealthy family with all provisions made for a liberal education.[6] His upbringing was notable for its "fervent puritanism," owing much to his stepmother and to his university tutor at Oxford, William Pemble. Leigh undertook a double apprenticeship, first at Magdalen Hall, Oxford (gaining both his BA and MA in 1620 and 1623, respectively), and then at Middle Temple where he studied law.

His public career was somewhat varied and colorful. He served as a Justice of the Peace of the county of Staffordshire intermittently from 1641 to 1645. He also joined the parliamentary army as officer of an infantry regiment in 1643. In 1645 he was elected to Parliament as an MP representing Stafford. As an MP he was especially engaged in ecclesiastical matters, serving on the committee for plundered ministers in 1646 and as a visitor for the regulation of Oxford University in 1647. In 1646 he was elected to the Westminster Assembly of divines to serve as a teller and subscribed to the Solemn League and Covenant, though he apparently preferred the primitive Episcopal form of government.[7] He was ejected from Parliament in Pride's Purge in 1648, returning briefly to serve on the restored Rump Parliament after the fall of the protectorate. Though he endorsed the restoration of Charles II in 1660, he became increasingly disenchanted with him and spent the final decade of his life in "a way of retirement."

Leigh's writing career is even more varied than his public

---

[6] John Sutton, "Leigh, Edward," in *Oxford Dictionary of National Biography*, ed. H. C. G. Matthew and Brian Harrison, 60 vols. (Oxford: Oxford University Press, 2004), 33:233-34. All biographical information on Leigh is taken from this source unless otherwise noted.

[7] Leigh suggests that he agrees with Richard Baxter on this matter. See Edward

career. He was something of a polymath, publishing two tomes on philology (a definitive lexicon of Greek and Hebrew words and a philological commentary on legal terms), two books on history (on the Roman and Greek emperors and on the history of England's kings), a book on the court system, a volume on educational curriculum, another on England's topography, and another on foreign travel, money, and the measurement of distance. In addition to these he also published various works of divinity including *Treatise of the Divine Promises* (1633), *The Saints Encouragement in Evil Times* (1648), *Annotations on Five Poetical Books of the Old Testament* (1657), and *A Systeme or Body of Divinity* (1662). Though not an ordained minister, Leigh would certainly fit the criteria that Herman Witsius envisioned for ministers: possession of a breadth of culture and learning. Leigh was "habituated to the reverent observation of nature, learned in history and languages, [and] well versed in the arts and in the skills of communication."[8] The latter may be assumed on account of his success both as a JP and MP.

Leigh's *Systeme or Body of Divinity*

Many seventeenth-century Protestant scholastics published works in non-scholastic genres in addition to their scholastic contributions.[9] Sutton observes that biblical exegesis was the leitmotif of most of Leigh's publications.[10] As we turn our attention to Leigh's great scholastic and systematic work of theology, it should be noted that

---

Leigh, *A Systeme or Body of Divinity* (London: William Lee, 1662), "To the Reader" (4). All page numbers appearing in parentheses are supplied by the present writer in that the pages are unnumbered in the original. It is not entirely clear whether Baxter was a Presbyterian or Episcopalian. Generally the scholarship concludes that he held to a primitive form of episcopacy. We may safely assume that Leigh held to the same, though he speaks very highly of Presbyterianism. See Ibid., 645-55. Cf. Irvonwy Morgan, *The Nonconformity of Richard Baxter* (London: The Epworth Press, 1946), 124-30.

[8] Muller, *After Calvin*, 117. In context Muller is giving a summary description of what the Reformed scholastic minister was expected to be. Leigh fits the expectation of the learned clergyman quite well.

[9] Muller, *After Calvin*, 77. Muller notes genres such as exegetical, catechetical, positive (non-disputative), and ascetic.

[10] *Oxford Dictionary of National Biography*, 33:233.

he also wrote a biblical commentary, a history of Christian martyrs, and a book on divine promises. This breadth of emphasis itself defies the caricature of a relentlessly rationalistic ecclesiastic.

The *Systeme* was expanded through four editions. The work grew from three books (132 pages) in 1646 to 10 books (1179 pages) by 1662, with the final edition comprising what may arguably have been the most complete and proper systematic theology in the English language at the time of its publication.[11] It bears a certain resemblance to other English works of divinity including William Perkins's *Golden Chaine* (1592), William Ames's *Marrow of Theology* (1623), and John Downame's *The Summe of Sacred Divinitie* (c. 1630). But Leigh's *loci* method is more explicit than that of his predecessors.[12] Also, the positive utilization of medieval scholastic sources is more conspicuous in Leigh than in his English forerunners. Does this not lend credence to the assertion that Protestant scholasticism became increasingly rationalistic and non-practical? Is not scholastic divinity fundamentally opposed to practical divinity as some recent historians have concluded? By considering Leigh's theological method and its implementation in his doctrine of God it will be shown that Protestant scholastic theology was not inherently adverse to practical divinity.

---

[11] A "faithfull Friend and Servant," denominated only as "T. B." (whom we may presume to be Thomas Barlow), prefixed the following sentiments to Leigh's *Systeme*: "I Have seriously read a good part of your Book, and am very well pleased both with the Matter and Method of it, and doubt not but it will be of exceeding great use for all that would be Protestants by Advice, and not by Chance; all that would examine, and be satisfied in the Grounds and Foundations of their Religion; indeed it will be for poore Divines (as I fear too many are like to be) rather a little Library, than a single Book, seeing they may have in it so many and so pertinent Proofs and Quotations put orderly in a readinesse for them." In Leigh, *Systeme*, following "To the Reader" (page unnumbered in original).

[12] He lays out the topics of his ten books as follows: (1) Scripture, (2) God (existence, essence, & triunity), (3) works of God, (4) the fall and sin, (5) salvation (recovery by Christ), (6) ecclesiology (and Antichrist), (7) union with Christ (Holy Spirit), (8) the ordinances (esp. baptism), (9) the Decalogue, and (10) glorification. Edward Leigh, *Systeme*, "To the Reader" (2-4). Muller maintains that the use of the *locus* method indicates an interrelationship between humanism and scholasticism. Muller, *After Calvin*, 73.

Edward Leigh's Method of Theology

1. Leigh's motives for composing his *Systeme* in the scholastic method

We have noted that Leigh's theology was scholastic.[13] Various motivations impelled the seventeenth-century Reformed theologians to adopt this method. Muller explains:

> . . . the rise of scholastic, confessional orthodoxy in the Reformed and Lutheran churches related both to polemical and pedagogical needs and, in the specific development of large scale theological systems, to the need for a detailed working-out of theological and philosophical problems raised or posed by the Reformation. Those needs . . . all relate to the broader task of the full appropriation of the substance of the catholic tradition and the identification of an institutional Protestant church as the church catholic.[14]

The Reformers did not intend to dispense with the theological traditions of the medieval church. Indeed, their criticisms of medieval scholasticism cannot be read as refutations of the scholastic method as such, but as what they perceived to be the aimless speculation of so many medieval theologians. In one sense, Protestantism needed time to articulate itself in relation to the catholic theological tradition as a whole. By the seventeenth century the general conclusion of Reformed theologians was that Protestantism stood firmly within the trajectory of the best of medieval theology.

Edward Leigh is certainly conscious of the need for Protantism to extensively articulate its doctrinal continuities and

---

[13] Muller offers the following definition of scholasticism: "In the standard scholarly definitions, 'scholasticism' does not refer to a particular theology or philosophy but to a *method* developed in the medieval schools in order to facilitate academic argument, specifically argument leading to the resolution of objections, the identification and use of distinctions, and the establishment of right conclusions." Muller, *After Calvin*, 75.

[14] Muller, *After Calvin*, 74.

discontinuities with the medieval tradition. He seeks to establish a Reformed catholicity as a Protestant answer to the Roman system. Consider his challenge: "Shall the Jesuitical and heretical party be so active for Popery, for errour, and shall not the Orthodox be as studious to hold fast and hold forth the Truth?"[15] There is a concern that Protestantism must oppose Rome by being equally comprehensive and scholarly in its theology. This expression, "as studious," sets the tone for Leigh's own method in his *Systeme*. He attempts to match the Papists in scholastic rigor, both in breadth and depth. Robust opposition warrants robust defense.

The system offered by Leigh may certainly be read as both a positive and negative (or polemical) piece of work. Positively, it aims to set out the Reformed faith in a full-bodied and detailed manner. In doing so Leigh demonstrates a great deal of continuity with the medieval scholastic method and doctrine. Muller calls this a "catholicizing tendency."[16] Protestantism is not to be defined merely by what it opposes, but also by what it teaches on every head of doctrine. Negatively, Leigh's *Systeme* is an attempt to displace Roman error with truth. It should be noted, however, that Leigh's approach is not overtly polemical.

Another reason that Leigh gives for writing his *Systeme* is to fill a gap in the English literature. He notes the paucity of English writers who had produced a complete system of doctrine:

> There are Calvins *Institutions*, Bullingers *Decads*, Zanchies *Works*, Gerhards *Common-places*, Ursins *Summe of Divinity*, and some others that have more fully handled the Body of Divinity, but there are fewer of our English Writers (unlesse Mr. Perkins of old, and B. Usher lately) who have largely and fully written in English this way.[17]

Leigh conceives his treatise as offering the Church of England a full-bodied Reformed system of theology in accord with the Westminster Confession of Faith.[18] By 1662 the need for this sort of

---

[15] Leigh, *Systeme*, "Epistle Dedicatory" (6).

[16] Muller, *After Calvin*, 145. Though Muller says this in relation to Turretin's *Institutes of Elenctic Theology* (1679-1685), it is equally relevant to Leigh's *Systeme*.

[17] Leigh, *Systeme*, "To the Reader" (1).

system would have been keenly felt in England inasmuch as the fear of a Roman takeover of the country was at a fever pitch.[19] English clergymen needed to have a firm grasp on their ecclesiastical credentials as Protestants in order to thwart this threat. This necessitated having a complete system of divinity that could match the traditional Roman theologies and establish a reasonable measure of continuity with the catholic tradition. So much for Leigh's historical motivations; we turn now to consider the purpose and method of his theology.

2. The purpose of theology

Before proceeding with the study of divinity it is crucial to grasp the object and goals involved. For Leigh the object and goal of theology are bound together. He writes, "Christians must chiefly study to know God."[20] By identifying God as the proper object of theology, Leigh locates himself squarely in the medieval and Reformed tradition. Muller suggests that, "Formal identification of the object or subject matter of theology by the Protestant scholastics, like their discussion of archetypal and ectypal theology, looks back to medieval models through the glass of the Reformation."[21] Francis Turretin, writing less than two decades after Leigh, explains what is meant by "object": "The object of any science is everything specially treated of in it, and to which all its conclusions relate."[22] Of the

---

[18] Numerous references to the Westminster Confession of Faith can be found throughout the *Systeme*.

[19] Charles II, suspected by many of a covert commitment to Romanism, had been restored in 1660. Leigh expresses earnest desire that the Reformed Churches in England not be weakened by their divisions and thus "accomplish their enemies great design." The enemy in this case was Rome. The Protestants needed doctrinal solidarity lest the Jesuits succeed in a takeover of England. For a clear indication of Leigh's anti-Roman agenda see *Systeme*, "The Epistle Dedicatory" (5-6).

[20] Leigh, *Systeme*, "To the Reader" (2).

[21] Richard A. Muller, *Post-Reformation Reformed Dogmatics*, 4 vols. (Grand Rapids: Baker Academic, 2003), 1:313-14. For Leigh's identification of the archetypal and ectypal distinctions in theology see *Systeme*, 2.

[22] Francis Turretin, *Institutes of Elenctic Theology*, ed. James T. Dennison, Jr., trans. George Musgrave Giger, 3 vols. (Phillipsburg, NJ: P&R Publishing, 1992-1997), I.5.1.

study of divinity he adds:

> Although theologians differ as to the object of theology, the
> more common and true opinion is that of those who refer it
> to God and divine things . . . i.e., God directly and indirectly
> (viz. God and the things of him . . . and subject to him . . .
> and tending to him . . .). Thus that all things are discussed in
> theology either because they deal with God himself or have
> a relation (*schesin*) to him as the first principle and ultimate
> end.[23]

Similarly, Leigh asserts that "God and his works are the matter or
parts of Divinity."[24] There is nothing original in this statement;
indeed, this was the common commitment of the catholic tradition,
both Roman and Protestant.

Among the Protestants this notion is expressed prior to Leigh in
William Perkins' *Golden Chaine*: "*Theologie* hath two parts: the first of
God, the second of his workes."[25] For both Perkins and Leigh the
study of God's works is still a way, though indirect, of coming to
know God himself. This identification of God and his works as the
object(s) of theology is in keeping with medieval catholic
scholasticism. For instance, Thomas Aquinas writes:

> Now all things are dealt with in holy teaching in terms of
> God, either because they are God himself or because they are
> relative to him as their origin and end. Therefore God is
> truly the object of this science.[26]

Though the foremost object of theology is God himself, the goal
of knowing God is not merely a striving after bare cognition.
Rather, God is also studied so that he might be obeyed and enjoyed.

---

[23] Turretin, *Institutes*, I.5.2.

[24] Leigh, *Systeme*, 144.

[25] William Perkins, *A Golden Chaine: or, The Description of Theology*, in *The Workes of That Famous and Worthy Minister of Christ in the Universitie of Cambridge, Mr. William Perkins*, 3 vols. (London: John Legatt, 1626), 1:11.

[26] Thomas Aquinas, *Summa Theologiae: Latin Text and English Translation, Introductions, Notes, Appendices and Glossaries*, ed. and trans. Thomas Gilby, vol. 1 (London and New York: Eyre & Spottiswoode and McGraw-Hill, 1964), 1a. 1, 7.

Thus, man's holiness and blessedness are also goals of the theological investigation. Leigh insists, "If God were more known, he would be more loved, feared, honoured, Trusted. God is *primum verum* which satisfies the understanding, and *summum bonum* which satisfies the will . . ."[27] Man's good is bound up with the study of God (or divinity). In fact, without the knowledge of God man cannot be happy. So Leigh states, including a reference to Ephesians 4:18, "To be ignorant of God is a great misery; *Being alienated from the life of God through the ignorance that is in them.* . . . Our welfare and happiness consists in the knowledge of God."[28]

This language of "happiness" echoes the answer to the first question of the Westminster Shorter Catechism, which affirms that the chief end of man is to glorify God and enjoy him forever. Thus Leigh maintains the goals of theology as being "first, the glory of God, the celebration or setting forth of God's infinite excellence, [and] second, man's blessedness."[29] Man's knowledge of God and the ensuing beatitude are to be directed ultimately to the glory of God as the chief end.[30] Still, salvation and eternal blessedness are listed by Leigh as the secondary goal.[31] There is a striking similarity between Leigh's expression of theology's aims and those of his Dutch contemporaries, Gisbertus Voetius and Herman Witsius. Writing of the latter two, Muller explains:

> Whatever the tools and categories or modes of approach to the materials of theology, theological study was viewed as having a single object, God and the Works of God, and as having a single goal, the glory of God in the salvation of believers.[32]

Leigh simply arranges the single goal of Voetius and Witsius as the primary and secondary aims of divinity. In this order of arrangement he follows an earlier Dutch theologian, Johannes

---

[27] Leigh, *Systeme*, "To the Reader" (2-3).
[28] Leigh, *Systeme*, 144.
[29] Leigh, *Systeme*, 5.
[30] Leigh, *Systeme*, 3.
[31] Leigh, *Systeme*, 3.
[32] Muller, *After Calvin*, 119.

Wollebius. Wollebius argues that since God is the primary object of theology he must also be its primary and final end. He adds, "A subordinate end of sacred theology is our salvation, which consists of communion with God, and enjoyment of him."[33] Leigh conceives the purpose of theology in the same way as his continental counterparts. Having considered the purpose of divinity, including its proper object and goals, the method of theology must still be explained. How should divinity proceed in order to attain these goals?

3. The character of theology

First, theology is theoretical and practical. Though Leigh's method is scholastic, the character of his theology is theoretical and practical in accordance with the purpose and goals discussed above. The terms "theory" (*theoria*) and "practice" (*praxis*) were well-defined by the Protestant scholastics. "Theory" did not mean mere rationalization, nor did "practice" indicate mere ethical action. The knowledge indicated by the term "theoretical" is not like the knowledge possessed in other sciences. God is not a set of facts or propositions to be known or discovered; rather he is to be the chief object of man's desire and should be beheld and admired for his own glory and worth (see below). This begins in part on earth, in a glass darkly, and is consummated in the eschatological knowledge of God. Medieval theologians characterized this consummate knowledge as the "vision of God" (*visio Dei*) or the "beatific vision" (*visio beatifica*). Except for beholding the resurrected Christ, this is not a vision of the eyes, but of the mind: "the *visio* is *cognition Dei clara et intuitive*, a clear and intuitive knowledge of God, an inward *actus intellectus et voluntatis*, or act of intellect and will."[34] This is the

---

[33] Johannes Wollebius, *Compendium Theologiae Christianae*, in *Reformed Dogmatics*, ed. and trans. John W. Beardslee III (New York: Oxford University Press, 1965), 35. Salvation entails beatitude. For Leigh, beatitude entails the *visio Dei*, which is to behold or contemplate God. This is an important point when asking what it means for theology to be practical.

[34] Richard A. Muller, *Dictionary of Latin and Greek Theological Terms: Drawn Principally from Protestant Scholastic Theology* (Grand Rapids: Baker Book House, 1985), 327.

final goal of theology.

But, as noted above, knowing God is not the only goal in divinity; love, fear, honor, and trust toward God are also theological aspirations. These practical aims are all aspects of salvation. Insofar as theology seeks the salvation of man it is practical: "since theology is a discipline taught and studied with an end in view, viz., the salvation of mankind, it can be called a *praxis*, i.e., a practical discipline."[35] So, Christian theology is at once theoretical (seeking the *visio Dei*, or *visio beatific*) and practical (seeking the salvation of men).

On the scholastic understanding of *theoria* and *praxis*, Muller offers the following description:

> The scholastics, both of the Middle Ages and the seventeenth century, understood both words in their basic etymological sense: *theoria* (from the Greek verb *theorein*, 'to look at') indicates something seen or beheld; *praxis* (from the Greek verb, *prassein*, 'to do') indicates something done or engaged in with an end in view. *Theoria*, then, is synonymous with *contemplation* or *speculation* and indicates the pure beholding of something. To the scholastic mind, this concept of a pure beholding, with no end in view other than the vision of the thing beheld, must be understood in terms of the *visio Dei* and the ultimate enjoyment of God (*fruitio Dei*) by man. *Praxis*, by contrast refers to an activity that leads toward an end: theology is understood as practical when it is understood as leading to a goal beyond itself, namely salvation, and is designed therefore to conduce to a righteous life and the love of God.[36]

In the seventeenth century this theoretico-practica conception of theology would have conflicted with the purely practical construction of the Socinians and later Remonstrants.[37] For instance, Benedict de Spinoza, a Dutch contemporary of Leigh's, wrote in the preface of his *Tractatus Theologico-Politicus*, "Revelation has

---

[35] Muller, *Dictionary*, 244.
[36] Muller, *PRRD*, 1:341.
[37] Muller, *After Calvin*, 141.

obedience for its sole object, and therefore, in purpose no less than in foundation and method, stands entirely aloof from ordinary knowledge."[38] He later adds, "The aim and object of Scripture is only to teach obedience." Indeed, the Scripture does not mean to teach knowledge, but merely to inspire obedience.[39] In Spinoza's view there is no place for a work like Leigh's *Systeme*. If theology is all in the "doing" then Leigh's hundreds of pages, seeking to carefully delineate the knowledge of God, is an entirely misguided project. Such was the challenge Leigh and his fellow Protestant scholastics faced. It is no wonder that they were so self-conscious about explaining the proper character of theology.

Leigh addresses this matter in a five page discussion at the outset of his work under the heading, "Of Divinity in General." In doing so he enters into the very concerns of the medieval scholastics. He writes, "It is a Question with the schoolmen, Whether Divinity be Theoretical or Practical."[40] Leigh's answer to the question is somewhat difficult to sort out. He does not explicitly express his position as a mixture of the two; rather he simply sets out both positions with little indication of his sympathy. On conceiving theology as practical he explains that it

> seems . . . rather to be practical, 1. Because the Scripture, which is the fountain of true Divinity, exhorts rather to practice then speculation. 1 *Tim.* 1.5. 1 *Cor.* 8.3. & 13.2. *Jam.* 1.22.24. hence *John* so often exhorts to love in his first Epistle. 2. Because the end of Divinity, to which we are directed by practical precepts, is the glorifying of God, and the eternal salvation of our souls and bodies, or blessed life, which are principally practical.[41]

He hastens on to set forth the theoretical position as found in Peter du Moulin.

Peter du Moulin in his Oration in the praise of Divinity, thus

---

[38] Benedictus de Spinoza, *The Chief Works of Benedict De Spinoza: A Theologico-Political Treatise and A Political Treatise*, trans. R. H. M. Elwes, 2 vols. (New York: Dover Publications, Inc., 1955), 1:9-10.

[39] de Spinoza, *The Chief Works*, 1:183.

[40] Leigh, *Systeme*, 2.

[41] Leigh, *Systeme*, 2.

determines the matter: That part of Theology which treateth of God and his Nature, of his Simplicity, Eternity, Infinitenesse, is altogether contemplative, for these things fall not within compasse of action: that part of which treateth of our manners, and the well ordering of our lives, is merely practick; for it is wholly referred unto action. Christianity is not a bare profession, or speculative science, but a work, a religion to live by, *John* 6.29. *Matth.* 11.12. *Tit.* 2.14. Theology is more contemplative then practick, seeing contemplation is the scope of action, for by good works we aspire unto the beatificall vision of God. . . . Divinity first dealeth with the understanding, yet thereby and principally woeth the will, it teacheth truth, and presseth goodnesse.[42]

We cannot underestimate these statements when attempting to understand Leigh's conception of the character of theology. On the one hand, he seems sympathetic to the argument that theology is practical. He insists that Christianity is not merely speculation, but a work and a religion by which to live. Thus, theology should account for both knowing *and* doing. But when asked which is more basic, it appears Leigh would argue that "knowing" or "understanding" is more basic because "doing" derives its motivation from what is known or seen:

The whole doctrine of Religion is called Theology, that is, a Speech or doctrine concerning God: to signifie that without the true knowledge of God, there can be no true Religion, or right understanding of anything."[43]

There seems to be an organic connection between the two. Without a vision of God (i.e., intellectual contemplation), how could man obey or enjoy him?

On the other hand, God is only truly known when he is obeyed. Man cannot be said to know God if the knowledge of God does not move him to keep God's commandments. Thus, Leigh describes divinity as a practical art:

It is such an art as teacheth a man by the knowledge of Gods

---

[42] Leigh, *Systeme*, 2.
[43] Leigh, *Systeme*, 2.

will and assistance of his power to live to his glory. . . . There is no true knowledge of Christ, but that which is *practical, since then everything is then truly known,* when it is known in the manner it is propounded to be known. But Christ is not propounded to us to be known theoretically but practically.[44]

This final comment is not prejudicing action over knowledge in the Spinozan sense, but rather emphasizes that the saving (true) knowledge of Christ is not merely notional.[45] Leigh is not contradicting his statements regarding knowledge as the proper compass of action; he simply wants to point out that the true knowledge of God *always* encompasses obedience. This would concur with the sentiment of Voetius, when he wrote that the study of divinity is "the art [or technique] of applying theology to use and practice, to the edification of conscience, and to the direction of the will and its affections."[46]

This interchange between *theoria* and *praxis* certainly influences Leigh's explanations of theology as *sapientia* (wisdom). Simply in asking whether divinity is to be categorized as *sapientia* or *scientia* (knowledge), he yet again displays his commitment to the scholastic method of reasoning.[47] He does not provide reasons for rejecting *scientia,* but we may assume that he simply reflects the increasing disuse of this term by the late seventeenth-century scholastics. *Scientia* had become increasingly associated with Cartesian rationalism in which knowledge was gained only through "mathematical or demonstrative certainty."[48] The Reformed insisted that "no single intellectual faculty or habit corresponds precisely with theology."[49] Turretin explains the difficulty of categorizing theology according to other various ways of knowing: "None of the intellectual habits . . . can constitute the true and proper genus of theology because they are all habits of knowing and theology is not

---

[44] Leigh, *Systeme,* 3, emphasis added.

[45] The context suggests that this is Leigh's intended meaning, even if he employs a slight overstatement at this point.

[46] Gisbertus Voetius, *Ta Asketika sive de exercitiis pietatis,* 12, in Muller, *After Calvin,* 116.

[47] Leigh, *Systeme,* 3.

[48] Muller, *PRRD,* 1:330-31.

[49] Muller, *PRRD,* 1:331.

a habit of knowing, but of believing."[50] He does not mean that theology does not convey true and certain knowledge, but rather that such knowledge is not had by way of empirical investigation. Rather, it is based on testimony.

Leigh reflects this same uneasiness with categorizing divinity according to the same terms as the secular disciplines. Theology differs from all other kinds of wisdom (*sapientia*) in "the manner of knowing, which in Divinity is singular and different from all other arts, *viz.*, by Divine Revelation."[51] This is exactly the argument Turretin made (see above) seventeen years later in relation to *scientia*. Still, Leigh sees fit to retain the term *sapientia* to describe theology. He appears to do this because he regards the term as holding together both *theoria* and *praxis*.[52] Christian wisdom, as derived from the Scriptures, is a "most certain knowledge" that touches "all those Offices of Piety in which we are obliged by God to our neighbor."[53] Clearly both theoretical and practical elements are operative in *sapientia*.

The question remains as to how *theoria* and *praxis* can be combined. Muller's description of these terms given above poses some difficult questions in connection with Leigh's understanding of the relation between knowing and doing. Leigh seems to deny that knowledge alone is real knowledge, concluding that God is only truly known when he is known practically. How does that fit with Muller's depiction of the scholastic conception of *theoria* as "pure beholding" with no other end in view than the vision of the thing beheld? The answer seems to lie in Leigh's construction of divinity's goals. For him, the *visio Dei* is not only a prerequisite for *praxis* (e.g., love, worship, and obedience toward God), but it is also

---

[50] Turretin, *Institutes*, I.6.4. This critique of classifying theology as *scientia* does not signify a disagreement with earlier Protestants, like William Perkins, who used the description quite freely. It was simply a way of responding to new challenges such as Cartesian philosophy. The scholastic method and conclusions of the late sixteenth century are substantially quite similar to those of the mid to late seventeenth century.

[51] Leigh, *Systeme*, 3.

[52] See the discussion on *sapientia* in Wolfhart Pannenberg, *Theology and the Philosophy of Science*, trans. Francis McDonagh (Philadelphia: The Westminster Press, 1976), 232.

[53] Leigh, *Systeme*, 3.

the goal of all *praxis* inasmuch as it is entailed within the *fruitio Dei* (the enjoyment of God). The movement, then, is from knowledge to practice to knowledge again. Thus, he explains that man aspires to the beatific vision of God *in his good works*. Now, this final eschatological "speculation," or beholding, of God will also be at once supremely practical in that it will constitute man's perfect communion with and conformity to God in love. *Knowing and beholding God is salvation in the ultimate sense.* Leigh describes this "fruition of glory": "This end has diverse names in Scripture, it is called, *The knowledge of God,* John 17.3. *Partaking of the Divine Nature,* 2 Pet. 1.4. *Likeness to God,* 1 John 3.2." He adds, "*Eternal Salvation,* the vision and fruition of God, is the chiefest good."[54] Salvation and conformity to God are often categorized as practical, yet in Leigh's scheme they are bound together with the theoretical knowledge of God in the *visio Dei.* This leads only to the conclusion that theology, though scholastic in method, is theoretico-practica in character.[55]

Second, theology subjects reason to revelation. Before considering the implications of this theoretico-practica notion of theology for Leigh's doctrine of God, it must also be understood how he relates revelation and reason. The portrait of Reformed scholastics as painted by Brian Armstrong assumes that reason and ratiocination are, at best, on par with Scripture in the scholastic method, and, at worst, used to subject the Scriptures to the powers of man's intellect. This charge does not hold with respect to Leigh's stated principles of theology in which Scripture is the *principium cognoscendi* and God is the *principium essendi.*[56]

In addition to affirming Scripture as the source of knowledge one can also detect the preeminence of the redemptive record in the very shape of Leigh's *Systeme.* The division of topics, beginning with Scripture and God, proceeds through the fall to redemption and finally to glorification. Muller explains this redemptive-historic

---

[54] Leigh, *Systeme,* 3.

[55] Turretin develops this position more extensively than Leigh in his *Institutes,* I.7.1-15. He writes, "We consider theology to be neither simply theoretical nor simply practical, but partly theoretical, partly practical, as that which at the same time connects the theory of the true with the practice of the good." Turretin, *Institutes,* I.7.2.

[56] Leigh, *Systeme,* 144. For his treatment of the authority of Scripture see *Systeme,* 6-37.

pattern of dogmatics:

> The synthetic model, by definition, began with first principles and then traced out its order through means of instrumentalities toward the ultimate goal: this model is reflected in the Reformed patterning of system to move from Scripture and God, the two *principia theologiae*, through the body of doctrine to the last things. Yet this model neither presses a central dogma on the Reformed system nor indicates a purely deductive approach: the topics of the system were elicited from Scripture, echoed the centuries-old assumptions concerning the basic topics in theology, and were given their content on the basis of rather painstaking reflection on Scripture and tradition.[57]

The whole construction of Leigh's *Systeme* refutes the accusation of being rationalistically executed and arranged.

Besides affirming Scripture as his source of knowledge and structuring his theology according to redemptive history, Leigh offers his readers five reasons for prizing Scripture: (1) Christ did so; (2) it is divinely inspired; (3) it is the sword of the Spirit and instrument by which he works; (4) it is surer than immediate revelation (2 Pet. 1:19); and (5) God has committed it to writing that it may be the standing rule of instruction and consolation.[58]

The difficulty lies in understanding how Leigh can profess such a high view of Scripture and yet produce a body of divinity that articulates itself so frequently in the language of medieval scholasticism and philosophy. He can be found arguing his point from metaphysics and philosophy in discussions about the boundaries of natural bodies and the nature of secondary and primary causes.[59] In speaking of God as the unmoved mover he even mentions with approval Plato, Aristotle, and "all the best Philosophers."[60] Thus, it is true that Leigh employs a strong use of reason and philosophy in his treatise. But this conspicuous use of

---

[57] Muller, *After Calvin*, 95.
[58] Leigh, *Systeme*, 5.
[59] Leigh, *Systeme*, 154.
[60] Leigh, *Systeme*, 154.

reason itself does not indicate that he elevated reason over revelation. At the opening of the same section where we find discussions of essences, bodies, and causal chains Leigh writes, "The weightiest testimony that can be brought to prove that there is a God, is to produce the Testimony of God speaking in his word."[61]

Leigh's use of reason and philosophy is instrumental, not principial. Muller explains this in relation to the Protestant scholastics:

> The presentation of logical or rational arguments in the context of faith and the typically scholastic recognition of a series of authorities are not supportive of rationalism unless reason is established as the primary authority and used as the foundation and source of the content of thought rather than as an instrument in argumentation.[62]

In relation to the doctrine of God, we may safely assume that Leigh would have agreed with Zanchius who wrote:

> For there are very many divine attributes that in my opinion cannot be sufficiently explained or even understood unless that which is offered to us by Philosophy is accepted and applied. For we do not immediately leave the School of Christ when we enter the Lycaeum. Nor do we confuse the sciences when we employ the *artes* in explaining Scripture.[63]

One final issue in relating revelation and reason has to do with how one arrives at theological conclusions. This is especially pertinent to Leigh's explanation of the doctrine of divine simplicity. He rejects any approach to divinity that is content simply to cite Scripture.[64] According to Leigh, Scripture demands adherence to

---

[61] Leigh, *Systeme*, 147. For Leigh, saving knowledge comes through testimony, not empirical investigation.

[62] Muller, *After Calvin*, 79.

[63] Cited in Harm Goris, "Thomism in Zanchi's Doctrine of God," in *Reformation and Scholasticism: An Ecumenical Enterprise*, eds. Willem J. van Asselt and Eef Dekker (Grand Rapids: Baker Academic, 2001), 124-25.

[64] Incidentally, in the seventeenth century the Socinians were notoriously fond of insisting that only what is explicitly set down in Scripture is to be believed;

more than what is expressly set down; whatever is a good and necessary consequence also passes as orthodox doctrine. He writes:

> Others deny consequences out of Scripture to be Scripture, nothing is Scripture (say they) but what is found there expressly. What is necessarily inferred is Scripture as well as what is literally expressed, *Levit.* 10.1. The Apostle proves the Resurrection by consequence. Paul and Apollo *Act.* 17.3. & 18.28, proved to the Jews by Scriptures that Jesus was the Christ, although in those Scriptures these very words are not found, but are deduced by a necessary consequence.[65]

Thus, the instrumental use of reason in deducing consequential doctrines is indispensable to arriving at a sound and biblical conclusion. Muller again:

> This argument [that theology consists both in scriptural principles *and* in conclusions drawn from them] was crucial to the scholastic Protestant definition of scripture as the cognitive principle (*principium cognoscendi*) of theology: the radical *sola scriptura* of the Reformers can be maintained only on the assumption that the theological system rests not only on statements drawn directly from scripture but also on logical conclusions resting on scriptural premises.[66]

It should not be surprising that Leigh promotes a strong instrumental use of reason; this is nothing less than what the Westminster Confession of Faith, which he prizes so highly, teaches:

> The whole counsel of God concerning all things necessary for his own glory, man's salvation, faith and life, is either expressly set down in Scripture, or by good and necessary consequence may be deduced from Scripture.[67]

Leigh's Theological Method as Applied to the Doctrine of Divine Simplicity

hence, their denial of the Trinity.

[65] Leigh, *Systeme*, "To the Reader" (2).

[66] Muller, *After Calvin*, 139.

[67] *Westminster Confession of Faith*, I.6.

Of all the doctrines wherein the Protestant scholastics might be charged with arid speculation and rationalism, none is more suspect than their treatment of God's simplicity. Is not their scholastic handling of this doctrine proof of their pronounced interest in metaphysical matters, and in abstract, speculative reasoning? It might be thought that even if Leigh were able to marshal a theoretico-practica construction of other doctrines, he certainly could not do so in his discussion of divine simplicity.

1. The explanation of the doctrine of divine simplicity

Leigh's account of God's simplicity offers no variation from that generally stated by the medieval catholic theologians:

> Simplicity is a property of God, whereby he is void of all composition, mixtion and division, being all Essence; whatsoever is in God, is God. Simpleness is the first property of God, which cannot in any sort agree to any creature.[68]

Leigh lists five ways in which God is free of composition: (1) Of quantitative parts, as a body; (2) Of essential parts, matter and form, as a man consists of soul and body; (3) Of a genus and difference, as every species; (4) Of subject and accidents, as a learned man, a white wall; (5) Of act and power, as the spirits.[69] The first four of these follow the same order found in Thomas Aquinas's *Summa Theologiae*.[70]

Of course Leigh, like his medieval and Reformed predecessors, had a very specific purpose in adopting this doctrine. He declares:

> God is absolutely Simple, he is but one thing, and doth not consist of any parts; he hath no accidents; but himself, his

---

[68] Leigh, *Systeme*, 166.

[69] Leigh, *Systeme*, 166.

[70] Thomas Aquinas, *Summa Theologiae: Latin Text and English Translation, Introductions, Notes, Appendices and Glossaries*, ed. Thomas Gilby, trans. Timothy McDermott, vol. 2 (London and New York: Eyre & Spottiswoode and McGraw-Hill, 1964), 1a. 3. 2, 3, 5, 6.

Essence and Attributes are all one thing, though by us diversly considered and understood. *If he did consist of parts, there must be something before him, to put those parts together; and then he were not Eternal.*[71]

That is to say, there would have been a point in God's existence when he was not the God he now is. Leigh references Isaiah 43:10 as evidence that nothing can be before God: "before me there was no God formed, neither shall there be after me."

If God were not simple he would not be the most perfect and ultimate being. Echoing Anselm and Aquinas, Leigh writes, "Everything the more simple . . . the more excellent."[72] The idea is that the less complex a thing is the less it depends for its nature on other things. Only God is absolutely simple, depending on nothing for his existence or essence. This is the thrust of the doctrine as found in Anselm, who writes:

But undoubtedly, whatever thou [God] art, thou art through nothing else than thyself. Therefore, thou art the very life whereby thou livest; and the wisdom wherewith thou art wise; and the very goodness whereby thou art good to the righteous and the wicked; and so of other like attributes.[73]

Compare this with Leigh's statement regarding God's attributes: "They are all Essential to God: for in him is no accident at all; whatsoever is in God, the same is God. Gods wisdome is Himself, and his Power is Himself."[74] There is no potentiality in God. He is pure act.[75] Theologically this is a way of expressing God's aseity, his total self-sufficiency. Indeed, his very name, Jehovah, signifies his "Perfect, Absolute and simple Being, of and by himself."[76] If God

---

[71] Leigh, *Systeme*, 166-67, emphasis added.

[72] Leigh, *Systeme*, 166. In the context Leigh qualifies this statement by explaining that this simplicity is in reference to mixture and not to the depths of complex wisdom found in the gospel.

[73] Anselm, *Proslogium*, chap. 12, in *St. Anselm: Proslogium; Monologium; An Appendix in Behalf of the Fool by Gaunilon; and Cur Deus Homo*, trans. Sidney Norton Deane (1903; reprint, La Salle, IL: The Open Court Publishing Company, 1948).

[74] Leigh, *Systeme*, 160.

[75] Leigh, *Systeme*, 158.

were not absolutely simple he could not be truly of and by himself. He would have to go to some more basic and eternal source than himself in order to constitute his essence. Thus, he would be dependent.

2. The scriptural argument for the doctrine of divine simplicity

Where Leigh advances the discussion of simplicity beyond the medieval scholastics is in his attempt to demonstrate it from Scripture. He does not criticize the medieval representation of the doctrine as speculative or overly philosophized; rather, he suffuses his discussion with Scripture references and short explanations of the passages. Of course, this scriptural emphasis did appear more prominently in Aquinas than in Anselm; but not so conspicuously as it does in Leigh.

An example of Leigh's use of Scripture is demonstrated in his treatment of the distinction of the divine attributes. In keeping with the traditional doctrine of God's simplicity he writes, "These Attributes differ not among themselves, nor from the Divine Essence."[77] Leigh cites support for this view in Isaiah 43:5, where God says to Israel, "Fear not; for I am with thee." Leigh's point is that God was with Israel in his merciful acts on their behalf. Thus, even though Israel perceived that God's *mercy* was with them, it was, of course, God himself who was there since his attributes are identical to him. Leigh explains the passage: "[God says] *For myself,* not for my Mercy; to teach us, that his Mercy is himself, and not different from his Essence, as it is with us."[78]

Another example of his attempt to ground the doctrine in Scripture is found in his explanation that God is all his attributes both concretely and abstractly. He states, "In God to be, to will, and to do are the same."[79] Leigh points to John 14:6 as evidence that God just is his attributes: "Jesus saith unto him, I am the way, the truth,

---

[76] Leigh, *Systeme*, 159. "Jehovah" is the only name of God treated in this context. Apparently Leigh does not follow what Richard Muller identifies as the frequent practice of the Reformed orthodox of framing their discussion of the divine attributes with a discourse on the divine names. See Muller, *After Calvin*, 75.

[77] Leigh, *Systeme*, 160.

[78] Leigh, *Systeme*, 160.

[79] Leigh, *Systeme*, 167.

and the life." In addition to this he compares 1 John 1:7 ("he is in the light") to 1 John 1:5 ("God is light, and in him is no darkness at all"). Leigh explains: "to have life, and be life; to be in the light, and be light, are the same. God is therefore called in the Abstract Light, Life, Love, Truth."[80] In support Leigh refers again to John 14:6 and to 1 John 4:8 ("God is love").

Though modern biblical exegetes may balk at the idea that these passages support the metaphysical conclusion that Leigh draws, historians must appreciate the Protestant scholastics' attempt to ground even their most penetrating metaphysical comments upon a right interpretation of the Scriptures. Here is no intellectualistic subversion of the Scriptures to reason, but rather an instrumental use of reason attempting to give expression to the metaphysical implications of particular passages. Thus, Leigh's treatment of divine simplicity is at once traditionally catholic and reformationally scriptural.

3. The practical use of the doctrine of divine simplicity

Can this traditional doctrine, even if it is truly built upon the Scriptures, really be useful or practical for the Christian? Leigh certainly thinks so. He mentions numerous benefits of understanding divine simplicity. First, it, possibly more than any other doctrine, highlights the Creator-creature distinction. Absolute simplicity does not agree in any way to creatures. Leigh writes of God:

> He is a Spiritual, Simple, and Immaterial Essence. His Essence is substantial, an Essence which hath a being in itself, not in another, simply and wholly immaterial (he is one most Pure and meer Act) but Incomprehensible goes quite beyond our knowledge; so that we cannot comprehend his Essence, nor know it as it is.[81]

---

[80] Leigh, *Systeme*, 167. William Perkins makes the case for God's simplicity from these very same texts. See his *Golden Chaine*, 11. Wilhelmus à Brakel (1635-1711) does likewise in *The Christian's Reasonable Service*, ed. Joel R. Beeke, trans. Bartel Elshout, 4 vols. (Grand Rapids: Reformation Heritage Books, 1992-1995), 1:99.

Of the properties in God he writes:

> In God they are Infinite, Unchangeable and Perfect, even the
> Divine Essence itself; and therefore indeed all one and the
> same, but in men and Angels they are finite, changeable and
> imperfect, meer qualities, divers, they receiving them *by
> participation only*, not being such of themselves by nature.[82]

Thus, the Creator-creature distinction is seen, in part, in that God is
simple and man complex.

The practical side of grasping the Creator-creature distinction is
that it humbles man, and puts the fear of God in his heart. Knowing
God in all his glory, such as the truth that he is simple and wholly
self-sufficient, demonstrates to man how little he knows and how
self-insufficient he truly is as God's creature.[83] Furthermore, the
truth that God is wholly independent and man entirely dependent
serves to make man's sin more offensive to him. Leigh writes, "The
cleare knowledge of God raiseth a mans thoughts greatly touching
the sinfullnesse of sinne."[84] He sees that his offenses are not
ultimately against another creature, but against one who is infinitely
more sufficient (as evidenced in his simplicity) and powerful. Yet
this view of God's simplicity is not only meant for humbling man,
but also for inspiring awe in him:

> The sight of God fils a man with large affections toward him,
> and makes a man desire greater friendship and familiarity
> with him, and also brings a man to submit to the will of God.[85]

Another benefit is that divine simplicity is the proof to man of
God's dependability. Consider how Leigh plies the doctrine of
simplicity for the comfort of the Christian: "This may minister
comfort to Gods people; Gods attributes are not mutable accidents,

---

[81] Leigh, *Systeme*, 158.

[82] Leigh, *Systeme*, 162, emphasis added.

[83] Leigh, *Systeme*, 162. Some, who conceive of "practical" as strictly referring to
action, may not accept that knowledge of God's self-sufficiency is truly practical.
For a challenge to the notion that "practical" only indicates action, see Pannenberg,
Theology and the Philosophy of Science, 232-33.

[84] Leigh, *Systeme*, 162.

[85] Leigh, *Systeme*, 162.

but his very Essence: His Love and Mercy are like himself, Infinite, Immutable and Eternal."[86] He appeals to simplicity to offer comfort and assurance to the believer. How can the Christian know that God will not change? The answer is that God's being is identical with his attributes. Leigh's point is that God is not contingent, so that he may suddenly (or gradually) be other than he is. Unlike a white wall or a learned man (which may still be a wall or a man even if no longer white or learned), God would no longer be God if he were to lose any one of his essential attributes. His nature is as sure as his existence; his being does not precede his essence, but rather they are identical in him. So Leigh can say by way of consolation and warning, "Here is a matter of joy and comfort to the good; Mercy and Love are Gods Essence . . . and of Fear and Terror to the wicked, because Gods Anger and Justice are his Essence, and he is Unchangeable."[87]

A final way in which the doctrine of simplicity is useful to the believer is that it shows him wherein his sufficiency lies. God is the ultimate source of all good. As it is denied that there is any potential in God (i.e., God is not becoming), which would contradict his simplicity, man may conclude that he is not inert in any sense. All his attributes are "actually and operatively" in him.[88] He is not waiting to become something other than he is or to actualize some dormant property. Thus, man can confidently seek all things from God. Leigh explains, "Gods wisdome is the fountain of wisdome to us: We are to seek eternal life from his Eternity."[89] Leigh references Romans 6:23 as proof: ". . . the gift of God *is* eternal life through Jesus Christ our Lord." His point is that man does not receive eternal life apart from God himself (esp. the Son in this case), who is *himself* eternal Life. Philosophically, Leigh is controverting the notion of Platonic Forms. But there is a practical thrust: "All these are in God objectively and finally; our holinesse looks upon his holinesse, as the face in the Looking-glasse on the man, whose representation it is; and our holinesse ends in his."[90] There is no

---

[86] Leigh, *Systeme*, 161, emphasis added.
[87] Leigh, *Systeme*, 167.
[88] Leigh, *Systeme*, 160.
[89] Leigh, *Systeme*, 160.
[90] Leigh, *Systeme*, 160.

"Form" of holiness to be found alongside of or back of God.

All of this means that man can trust God for all his needs because God is the ultimate source of all goodness. Put another way, man's trust in God as "good" does not depend on the sturdiness of the more basic and universal abstract idea of goodness lying back of God. There are no universal notions or standards outside of or back of him. Were that the case man would have to have a more basic faith and confidence in those universals in order to be able to rely on God. Divine simplicity is a way of explaining that God is all of his attributes in the absolute sense. This is the reason that God can swear by none higher than himself.[91] There is nothing more sure, dependable, or absolute than him. Thus Leigh says that man's holiness "ends" in God's holiness; the believer has the supply of all he needs for life and godliness in God's nature. But this only holds if God's nature is simple. Such is the practical thrust of Leigh's teaching on divine simplicity.

Conclusion

In answer to the opening question, it would appear that scholastic theology is in no way opposed to practical divinity in the thought of the Protestant scholastics. Even its exacting divisions, questions, and conclusions can serve to foster a religion of the heart. In truth, because practical theology falls *within* the compass of theoretical theology the scholastic method was probably better suited to cultivate heart religion than the purely practical approaches of the Socinians and Remonstrants. In Leigh there is no divide between theology and piety. As he puts it, "Our welfare and happiness consists in the knowledge of God," which, "in the life to come is called the Beautiful vision."[92]

---

[91] Leigh, *Systeme*, 167.
[92] Leigh, *Systeme*, 144.

Chapter 13

"Eternally Begotten of the Father"

An Analysis of the Second London Confession
of Faith's Doctrine of the Eternal Generation
of the Son

Stefan T. Lindblad[*]

According to James M. Renihan, the Second London Confession of
Faith

> may perhaps best be understood against its historical and
> theological backgrounds. It did not appear *de novo*, the
> product of a sudden burst of theological insight on the part
> of an author or authors, but in the tradition of good
> Confession making, it is largely dependent on the statements
> of earlier Reformed Confessions.[1]

[*] Stefan T. Lindblad is a pastor of Trinity Reformed Baptist Church, Kirkland,
WA, and a Ph.D. Candidate in Historical and Systematic Theology at Calvin
Theological Seminary, Grand Rapids, MI. Portions of this essay previously
appeared under the same title as the annual circular letter for the Association of
Reformed Baptist Churches of America (April 2013) and can be accessed here:
http://s3.amazonaws.com/churchplantmedia-cms/arbca_carlisle_pa/circular-
letter-2013-final-edit-2.pdf. I am grateful to James Dolezal, Kevin Giles, and
Andrew McGinnis for their helpful comments on the previous version.

[1] James M. Renihan, *Edification and Beauty: The Practical Ecclesiology of the
English Particular Baptists, 1675-1705*, Studies in Baptist History and Thought 17
(Milton Keynes, UK: Paternoster, 2008), 18. This reflects the more recent interest in
the contextualized study of Reformed theology in the early modern era. For
indispensable summaries of the pertinent historiographical and methodological
issues see esp. Richard A. Muller, "Reflections on Persistent Whiggism and Its
Antidotes" in Alister Chapman, John Coffey, and Brad S. Gregory, eds., *Seeing
Things Their Way: Intellectual History and the Return of Religion* (Notre Dame, IN:

Rigorously defended in his writings and lectures, this statement ably summarizes one of Dr. Renihan's oft-repeated methodological canons for the study of the 2LCF. He has consistently maintained that in order to apprehend the intended meaning of the Confession we must understand something of its original historical and theological context(s), in particular the "earlier Reformed Confessions" that served as source documents for the 2LCF, as well as Reformed theology of the sixteenth and seventeenth centuries more generally. This seemingly obvious, yet often overlooked, presupposition for the study of the Confession has proven invaluable for my pastoral ministry in a confessional church and for my own research in Reformed Christology of the confessional era. It is but a small token of my gratitude for Jim's faithful instruction, scholarly example, and continued friendship to present the following analysis of the 2LCF's doctrine of eternal generation to our beloved Doctor on the occasion of his sixtieth birthday.

The framers of the 2LCF self-consciously adopted the order, as well as the majority of the language and content, of the Westminster Confession of Faith (WCF) and the Savoy Declaration (SD), in part, "to manifest our consent with both, in all the fundamental articles of the Christian Religion, as also with many others, whose orthodox confessions have been published to the world."[2] Thus while departing from these major source documents on certain distinguishing doctrines, the methodological commitment and theological content of the 2LCF indicate its place alongside the other Reformed symbols of the sixteenth and seventeenth centuries.[3] As these confessional standards have been regarded as noteworthy for their biblical and churchly trinitarianism, the same may be said of the 2LCF.[4] The doctrine of the Trinity articulated in the 2LCF is

---

University of Notre Dame Press, 2009), 134-53; Richard A. Muller, *Calvin and the Reformed Tradition: On the Work of Christ and the Order of Salvation* (Grand Rapids: Baker Academic, 2012), 13-50; and Willem J. van Asselt, "Scholasticism Revisited: Methodological Reflections on the Study of Seventeenth Century Reformed Thought," in Chapman, Coffey, and Boyd, *Seeing Things Their Way*, 154-74.

[2] *A Confession of Faith, put forth by the elders and brethren of many congregations of Christians (baptized upon profession of their faith) in London and the Country* (London: for Benjamin Harris, 1677), preamble, unnumbered page 4.

[3] For a detailed historical analysis of the provenance, sources, and authorship of the 2LCF, see Renihan, *Edification and Beauty*, 1-29.

catholic and Reformed, an essential topic of which is the doctrine of the eternal generation of the Son: "the Son is eternally begotten of the Father" (2LCF 2.3; cf. 8.1). While an exhaustive historical analysis of the doctrine would be beneficial, as would some discussion of the contemporary disputes regarding the doctrine that have arisen in the context of the debate regarding gender roles in the family and in church, such topics lie beyond my present scope. The narrow concern of what follows is the 2LCF's formulation of the doctrine of the eternal generation of the Son. I will argue that, when understood in the larger context of the Confession's doctrine of God, the 2LCF affirms the classical doctrine of the eternal generation of the Son as a fundamental article of the Christian faith, particularly, however, as it was argued exegetically, formulated positively, and defended polemically by confessional Reformed orthodoxy of the sixteenth and seventeenth centuries.

The State of the Question: The Confessional Reformed Doctrine of the Trinity and Contemporary Anachronisms

Two separate scholarly trends coalesce to underline the importance of the following analysis of the 2LCF's doctrine of eternal generation. First, despite extensive discussion of the patristic codification of the doctrine of the Trinity, including the Son's eternal generation, until recently little attention had been given to the detailed argumentation of the Reformers and their orthodox successors. Prior to Richard Muller's extensive analysis, the regnant paradigm was that the Reformed orthodox for various reasons — the supposed deleterious effects of a recrudescent scholasticism and speculative rationalism, preoccupation with a causal predestinarian metaphysic, or undue emphasis on the doctrine of the divine essence — had relegated the doctrine of the Trinity to an afterthought.[5] As a much needed corrective to such dogmatically

---

[4] Richard A. Muller, *Post-Reformation Reformed Dogmatics: The Rise and Development of Reformed Orthodoxy, ca. 1520-1725*, vol. 4, *The Triunity of God* (Grand Rapids: Baker, 2003), 103-04, hereafter cited as *PRRD*. Cf. Robert Letham, *The Westminster Assembly: Reading Its Theology in Historical Context* (Phillipsburg, NJ: P&R Publishing, 2009), 164-69.

driven anachronisms, Muller demonstrates at length that the doctrine maintained a significant place in the thought of the Reformed orthodox and, more importantly, that the theologians of the era argued the catholic doctrine of the Trinity on extensive exegetical grounds, especially against the rising tide of antitrinitarianism.[6] Similarly, several studies—especially those of Goris, Beck, Rehnman, Muller, and my own work on Leigh's doctrine of God—have redressed the errors of this older line of scholarship and offered a more contextualized reading of the development of the Reformed orthodox doctrine of God, including the doctrine of the Trinity.[7]

---

[5] These wide ranging anachronisms occur across the spectrum of twentieth-century theology and historiography. See Karl Barth, *Church Dogmatics*, eds. G. W. Bromiley and T. F. Torrance, 4 vols. (Edinburgh: T. & T. Clark, 1936-1975), I/1, 300-01; Otto Gründler, "Thomism and Calvinism in the Theology of Girolamo Zanchi (1516-1590)" (Th.D. dissertation, Princeton Theological Seminary, 1961), 19-23, 94-120, 158-59, translated as *Die Gotteslehre Girolami Zanchis und ihre Bedeutung fur seine Lehre von der Pradestination* (Neukirchen: Neukirchner Verlag, 1965); Brian G. Armstrong, *Calvinism and the Amyraut Heresy: Protestant Scholasticism and Humanism in Seventeenth-Century France* (Madison, WI: University of Wisconsin Press, 1969), 32, 38-42; Otto Weber, *Foundations of Dogmatics*, trans. Darrell Gudder, 2 vols. (Grand Rapids: Eerdmans, 1981-1982), 1:349-51; Thomas F. Torrance, *Scottish Theology: From John Knox to John McLeod Campbell* (Edinburgh: T. & T. Clark, 1996), 131-33; Alister E. McGrath, *Reformation Thought: An Introduction*, third edition (Oxford: Blackwell, 1999), 140-41; Thomas F. Torrance, "The Distinctive Character of the Reformed Tradition," *Reformed Review* 54/1 (Autumn 2000): 5-6; and with some caveats, Letham, *The Westminster Assembly*, 109, 164-65. For general critiques of this line of scholarship, see Richard A. Muller, *After Calvin: Studies in the Development of a Theological Tradition* (Oxford: Oxford University Press, 2003), 63-102; Richard A. Muller, "The Problem of Protestant Scholasticism—A Review and Definition," in Willem J. van Asselt and Eef Dekker, eds., *Reformation and Scholasticism: An Ecumenical Enterprise* (Grand Rapids: Baker Academic, 2001), 45-64; and with reference to the doctrine of God, Muller, *PRRD*, 3:154-59.

[6] Muller, *PRRD*, vol. 4. Cf. Carl R. Trueman, *John Owen: Reformed Catholic, Renaissance Man* (Surrey, UK: Ashgate, 2007), 47: "The contributions of the Reformed orthodox to Trinitarian theology are not marked so much by innovative critique of the dominant tradition but rather defence of that tradition in the face of radical attacks by those who rejected the creeds and who saw patristic theology as reflecting declension from, and perversion of, the pristine gospel of the New Testament."

[7] Harm Goris, "Thomism in Zanchi's Doctrine of God," in van Asselt and Dekker, *Reformation and Scholasticism*, 121-39; Andreas J. Beck, "Gisbertus Voetius (1589-1676): Basic Features of His Doctrine of God," in van Asselt and Dekker,

Several other recent works have shed light on the historical and theological milieu in which the 2LCF affirmed the classical doctrines of the Trinity and the eternal generation of the Son. Of particular importance are Trueman's analysis of John Owen's doctrine of the Trinity, Lim's study of the trinitarian polemics that profoundly affected the theological and ecclesiastical landscape of seventeenth-century England, and Ellis' historical and theological analysis of the Reformed doctrine of the Son's aseity.[8] Also of note is the renewed attention given to these doctrines as enshrined in the Westminster Standards.[9] Fesko, in particular, not only joins the chorus against Robert Reymond's mistaken claim that the trinitarianism of Calvin and, to some extent, the WCF developed as an alternative to the creedal formulae of Nicaea (325) and Constantinople (381), but he also offers a contextualized reading of the internecine Reformed discussion of the doctrines of the Son's aseity and eternal generation. He concludes that while there was certainly diversity of expression, there was nevertheless broad agreement on these topics

---

Reformation and Scholasticism, 205-26; Sebastian Rehnman, "Theistic Metaphysics and Biblical Exegesis: Francis Turretin on the Concept of God," *Religious Studies* 38 (2001): 167-86; Richard A. Muller, "Unity and Distinction: The Nature of God in the Theology of Lucas Trelcatius, Jr," *RRR* 10.3 (2008): 315-41; and Stefan T. Lindblad, "Of the Nature of God: The Inter-relation of Essence and Trinity in Edward Leigh's *A Systeme or Body of Divinity* (1662)," *Journal of the Institute of Reformed Baptist Studies* (2014): 95-124.

[8] Carl R. Trueman, *The Claims of Truth: John Owen's Trinitarian Theology* (Carlisle, UK: Paternoster, 1998); Trueman, *Reformed Catholic*, 35-66; Paul C. H. Lim, *Mystery Unveiled: The Crisis of the Trinity in Early Modern England* (Oxford: Oxford University Press, 2012); and Brannon Ellis, *Calvin, Classical Trinitarianism, and the Aseity of the Son* (Oxford: Oxford University Press, 2012). See also Philip Dixon, *Nice and Hot Disputes: The Doctrine of the Trinity in the Seventeenth Century* (London: T & T Clark, 2003); Brian K. Kay, *Trinitarian Spirituality: John Owen and the Doctrine of God in Western Devotion* (Eugene, OR: Wipf & Stock, 2008); and Joel R. Beeke and Mark Jones, *A Puritan Theology: Doctrine for Life* (Grand Rapids: Reformation Heritage Books, 2012), 85-100.

[9] Letham, *The Westminster Assembly*, 164-73; J. V. Fesko, *The Theology of the Westminster Standards: Historical Context and Theological Insights* (Wheaton, IL: Crossway, 2014), 170-84; and Chad van Dixhorn, *Confessing the Faith: A Reader's Guide to the Westminster Confession of Faith* (Edinburgh; Carlisle, PA: The Banner of Truth, 2014), 37-40. On the debate at the Assembly regarding the Son's aseity and eternal generation, see Chad van Dixhorn, "Reforming the Reformation: Theological Debate at the Westminster Assembly 1643-1652," 7 vols. (Ph.D. diss., Cambridge University, 2004), 1:245-49.

---

among theologians of the era, the notable exception being Arminius who denied altogether that the Son is *autotheos* and espoused a form of ontological subordination.[10]

Despite this growing corpus of scholarly literature on the Reformed orthodox doctrines of the Trinity and the Son's eternal generation, there is as of yet no study that addresses directly the thought of the seventeenth-century Particular Baptists or their confessional documents. This is all the more significant given that 2LCF 2.3 does not adopt the language of WCF 2.3 or SD 2.3 verbatim, incorporating some of the language of the First London Confession of Faith (1646 revision, hereafter 1LCF). The Particular Baptists also appealed to the creedal and confessional doctrine of the Son's eternal generation in their polemic against Thomas Collier, a one-time Particular Baptist evangelist turned radical antitrinitarian.

There is a second line of scholarship that, at least indirectly, bears upon the following analysis of the 2LCF's doctrine of eternal generation. Contemporary systematic theology has penned a large swath of literature on the doctrine of the Trinity. One of the major questions addressed in this burgeoning trinitarian discussion has been whether and to what extent the doctrine of the Trinity is capable of generating social, political, and ethical constructs [11] Having assumed such a thing is possible and sound, participants on both sides of the gender debate have argued that the eternal relation of the Father and the Son entails their respective position.[12] In doing

---

[10] Fesko, *Westminster Standards*, 170-84. Contra Robert Reymond, see also Paul Owen, "Calvin and Catholic Trinitarianism: An Examination of Robert Reymond's Understanding of the Trinity and His Appeal to John Calvin," *CTJ* 35 (2000): 262-81; Letham, *The Westminster Assembly*, 94, 166-73; and Robert Letham, *The Holy Trinity: In Scripture, History, Theology, and Worship* (Phillipsburg, NJ: P&R Publishing, 2004), 252-68.

[11] For analysis and critique of this trend, see Thomas H. McCall, *Which Trinity? Whose Monotheism? Philosophical and Systematic Theologians on the Metaphysics of Trinitarian Doctrine* (Grand Rapids: Eerdmans, 2010), 224-27; and Stephen Holmes, *The Quest for the Trinity: The Doctrine of God in Scripture, History, and Modernity* (Downers Grove, IL: IVP Academic, 2011), 1-32.

[12] On the egalitarian side, see Gilbert Belizekian, "Hermeneutical Bungee-Jumping: Subordination in the Godhead," *JETS* 40 (1997): 233-53; Stanley Grenz, "Theological Foundations for Male-Female Relationships," *JETS* 41 (1998): 615-30; and Kevin Giles, *The Trinity and Subordinationism* (Downers Grove, IL: InterVarsity,

so, some proponents of male headship (i.e., complementarianism) have rejected the classical and confessional doctrine of eternal generation on the grounds that it is unbiblical, speculative, even pro-Arian.[13] The purpose of drawing attention to this particular modern theological and ethical discussion is not to enter the fray, at least not in this essay. My intention is merely to point out that much of this literature is riddled with historical caricatures and misunderstanding; even when correction has been supplied, the anachronisms persist.

The following analysis of 2LCF 2.3 will demonstrate not only that the classical doctrine of the Son's eternal generation was formulated in order to uphold the full deity of the Son, and so maintain the doctrine of the unity of the divine essence, but also that this particular doctrine, which was carefully defined in the patristic era and confessed as orthodox for centuries, was by the Reformed orthodox, and so the Particular Baptists, confessed as a fundamental article of the Christian faith elicited from, explained, and defended on the basis of Holy Scripture.[14]

2002). On the complementarian side, see Stephen D. Kovach and Peter R. Schemm, Jr., "A Defense of the Doctrine of the Eternal Subordination of the Son," *JETS* 42 (1999): 461-76; Wayne A. Grudem, *Systematic Theology: An Introduction to Biblical Doctrine*, rev. ed. (Grand Rapids: Zondervan, 2000), 248-52; Bruce A. Ware, "How Shall We Think about the Trinity?," in *God Under Fire: Modern Scholarship Reinvents God*, eds. Douglas F. Huffman and Eric L. Johnson (Grand Rapids: Zondervan, 2002), 269-77; Bruce A. Ware, *Father, Son, and Holy Spirit* (Wheaton, IL: Crossway, 2000), 71-87; and Bruce A. Ware and John Starke, eds., *One God in Three Persons: Unity of Essence, Distinction of Persons, Implications for Life* (Wheaton, IL: Crossway, 2015).

[13] Grudem, *Systematic Theology*, 1233-34; Ware, *Father, Son, and Holy Spirit*, 162, n. 3; John S. Feinberg, *No One Like Him: The Doctrine of God* (Wheaton, IL: Crossway, 2001), 488-92; J. P. Moreland and William Lane Craig, *Philosophical Foundations for a Christian Worldview* (Downers Grove, IL: InterVarsity, 2003), 594; and Mark Driscoll and Gary Breshears, *Doctrine: What Christians Should Believe* (Wheaton, IL: Crossway, 2010), 27-28. Against this rejection of the doctrine of eternal generation, see Keith E. Johnson, "Augustine, Eternal Generation, and Evangelical Trinitarianism," *TJ* 32 (2001): 141-63; Letham, *Holy Trinity*, 383-89; McCall, *Which Trinity*, 175-88; Kevin Giles, *The Eternal Generation of the Son: Maintaining Orthodoxy in Trinitarian Theology* (Downers Grove, IL: InterVarsity, 2012); and D. Glenn Butner, "Eternal Functional Subordination and the Problem of the Divine Will," *JETS* 58/1 (2015): 131-49.

[14] This is not to suggest that there has been complete unanimity on every specific aspect of the doctrine of the Son's eternal generation; it is, however, the

One in Trinity and Trinity in Unity

The 2LCF's doctrine of the eternal generation of the Son does not reside in either a historical or theological vacuum. Recognizing the various contexts of this confessional doctrine is vital to a proper analysis. The immediate confessional context is the paragraph on the Trinity (2.3), itself situated in the chapter on the nature of God. Within the 2LCF the doctrine of the Son's eternal generation is formulated on the basis of Scripture. It was understood by the Particular Baptists to be a fundamental article of the counsel of God "expressly set down or necessarily contained in Holy Scripture" (1.6), argued by way of the analogy of Scripture (1.9), and thus received by faith (1.10). The doctrine is briefly mentioned in subsequent chapters of the 2LCF, since it has implications for the doctrines of the covenant of redemption (7.3) and the Mediator's person and office (esp. 8.1-2). Moving out from this confessional epicenter, however, is the broader historical-theological framework provided by the 2LCF's source documents, the 1LCF, the WCF, and the SD, as well as the theology both of the seventeenth-century Particular Baptists and high Reformed orthodoxy. Quite obviously the theology of this specific era reflects the codification of Reformed theology by the second generation Reformers (ca. 1535 ca. 1565) and its further elaboration and defense by the early Reformed orthodox (ca. 1565-ca. 1640). In light of the doctrine under consideration, it is also necessary to bear in mind that Reformed trinitarianism stands in basic continuity with patristic and medieval antecedents—not only individual theologians such as Athanasius, Augustine, Anselm, and Aquinas, but especially the formulae of the councils of Nicaea (325) and Constantinople (381), the 4th Lateran Council (1215), the Council of Lyons (1274), and the Council of Florence (1438-1442).[15] A more lengthy analysis of the 2LCF's doctrine of

---

case that orthodox Christian theology from the fourth century through the early modern era unanimously affirmed that the Son is "begotten before all worlds . . . begotten, not made."

[15] A brief summary of the teachings of the medieval theologians and councils may be found in Muller, *PRRD*, 4:17-58. For an accessible treatment of the ancient creeds, see Carl R. Trueman, *The Creedal Imperative* (Wheaton, IL: Crossway, 2012), 81-108.

eternal generation would examine the significance of these interrelated contexts. For our purposes we are necessarily limited to only a few examples showing that the 2LCF's doctrine of eternal generation belongs to this stream of classical and Reformed trinitarian thought. The primary focus in this section is the contextual constraints of the 2LCF itself, especially chapter 2.

This chapter adopts the standard scholastic arrangement of the doctrine of God, the exception being that unlike the large scale theological systems of late medieval and Reformed scholasticism the 2LCF, as also the WCF and SD, does not begin with a separate topic devoted to God's existence.[16] The 2LCF focuses on two topics: what is God (i.e., divine essence and attributes; 2.1-2), and what sort of God he is (i.e., the distinction of the three persons; 2.3). This structural order does not suggest that the doctrine of the Trinity is of secondary importance to the confessional doctrine of God. The 2LCF employs a logical order, deemed necessary for pedagogical purposes, in which it first sets forth what distinguishes the one, simple, infinite God from finite creatures (2.1-2), and secondly the personal properties of the three personal subsistences in this one infinite and divine essence (2.3). The opening clause of this paragraph not only confirms that the 2LCF is articulating this traditionary doctrine of God, but also establishes clearly that the Particular Baptists understood the two topics of this chapter to be necessarily interrelated or interdependent. There is no imbalance in the 2LCF between God's essential properties (2.1-2) and his personal properties (2.3).[17] God is in himself all absolute (i.e., essential) and relative (i.e., personal) perfection.

In fact, 2LCF 2.3 teaches in several ways that what has been said of God's essential perfection in 2.1-2 is necessarily predicated of the God who is one in Trinity. We will see momentarily why the 2LCF takes pains to do so, but generally speaking this paragraph underscores that whatever Scripture predicates of the one, true, and

---

[16] Though, note Q. 2-3 of the Baptist Catechism in James M. Renihan, *True Confessions: Baptist Documents in the Reformed Family* (Owensboro, KY: RBAP, 2004), 196-97. More than likely this omission in the 2LCF is not indicative of any aversion to the topic on the part of the Particular Baptists, but is due to the genre difference between theological system and confessional symbol.

[17] Contra Letham, *Westminster Assembly*, 165.

living God, is also predicated of the Father, the Son, and the Spirit, even though what is proper to each subsistence (e.g., eternal generation) is not and may not be predicated of the divine essence. William Ames, whose writings had a pronounced influence on the shape of Particular Baptist theology, states this rule of predication succinctly:

> The same essence is common to the three subsistences; wherefore, as concerning the essence, each singular subsistence is said rightly to be of itself. Nothing, moreover, is attributed to the essence, which may not be attributed to each singular subsistence, as concerning its essence. But those things that are properly attributed to each singular subsistence, as concerning its subsistence, may not be attributed to the essence.[18]

The 2LCF, therefore, goes to great lengths to teach both the unity and distinction of the divine nature; that is, the triune God is one, simple, fully actualized, eternal, and infinite essence and at the same time the persons of the Trinity are distinct or distinguished. Adopting some language from 1LCF, the Particular Baptists state that the Father, the Son, and the Holy Spirit are three personal subsistences "in this divine and infinite Being." The persons are not outside of or distinct from the essence; they are distinct from one another *within* the one essence. Secondly, these three subsistences are said to have in common the one essence and thus all the essential divine attributes: they are "of one substance, [of one] power, and [of one] eternity." They are not of *like* essence (*homoiousion*), nor are they of different essences (*heteroousion*), but are of the same essence (*homoousion*), and therefore of the same essential omnipotence and eternity. Third, again depending on the

---

[18] William Ames, *Medulla Theologica* (Amsterdam: John Jansson, 1634), 16. Cf. William Ames, *The Marrow of Sacred Divinity* (London: Edward Griffin, 1639), 15. The formative significance of Ames's *Medulla* on the Particular Baptists is evident from its use as a source document for the 1LCF, as well as from its citation by Nehemiah Coxe in his polemical work against Thomas Collier. See Nehemiah Coxe, *Vindiciae Veritatis, or a Confutation of the heresies and gross errours asserted by Thomas Collier in his additional word to his Body of Divinity* (London: for Nathaniel Ponder, 1677), 8, margin.

1LCF, each personal subsistence is said to have "the whole divine essence," though each in a distinct manner—the Father as neither begotten nor proceeding, the Son as begotten of the Father, and the Spirit as proceeding from the Father and the Son. Yet, they are not three essences, or three gods, for the divine essence is numerically one and "undivided." Finally, after stating how the three personal subsistences are simultaneously distinct but related—not begotten, begotten, proceeding—the 2LCF states again, rather clearly and succinctly, that these *personal* and *relative* properties in no way undermine God's essential unity, equality, and eternity. Father, Son, and Holy Spirit are "all infinite, without beginning, therefore but one God, who is not to be divided in nature and Being: but distinguished by several peculiar, relative properties, and personal relations." Several observations are in order regarding this very precise and nuanced formulation of the doctrine of the Trinity, particularly as it provides the proper framework in which to understand the 2LCF's confession of the doctrine of the Son's eternal generation.

1. The common, undivided divine essence

In this chapter the 2LCF identifies its doctrine of the Trinity, and so also its doctrine of the Son's eternal generation, as pro-Nicene. To say, "In this divine and infinite Being there are three subsistences . . . of one substance, power, and eternity . . ." is to say that the unity of the persons is essential rather than volitional. That the unity of the Father and the Son was established by an act of divine will was the argument of both the Arians and semi-Arians of the fourth century: the Son was *like* God because of the Father's will to create or make the Son. Those who affirmed the *homoousion* of Nicaea argued instead that the Father and the Son are of the same essence. Constantinople extended this affirmation to the person of the Spirit.[19] Thus, the 2LCF argues that the three subsistences in the one infinite and divine essence are of one substance, and therefore of one power and one eternity. Though this teaching is affirmed everywhere by

---

[19] Khaled Anatolios, *Retrieving Nicaea: The Development and Meaning of Trinitarian Doctrine* (Grand Rapids: Baker, 2011), 15-31.

orthodox trinitarianism, it is expressed quite clearly by the so-called Athanasian Creed:

> And the catholic faith is this: that we worship one God in Trinity and Trinity in Unity; neither confounding the persons nor dividing the substance. For there is one Person of the Father, another of the Son, and another of the Holy Spirit. But the Godhead of the Father, of the Son, and of the Holy Spirit is all one, the glory equal, the majesty coeternal.

This is precisely the teaching of 2LCF 2.3.[20] In which case, by wholeheartedly agreeing with such statements of trinitarian orthodoxy, the 2LCF rejects what creedal orthodoxy had always rejected, namely, the notion that eternal generation implies or entails the Son's subordination in the Godhead.

The claim that each personal subsistence has the whole divine essence, yet the essence is undivided, is significant in two respects. First, that the 2LCF borrows all of this language, except for the term subsistence, from the 1LCF suggests that in 1646, 1677, and 1689 the Particular Baptists were eager to avoid any and all association with the rather vocal antitrinitarian movements of the era.[21] By 1677, in fact, they were compelled to answer the radical antitrinitarianism of Thomas Collier, a one-time Particular Baptist evangelist.[22] Stated positively, the Particular Baptists were eager to demonstrate their orthodoxy on this fundamental article of the Christian faith in view of both accusations to the contrary and the heretical views of a former minister in their communion of churches. They thus cut off at the root any charge of modalism, Sabellianism, or subordinationism, whether in ancient or early modern forms, by

---

[20] Individual theologians among the Particular Baptists also affirmed such creedal orthodoxy, as evidenced by Hercules Collins' unqualified recommendation of the Nicene Creed, the Athanasian Creed, and the Apostles' Creed in *An Orthodox Catechism: Being the sum of Christian Religion, contained in the law and the gospel* (London: 1680), preface, unnumbered pp. 6-7.

[21] On seventeenth-century antitrinitarianism in England, see Lim, *Mystery Unveiled*, 16-123.

[22] Coxe, *Vindiciae Veritatis*, 1-27. Cf. James M. Renihan, "Thomas Collier's Descent in Error: Collier, Calvinsim, and the Second London Confession," *Reformed Baptist Theological Review* I:1 (January 2004): 67-83.

affirming that each personal subsistence has the whole divine essence. By stating also that the essence is yet undivided they were precluding the charge of tritheism. In fact, in these few words the 2LCF reasserts not only the doctrine of the unity of God's essence (cf. 2.1, ". . . one only living, and true God"), but also the doctrines of divine simplicity (cf. 2.1, "without . . . parts") and pure actuality (cf. 2.1, "a most pure spirit"), now, however, in the context of the doctrine of the Trinity. Though in the divine essence there is a Trinity of persons, three fully divine subsistences distinct from one another by virtue of certain personal and relative properties, the infinite and divine essence is numerically one, without composition, accidents, succession or mutation, and therefore, incapable of any kind of essential division, derivation, or gradation. God is what he is. He is his essence, and therefore, he can neither be divided nor become greater, lesser, or another thing. Hence, Father, Son, and Spirit are distinguished one from another, but the common essence is undivided. Jerome Zanchi—a significant early Reformed orthodox theologian who devoted a large portion of his career to articulating and defending the doctrine of the Trinity—states the same truth in a rather simple and straightforward manner.

> Being, then, instructed by God in Holy Scripture . . . which is his own Word, we believe, that there is only one God, that is, one most simple, indivisible, eternal, living, and most perfect essence subsisting in three *hypostasis*, or persons (as the church has typically said), the eternal Father, the eternal Son, and the eternal Holy Spirit, truly distinct from each other, but without all manner of division . . . So thus we believe, and are taught from the Holy Scripture, that the Father is true and perfect God, the Son also is God, and the Spirit is God; and yet God is not multiplied, but there is only one Jehovah.[23]

Understood in this way, this clause is significant, secondly, because it draws attention to the *uniqueness* both of God's essential unity and of the distinction of the persons in the Godhead. By

---

[23] Hieron. Zanchius, *De religione Christiana, fides* (1588) in *Operum theologicorum D. Hieronymi Zanchii, tomus octavus* (Geneva: John Tornaes, 1649), col. 484.

stating that the one, infinite God is a Trinity of personal subsistences, each having the whole divine essence, but without any division of the divine essence, the 2LCF argues against the strict identity of essence and subsistence (or person). The terms *God, Being, essence, or nature* were not understood as if they described a genus or class of which Father, Son, and Spirit are three essences, for instance, in the same way that the genus or class of humanity includes a number of distinct, individual beings (or essences). The common humanity of three human persons is a unity of genus (i.e., generic unity) or a unity of species (i.e., specific unity) that can be and is divided. God, however, is an *infinite* and *divine* being. He is not limited as is every created, finite being (e.g., by space, time, composition, potentiality, etc.). As such, the divine unity is a numerical unity, incomparable to anything in the created order. Drawing on Deuteronomy 6:4 and 1 Corinthians 8:4, Bucanus answers the question, "How is God said to be one?" by noting, "Neither by a genus, nor species, but in essence and in number, or in his nature (*ratione naturae*); which essence is only one and indivisible."[24] The persons of the Trinity are distinct, then, not as are individual human persons, out of or apart from the essence; instead, they are distinct within the essence, according to their distinct manner of subsistence. Wollebius explains:

> The divine person is neither the species of God or of the Deity, nor a part of Him, nor a thing apart from the Deity, nor a bare relation, nor only the manner of susbsisting, but the essence of God, with a certain manner of subsisting.[25]

The divine nature, according to the Reformed orthodox, has a manner of subsistence that is very different from that of any created being. Muller summarizes Reformed orthodox thought on this point:

> Specifically, *ousia* or *theotos* refers to the unity of the

---

[24] William Bucanus, *Institutiones theologicae, seu locorum communium Christianae religionis, ex Dei verbo, et praestissimorum theologorum orthodoxo consensu expositorum . . .* (Bern: John and Isaiah le Preux, 1605), 4.

[25] Johannes Wollebius, *Christianae theologiae compendium* (Basel: John Jacob Genath, 1626), 20-21.

Godhead in a manner different than the reference of the common essence of humanity to individual human beings — whereas divinity, as Father, Son, and Spirit, is numerically one God, human beings, one in essence, are numerically many.[26]

The 2LCF thus assumes what was common among the Reformed orthodox: the Father is infinite and divine, having the whole divine essence; the Son is infinite and divine, having the whole divine essence; and the Spirit is infinite and divine, having the whole divine essence. Yet they are not three essences, for the common essence is undivided. As for what appears to be the logical contradiction here — speaking of one in three, or three in one — Owen appeals to the distinction between the infinite God and finite creatures.

Distinction of persons (it being in an *Infinite* substance) doth no way prove difference of Essence between the Father and the Sonne. Where Christ as Mediatour is said to be another from the Father, or God, spoken *personally* of the Father, it argues not in the least, that he is not partaker of the same nature with him. That in one Essence there can be but one person, may be true where the Substance is *Finite*, and limited, but hath no place in that which is *infinite*.[27]

This also means that God is not a quaternity: three persons and the essence itself. The divine essence is not distinct from the persons as a thing. In the Trinity there is another and another (*alius et alius*), not another thing and another thing (*aliud et aliud*). The Father and the Son, for instance, are distinguished from one another *personally*, as to their distinct manner of subsistence in the divine essence, but not

---

[26] Muller, *PRRD*, 4:175.

[27] John Owen, *Vindiciae Evangelicae or The Mystery of the Gospell Vindicated, and Socianisme Examined, in the consideration, and confutation of a Catechisme, called A Scripture Catechisme, written by J. Biddle, M. A. And the Catechisme of Valentinus Smalcius, commonly called the Racovian Catechisme* . . . (London: Leon. Lichfield, 1655), 139. The same statement appears, almost verbatim, in John Owen, *A Brief Declaration and Vindication of the Doctrine of the Trinity: As also the Person and Satisfaction of Christ* (London: 1669), 58-59.

as separate things from or out of the divine essence. Since they each have the same undivided nature or essence, Leigh explains:

> They differ not in their Natures as three men or three Angels differ, for they differ so as one may be without the other; but now the Father is not without the Sonne, nor the Sonne without the Father, so that there is the same numerical Essence.[28]

This careful statement of the unity and distinction of the divine nature has two far reaching implications. First, the Son, as eternally begotten of the Father, is personally distinct from the Father, but not of a lesser, different, or subordinate essence. The Father, though he is first in the order of subsistence and in the order of historical operations (cf. 1 Cor. 8:4-6), is not primary essence and the Son a secondary or other essence. "To argue otherwise," Muller notes, "is to claim real or substantial distinctions between the persons, to reduce the unity of the persons to a generic unity . . . and to produce either a form of tritheism or a radical subordinationism."[29] Secondly, the personal property of the Son — to be eternally begotten of the Father — must be understood as the begetting of an infinite and divine subsistence (not essence) *within* the one, eternal, undivided, infinite and divine Being. Whatever the analogy between human begetting and divine begetting, the former is of a *finite* essence belonging to a finite genus or species (i.e., humanity) and therefore cannot be the measure of the latter. Nehemiah Coxe, a Particular Baptist pastor and likely one of the editors of the 2LCF, makes this very point against Thomas Collier's denial of the doctrines of the Trinity and the Son's deity, echoing the language and substance of 2LCF 2.3.

> Now unto these relative properties [of each divine subsistence] belong all imaginable perfection, but no imperfection because they are in God: Therefore as considered in him they do infer personality, because a

---

[28] Edward Leigh, *A Systeme or Body of Divinity* (London: A.M. for William Lee, 1662), 253. Cf. Bucanus, *Institutiones theologicae*, 4-6.

[29] Muller, *PRRD*, 4:179-80.

personal subsistence, is the most perfect manner of being in the whole reasonable nature . . . Though in our conception of personality in the Divine nature, we must separate from it whatsoever imperfection is seen in a created person: Every created person hath a limited essence distinct and distant from one another: But all the increated [uncreated] persons in the Deity have the same immense undivided essence, and are the one Eternal immortal invisible only wise God.[30]

The collation of biblical texts cited by the 2LCF indicate that this doctrinal formulation was not understood to be the fruit of rationalism, but instead was elicited from the *principium cognoscendi theologiae*, Holy Scripture (cf. 2LCF 1.6), as interpreted according to the Protestant principle of the analogy of Scripture (cf. 1.9). God's proper or essential name, "I am" (Exod. 3:14), reveals that he alone is "infinite in being, and perfection" (cf. 2.1). God is essential or absolute perfection: he is one, simple, infinite, and divine essence. Yet, John 14:11 and 1 Corinthians 8:6 interpreted side by side establish that this divine name is properly predicated of the Father, the Son, and the Spirit for two reasons: first, because of the unity of the divine essence and the mutual indwelling (*perichoresis*) of Father, Son, and Spirit in the one divine essence (John 14:11); and, secondly, because Scripture ascribes divine names and divine operations in common to both the Father and the Son (1 Cor. 8:6). The Father, the Son, and the Spirit each have the whole divine essence. The Son, therefore, has in common with the Father and the Spirit all the essential properties of the divine essence (2.1-2). He is *very God*, eternal, immense, Almighty, perfect, and infinite. For God is one in Trinity. At the same time, the Father, the Son, and the Spirit are not three slices of one pie, three parts of an apple, three forms of water, or three individual essences of one generic essence, since the one God who reveals himself as "I am" is neither distributed into three parts or components, nor divided into three graded essences or ranked persons: God is Trinity in Unity.

---

[30] Coxe, *Vindiciae Veritatis*, 7. On Coxe as a probable editor of the 2LCF, along with his co-pastor William Collins, see Renihan, *Edification and Beauty*, 22-26.

2. One essence, three subsistences: the confessional language of unity and distinction

The 2LCF, in fact, carefully safeguards this understanding of the unity of the divine essence and the distinction of the persons by adopting the rather technical vocabulary of one *Being* (or nature, essence) and three *subsistences*. Tritheism says that Father, Son, and Spirit are three different *essences* of the genus God. Modalism and Sabellianism argue that the one divine essence or person manifests itself in three modes or roles externally, in the works of creation (Father), redemption (Son), and sanctification (Spirit), while subordinationism claims that the one divine essence is marked by a gradation of degree or rank. Orthodox trinitarianism rejected these formulations, teaching instead that the distinction of persons is intrinsic to the Godhead. *Within* the one infinite and divine *Being* (or essence) there are three consubstantial, coequal, and coeternal *persons* or *personal subsistences*. Among the Reformed orthodox, the terms person and subsistence were understood to be roughly equivalent; both are attempts to describe the distinction of persons in the Godhead. Yet certain Reformed theologians argue that *subsistence* is preferable because it expresses more precisely than the loaded term *persona* the import of the Greek term *hypostasis*, a term with biblical precedent (Heb. 1:3).[31] Coxe not only uses *subsistence* in his disputation against Collier, but appeals to this biblical text as supplying the "warranty of this term," arguing on trinitarian grounds that as *hypostasis* is applied to the Father so it also rightly used of the Son and the Spirit.[32] It is frequently the case, moreover, that theologians who employ the term person explain it by use of the word subsistence. Polanus, for example, writes, "A person of the Deity is a subsistence having by nature the whole divine essence, but having properties that are incommunicable from one distinct

---

[31] Wollebius, *Compendium*, 20; Francis Cheynell, *The Divine Trinunity of the Father, Son, and Holy Spirit: or, the blessed Doctrine of the three coessential subsistents in the eternal Godhead without any confusion or division of the distinct Subsistences, or multiplication of the the most single and entire Godhead* . . . (London: T. R. and E. M. for Samuel Gellibrand, 1650), 83-84.

[32] Coxe, *Vindiciae Veritatis*, 7. Coxe appears to be appropriating the argumentation of Ames for the purpose of his polemic against Collier. See Ames, *Medulla theologica*, 18.

person to another."[33] Wollebius makes the same point: "The persons of the Deity are subsistences, each of whom has the whole essence of God, differing in their incommunicable properties."[34] The 2LCF thus employs the term subsistence, with precedent in the Reformed tradition "as a precise description of the way the persons related to the essence of God."[35]

By itself subsistence was used to speak of a being's mode or manner of existence. So, for example, the 2LCF uses this term to speak of the manner of God's essential self-existence: he subsists in and of himself eternally (cf. 2.1). As used in the doctrine of the Trinity, however, the term describes the personal mode or manner of existence of the Father, the Son, and the Holy Spirit, *within* the one divine nature. Used of these three *personally*, therefore, it underscores that they are simultaneously *distinguished* one from another and *related* one to another *personally* without division of the divine essence. To say, for example, that the Son is a subsistence in the one God is to say that he has his own personal manner of existence within the Godhead, by which we know, on the one hand, that he is neither the Father nor the Spirit and, on the other hand, that he is eternally related to the Father and the Spirit in the one, common divine essence. Coxe exemplifies the significance of this terminology by stating that God

> is the Divine essence, *subsisting* in three relative properties: the relative property of the Father is to beget . . . The relative property of the Son is to be begotten; The relative property of the Holy Spirit is *to be breathed*, or to *proceed* from the Father and the Son . . .[36]

---

[33] Amandus Polanus von Polansdorf, *Partitiones theologicae* (1590; Geneva: Peter Albert, 1623), 25. Cf. Zacharius Ursinus, *Corpus doctrinae Christianae* (Hanover: 1634), 131, 134; William Perkins, *A Golden Chaine: or, the description of theologie, containing the order of the causes of salvation and damnation, according to Gods word* in *The Workes of that famous and worthy minister of Christ in the Universitie of Cambridge, Mr. William Perkins*, vol. 1 (London: John Legatt, 1612), 14; and Leigh, *Body of Divinity*, 253-54.

[34] Wollebius, *Compendium*, 20.

[35] Muller, *PRRD*, 4:184. Cf. 2LCF 8.2, which uses the term "person" with respect to the Son.

[36] Coxe, *Vindicae Veritatis*, 6-7. Coxe appears to have borrowed significantly from Ames at this point. Cf. Ames, *Medulla*, 17; Ames, *Marrow*, 15-16.

This technical vocabulary—essence and subsistence—is thus designed to maintain "the utter unity of the divine being while at the same time safeguarding with precision the way in which the one essence is also three."[37] This is why the 2LCF goes on to state, again incorporating the language of the 1LCF, that the three subsistences, Father, Son, and Spirit, are "all infinite, without beginning, therefore but one God who is not to be divided in nature and Being; but distinguished by several peculiar, relative properties, and personal relations." This statement makes explicit what is entailed in the language of three subsistences in one essence, or one essence in three subsistences. The Son, for instance, is distinct, not from the essence, but from the Father and the Spirit as a personal subsistence within the essence. He is distinguished, in other words, by personal properties that are unique, incommunicable, or "peculiar" to his individual subsistence. It can only be said of the Son that he is the Son "eternally begotten of the Father." This also describes the manner of his "personal relation" to the Father. The Son is not a different thing from the Father. As subsistences in the divine essence these three are necessarily related, but in such a manner that neither the essence is divided nor the persons confounded. Thus, to be a personal subsistence in the Godhead is to be distinguished from the other personal subsistences *personally*, but not divided *essentially*. Father, Son, and Spirit are three fully divine and infinite *subsistences* within the one, undivided, infinite and divine Being or nature. We will address the implications of this for the doctrine of the Son's eternal generation more fully in the next section. At this point, however, we note that the 2LCF is intent on highlighting what the Particular Baptists, and the Reformed orthodox more broadly, regarded as a fundamental, albeit incomprehensible, truth revealed in Holy Scripture: the one God is Trinity, and Trinity in Unity. Cheynell expresses this point rather succinctly.

> We do believe that God is one, most *singly and singularly one*, and *an only one*: The unity of the Godhead is not a *generical*, or a *specifical* unity, but a most singular unity . . . All the three Persons have one and the same single and infinite

---

[37] Muller, *PRRD*, 4:184.

Godhead, and therefore must needs *mutually subsist* in one another, because they are all three one and the same infinite God. *Three consubstantial, coessential, coeternal, coequal Persons, are distinguished, but not divided, are united, but not confounded;* united in their *one* nature, not confounded in their distinct subsistences; nay though their subsistence is in one another, yet their subsistences are distinct, but their nature most singularly the same; nay *the divine nature is as singular as any one of the singular subsistences,* and yet whatever is proper to the Divine nature is common to all three of these Divine subsistences; and the Divine nature doth not subsist out of these three Divine subsistences.[38]

With these contextual constraints in view, then, I turn next to the doctrine of eternal generation more narrowly considered.

The Eternal Generation of the Son

The intent of the previous section has been to underscore that when the 2LCF speaks of the Son's personal subsistence, of what distinguishes him as the Son from the Father and the Spirit, it does not do so in the abstract. It was, in fact, common among the Reformed orthodox to aver, especially against the antitrinitarianism of the age, that the Son is not and cannot be separated or divided from his relation to the Father and the Spirit within the one, common divine essence. "When we describe the Divine nature," argues Cheynell against John Biddle, "we should not abstract it from the three Persons; and when we describe a Divine Person we should not abstract him from the Divine Nature."[39] For the

---

[38] Cheynell, *Divine Trinunity*, 42.

[39] Cheynell, *Divine Trinunity*, 80, emphasis original. In email correspondence Dr. James M. Renihan reminded me that Cheynell's rule is reminiscent of the words of Gregory Nazianzen, a fourth century Greek theologian and key figure at the Council of Constantinople (381): "No sooner do I conceive of the One than I am illumined by the splendor of the Three; no sooner do I distinguish Them than I am carried back to the One." Cf. John Owen, *Of Communion with God the Father, Sonne, and Holy Ghost, each person distinctly in love, grace, and consolation: or The saints fellowship with the Father, Sonne, and Holy Ghost, unfolded* (London: A. Lichfield,

theologians of the era, including the 2LCF, to speak of the Son's distinct subsistence, his personal manner of existence or his peculiar, incommunicable properties, was to speak of the Son in the concrete, as he subsists in the one divine essence, himself having the whole divine essence, and therefore, of one essence, of one power, and of one eternity with the Father and the Spirit. While he is distinguished as the Son, then, it was deemed necessary to maintain the doctrine of the unity of the divine essence, in accord with such biblical texts as John 10:30 and 14:11.

With that said, we have noted at some length that the 2LCF formulates the doctrine of the Trinity so as to emphasize *that* the Son is distinct from and related to the Father and the Spirit as to his personal subsistence. The key question, however, remains: According to the 2LCF, *what* distinguishes the Son? *How* is he distinct *personally*? What are his peculiar relative properties and his personal relation? Coxe answers: "The relative property of the Son is to be begotten."[40] This is precisely the point of the language of 2LCF 2.3, that "the Son is eternally begotten of the Father." To understand the intent of this language, this section will consider both the theological content and the biblical foundation of the doctrine of eternal generation, as argued by the 2LCF and Reformed orthodoxy.

1. Theological content

In addition to his proper name, "Son," which is incommunicable, the Son is personally distinguished from and personally related to the Father, according to the 2LCF, by reason of this incommunicable property: he is "eternally begotten of the Father." Only the Son is the Father's proper Son, and only the Son is begotten of the Father. Yet because he is begotten *of the Father*, he is eternally and personally related to the Father within the divine essence. In order to understand what the 2LCF intends by this language, it is helpful to observe how Owen approached the subject, even though he states his formulation of the doctrine in his polemic against the

---

1657), 6, margin.

[40] Coxe, *Vindiciae Veritatis*, 7.

argumentation of Biddle that the classical doctrine of eternal generation is a logical impossibility. Owen begins by noting that such an argument is "the fruit of measuring *Spirituall* things by *carnall*; *infinite* by *finite*; God by our selves; the object of *Faith*, by corrupted Rules of corrupted *Reason*." Owen insists, however, that because Scripture plainly teaches that the Son is *eternally* begotten of the Father, and that he is the Father's proper or natural Son, it is neither valid nor sound to object to the doctrine by measuring what is supernatural and infinite according to what is physical and finite. "What is *impossible* in *finite*, limited Essences," he writes, "may be possible & convenient to that which is *infinite* & *unlimited*; as is that whereof we speake." A positive definition of the doctrine follows:

> We say then, that in the Eternall Generation of the Son, the *whole* Essence of the Father is communicated to the Sonne, as to a *personall existence* in the same Essence without multiplication or division of it; the same essence continuing still *one* in number; and this without the least shew of *impossibility* in an infinite essence. All the Arguments that lye against it, being taken from the Propertys and attendencys of that which is finite.[41]

Though the 2LCF does not use the word *communication*, that is surely the intended meaning of the term it does use: "begotten."[42] It is imperative to note, however, what Owen and the Particular Baptists do not say. It is not the divine essence that begets or is begotten; if that were the case the divine essence would be divided. Polanus clarifies this very point by an appeal to the simplicity of the divine essence.

> The divine essence neither begets, nor is begotten: for that which begets, is, as to the thing itself, distinguished from that which is begotten; now the divine essence, which is one and most simple, is not in a real manner (*realiter*) distinguished from itself.[43]

---

[41] Owen, *Vindiciae* Evangelicae, 232-33.
[42] Cf. Fesko, *Westminster Assembly*, 179-81.
[43] Polanus, *Partitiones*, 26.

The need for such clarification was, in part, the common Socinian objection to the doctrine of eternal generation. Bucanus explains and answers this objection:

> Ob: The essence of the Father is communicated to the Son by generation. Therefore there is one essence in the Father, another in the Son, because there is one essence begetting, and another begotten. R: We must distinguish between generation and communication. Now, the person begets and is begotten. Indeed, the essence neither begets nor is begotten, but is communicated.[44]

For the essence absolutely to beget or absolutely to be begotten would divide the indivisible essence. Rather, the Father begets the Son; the Son is begotten of the Father. At the same time, however, the Father does not beget the Son out of his (the Father's) personal subsistence. For the Father to communicate his person to the Son would mean that the Son just is the Father, or the Father just is the Son. This compromises the distinction of the persons. Instead,

> The divine persons are distinguished by their inward and personal actions. The Father did from all Eternity communicate the living essence of God to the Son, in a most wonderfull and glorious way.[45]

Of tremendous significance for understanding the 2LCF's doctrine, then, is the very point established in this same paragraph, that Father, Son, and Holy Spirit "each have the whole divine essence." The manner in which the Father, as the Father, has the whole divine essence is "of none," since he is "neither begotten nor proceeding." The manner in which the Son, as the Son, has the whole divine essence is by the Father's "inward and personal" act of begetting or communication. The question the doctrine of eternal generation answers is this: How does the Son have the whole divine essence, but in such a manner that the one common essence is not divided and the distinct persons are not confounded? The

---

[44] Bucanus, *Institutiones*, 12.
[45] Cheynell, *Divine Trinunity*, 188-89.

theologians of the era argued that the answer is simple, yet profoundly mysterious: the Son, as to his personal subsistence in the divine essence (i.e., as the Son), has the whole divine essence because the Father *personally* communicated *his* whole essence (i.e., the whole divine essence the Father has of himself) to the Son *personally*. Having affirmed that the very essence and nature of God is in Christ, so that he is God, Zanchi defines eternal generation in these very terms, at the same time affirming that the Son, as he is God, is *autotheos*, of himself.

> Indeed, from whom does he then have [the whole divine essence]? Of himself, or of another? If you say of himself simply, then he has not been generated of the Father. For what is it to be the Son generated of the Father, if not God of God, light of light, very God of very God, as the fathers at the Council of Nicaea defined it from the word of God? He is, most certainly, generated of the Father. Therefore, he has his essence and whatsoever he is of the Father. Yet in what manner does he have this? By being begotten of the Father. He is therefore generated of the substance of the Father. This generation, however, is eternal, so that God the Father was never without God the Son. Likewise, generation is most perfect, so that the Father's whole essence is communicated to the Son without any diminution, alteration, or mutation, but the whole yet remains in the Father. And, therefore, one is not able to say that the Son's essence is derived, created, or essentiated from the essence of the Father, since the simple essence that is in the Father is communicated fully to the Son. It is for this reason one may accept the language of certain pious persons that the Son, as he is God, is of himself, that is, the essence that is in the Son is not of another essence, but is self-existent. For it is neither created nor properly speaking generated, as if it were another thing, but the same is communicated.[46]

We may also note the way Perkins states the doctrine in keeping

---

[46] Hie. Zanchius, *De tribus Elohim, Aeterno Patre, Filio, & Spirtum Sanctum* . . ., in *Omnium Operum Theologicorum*, col. 249.

with the language of Nicaea, maintaining both the Son's eternal generation as the Son and his aseity as fully divine:

> In the generation of the Sonne, these properties must be noted: I. He that begetteth, and he that is begotten are together, and not one before another in time. II. He that begetteth, doth communicate with him that is begotten, not some one part, but his whole essence. III. The Father begot the Sonne, not out of himselfe, but within himselfe . . . The incommunicable property of the Father, is to be unbegotten, to bee a Father, and to beget . . . The two other persons have the Godhead, or the whole divine essence, of the Father by communication . . . The Sonne is the second person, begotten of the Father from all eternity . . . Although the Sonne bee begotten of his Father, yet nevertheless, he is of and by himselfe very God: for he must be considered either according to his essence, or according to his filiation or Sonneship. In regard of his essence, he is (*autotheos*) that is, of and by himselfe very God: for the Deitie which is common to all the three persons is not begotten. But as he is a person, and the Sonne of the Father, hee is not of himselfe, but from another: for hee is the eternall Sonne of his Father. And thus he is truely said to be *very God of very God*.[47]

The 2LCF, therefore, affirms that the Son's eternal generation is to be understood as the Father's necessary, eternal, supernatural, and incomprehensible personal act of communicating his whole essence to the Son, as to the Son's personal subsistence, without any imperfection, dependence, succession, multiplication, mutation, causation, derivation, confusion, or division, either of the one common divine essence or of the distinct personal subsistences of the Trinity.

While it is tempting to construe this generation in terms known to us, namely on analogy with human procreation or the grace of adoption, the 2LCF argues against such an analogy by the way in which it frames, both contextually and linguistically, the doctrine. Specifically, the 2LCF argues that the Son is *eternally* begotten of the Father. He is, as the 2LCF later states, "infinite, without beginning."

---

[47] Perkins, *Works*, 1:14.

He is neither created nor made, as if he were another thing external to the divine essence or another thing caused by the Father. The Son's generation is without beginning, without end, and without succession. As such, the Son is necessarily and eternally begotten of the Father within the unity of the Godhead.[48] The Son's filiation is an *ad intra* personal work of the Father, the person begetting, and an *ad intra* personal work of the Son, the person begotten. For this reason, it is also necessary, rather than voluntary, and is, as Zanchi said, most perfect. To this relative property of the Son, Coxe notes succinctly, "belongs all imaginable perfection, but no imperfection," precisely because the Son is begotten of the Father "in God."[49]

Because the Son's generation is eternal, internal, necessary, and most perfect, its manner — that is, how the Father communicates his essence to the Son — is regarded as "supernatural" (*hyperphysical*) and therefore "ineffable."[50] Pictet, in fact, states this in the strongest possible terms: "Here the understanding of not only of men, but of angels, is at a loss; here we must lay our hands upon our lips, and be silent."[51] The point being made is that the Son's eternal generation cannot be construed in the very same way as the begetting of human procreation, or the begetting entailed in the graces of regeneration and adoption. Every act of begetting is an act of communication from the one begetting to the one begotten: yet here is where the analogy begins and ends. For in the birth of a human son, a father communicates the seed of life, which produces another thing with its own distinct essence. The generic human essence is divided, as a human father communicates that essence out of himself, not within himself. So, in time, there is one before (a human father) and another after (a human son). By virtue of being begotten, a human son moves from a state of potentiality (or non-existence) to another state of potentiality (a living, growing, changing human being). In the case of regeneration, a communication of grace renews the component parts of the soul. So

---

[48] Cheynell, *Divine Trinunity*, 189.

[49] Coxe, *Vindiciae Veritatis*, 7.

[50] Lucas Trelcatius, Jr., *Scholastica et methodica locorum communium S. Theologiae Institutio, didactice & elenctice in epitome explicata* (London: John Bill, 1604), 22.

[51] Benedict Pictet, *Christian Theology*, trans. Reyroux (Geneva: 1696; London: 1834), 114.

also with adoption: a new status is communicated by divine grace, before which one was a servant in sin and after which one is an adopted son of God. Every imperfection accruing to finite acts of generation or begetting must be removed, negated, so to speak, in order to apprehend something of this infinite mystery of the Son's generation.[52] For not only is he the natural (not adopted) and eternal (not created) Son of God, but is also *eternally* begotten of the Father within the divine essence.[53] This divine act of generation within the Godhead is not one of mutation or creation. Nothing new is produced or caused. The Son is not derived from the Father or propagated by the Father as another thing. He is not thereby subject to succession or change, moving from non-existence (potentiality) to existence (actuality). He is thus not other than or less than the Father in degree, rank, or authority. All manner of ontological subordination is precluded. Neither, moreover, is the divine essence subject to change, succession, multiplication, or division. Having argued already that this generation takes place within the unity of the Godhead, and is therefore perfect, Cheynell states the significance of all these negations.

> The Father did beget his Son without change or motion after a most glorious and wonderfull manner; there can be no change, no motion, or succession in this eternall and most perfect generation. The Essence of God is spirituall, John 4.24, and therefore the Son is not begotten of the Father's seed, or any material substance, because God is a single and most pure Act, who doth beget a Son within himself Essentially one with himself, and therefore his Son doth not subsist out of himself, John 14.10, John 10.30, for an infinite nature cannot be poured forth beyond itself. There can be no essential change in the Son by this generation, because the generation is eternall, and the nature which is communicated by generation is unchangeable; the Father did unchangeably beget his Son, and his Son is unchangeably begotten, there is no shadow of changing or turning either in the Father of lights, or the Son of

---

[52] Coxe, *Vindiciae Veritatis*, 7.
[53] Collins, *Orthodox Catechism*, 13.

righteousness, because they are the one and the same unchangeable Jehovah, James 1.17, Malach. 3.6. They are too carnal and base who make an unworthy and odious comparison between the material generation of a weak man, and this more than spirituall and supernatural generation. The eternall and unchangeable Father doth beget an eternall and unchangeable Son according to the perfection of his eternall, unchangeable, infinite nature. The Father doth beget his Son naturally, and therefore in a way agreeable to his unchangeable Nature; if the Son were not necessarily begotten, his being would not be necessary, and then his Essence would not be divine.[54]

When the 2LCF, therefore, indentifies the order of the divine subsistences, although it does not employ the technical term *taxis*, it avoids conceiving of the Son's generation, as well as the Spirit's procession, as if it entailed any essential subordination or personal gradation. Coxe avers against Collier's subordinationism that the order is one of "eternal origination," in which "there is no priority of time or nature."[55] Coxe here reflects the teaching of Reformed orthodoxy.[56] The order of the divine persons, explains Ursinus, is not a temporal order, but an order of existence, in which "no person is before or after the others in time (*tempore*), dignity (*dignitate*), or degree (*gradu*), but only in the order in which they exist."[57] Drawing upon a number of biblical citations (Isa. 63:7-8; Matt. 3:16-17; and John 15:26), Trelcatius contrasts the way in which the persons of the Trinity are distinct from one another, as to order, number, and mode of working (*ordine, numero, et modo agendi*), with any and all notions of degree, state, or dignity (*gradu, statu, aut dignitate*).[58] The language simply clarifies what is latent in the Reformed discussion of the distinct personal properties of each divine subsistence, as they exist within the undivided divine essence. *Taxis* is simply an irreversible order by which the Father is distinguished personally

---

[54] Cheynell, *Divine Trinunity*, 195-96.
[55] Coxe, *Vindiciae Veritatis*, 7. Cf. Ames, *Medulla*, 16.
[56] Cf. Polanus, *Partitiones*, 25-26; Bucanus, *Institutiones*, 12.
[57] Ursinus, *Corpus doctrinae*, 136.
[58] Trelcatius, *Scholastica et methodica*, 22; Cf. Perkins, *Works*, 1:14.

by his incommunicable property of being neither begotten nor proceeding, the Son by his incommunicable property of being begotten of the Father, and the Spirit by his incommunicable property of proceeding from both the Father and the Son.[59] What is more, as Trelcatius' comments indicate, when understood as the personal *ad intra* acts of the Godhead, these distinctions form the trinitarian foundation of the personal *ad extra* works, the appropriated works, of the persons of the Trinity. The 2LCF adumbrates these distinctions when making mention of the Son's personal properties at the outset of its formulation of the doctrine of the Mediator's person and office. "It pleased God," according to 2LCF 8.1, "in his eternal purpose, to choose and ordain the Lord Jesus *his only begotten Son*, according to the Covenant made between them both, to be the Mediator between God and Man."[60] As such, the Son's personal works of incarnation and mediation, though willed by God as an essential *ad intra* work, terminate upon and are appropriate to the Son, rather than the Father or the Spirit, precisely because he is the only begotten Son.

Even though the Particular Baptists, and more broadly the Reformed orthodox, insist that we are limited in what we can say regarding *how* the Father communicates his whole essence to the Son, they likewise insisted *that* the Father does so necessarily, indeed, in a truly eternal, spiritual, supernatural, immutable, perfect, infinite, and therefore, ineffable and incomprehensible manner within the unity of the Godhead. The doctrine, they argued strenuously, cannot be dismissed on the grounds of our inability to comprehend, especially since they were convinced that God had revealed in Scripture for believers to apprehend and confess that the Son is the consubstantial, coequal, and coeternal Son of the Father, "begotten before all worlds . . . begotten, not made."

2. Biblical foundations and exegetical argumentation

The Reformed orthodox argued, as Wollebius summarizes, that

---

[59] Ursinus, *Corpus doctrinae*, 136-37; Trelcatius, *Scholastica et methodica*, 22; and Coxe, *Vindiciae Veritatis*, 7.

[60] See also Wollebius, *Compendium*, 28-30. Cf. Muller, *PRRD*, 4:257-60.

"The dogma of the Trinity is not merely a tradition of the church, but a doctrine expressed in the Holy Scripture."[61] Moreover, they consistently maintained that this is a revealed mystery rather to be adored than enquired into by reason, since the triune God is infinite and incomprehensible.[62] For such reasons, Coxe emphasized *pace* Collier the limitation of reason, the sufficiency of revelation, and the necessity of faith.

> The Scripture doth also instruct us concerning the subsistence of God, or the manner of his being; and this is such a glorious mystery as by his word only is revealed to us; we cannot by reason comprehend it, but ought to adore it; and by Faith rest in his testimony concerning it.[63]

As Cheynell confronted the difficulty of discussing the distinction of the persons of the Trinity, he went so far as to invoke divine aid.

> This question concerning the Distinction of the Divine Nature and these three most glorious persons which subsist in it, is the most difficult point in all Divinitie, and therefore I humbly beg the assistance of all these glorious persons, that I may conceive and write judiciously and reverently of this profound and glorious Mysterie of Faith.[64]

The Particular Baptists and Reformed orthodox alike confessed that what is to be known of God, and so what is to be known of the eternal generation of the Son, is communicated to us, not that we might speculate according to our finite, even sanctified, reason, but that the church would believe God's sufficient self-revelation in Holy Scripture. For this reason, the Reformed orthodox sought to articulate and defend the doctrine of the Son's eternal generation on

---

[61] Wollebius, *Compendium*, 21.

[62] Theodore Beza, *Theses theologicae in schola Genevensi ab aliquot Sacarum literarum studios sub DD. Theod. Beza & Antonio Fayo S.S. Theologiae professoribus propositae & disputatae* (Geneva: Vignon, 1586), 3; John Downame, *The Summe of Sacred Divinitie Briefly and Methodically Propounded* (London: William Stansby, 1625), 33-34; and Leigh, *Body of Divinity*, 266.

[63] Coxe, *Vindiciae Veritatis*, 6.

[64] Cheynell, *Divine Trinunity*, 97.

the basis of Scripture, the *princium cognoscendi theologiae.*

Considered in the context of the 2LCF itself, the Particular Baptists were convinced that the doctrine is "expressly set down" and "necessarily contained" in Scripture (1.6). They argued that a doctrine was to be believed only on the authority of God speaking in Scripture (1.10). Thus, following the WCF and the SD, they cited John 1:14, 18 as the *sedes doctrinae*, the primary biblical foundation of the doctrine.[65] At the same time, neither the Particular Baptists nor the Reformed orthodox argued that the doctrine rested entirely on these two texts. Rather, they were convinced that the doctrine was taught clearly and sufficiently across Holy Scripture.

A brief word is in order regarding the 2LCF's practice of citing biblical texts. To call this a "proof-texting method" in the modern derogatory sense is misleading. By citing specific texts in support of their statements, the authors of the Confession were indicating their adherence to methods of biblical interpretation and doctrinal formation that was characteristic not just of Reformed orthodoxy but also of the whole sweep of pre-critical exegesis. The texts cited here by the 2LCF are regarded as the primary seat of the doctrine, the primary (not exclusive) place in Scripture where the doctrine was either explicitly taught or "by just consequence deduced."[66] By citing these texts the 2LCF was not arbitrarily appealing to texts out of context. Rather, as with the other confessional symbols of the era, the 2LCF was drawing on the interpretation of these texts as argued in the biblical commentaries and annotations of the era. The statement of the Confession is thus a doctrinal result resting on the foundation of Scripture and its proper interpretation. The biblical texts cited thus point in two directions: back to biblical interpretation and forward to doctrinal formulation. Such texts, the *dicta probantia* or "proving statements," function as the necessary link between biblical interpretation and doctrinal formulation. A confession was not designed to reproduce the work of biblical interpretation, but to affirm its fruit, given that Scripture was the

---

[65] Richard A. Muller, *Dictionary of Latin and Greek Theological Terms: Drawn Principally from Protestant Scholastic Theology* (Grand Rapids: Baker, 1985), 278, defines *sedes doctrinae* as "*a seat of doctrine*: the particular text of Scripture used as the primary foundation of a doctrine."

[66] Coxe, *Vindiciae Veritatis*, 9.

only authoritative and sufficient foundation for every doctrinal topic and for a system of theology as a whole. Thus, when the 2LCF cited John 1:14, 18, it was not employing a crude form of proof-texting, but was instead reflecting a whole tradition of interpretation understood to be utterly indispensable and foundational for this doctrinal construct.[67]

The Particular Baptists agreed with the WCF and the SD that the doctrine of eternal generation rested primarily upon the explicit identification of the Son as *monogenes* (*unigenitus*) in John 1:14, 18. The biblical commentaries and annotations of the era argue the point exegetically. Although the so-called Westminster Annotations bear no direct relation to the *dicta probantia* cited by the WCF, they do provide an index of the interpretation that served as the biblical rationale for the Confession's citation of these two Johannine texts. The appellation *unigenitus*, only begotten, in John 1:14 is understood to confirm the full deity of the Son. Citing the patristic commentator Fulgentius, *unigenitus* is further defined in distinction from *primogenitus*, first begotten:

> in that Divine and Incomprehensible generation, in which before all times he is God of God, he is the onely begotten, the Son by nature: but in this generation wherein he became flesh, he is the first-born of every creature, or the first-born among many brethren, Rom 8.29, that is, of those whom he vouchsafed, through faith, to adopt his brethren.[68]

The annotation on John 1:18 does not repeat this interpretation, but does argue, citing John 13:22-23 and John 10:30, that the language

---

[67] For a helpful survey of the dependence of theological formulation on biblical interpretation, see Muller, *PRRD*, 2:442-520, esp. 502-20; and Richard A. Muller, "Scripture and the Westminster Confession," in Richard A. Muller and Rowland S. Ward, *Scripture and Worship: Biblical Interpretation and the Directory for Public Worship*, The Westminster Assembly and the Reformed Faith, vol. 1, ed. Carl R. Trueman (Phillipsburg, NJ: P&R Publishing, 2007), 59-82.

[68] *Annotations upon all the books of the Old and New Testament: this third, above the first and second, edition so enlarged, as they make an entire commentary on the Sacred Scripture: The like never before published in English. Wherein the text is explained, doubts removed, Scriptures parallel'd, and various readings observed; by the labor of certain learned Divines thereunto appointed, and therein employed* (London: Evan Tyler, 1657), in loc., John 1:14.

"the bosom of the Father" teaches that the Father and his only begotten Son are one in nature, omniscience, will, and knowledge.[69] The Dutch Annotations, commissioned by the Synod of Dort, adopt a similar interpretation of both texts, albeit with far greater brevity. Of particular note is that the Son's generation is identified as eternal, its manner unspeakable, and as the generation of one who is "of one essence with the Father, beloved of him."[70]

Of some significance among the Reformed orthodox is the proper translation of the term *monogenes*. Beza is illustrative of the point. He argues against Erasmus, who, following the late Medieval commentator Lorenza Valla, read *unicus* as a suitable rendering of *monogenes*. Beza adopts the translation *unigenitus*, only begotten, on account of John's singular use of the term. For while *unicus* may refer to a human child of distinction, and so may simply distinguish a son from his father's other offspring, *unigenitus* better reflects the emphasis of the Gospel writer, namely that *monogenes* is said properly only of Christ's divine nature, and not his human nature.[71] The 2LCF's use of this term, only begotten, and the citation of these two Johannine texts as the *sedes doctrinae* of the Son's eternal generation is not therefore without linguistic and exegetical rationale.

At the same time, a number of other biblical texts were understood to serve as *dicta probantia* for the doctrine, if not by way of express teaching, as in the case of John 1:14, 18, certainly by good and necessary consequence. As Muller has observed, the Reformed orthodox interpreted several texts along both positive and disputative lines.[72] Serving the positive formulation of the doctrine, for example, is the Westminster Annotations' comment on John

---

[69] *Annotations upon . . . the Old and New Testament*, in loc., John 1:18.

[70] Theodore Haak, *The Dutch Annotations upon the whole Bible: or, all the Holy Canonical Scriptures of the Old and New Testament, together with, and according to their own translation of all the text: as both the one and the other were ordered and appointed by the Synod of Dort, 1618, and published by authority, 1637* (London: Henry Hills, 1657), in loc., John 1:14, 18.

[71] Theodore Beza, *Novum D. N. Jesu Christi Testamentum. A Theodoro Beza versum, ad veritatem Graeci sermonis e regione appositi, cum eiusdem annotationibus, in quibus ratio interpretationis redditur* (Basel: Nicholas Barbir and Thomas Courteau, 1559), 271.

[72] Muller, *PRRD*, 4:283-88.

5:25-26. The text

> rendereth a reason of that he said the dead shall hear the
> voice of the Son of God, and live: because God the Father,
> who is the eternal Fountain of Life, communicateth his
> whole essence to the Son: so that, as he is the eternal Word
> and Wisdom of God, He hath all things of himself.[73]

The Reformed orthodox develop the argument positively also,
Muller notes, on the basis of an explicit reference to the Son's
generation in Psalm 2:7, the identification of the Son as beloved
(Matt. 3:17; 17:5), the proper name of the Son (John 5:18; Rom. 8:32),
the use of *unigenitus* throughout John's writings (John 1:14, 18; 3:15,
18; 1 John 4:9), the description of the Son as the glory and express
representation of the Father (Col. 1:15; Heb 1:3), and the
identification of the Son as the Wisdom "begotten of God" (Prov.
8:24-25 in conference with John 1:14).[74] Though the interpretation of
some of these texts was disputed among the Reformed orthodox,
notably Psalm 2:7, they nevertheless regarded a large collation of
biblical passages as either teaching or confirming this doctrinal
formulation.

   Much of this positive interpretive argumentation was put to use
by the Particular Baptists and the Reformed orthodox in polemic
against various antitrinitarians. Coxe, for example, invokes Psalm
2:7, John 1:14, 3:16, Proverbs 8:22-25, and Hebrews 1:3 against
Collier's denial of the classical and confessional doctrines of the
Trinity, the deity of the Son, and eternal generation.[75] One of the
more extensive exegetical arguments concerning the doctrine of
eternal generation specifically was developed by Cheynell in his
polemic against Biddle.[76] In this context, Cheynell argues four
conclusions regarding the doctrine of eternal generation, all of them
elicited and argued from the *dicta probantia* commonly employed by

---

[73] *Annotations upon . . . the Old and New Testament*, in loc., John 5:26.

[74] Muller, *PRRD*, 4:287-88.

[75] Coxe, *Vindiciae Veritatis*, 7, 11-12, 21.

[76] Owen's far more extensive polemical treatment of many of these same texts
is developed in Owen, *Vindiciae Evangelicae*, 231-46. For an analysis of the context of
Cheynell's and Owen's shared polemic against Biddle, see Lim, *Mystery Unveiled*,
172-216.

the Reformed orthodox. First, Psalm 2:7 collated with Hebrews 1:3-6 grounds the claim that "the Father did beget his Son." Against the objection that these texts refer only to a temporal begetting, Cheynell appeals to Matthew 3:17, 19:5, Acts 13:32-33, and Romans 1:4 to argue the point that Christ's anointing, transfiguration, and resurrection are not the cause of his sonship or generation, but are rather the manifestation of his eternal sonship and eternal generation.[77] Second, that the Son's generation is eternal is argued on the basis of Proverbs 8:22-25 as interpreted alongside Micah 5:2, John 1:1-3, John 17:5, Colossians 1:15, and Revelation 1:18. Not all of these texts are understood to teach the doctrine explicitly. Instead, because they attribute to the Son the divine attribute of eternity they confirm that his generation is necessarily eternal.[78] Third, that the Son is begotten of the Father in the unity of the Godhead is a point Cheynell argues from Romans 8:32 and John 5:18. Christ is the Father's "own" or "proper" Son, and the Father is Christ's "own" or "proper" Father. John 5:18 demonstrates that

> the Jews did well understand the force and importance of that expression, for say they, in that he said God is his own Father, he hath made himself equall with God; and therefore the phrase doth import that *he* is the *Naturall* and *Coessentiall* Son of God, else he could not be *Coequall* with his Father.

John 5:26 is, again, significant:

> God hath but one Coessentiall Son, to whom he hath given to have *life in himself*, John 5.26. because the Divine Nature, which is *life* itself is communicated to the Son by this eternall and ineffable generation. It is proper to *living* creatures to communicate their nature by generation in their low and imperfect way; but the great God who is not subject to imperfection, doth after the most glorious and perfect manner beget a Son in the unity of his own *living* Essence, who is therefore called the Son of the *living* God, that is the Naturall and Coesentiall Son of God, who hath the same

---

[77] Cheynell, *Divine Trinunity*, 191-93.
[78] Cheynell, *Divine Trinunity*, 193.

Divine Life, Nature, Essence with the Father . . . The same single and infinite Essence is in the Father, Son, and Holy Ghost; the whole undivided and indivisible essence of God dwels in the Son in its fulnesse and infinite perfection.[79]

In view of the previous three points, Cheynell concludes that because God is spiritual (John 4:24) and immutable (James 1:17), the Son's generation by the Father is spiritual, devoid of all change, motion, and succession.[80]

While 2LCF 2.3 only cites two biblical texts as the foundation for the doctrine of eternal generation, the Particular Baptists hereby do not suggest that these are the only two biblical texts that teach or confirm this doctrinal formulation. They cited John 1:14, 18 as the *sedes doctrinae* of the Son's eternal generation in such a way as to point beyond these texts to a larger interpretive tradition of a number of other places of Scripture that, when collated and argued according to the analogy of Scripture, provided the necessary and sufficient biblical foundation for the doctrine.

Conclusion

The Particular Baptists confessed that Jesus is the Christ, the Son of the living God, begotten before all worlds, begotten, not made. Their articulation of this doctrine, in the context of the doctrine of the Trinity (2LCF 2.3), was hardly original. The theological content, the biblical foundations, even the language itself is unoriginal. As I have argued, the Particular Baptists confessed the catholic doctrine of eternal generation in the same manner and by way of the same biblical, theological, and polemical argumentation as their confessional Reformed counterparts. As did the Reformed orthodox generally, the 2LCF confessed that the Son's generation of the Father within the undivided divine essence was eternal, necessary, immutable, perfect, and so incomprehensible. Far from engaging in unbiblical rationalization or metaphysical speculation, they regarded this doctrine as a divinely revealed mystery, one founded

---

[79] Cheynell, *Divine Trinunity*, 193-95.
[80] Cheynell, *Divine Trinunity*, 195-96.

upon the express teaching of Holy Scripture and to be defended against all error on the same foundation. They did so, in fact, believing the doctrine to be not only a fundamental article of the Christian faith, but necessary to the Christian's faith. Indeed, they conclude 2LCF 2.3, adopting the language of SD 2.3, by confessing that this doctrine of the Trinity, including the doctrine of the Son's eternal generation, "is the foundation of all our Communion with God, and comfortable dependence upon him."

Chapter 14

The Temple Repair'd

Hercules Collins[*]

That Scripture which I shall lay for the Foundation of my Discourse is 2 Tim. ii. 15. *Study to shew thy self approved unto God, a Workman that needeth not be ashamed, rightly dividing the Word of Truth.* [1]

By way of Division: We consider those words are an exhortation. (1.) The Duty exhorted unto is *Study.* (2.) The End and Design of it is, that he may approve himself to God, and to all good Men, as a good Workman, *rightly dividing the Word of Truth.* And then we have (3.) The Advantage that follow it; all such will be delivered from Shame, and gain Honour and a holy Boldness in the Faith: For there is a Figure in the Text, where there is more intended than expressed. The Scripture speaks after the same manner in several places, as where it is said, *he will not break the Bruised Reed;* that is, he will strengthen the Soul under all its Temptations.

Doctrine of the Text

We shall now raise some Observations, which are express'd and implied in the words.

Doct. 1. *That Study is an Ordinance of God.*

Doct. 2. *That the Scriptures of Truth are the Foundation of a Minister's Study.*

---

[*] Hercules Collins (1646/7-1702) was a British Particular Baptist pastor and author of *An Orthodox Catechism.* Edited by Samuel Renihan.

[1] This sermon, abbreviated and edited, comes from Hercules Collins, *The Temple Repair'd: Or, An Essay to revive the long-neglected ordinances, of exercising the spiritual Gift of Prophecy for the Edification of the Churches; and of ordaining Ministers duly qualified* (London: William and Joseph Marshall, 1702).

Doct. 3. *Mens great Design and End in Study should not be to get Mens Hums and Applause by quaint and eloquent speech, but above all to please God, and win Souls.*

Doct. 4. *Those that study so as to approve themselves to God their Master, and rightly divide the Word of Truth, will be delivered from all Shame, and rather gain themselves Honour and holy Boldness.*

Doct. 5. *All Persons who will undertake to preach without Study, are not like to approve themselves to God their Master, nor rightly divide the Word of Truth, but rather expose themselves and the Cause of God in their hands to Shame and Contempt.*

Now I shall sum up all into one Doctrine.

Doct. *That it is the Duty of every Gospel-Minister so to study as they may approve themselves to God; and so divide the Word of Truth, that they may not be ashamed, but rather have the Honour that belongs to that calling.*

Exposition of the Doctrine

In speaking to this Proposition I shall use this Method. 1st. I shall explain the Point. 2*dly*. Lay down one Proposition. 3*dly*. Shew who are good Workmen. 4*thly*. Give the Reasons why they should so study 5*thly*. Improve the Doctrine.

I. By way of Explanation. When the Apostle saith *rightly dividing the Word of Truth*, you must know it is a Metaphorical Expression, a borrowed Saying, whether it be from the Priest's cutting the Sacrifices, so as all had their proper shares; or from the Parents dividing the Dish amongst several Children; or from the Carpenter who divides his Timber by a right Line: The word imports thus much, that Ministers should so divide the Word of Truth, as to give every one their due Portion. It is prophesied of Christ, *The Lord hath given me the Tongue of the Learned, that I should know how to speak a word in season to him that is weary.* Every one must have his Portion. You must seek the Sinner's Conversion, the ignorant Man's Instruction. *The good Shepherd will seek that which is lost, raise them that are fallen, and bind up the broken in Heart with God's sweet Promises, and labour to bring them to the Fold that have been driven away, heal and strengthen those that are sick.* Thus every one is to have his Portion rightly divided to him. In a word, Som must be fed *with*

Milk, some with strong Meat: Food for strong Men, and Milk for Babes (Ezek. 34.4, 16. Heb. 5.12).

II. The second General Head is to lay down one Proposition, which is this;

That it's God alone by the Inspiration of his Holy Spirit can make Men able Ministers of the New Testament: This is proved by Christ's words to *Paul,* who said unto him, *I have appear'd unto thee for this purpose, to make thee a Minister and a Witness both of those things thou hast seen, and in those things in which I will appear unto thee* (Acts 26.16). St. *Paul* acknowledgeth, when he saith, *Christ hath made us able Ministers of the New Testament* (2 Cor. 3.6.). And tho it be granted that human Literature is very useful for a Minister, yet it is not essentially necessary; but to have the Spirit of Christ to open the Word of Christ is essentially necessary: For altho it is possible to make an exact Translation of the Scriptures out of many learned Languages, and given an exact Grammatical Construction of the same, yet if this Man be void of the Spirit of Christ, he cannot know or understand the Mysteries contain'd in God's Word. Every rational Man will acknowledg the truth of that Sentence of the Apostle *Paul, As no Man knoweth the things of a Man, save the Spirit of a Man within him; even so the things of God knoweth no Man but the Spirit of God* (1 Cor. 2.11). Thus puts me in mind of a Saying of a worthy Minister at a Person's Ordination above four and twenty years ago; Tho I understood Latin and Greek, Philosophy, Logick, and Rhetorick, &c. yet before Conversion I was as ignorant of Christ as a wild Ass's Colt.

III. We shall labour to shew you who are good Workmen.

1. A good Workman will lay a good Foundation for his Superstructure. St. *Paul* saith, *As a wise Master-builder I have laid the Foundation, which was Christ alone, and no other Foundation can any one lay for the Salvation of immortal Souls* (1 Cor. 3.10.). All others that build upon any thing but him, are *foolish Builders, and build upon the Sand; and when the Storms arise, the House falls; and great will be the Fall* (Mat. 7.26, 27.) of any that that fall into Hell for want of building upon Christ their Foundation; for they only are truly wise that build their Happiness upon Christ crucified (1 Cor. 2.2.). This is that *Rock upon which whosoever builds, the Gates of Hell shall not prevail against him* (Mat. 16.18.); that is, the Rage, Malice, and Power of the Devil's Kingdom.

The Temple Repair'd

2. Such are good Workmen in the Mysteries of the Gospel who build a good Structure upon this good Foundation; that is, *Gold, Silver, precious Stones, not Wood, Hay, and Stubble* (1 Cor. 3.12.): We must take care that we do not build upon this Foundation bad Works, and an evil Life, and say Christ is our Foundation; neither must we build upon it unsound Doctrine, nor stuff our preaching with Human Art, Rhetorical Ornaments, Philosophical Questions or Reasons, for that is all Wood, Hay, and Stubble, and must be burnt up; but we must continue to preach the pure, divine, sound, and precious Doctrine of the Gospel, in a way conformable to the Substance of it, and build upon it a good Life, which is like Gold, Silver, and precious Stones that will abide the Trial.

3. A good Workman in the Gospel lays his Work well together, or else it wants that Profit and Beauty that otherwise it would have; our Discourses should hang as it were in a Link or Chain. Thus it is in all our Saviour's Sermons, and *Paul's* Epistles; there is a wonderful Coherence and Dependance of one thing upon another. When we name a Text we should not take our farewel of it, as too many do, and not return to it again in our whole Discourse; but we should closely follow the Scope and Design of the Spirit of God in that Text, with that Order and Connexion of the Parts, that it may look beautiful and prove profitable.

4. He is a good Workman in the things of God, that uses proper ways and means to prove a Theme or Proposition by. A Carpenter hath his proper Tools to do his Work withal; he doth not take a Mallet when he wants a Chizel, nor a Saw when he wants a Hammer, but uses such proper Tools as will effectually do his Work: As for Example, suppose your Proposition was this, That it is the Duty of every Man to love and praise God. Now to prove this, we argue as King *David* did, (1.) from our Creation: *The Lord is our Maker, let us therefore worship and bow down before him: Because he hath made us, we should enter into his Gates with Thanksgiving, and into his Courts with Praise* (Psal. 95.7. Ps. 100.3, 4). (2.) We ought to love and honour God superlatively, because this was the great End of our Creation: *God hath made all things* (saith *Solomon*) *for himself. The four and twenty Elders acknowledg that God is worthy to receive all Glory, Honour, and Power, because he created all things* (Prov. 16.4. Rev. 4.) (3.) We not only argue from the Author of our Being, and the End of our

Being, but from the lesser to the greater: As if it be the Duty of Children to honour their Parents, and the Duty of Subjects to honour their Prince; how much more is it the Duty of a Creature to honour its Creator? Again, if Men will bestow any Pains and Cost to prevent sickness and Death on their Bodies, how much more should we labor after the Salvation of our Souls?

5. We count them good Workmen that do their Work well, and a great deal too. Indeed there are some very good Workmen that do their Work well, but do a very little. Others again may speak a great many Words in a Sermon, who have but little Matter: He is most accepted that brings the best Bread and a full Meal. Some can deliver more Matter in half an hour to the profit of their Hearers, than others can in a whole hour. As some Persons do their Work so bad as makes some almost sick to see it, so some may preach as to make the Hearers sick to hear it: And yet some are so conceited of their own Abilities, that there is no room for Instruction. To be sure this is true, he doth the best Work and the most Work, that labours most in his Study, with a dependance upon God for a Blessing.

IV. The Reasons of the Point, in which I shall be very brief.

1. We should study to be good Workmen, because our Work is of the highest nature. Men that work among Jewels and precious Stones, ought to be very knowing of their business. A Minister's Work is a great Work, a holy Work, a heavenly Work. Hence the Apostle saith, *Who is sufficient for these things?* (2 Cor. 2.16.) O how great a Work is this! What Man, what Angel is sufficient to preach the Gospel as they ought to preach it! You work for the highest End, the Glory of God, and the good of immortal Souls; you are for the beating down of the Kingdom of the Devil, and enlarging and exalting Christ's Kingdom: and *he that winneth Souls* (saith *Solomon*) *is wise* (Prov. 11.30); that is, he that draweth them to God, and to the Love of him, sweetly gaineth and maketh a holy Conquest of them to *Jehovah*.

2. We should study to be good Workmen, because you will be the better able to give a good account to your Master, *an Account with Joy and not with Grief* (Heb. 13.17), having been faithful Watchmen over your Flocks. *Paul*, boldly declares it, that *he was clear from the Blood of all Men, and had not shunn'd to declare the whole Counsel of God* (Acts 20.27, 28.); and it is his Counsel to the Elders at

Ephesus, To take heed to themselves, and to all the Flock over which the Holy Ghost had made them Overseers. And in so doing there may be expected an approving of God, and a *Well done good and faithful Servant, enter into the Joy of thy Lord* (Mat. 25.23.), that is, into everlasting Happiness.

V. The Use and Application.

1. By way of information. If it be the Duty of Gospel Ministers to study to divide the Word of God aright, then we fairly and naturally infer, that it is their Sin that preach and neglect Study. You may easily perceive from the Pulpit whether the Man hath wrought hard at his Study the week before, or not. We may say of Sermons as some do of pieces of Work amongst Men: We say of some Work, there is no Labour, there is no pains in it, it is a very slight thing. But it may be said of others on the contrary, this is a good piece of Work, this is well wrought, here is Labour in this, this is substantial Work. As there are too few painful Labourers, so I fear there are too many Loiterers concern'd in this glorious Imployment; the Holy Ghost speaks of some *Watchmen sleeping, loving to slumber* (Isa. 56.10).

2. This Doctrine refutes the Opinions of those that think it unlawful to study to declare God's Mind, and will contemptuously speak against it, as if we were to preach by Inspiration, as the Prophets and Apostles of old did. What can be a better Confutation of those Men than our Text? which commands Ministers *to study to shew themselves good Workmen; and to meditate in God's Law day and night* (2 Tim. 2.15. Psal. 1.2-3.). To meditate in the Law, the revealed Word of God, the Rule of Life, so as to draw the Ground of our Faith, and the Comfort of Conscience out of the Promises of Grace.

3. This affords us a Use of Caution. If it be Ministers Duty to study, then be cautioned against Idleness in the great things of God, and the Concerns of immortal Souls; the Lord hath often reproved idle Shepherds. There is so much precious time spent in the World and Pleasures thereof, that there is a very small remnant of the Week left, I fear by too many, so that they have not sufficient time to improve the Talent God hath given them; and what can be expected then but a lean Discourse, if not a confused one, when the Sabbath comes?

4. This affords a Use of Consolation. If Shame will attend them

that are lazy and idle in the things of God, then Honour and Praise will follow those that are true Labourers in the Lord's Vineyard. *Those that rule well, and labour in the Word and Doctrine, are counted worthy of double Honour, and to be esteemed very highly for their Works sake* (1 Tim 5.17. 1 Thess. 5.13.). Let all faithful Labourers rejoice, you shall have Peace in your own Consciences, you will have the Praise of the Churches, and all Saints; and, which is best of all, God's Approbation at last, *Well done good and faithful Servants* (Mat. 25.23.).

An Additional Word to the Churches

1. Let the necessity of a Gospel-Ministry lie with weight upon your Hearts; that there is such a necessity appears (1.) from a special Institution of God, who is said to have *set or constituted Teachers in his Church*, and has *given* them to her as a part of her Dowry: There are *sent forth by the Lord of the Harvest*; who alone giveth *Pastors* to the Church; the Ministry is received of the Lord, and it is the *Holy Ghost that maketh them Overseers* (1 Cor. 12.28. Ephes. 4.11. Mat. 9.38. Jer. 3.14. Col. 4.17. Acts 20.28.). Now that which God hath instituted and appointed in his Church ought to be accounted necessary, and therefore a Gospel Ministry ought to be so esteemed.

(2.) The Titles given to Ministers import Services of absolute necessity, which the Scripture calls by many Names, but not intending any Preheminence in Office: They are call'd *Elders* to signify their Gravity, decent and reverend Behaviour; at other times *Bishops, Overseers, Watchmen* (Acts 20.28. Heb. 13.17.), because their Work is to take the Oversight of the Church, and *watch for their Souls*. They are also call'd *Pastors*, because they are to feed the Flock with the *Words* of eternal Life: Also *Stewards of the Mysteries of God*: Sometimes *Angels, Ambassadors*, Persons sent from God to publish Peace: Moreover, they are call'd *Planters and Builders* (Jer. 3.14. 1 Cor. 4.1. Rev. 1.20. 2 Cor. 5.20. 1 Cor. 3. 7, 9.); all which Metaphorical Expressions import Services of absolute necessity; therefore let every Church look to it, that such Officers be continued in the Church.

(3.) There are necessary Ordinances to be administered in the Church of Christ till the end of the World, therefore Ministers are necessary: They are to proclaim *Remission of Sins in Christ's Name* (Acts 13.38), to press the Doctrine of *Repentance from dead Works, and Faith in our Lord Jesus Christ* (Heb. 6.1, 2.); they are *to bring good tidings to the meek, turning Men from Darkness to Light* (Rom. 10.15. Acts 26.18.), *speaking a word in season to the weary* (Isa. 50.4.), *edifying the Body of Christ, and perfecting the Saints, nourishing men in the words of Faith* (Eph. 4.11, 12.): The *word of Reconciliation* (2 Cor. 5.20.) is committed to them, the Administration of Baptism, and the Lord's Supper, all these are necessary in the Church, and therefore all Churches ought to imitate the Apostles, who took a special care for a standing Ministry in the Church; hence they took care *to ordain Elders in every Church* (Acts 14.23.): So *Paul* exhorted *Timothy* to *commit the things he had heard of him to faithful Men, who should be able to teach others also* (2 Tim. 2.2.): And *Paul* tells *Titus, left I thee in Crete, that thou shouldst ordain Elders in every City, even as I appointed thee* (Tit. 1.5.).

2. Let the Churches be cautioned for the Honour of God, the Glory of the Cause in their hands, and the good of their own Souls, against calling to Office an ignorant, unlearned, unexperienc'd Person: *The Priest's Lips should preserve Knowledg, and they shall seek the Law at his Mouth* (Mal. 2.7.). Pastors are to feed the People with Knowledg and Understanding: *Paul* tells the *Ephesians* when they come to *read his Writings*, they should *understand his Knowledg in the Mysteries of Christ* (Ephes. 3.4.). When *the blind lead the blind, they both fall into the Ditch* (Mat. 15.14.). It was *Jeroboam's* Sin to make some of *the lowest of the People Priests* (1 King. 12.31.). But when I said, beware of calling unlearned Men, I mean such *unlearned* as *Peter* speaks of, *who wrest the Scriptures to their own Destruction* (2 Pet. 3.16.). *Peter* did not mean by unlearned Men, Men who wanted human Learning; for then, as one saith, he must of necessity condemn himself; for he was a Man in the sense of the great Council that wanted this Learning, so that he must lie under that blame which he lays upon others: But to be learned in *Peter's* sense, was to be *taught of God as the Truth is in Jesus, and by the Spirit to understand the deep things of God* (Eph. 4.20, 21. 1 Cor. 2.10.); and through a saving knowledg of Christ to be well establish'd, in opposition to those unstable Ones he speaks of: They must be men zealous for the Glory of God, sensible of the Interest of Souls, exemplary to the

Flock, able to speak experimentally of the Ways of God, of the Devices of Satan, and the Deceit of Lust, and the Issues and Events of Temptations, and to understand Consolations of the Holy Spirit: A Person of such able Parts, as that he may be *apt to teach* (1 Tim. 3.2.) and speak a word in season (Isa. 50.4.), to *shew a Man his Uprightness* (Job 33.23.), to *convince Gainsayers*, and *to use sound Speech which cannot be condemned* (Titus 1.11; 2.8.). Thus his Teaching is to be Divine Teaching. The Holy Ghost came down upon the Apostles in the day of *Pentecost* to fit them for this glorious Work (Acts 2.1, 2, 3.). That Unction and Divine Anointing which may make a Person a true Believer, may not be sufficient to make him a Minister. The Holy Ghost is call'd the *Promise of the Father* (Acts 1.4, 8.), not only as to make Persons Believers, but to make them Ministers, by a *Divine Power from on high*, that they may be the better able to be Witnesses for Christ, and serve his Church. 'Tis not enough to have the *Thummim* of Integrity, but we must also have the *Urim* of Knowledg.

3. Let the Churches be exhorted to go to the Lord of the Harvest to beseech him that he would *send more Labourers into his Harvest* (Mat. 8.37, 38.): What abundance of able Ministers hath God removed out of this City those thirty years last past? and it is well if the Churches can say that their places are fill'd up: Pray hard that God would send *Joshua's* and *Elisha's* in the room of those *Moses's* and *Elijah's* which he hath removed.

4. Give that Honour and Respect to your Ministers and Pastors that God allows; God accounts it an honourable place. If Honour is to be given to a King, who is a Protector of the Body, shall they be denied it that watch for Mens Souls (Heb. 5.4.)? It is the Apostle's Counsel to the Church at *Thessalonica*, to *know them which labour among you, and are over you in the Lord, and admonish you: And to esteem them very highly for their Works sake* (1 Thess. 5.12, 13.). *Let the Elders* (saith Paul) *that rule well, be counted worthy of double Honour, especially they who labour in the Word and Doctrine* (1 Tim. 5.17.). *So* (saith he) *obey them who have the Rule over you, and submit your selves* (Heb. 13.17.): not that they are *Lords over God's Heritage* (1 Pet. 5.3.), to be rul'd in a Lordly way, and by Force and Rigor, seeing they are a voluntary People, and to be govern'd with their own Consent.

5. Bless God for those faithful Ministers he hath given you; take

heed you do not sin them away and the Gospel together; provoke not God to send *a Famine of the Word* (Amos 8.11, 12.), and remove the Gospel from *England* and *London,* as he did from *Jerusalem* (Mat. 21.43.), and the Churches in *Asia* and *Africa;* even there where the Gospel did seriously shine, those very places are overspread with Heathenism and Mahometanism. Pray that the Word *may have free course, and may run and be glorified* (2 Thess. 3.1, 2.) in the Sinners Conversion, and Saints Perfection. God hath promised to take *away the Heart of Stone, and give a Heart of Flesh; but* (saith he) *for these things I will be sought unto by the House of Israel,* the Church of God (Ezek. 35.26, 27.). And if we find the Womb of Conversion much shut up, for the Church to set apart a day of Humiliation upon that account, and to pray that a *Door of Faith may be open* (Acts 14.27.). Some can speak by Experience that God hath own'd this Practice. Beg for greater degrees of his Holy Spirit to be pour'd upon your Ministers, that God would give them a double Portion, that they may every way answer their honourable Titles, who are call'd *the Salt of the Earth, and the Light of the World* (Mat. 5.13, 14, 16.).

Chapter 15

Escaping the Condemnation of the Devil

An Urgent Call for Spiritual Maturity

in the Ministry

Jason Walter*

I have been privileged to know Jim Renihan in a variety of roles: first as my pastor, then as my professor, now as my fellow-elder, and throughout each of these as my adviser, encourager, and friend. As one who was ordained to ministry while still certainly characterized, like Timothy, by "youth" (1 Tim. 4:12), I have felt safe having a man like Jim as my fellow-elder. His example, experience, knowledge, and wisdom have been used of God to help keep me from falling into the condemnation of the devil.

Introduction

> The way appointed by Christ for the calling of any person, fitted and gifted by the Holy Spirit, unto the office of bishop or elder in a church, is, that he be chosen thereunto by the common suffrage of the church itself . . . .

So reads Paragraph 9 of the 26th chapter of the 2LCF, giving expression to what has ever been a Baptist—particularly a Reformed Baptist—distinction: each church chooses its own pastors. This is a high privilege; but, as with all high privileges, it is also a grave responsibility, a responsibility that falls not just upon the

---

* Jason Walter, M.Div., Westminster Seminary California, is a pastor of Christ Reformed Baptist Church, Vista, CA.

church as a whole but also upon each member individually. As such, it is the solemn duty of every member to be acquainted intimately with the scriptural qualifications of the office of the pastor and to be able to exercise godly discernment in determining whether or not a candidate for ministry meets those qualifications. Great harm has been done to the glory and cause of Christ by unqualified men who have nevertheless held this office; and the blame for such harm may justly be shared by those who, through lack either of diligence or discretion, placed them into it.

Examples abound of contemporary "job descriptions" for pastors that emphasize none of the scriptural requirements: no examples need be given here. Suffice it to say that Reformed Baptists ought to give just weight to the pastoral qualifications enumerated in Scripture, "the only sufficient, certain, and infallible rule in all saving knowledge, faith, and obedience" (2LCF 1.1). Though to choose one among those qualifications as more important than the rest would be unwise and impossible, one does seem to stand out as particularly worthy of attention both by the emphasis afforded to it by the Apostle Paul and by the lack of emphasis afforded to it by many modern evangelical churches: the requirement that an overseer "not be a recent convert" (1 Tim. 3:6).[1] Put positively, this is a requirement for spiritual maturity in the pastorate,[2] and a solemn warning is appended to it: "or he may become puffed up with conceit and fall into the condemnation of the devil." As the interpretation of this verse has been much debated and its application often disregarded, it deserves the careful attention of all who are concerned for the good of the church and the purity of its ministry. This study will proceed with an exegetical analysis of this verse and then offer some suggestions by way of practical implementation, drawing insights and exhortations especially from our Reformed and Reformed Baptist forbears.

---

[1] Unless otherwise noted, all English Scripture citations are from the English Standard Version (Wheaton, IL: Crossway, 2001).

[2] This study will assume the equivalency of office indicated by the scriptural terms ἐπίσκοπος and πρεσβύτερος. Cf. 2LCF 26.8. See also John Owen, *The True Nature of a Gospel Church and its Government* in *The Works of John Owen*, ed. William H. Goold, vol. 16 (1850-1853; reprint, Edinburgh; Carlisle, PA: Banner of Truth, 1997), 44-46.

Exegetical Analysis

1. The context

Paul's purpose in writing his first letter to Timothy is quite clear:

> I hope to come to you soon, but I am writing these things to you so that, if I am delayed, you may know how one ought to behave in the household of God, which is the church of the living God . . . (1 Tim. 3:14-15)

Paul had left Timothy in Ephesus in order to help further establish the church there, especially to oppose certain false teachers that were troubling the Ephesian believers (1 Tim. 1:3ff.). The qualifications for the office of overseer that are given in 3:2-7 are introduced in 3:1: "The saying is trustworthy: If anyone aspires to the office of overseer, he desires a noble task." This is the second of Paul's five so-called "faithful sayings" in the Pastoral Epistles, sayings that were apparently common within the first-century churches and that Paul validates and commends to his readers with his apostolic approval.[3] The formula πιστὸς ὁ λόγος ("the saying is trustworthy") is "one of emphasis as well as one of citation."[4] By using it in 3:1, Paul is highlighting the following saying, drawing Timothy's (and the church's) attention to it, and proclaiming it to be both true and important.[5] Each of the other four instances of that formula (1 Tim. 1:15; 4:9; 2 Tim. 2:11; Tit. 3:8) refer to sayings that summarize basic and vital Christian truths, truths about the gospel itself or about the necessity of godly living. By applying it to the saying of 1 Timothy 3:1b, Paul places its importance on the same

---

[3] See the landmark study of these sayings by George W. Knight III, *The Faithful Sayings in the Pastoral Letters* (Grand Rapids: Baker Book House, 1979).

[4] Knight, *Faithful Sayings*, 22.

[5] That the formula refers to what follows and not to what precedes it is all but universally acknowledged by the commentators. See the survey in Knight, *Faithful Sayings*, 52-54. For the opposing minority view, see Jerome D. Quinn and William C. Wacker, *The First and Second Letters to Timothy: A New Translation with Notes and Commentary*, The Eerdmans Critical Commentary (Grand Rapids: William B. Eerdmans Publishing Company, 2000), 240-42.

level as that of the other sayings. For Paul, the church's recognition of the dignity and intrinsic value of the pastoral office is indeed that basic. In the overall context of the book, this implies that Paul viewed the appointment of qualified pastors as essential to the proper functioning of the church as well as to its protection against the false teaching of those who were not so qualified. The office of overseer is emphatically a καλοῦ ἔργου (lit. "good work"), and aspiration to it is emphatically commendable.

The list of pastoral qualifications that follows in verses 2-7 is connected with the faithful saying of verse 1 by the inferential particle οὖν, "therefore." Precisely because there is such dignity and value in the office, those who occupy it "must" (δεῖ) be duly qualified; they must meet these rigorous standards.[6] The structure of this list is enlightening. Verses 2-6 comprise one long sentence in the original, all governed by the initial δεῖ in verse 2. Verse 7 begins a new sentence with a separate δεῖ in the main clause. The initial qualification that the overseer be "above reproach" (ἀνεπίλημπτος), seems to be the overarching requirement, the rest of the requirements expounding the specific ways in which the initial qualification would manifest itself. The requirement in the new sentence of verse 7 that the overseer "be well thought of" is conceptually parallel to this overarching requirement of verse 2 but

---

[6] Several form critics, especially Dibelius and Conzelman, have argued that this and other NT lists of virtues and vices follow stereotyped formats that were common in the culture and that they therefore contain very little that is especifically "episcopal" or even specially Christian. See Martin Dibelius and Hans Conzelman, *The Pastoral Epistles*, Hermeneia (Philadelphia: Fortress Press, 1972), 50-53. For a helpful survey and critique of these conclusions, see David A. Mappes, "Overseers as Stewards and the Qualifications for Leadership in the Pastoral Epistles," *Bibliothecra Sacra* 160 (April-June 2003): 202-18; John K. Goodrich, "Moral Virtues Associated with Eldership," *Zeitschrift für die neutestamentliche Wissenschaft und die Kunde der älteren Kirche*, 104:1 (2013): 77-97; George W. Knight III, *The Pastoral Epistles: A Commentary on the Greek Text*, The New International Greek Testament Commentary (Grand Rapids: William B. Eerdmans Publishing Company, 1992), 151-52; Philip H. Towner, *The Letters to Timothy and Titus*, The New International Commentary on the New Testament (Grand Rapids: William B. Eerdmans Publishing Company, 2006), 240-41. Mounce, in particular, demonstrates clearly how the list in 1 Tim. 3:2-7 is perfectly adapted in its specific context to contrast with the various characteristics of the false teachers at Ephesus in William D. Mounce, *Pastoral Epistles*, vol. 46 of Word Biblical Commentary (Nashville: Thomas Nelson Publishers, 2000), 153ff.

with respect specifically to those outside the church, indicating that verses 2-6 specify the ways in which he must be "above reproach" or "well thought of" within the church itself.[7] The requirement of verse 6, then, is the final one of its sentence and of the requirements under the internal evaluation of the church.

The qualification given in verse 6 is further highlighted within this list by being the only one to include a solemn threat of judgment if it be found lacking: "the condemnation of the devil." The exact nature of this judgment will be discussed below. The requirement of verse 7 also includes a warning against the "snare of the devil," but not an explicit threat of judgment. This, along with its position as the ultimate qualification in the initial list, marks out the requirement of spiritual maturity in verse 6 as particularly worthy of note.

2. The requirement

The basic requirement of verse 6 is expressed in negative fashion: μὴ νεόφυτον. Νεόφυτος (from which, through the Latin, comes the English word "neophyte") literally refers to a "newly planted" plant (LXX Job 14:9; Psalm 127:3 [ET 128:3]; 143:12 [ET 144:12]; Isa. 5:7). Presumably building off of the many agricultural metaphors in Scripture (e.g., Isa. 5:1-7; Mark 4:3-20; 1 Cor. 3:9; etc.), this uniquely Christian metaphorical usage[8] obviously refers to one who has only recently come to the faith, who has had "insufficient time to put down roots and grow up in Christ."[9]

The concern here is evidently that of one's spiritual maturity and not necessarily of one's physical age: after all, Timothy himself, at the time of this epistle's writing, could still be characterized by

---

[7] William Hendiksen, *Exposition of the Pastoral Epistles*, New Testament Commentary (1957; reprint, Grand Rapids: Baker Academic, 2007), 119.

[8] *Greek-English Lexicon of the New Testament and Other Early Christian Literature*, 3rd ed., ed. Frederick William Danker (Chicago: University of Chicago Press, 2000), 669. All subsequent metaphorical usages to denote a recent convert depend upon this one instance in 1 Tim. 3:6. Cf. *A Patristic Greek Lexicon*, ed. G. W. H. Lampe (New York: Oxford University Press, 1961), 905.

[9] John R. W. Stott, *The Message of 1 Timothy and Titus*, The Bible Speaks Today (Downers Grove, IL: InterVarsity Press, 1996), 98.

νεότης ("youth"), a potential liability that could be compensated for by exemplary piety (1 Tim. 4:12). At the same time, however, physical age cannot be entirely discounted. Both in Hebrew (זָקֵן) and in Greek (πρεσβύτερος), the word for "elder" originally denoted advanced physical age, and there is sufficient evidence that within the Jewish and Greco-Roman worlds the age of thirty was generally considered the minimum to be qualified as such in either the general or technical senses.[10] The consensus of scholars estimates Timothy even to have been in his mid-thirties at the time at which Paul wrote him this first letter.[11] It must be stressed, however, that no precise age or interval of time since conversion is ever stipulated by Paul or any other New Testament author. It is left to the discretion of the church to decide whether or not someone has attained sufficient spiritual maturity no longer to be considered a νεόφυτος and therefore to meet this qualification for the office of ἐπίσκοπος/πρεσβύτερος.[12]

---

[10] Ed Glasscock, "The Biblical Concept of Elder," *Bibliothecra Sacra* 144 (January-March 1987): 66-78; J. Behm, "νέος" in vol. 4 of *Theological Dictionary of the New Testament*, ed. Gerhard Kittel, trans. Geoffrey W. Bromiley (1967; reprint, Grand Rapids: William B. Eerdmans Publishing Company, 2006), 897; BDAG, 863.

[11] Knight, *Pastoral Epistles*, 205.

[12] The claim is often made and repeated that this requirement is further relativized and perhaps even negated in relation to the respective age of each church based upon the fact that it is not found in the list of elder qualifications in Tit. 1:5-9, the church in Crete presumably being younger than that in Ephesus and therefore without any ministerial candidates who could meet this standard. Towner argues that the Ephesian believers "had the luxury of being more selective in its choice of leaders than was the case in the pioneering situation in Crete." Cf. Towner, *Timothy and Titus*, 257. Similarly Mounce, *Pastoral Epistles*, 153-54, 181; Donald Guthrie, *The Pastoral Epistles: An Introduction and Commentary*, 2nd ed. Tyndale New Testament Commentary (1990; reprint, Grand Rapids: William B. Eerdmans Publishing Company, 2000), 94. This point seems speculative to the present author. Proper evaluation of potential elders according to the rest of the stringent requirements listed in Titus 1 would in itself necessitate the passage of considerable time and the attainment of a high degree of spiritual maturity in those being evaluated. As Johnson rightly observes, even "a period of two years would be more than long enough to enable such comparative criteria" as that found in the verse under consideration. Cf. Luke Timothy Johnson, *The First and Second Letters to Timothy: A New Translation with Introduction and Commentary*, The Anchor Bible (New York: Doubleday, 2001), 216.

3. The warning

The reason given for this negative requirement is expressed also in a negative form, by means of a negative purpose clause introduced by ἵνα μή. The potential danger to be avoided is described by the verb τυφόω. The exact significance of τυφόω is debated. The word appears in the New Testament only in the Pastorals, the other two instances (1 Tim. 6:4; 2 Tim. 3:4) directly describing false teachers. Apparently deriving from τύφω, "to give off smoke," suggested translations have varied. If the signification of τυφόω is taken as being *filled* with smoke, then translations such as "be puffed up, conceited" result, indicating that the basic danger confronting the neophyte overseer is pride.[13] If the signification of τυφόω is taken as being *enveloped* in smoke, then translations such as "be blinded, foolish" are preferred and the danger is seen to be that of ignorance rather than of pride.[14] A third definition is suggested in BDAG, "be mentally ill," which Quinn and Wacker take to be the "root meaning."[15] Perhaps the best modern English gloss would be "to be delusional" since this would encapsulate all three nuances. Such "delusion" would imply not just pride, but a specific kind of pride that results from an unrealistic estimate of one's own importance. It would also, therefore, imply blindness or foolishness, but again of a specific kind that is both produced by and productive of pride. Based on further examples from Josephus, the church Fathers, and contemporary secular literature, Luke Timothy Johnson offers the translation "false sense of his own importance" and further describes τυφόω as "a term that is used frequently in moral discourse figuratively for the sort of arrogance that derives from a sense of superior station, whether political or moral."[16] If this is indeed its significance in 1 Timothy 3:6, one can easily recognize such a danger in the case of a new

---

[13] BDAG, 1021, definition 1; *Greek-English Lexicon of the New Testament: Based on Semantic Domains*. ed. J. P. Louw and E.A. Nida. 2nd ed. (New York: United Bible Societies, 1989), 765.

[14] BDAG, 1021, definition 2; Mounce, *Pastoral Epistles*, 181; Knight, *Pastoral Epistles*, 251.

[15] BDAG, 1021, definition 3; Quinn and Wacker, *Timothy*, 264.

[16] Johnson, *Timothy*, 216. See the similar conclusions of Ceslas Spicq, vol. 3 of *Theological Lexicon of the New Testament*, ed. and trans. James D. Ernest (Peabody, MA: Hendrickson Publishers, 1994), 388-89.

convert who has prematurely been elevated to such a "noble" office as that of overseer.

Disastrous as such a state of mind would be in itself, it is not the ultimate danger facing the νεόφυτος. The participle τυφωθεὶς stands in causal relationship to the main verb of the negative purpose clause, ἐμπέσῃ. The ultimate danger is that he might "fall into the condemnation of the devil." The meaning of this phrase is doubtless the most contentious point of interpretation within this verse, the three possibilities having been noted and debated at least since Calvin's time.[17] The three possible interpretations of the phrase κρίμα τοῦ διαβόλου are: 1) the accusation of some nameless, human "slanderer," taking διάβολος not as a reference to Satan but in its original, literal sense; 2) the condemnation that the devil pronounces or enforces, taking the genitive as subjective; or 3) the condemnation which the devil has received or will receive, taking the genitive as objective. Of these options, the first has the least to commend it and has been rejected by the majority of commentators. Though διάβολος is used three times in the Pastoral Epistles in its literal adjectival sense of "slanderous," each time it is anarthrous (i.e., without an article) and plural. In all thirty of its New Testament occurrences in which διάβολος is singular, articular, and substantival, the reference is clearly to Satan, as it is in 1 Timothy 3:6.[18] In addition, as Calvin observed, κρίμα implies far more than mere "slander."[19]

But is this κρίμα τοῦ διαβόλου one that the devil somehow initiates or carries out, or is it one into which he himself falls? Those who argue in favor of taking the genitive as subjective point mostly to the parallel phrasing in the warning appended to the requirement of verse 7: ἵνα μὴ εἰς ὀνειδισμὸν ἐμπέσῃ καὶ παγίδα τοῦ διαβόλου. The negative purpose clause is the same as in verse 6, as is the verb and the genitive construction. Παγίδα τοῦ διαβόλου is clearly a subjective genitive phrase, the snare being laid by the devil, not one into which the devil has fallen.[20] On this understanding, the substance of

---

[17] John Calvin, *Commentaries on the Epistles to Timothy, Titus, and Philemon,* trans. William Pringle, in *Calvin's Commentaries,* vol. 21 (reprint, Grand Rapids: Baker Books, 2003), 84.

[18] Knight, *Pastoral Epistles,* 163-64.

[19] Calvin, *Timothy, Titus, and Philemon,* 84.

the κρίμα would be either exposure to the judicial accusations of Satan (Zech. 3:1; Rev. 12:10) or the kind of judgment that Satan is permitted to carry out on those who have been "handed over" to him after excommunication such as had already befallen two of the false teachers in Ephesus (1 Tim. 1:20; cf. 1 Cor. 5:5).[21]

The majority of commentators take the objective genitive view.[22] In favor of this position are the following considerations: First, it is more in keeping with the most common meaning of κρίμα, that of a legal ruling or verdict, usually an unfavorable one.[23] It is more than just an accusation. Second, the objective sense is more in keeping with the overall biblical portrayal of the devil. Satan is certainly "the accuser of the brethren," but he is not their condemner. He may play the part of prosecutor, but God alone is Judge. And while, on occasion, God may use other agents to carry out his sentences, the κρίμα is still his and not the agent's. Also, there is far more emphasis in Scripture on Satan's being condemned than on his participation in the condemnation of others.[24] Third, the objective sense is more in keeping with the correlation between the κρίμα and its cause, the delusional self-importance of the object of the condemnation. Traditionally, Satan's own condemnation and fall is attributed to the same kind of τῦφος as is warned against here in 1 Timothy 3:6, making the parallel and warning all the more striking.[25] This last consideration also hints at what would be the nature of the κρίμα

---

[20] Towner, *Timothy and Titus*, 258; I. Howard Marshall, *A Critical and Exegetical Commentary on the Pastoral Epistles*, International Critical Commentary (New York: T&T Clark LTD, 1999), 482.

[21] Quinn and Wacker, *Timothy*, 265.

[22] Patrick Fairburn, *A Commentary on 1 & 2 Timothy and Titus*, Geneva Series Commentary (1874; reprint, Edinburgh; Carlisle, PA; Banner of Truth Trust, 2002), 144; Guthrie, *Pastoral Epistles*, 94; Stott, *1 Timothy and Titus*, 99; Calvin, *Timothy, Titus, and Philemon*, 84; Hendriksen, *Pastoral Epistles*, 127; Johnson, *Timothy*, 216.

[23] BDAG, 567; Louw and Nida, *Semantic Domains*, 556.

[24] Hendriksen, *Pastoral Epistles*, 127-28, n. 63.

[25] There is evidence that at least some Jewish contemporaries of Paul may have interpreted passages such as Isa. 14:12 and Ezek. 28 and the pride of the rulers condemned therein as applying to the fall of Satan, an interpretation that seems supported by the allusions Jesus made to Isa. 14:12 in his discussions on Satan in Luke 10:18 and John 8:44. See David W. Pao and Eckhard J. Schnabel, "Luke," in *Commentary on the New Testament Use of the Old Testament*, ed. G. K. Beale and D. A. Carson (Grand Rapids: Baker Academic, 2007), 318; and Andreas J. Köstenberger, "John," in *Commentary on the New Testament Use of the Old Testament*, 458.

here threatened. It is unlikely to be final, eternal condemnation: the genuineness of the conversion, however recent and however unfit for office the neophyte may have proven, is not necessarily called into question. Rather, given the parallel with the fall of Satan, the threatened judgment is more likely to consist of a similar loss of station and office.

Given that the argument in support of the subjective understanding from the parallel with the subjective genitive in verse 7 is far from conclusive (it is unlikely that Paul would even have thought in terms of different categories of genitives), the objective genitive view seems the most likely option. Whichever option one concludes most probable, however, as Quinn and Wacker observe, "The general sense is clear. [The deluded neophyte] will come to a bad end."[26] Though significantly understated, their point is taken: the threat of falling into the condemnation of the devil, whether through excommunication, through being discharged from office, or through both, is one that is calculated to arrest attention and provoke serious, cautious reflection. Such is the urgent and grave necessity for spiritual maturity in those desirous of this high office.

Practical Implications

Given the responsibility of Reformed Baptist churches to evaluate ministerial candidates, a few words of suggested application from what has been considered in 1 Timothy 3:6 appear to be in order, words addressed to the aspiring pastor and to the evaluating church respectively. Here, wisdom will be sought from Reformed writers of the past, and especially from those late seventeenth- and early eighteenth-century Particular Baptist authors who were contemporaries of the publication of the 2LCF. As even John Owen felt it necessary to lament in his day with respect to these pastoral qualifications, "It were to be wished that what is of this kind expressed in the rule, and which the nature of the office doth

---

[26] Quinn and Wacker, *Timothy*, 265. Towner, though ultimately siding for the subjective genitive, similarly concludes that "in choosing one solution over another little is lost." Cf. Towner, *Timothy and Titus*, 258.

CHAPTER 15 • *Jason Walter* | **365**

indispensably require, were more exemplified in practice than it is."[27]

1. Implications for the aspiring pastor

It is important to realize that this requirement for spiritual maturity in the ministry is given not just for the good of the church but also, and especially, for the good of the minister's own soul. He is the one threatened with the κρίμα τοῦ διαβόλου. He himself should take this qualification with the utmost seriousness. Several further applications to the aspiring pastor are hereby implied and encouraged.

First, those who aspire to be pastors need to make a sober estimation of the magnitude of the office to which they aspire. While the work of the office itself and aspiration to it are unequivocally good things (1 Tim. 3:1), still this commendable desire must be balanced by a proper understanding of the weight of responsibility that is involved in being an overseer in the church of the living God. This desire, therefore, ought to be no casual, thoughtless whim but a settled, considered longing to be of use to the kingdom, despite the personal sacrifices and even the personal dangers that such service will entail. It certainly ought not to be an expression of one's own lust for preeminence and glory, for that would inevitably lead to the precise kind of delusional arrogance so solemnly warned against in this passage. "If anyone aspires to the office of overseer, he desires a noble task," indeed. But the warning of James ought to be kept equally in mind: "Not many of you should become teachers, my brothers, for you know that we who teach will be judged with greater strictness" (James 3:1). Calvin's estimation is correct: a proper assessment of the responsibility and accountability of such an office seems more likely to inspire terror than to stir ambition. He writes:

> It is no light matter to be a representative of the Son of God, in discharging an office of such magnitude, the object of which is to erect and extend the kingdom of God, to procure the salvation of souls which the Lord himself hath

---

[27] Owen, *Church*, 47.

Escaping the Condemnation of the Devil: An Urgent Call for Spiritual Maturity...

purchased with his own blood, and to govern the Church, which is God's inheritance.[28]

He continues in this vein:

If any one object, that the government of the church is a matter of so great difficulty, that it ought rather to strike terror into the minds of persons of sound judgment than to excite them to desire it; I reply, that the desire of great men does not rest on confidence of their own industry or virtue, but on the assistance of "God, from whom is our sufficiency," as Paul says elsewhere (2 Cor. 3:5).[29]

Such a conviction of the appointment and empowering of God is indeed the only motive strong enough to sustain one in this high and often difficult calling. Mere ambition or pride will never suffice. As Thomas Murphy has observed, "A very high appreciation of his office is one of the first qualifications for him who would be an efficient pastor."[30] The seventeenth-century Baptist Benjamin Keach adds this solemn exclamation:

And O! with what trembling should this Work be undertaken, 'tis a mighty Trust, and Woe to them that seek themselves, and not the Honour of God and Jesus Christ herein.[31]

Second, those who aspire to be pastors need to make an honest evaluation of their own readiness for the office. The irony here is that it will generally be the one who is indeed deluded by a sense of self-importance who will consider himself ready, while the one who feels least sufficient for the task is likely the most qualified. Still, Paul's list of pastoral qualifications is given not only to the church

---

[28] Calvin, *Timothy, Titus, and Philemon*, 74.

[29] Calvin, *Timothy, Titus, and Philemon*, 75.

[30] Thomas Murphy, *Pastoral Theology: The Pastor in the Various Duties of His Office* (1877; reprint, Willow Street, PA: Old Paths Publications, 2001), 27.

[31] Benjamin Keach, *The Display of Glorious Grace: or, The Covenant of Peace, Opened* (London: S. Bridge, 1698), 148.

to help it evaluate the readiness of a candidate but also to the candidate to help him evaluate himself. Especially important, as has been discussed, is this requirement of spiritual maturity, the chief marker of which is humility (as the chief marker of spiritual immaturity is pride). As R. B. Kuiper noted:

> A Christian virtue on which Scripture puts especial emphasis as a requisite for the office of elder is humility. This emphasis is not difficult to account for. Just because the office is so exalted and honorable, only the humble man is fit to hold it. Any other man, if chosen to this high office, will almost certainly be overcome by pride.[32]

Once again, however, the proud man will generally consider himself sufficiently humble, whereas the truly humble man will continue to see distressing remnants of pride. Charles Bridges, however, considered such feelings of inadequacy more an indication of one's readiness for the office than otherwise:

> There is something so fearfully responsible in entering upon this work with incompetent abilities, that the man can scarcely have felt any serious concern for his own soul, for the immortal interests of his fellow-sinners, or for the welfare of the Church of God, whose mind had not been more or less exercised upon the ground of personal unfitness.[33]

In none of these qualifications will even the holiest of men come anywhere near perfection, but they must be present in sufficient degree before any man should feel himself ready to enter this office. There is a degree of subjectivity here, to be sure; but that is one of the reasons why God has not left the candidate alone in determining his readiness and has not permitted the candidate's own evaluation to be definitive. The definitive evaluation belongs to

---

[32] R. B. Kuiper, *The Glorious Body of Christ: A Scriptural Appreciation of the One Holy Church* (Grand Rapids: William B. Eerdmans Publishing Company, 1966), 147-48.

[33] Charles Bridges, *The Christian Ministry with an Inquiry into the Causes of its Inefficiency* (1830; reprint, Edinburgh; Carlisle, PA: Banner of Truth Trust, 1976), 24.

the gathered church.

Third, those who aspire to be pastors need to be patient with and submissive to the evaluation and decision of the church. Impatience and the lack of a submissive attitude in this respect would be clear warnings of the precise kind of pride and immaturity that would disqualify a man from pastoral office anyway. They would also be indications that the candidate's motives for seeking the office were incorrect. Such a one is manifestly driven by selfish ambition and not by a desire simply to serve. Again, Calvin's insights are helpful. He maintains that those truly qualified with the requisite humility and maturity

> do not thrust themselves forward, and do not, even by their own wish, make themselves bishops, but are only ready to discharge the office, if their labours shall be required. And if it turn out that, according to the lawful order, they are not called, let them know that such was the will of God, and let them not take it ill that others have been preferred to them. But they who, without any selfish motive, shall have no other wish than to serve God and the Church, will be affected in this manner, and, at the same time, will have such modesty that they will not be at all envious, if others be preferred to them as being more worthy [34]

2. Implications for the evaluating church

The church also (especially Reformed Baptist churches) has solemn duties with respect to these matters. Our Puritan and Particular Baptist forefathers appear to have had a higher awareness of and regard for these duties than do many churches today. According to Owen, the foremost theologian of the Independents to whom our Baptist ancestors were deeply indebted for much of their ecclesiology,[35] the evaluation and selection of its pastors

---

[34] Calvin, *Timothy, Titus, and Philemon*, 74-75.

[35] Though with notable exceptions, see James M. Renihan, *Edification and Beauty: The Practical Ecclesiology of the English Particular Baptists, 1675-1705*, vol. 17 of *Studies in Baptist History and Thought* (Euguene, OR: Wipf and Stock Publishers,

is *the chief trust* that the Lord Christ hath committed unto his churches; and if they are negligent herein, or if at all adventures they will impose an officer in his house upon him without satisfaction of his meetness upon due inquiry, it is a great dishonour unto him and provocation of him. Herein *principally* are churches made the overseers of their own purity and edification.[36]

These are strong words, but our Baptist forebears evidently agreed with this sentiment. This duty and the care with which it is to be exercised are discussed by Benjamin Keach,[37] Nehemiah Coxe,[38] and Hercules Collins.[39] These ideas also find forceful expression in a book published in 1689 in defense of pastoral compensation entitled, *The Gospel Minister's Maintenance Vindicated*.[40] The work is anonymous but was published "with a recommendatory preface signed by eleven London [Baptist] pastors."[41]

First, the church must have a proper estimation of the dignity and duties of the pastoral office. Such an estimation is foundational and indispensable. If a church has a low view of this office or is ignorant concerning the way in which especially a church's official ministry affects the entire body, it will inevitably be lax in its method of filling it. The seventeenth-century Particular Baptists never tired of calling congregations to hold the pastoral office in the

---

2009), especially 63-87. Still, most of 2LCF chapter 26, "Of the Church," is taken and adapted from the Independent's Savoy Platform of Polity. See the comparison of the two documents in *True Confessions: Baptist Documents in the Reformed Family*, ed. James M. Renihan (Owensboro, KY: Reformed Baptist Academic Press, 2004), 163-75.

[36] Owen, *Church*, 55, emphasis added.

[37] Keach, *Display*, 147-48.

[38] Nehemiah Coxe, *A sermon Preached at the Ordination of an Elder and Deacons in a Baptized Congregation in London* (London: Thomas Fabian, 1681), 19-21.

[39] Hercules Collins, *The Temple Repair'd: or, An Essay to Revive the Long-Neglected Ordinances, of Exercising the Spiritual Gift of Prophecy for the Edification of the Churches; and of Ordaining Ministers duly Qualified* (London: William and Joseph Marshal, 1702), 52-56.

[40] *The Gospel Minister's Maintenance Vindicated* (London: John Harris, 1689), 7-10.

[41] Renihan, *Edification and Beauty*, 104, n. 58. Renihan cites arguments that Benjamin Keach was the actual author.

Escaping the Condemnation of the Devil: An Urgent Call for Spiritual Maturity...

highest of regards. Keach speaks of "that great Dignity God hath conferred upon his Faithful Ministers, they represent the Person of Jesus Christ: O what greater Honour than this can be conferr'd on Men?" He then applies this to the congregation:

> Moreover, this Title [of Ambassador] should procure an high and honorable esteem of *Ministers* . . . especially such whom they have been Instruments to bring to accept of Peace, should highly value them.[42]

Collins speaks similarly:

> Give that Honour and Respect to your Ministers and Pastors that God allows; God accounts it an honourable place. If Honour is to be given to a King, who is a Protector of the Body, shall they be denied it that watch for Mens Souls?[43]

Coxe also reminds the church that they owe to their pastor "great Love, Respect, and Honour," giving them this motivation:

> 'Tis the Business of your Salvation, and the Concern of your precious and immortal Souls that the Minister is imployed in; and therefore it is much more your own Interest than his, that you should make Conscience of your Duty.[44]

The spiritual health and maturity of a church will in large measure depend upon the spiritual health and maturity of her pastors. The converse is also true. Murphy observed:

> the piety of a church will generally rise about as high as that of its minister. . . . How can it be otherwise, since his ministrations permeate the whole life of the body? He is the appointed agent for edifying the people of God in their most holy faith, and their spirituality cannot be expected to rise

---

[42] Keach, *Display*, 147.
[43] Collins, *Temple Repair'd*, 57.
[44] Coxe, *Sermon*, 32, 44.

higher than his. There doubtless are exceptions, but the general rule is, that the measure of devotedness in any particular church may be gauged by that of the pastor's heart.[45]

A church that has a similarly high view of the nature and importance of the pastoral office will take great care to place in it only a man of sufficient and proven spiritual maturity, if for no other reason than the sake of its own progress in spiritual maturity.

Second, the church must conduct patient and careful examination of candidates for the ministry. As spiritual maturity can be developed only over time, so it can be manifested only over time. "Do not be hasty in the laying on of hands" (1 Tim. 5:22). Without succumbing to an attitude of undue suspicion, the church must remember that it is all too easy to make and to receive a good but misleading first impression. Patience in this process of evaluation is sorely needed. Yet, when a church has been laboring for a long while without a pastor, or when a pastor has been laboring for a long while without a fellow elder, the temptation can be strong to forego a lengthy and rigorous examination of candidates. Yet, as Owen states quite forcefully:

> It can never be the duty of the church to call or choose an unmeet, an unqualified, an unprepared person unto this office. No pretended necessity, no outward motives, can enable or warrant it to do so. . . . And this has been one of the great means of debasing the ministry and of almost ruining the church itself . . . whence there hath not been a due regard unto the antecedent preparatory qualifications of those who are called unto the ministry.[46]

In another place, Owen decries the presumption of ordaining men whom Christ has not qualified with the requisite gifts, speaking of such an action in terms of a usurpation of Christ's own prerogatives as the only head of his church:

for if the whole authority of the ministry be from Christ, and

---

[45] Murphy, *Pastoral Theology*, 48.
[46] Owen, *Church*, 54.

if he never give it but where he bestows these gifts with it for its discharge, as in Eph. iv. 7, 8, etc, then to call any to the ministry whom he hath not so previously gifted is to set him aside, and to act in our own name and authority.[47]

This is perfectly in keeping with the Confession's emphasis on the unique and incommunicable nature of Christ's lordship over his church:

The Lord Jesus Christ is the Head of the church, in whom, by the appointment of the Father, all power for the calling, institution, order or government of the church is invested in a supreme and sovereign manner. (2LCF 26.4)

This prerogative clearly includes the appointment of officers within his church (2LCF 26.8), an appointment that is confirmed by the church through the careful recognition of their having been "fitted and gifted by the Holy Spirit" (2LCF 26.9). The usurpation of Christ's royal prerogative in this as in other matters is what earned the Pope the ignominious title of "antichrist" (2LCF 26.4). Accordingly, the author of *The Gospel Minister's Maintenance Vindicated* does not hesitate to call the ordination of elders without proper proof of their giftedness a "sin" because it violates "the Rules given by Christ." He continues:

How greatly then must those churches be to blame, that unconcernedly live in the neglect of so great a Duty, upon which the Edification of the Church, and her Wellbeing so much depends. . . .[48]

This duty of patient and careful examination of candidates for the ministry was seen as no light responsibility.

According to Owen, proper evaluation of a prospective pastor includes two steps: first, by an examination of the *"evidence* given of

---

[47] John Owen, ΠΝΕΥΜΑΤΟΛΟΓΙΑ *or, A Discourse Concerning the Holy Spirit*, in *The Works of John Owen*, ed. William H. Goold, vol. 4 (1850-1853, reprint, Edinburgh; Carlisle, PA: Banner of Truth, 1997), 495.

[48] *Minister's Maintenance*, 7-9.

the qualifications in him."[49] This obviously requires relatively extensive personal knowledge of the aspirant:

> The church is not to call or choose any one to office who is not known unto them, of whose frame of spirit and walking they have not had some experience; not a novice, or one lately come to them.[50]

Notice the allusion to 1 Timothy 3:6. Notice, also, that what is under examination firstly is not the candidate's intellectual achievements or preaching abilities, but his character, his piety, his spiritual maturity. This is not at all to take away from the need for an educated ministry. It is just to remind that there is something more, something deeper that is necessary to qualify a man for ministry. All pastors must be scholars, but not all scholars should automatically be made pastors. Spiritual maturity, along with its attendant virtues, is paramount; and *time*, Coxe notes, is necessary to the proving and manifestation of a man's true virtue and steadfastness.[51] Owen, though, recognizes that intimate acquaintance with each potential pastor may not always be a luxury enjoyed by every congregation, and so he allows a wise concession: "Where there is a defect of this personal knowledge, from want of an opportunity, it may be supplied by testimonies of unquestionable authority."[52]

A candidate's fitness for ministry is also to be determined "by *a trial of his gifts for edification*." This duty of trial cannot be transferred from the church to any other party: "every true church of Christ, that is so in the matter and form of it, is able to judge in some competent measure what gifts of men are suitable unto their own edification." Yet an associational relationship with other churches can be a great help in such trials:

> But yet, in making a judgment hereof, one *directive means* is the advice of other elders and churches; which they are

---

[49] Owen, *Church*, 54, emphasis original.
[50] Owen, *Church*, 54.
[51] Coxe, *Sermon*, 21.
[52] Owen, *Church*, 55.

obliged to make use of by virtue of the communion of churches, and for the avoidance of offence in their walk in that communion.[53]

Such a trial period or "probation" was viewed as a nonnegotiable necessity by our Baptist forefathers. Quoting 1 Timothy 3:6, Coxe writes, "This is the Rule of Trial that all churches are bound to have in their Eye, and diligently attend to, in the Election of Elders; and when they do so, Christ approves their choice . . . "[54] They argued such a trial period to be mandatory not only from their exegesis of 1 Timothy 3:6 but also by analogy with the requirement of a trial for potential deacons in 1 Timothy 3:10: "And let them also be tested first; then let them serve as deacons if they prove themselves blameless." This is a classic argument from the lesser to the greater: if such care is required in evaluating one for the lesser office of deacon, then how much more should it be required in evaluating one for the greater office of pastor.[55]

The trial consists simply in "a diligent comparing of the Qualifications of the Persons, with the Characters of one meet for such an Office which [Paul] before set down."[56] The scriptural requirements were the primary criteria, including the requirement that a pastor be "able to teach" (1 Tim. 3:2), the proper evaluation of which demanded hearing the candidate preach on multiple occasions.[57] According to James Renihan, in the seventeenth-century Particular Baptist churches, the length of the probation period could vary from three months to two years.[58] Collins makes reference to some churches in which "Some have been Probationers all their days" and in other churches for "ten or twenty years," though he evidently disagrees with this practice, calling it a "matter of Lamentation."[59] The length of the trial period must be determined by the discretion of the church as the time needed in order to be satisfied that the candidate has demonstrated sufficient spiritual

---

[53] Owen, *Church*, 55, emphasis original.
[54] Coxe, *Sermon*, 21. See also *Minister's Maintenance*, 8 and Keach, *Display*, 136.
[55] Collins, *Temple Repair'd*, 9.
[56] Coxe, *Sermon*, 11-12.
[57] Collins, *Temple Repair'd*, 9-13.
[58] Renihan, *Edification and Beauty*, 102.
[59] Collins, *Temple Repair'd*, 58.

maturity to qualify him for pastoral office, though the caution of Hercules Collins is wise: "a little time will not discover these gifts" sufficiently.[60]

Conclusion

First Timothy 3:6 makes spiritual maturity an absolute requirement for qualification to official ministry. Solemn consequences, both to the pastor himself and by implication to his church, are threatened if such a qualification prove to be lacking. This requirement sorely needs to be stressed far more than it often is. In a day and a culture in which, particularly in pastoral leadership, youth is clearly preferred over age, the new over the old, "freshness" over experience, enthusiasm over wisdom, personality over qualification—in a word, marketability over maturity—both potential pastors and searching churches need to emphasize the ministerial requirements that the Scriptures and that our Reformed and Baptist forefathers emphasized.

---

[60] Collins, *Temple Repair'd*, 9.

Chapter 16

The Regulative Principle of the Church

Sam Waldron[*]

Jim Renihan is one of those brothers that I call or write when I have a theological question. His theological and historical insight and learning have many times improved and corrected my own work. It is a privilege to have a part in a volume written in his honor. May God continue to bless and prosper his labors for the Lord.

Introduction

It is an understatement to say that the regulative principle has been the subject of much discussion in recent years. Many in the Reformed resurgence have adopted (as they should have) the regulative principle as part of the Reformed and Puritan tradition to which they are self-consciously returning.[1] Others have recoiled from it and sought to distance themselves from it.[2] Still others have

---

[*] Sam Waldron, Ph.D. Southern Baptist Theological Seminary, has been married for 40 years to his dear wife, Charlene. His dissertation entitled, *Faith, Obedience, and Justification: Recent Evangelical Departures from Sola Fide* has been published by RBAP. He is now one of the pastors of Grace Reformed Baptist Church, Owensboro, KY. He serves as the Dean and Professor of Systematic Theology at Covenant Baptist Theological Seminary. He is the author of *A Modern Exposition of the 1689 Baptist Confession, The End Times Made Simple, A Reformed Baptist Manifesto* with Richard Barcellos, *A Man as Priest in His Home*, and *Two Things You Must Do To Be Saved*. This chapter is a slightly revised version of material that appeared in *Going Beyond the Five Points* and is used with permission.

[1] Mark Dever in *The Deliberate Church* adopts the regulative principle. See particularly chapter 2.

[2] Mark Driscoll, http://marshill.com/media/religionsaves/regulative-principle; Steve Schlissel, http://www.messiahnyc.org/ArticlesDetail.asp?id=89 illustrate this tendency; R. J. Gore, *Covenantal Worship: Reconsidering the Puritan Regulative Principle* (Phillipsburg, NJ: P&R Publishing, 2002).

(in my opinion) embraced the phrase, but so re-interpreted it that it means something quite different from what it has meant in the tradition.[3] My own response to the regulative principle is that it forms an important and even basic feature of both the Reformed tradition and biblical teaching. I do believe, however, that the regulative principle is in need of some clarification, but clarification which, I think, is suggested by the tradition itself. I will strive both to state and clarify the regulative principle by means of the following headings: historical meaning, ecclesiastical framework, biblical support, multifaceted function, and necessary limitation.

Historical Meaning

There are certain theological words and phrases which gain such a clear and defined meaning in the history of theology and to affirm that one holds to them is tantamount to affirming their meaning in that history. To affirm such words and phrases and not hold to their historical meaning is simply to mislead both ourselves and others as to our real theological convictions. For instance, to affirm the Trinity, but to hold views which have more in common with historic modalism than with trinitarianism (as some contemporary modalists do) is to deceive ourselves and mislead others.[1] Again, to affirm *sola fide*, but hold views which are parallel to those of Rome (as do some modern evangelicals and devotees of the new perspective on Paul) is frankly deceptive.[5] Similarly, to affirm the regulative principle of worship, and yet hold views which are more like the normative principle held by the opponents of the regulative principle, is simply misleading.

The backdrop of the debates over the regulative principle among

---

[3] This is my opinion of John Frame's *Worship in Spirit and Truth* (Phillipsburg, NJ: P&R Publishing 1996).

[4] Many believe that this is what T. D. Jakes and other modalists are doing today. Cf. his "Elephant Room 2" discussion with Mark Driscoll and James MacDonald. http://www.theelephantroom.com/category/featured/.

[5] In my doctoral dissertation, I show that this is what a number of modern evangelicals are doing. Cf. Sam Waldron, *Faith, Obedience, and Justification: Current Evangelical Departures from Sola Fide* (Palmdale, CA: Reformed Baptist Academic Press, 2006).

Protestants must, of course, be found in the debates over *sola Scriptura* which came to light at the time of the Reformation. The conflict between the two viewpoints, which at the Reformation became characteristic of Romanism and Protestantism respectively, had in the centuries prior to the Reformation been crystallizing in Medieval theology.[6] When the Reformation churches affirmed *sola Scriptura*, the question had to be asked whether the Scriptures alone were sufficient to regulate the worship of the church or whether, on the other hand, tradition might have a place in ordering the government and worship of the church. This question gave rise to two answers on the part of the churches of the Reformation. Some gave tradition substantially no part in this construction process. This view became known as the *regulative principle*. Others regarded tradition as having a part to play in constructing the worship and government of the church. This became known as the *normative principle*.

The distinction between these two principles for the regulation of worship first emerged in the controversies between the Reformed and Lutheran churches in Europe. The "Conservative Reformation" of Luther adopted the policy of preserving the worship of Medieval Catholicism except where it contradicted Scripture. Calvin, on the other hand, adopted the principle that said the contents of worship had to have warrant in Scripture in language that seems the same as that in which the Puritans later stated the regulative principle.

The claim is made by some that Calvin's views were different from those of the Puritans. Thus, there is some debate about Calvin and his relation to the regulative principle of worship.[7] While it is true that one can point out differences of application between Calvin and the English Puritans, there is little doubt in my mind that Calvin articulated clearly what became known as the regulative principle of worship. Quotations from Calvin in support of this may be and have been given at length[8], but perhaps the clearest and classic quotation is

---

[6] Heiko Oberman, *Forerunners of the Reformation* (Cambridge, England: James Clarke & Co., 1967), 51-120.

[7] See the argument of Gore in *Covenantal Worship*, 53-90. In my and others' opinions Gore only succeeds in proving that there are differences of application, but not a difference in principle between Calvin and the Puritans. Cf. the critical comments about Gore's book by T. David Gordon in the article entitled, "The World's Ruined: The Regulative Principle of Worship," *Modern Reformation* (2003 Sept./Oct., Vol. 12): 5.

the following from his work entitled, *The Necessity of Reforming the Church*:

> Moreover, the rule which distinguishes between pure and vitiated worship is of universal application, in order that we may not adopt any device which seems fit to ourselves, but look to the injunctions of Him who alone is entitled to prescribe. Therefore, if we would have Him to approve our worship, this rule, which he everywhere enforces with the utmost strictness, must be carefully observed. For there is a twofold reason why the Lord, in condemning and prohibiting all fictitious worship, requires us to give obedience only to his own voice. First, it tends greatly to establish His authority that we do not follow our own pleasure, but depend entirely on his sovereignty; and, secondly, such is our folly, that when we are left at liberty, all we are able to do is go astray. And then when once we have turned aside from the right path, there is no end to our wanderings, until we get buried under a multitude of superstitions. Justly, therefore, does the Lord, in order to assert full right of dominion, strictly enjoin what he wishes us to do, and at once reject all human devices which are at variance with his command. Justly, too, does He, in express terms, define our limits, that we may not, by fabricating perverse modes of worship, provoke His anger against us. I know how difficult it is to persuade the world that God disapproves of all modes of worship not expressly sanctioned by His Word. The opposite persuasion which cleaves to them, being seated, as it were, in their very bones and marrow, is, that whatever they do has in itself a sufficient sanction, provided it exhibits some kind of zeal for the honour of God. But since God not only regards as fruitless, but also plainly abominates, whatever we undertake from zeal to His worship, if at variance with His

---

[8] Note the multitude of quotations brought forward by Brian Schwertley in his appendix on Calvin and the regulative principle in his article, "Sola Scriptura and the Regulative Principle of Worship," http://www.reformedonline.com/view/reformedonline/sola_a.htm.

command, what do we gain by a contrary course? The words of God are clear and distinct: "Obedience is better than sacrifice." "In vain do they worship me, teaching for doctrines the commandments of men," (1 Sam. xv. 22; Matth. xv. 9). Every addition to His word, especially in this matter, is a lie. Mere "will worship" (*ethelothreskeia*) is vanity. This is the decision, and when once the judge has decided, it is no longer time to debate.[9]

This principle articulated by Calvin and the Reformed against Luther and the Roman Catholics was given sharp focus in the debates between the Puritans and Anglicans in late sixteenth- and seventeenth-century England. It was given its classic and definitive statement in Reformed confessions formulated in the seventeenth century in Britain. It is stated in identical language at 21.1 in the WCF and at 22.1 in the 2LCF.

The light of nature shews that there is a God, who hath lordship and sovereignty over all; is just, good and doth good unto all; and is therefore to be feared, loved, praised, called upon, trusted in, and served, with all the heart and all the soul, and with all the might. But the acceptable way of worshipping the true God, is instituted by himself, and so limited by his own revealed will, that he may not be worshipped according to the imagination and devices of men, nor the suggestions of Satan, under any visible representations, or any other way not prescribed in the Holy Scriptures.

This Puritan statement may best be understood by contrasting it with the statement of the Church of England found in the 39 Articles. The Twentieth Article of the Church of England's Thirty Nine Articles states: "The Church hath power to decree rites or ceremonies and authority in the controversies of the Faith. And yet it is not lawful for the Church to ordain anything contrary to God's Word written."[10]

---

[9] John Calvin, "The Necessity of Reforming the Church," in *Selected Works* (1844; reprint, Grand Rapids: Baker Book House, 1983), 1:128-29.

[10] James Bannerman, *The Church of Christ*, 2 vols. (Edinburgh: The Banner of Truth Trust, 1960), 1:339.

G. I. Williamson helpfully and popularly states the Puritan principle exemplified in the Confession: "What is commanded is right, and what is not commanded is wrong."[11] James Bannerman provides this helpful contrast between the Puritan doctrine on this matter (contained in our Confession) and the Anglican doctrine.

> In the case of the Church of England, its doctrine in regard to Church power in the worship of God is, that it has a right to decree everything, except what is forbidden in the Word of God. In the case of our own Church, its doctrine in reference to Church power in the worship of God is, that it has a right to decree nothing, except what expressly or by implication is enjoined by the Word of God.[12]

Williamson helpfully illustrates the difference between the Anglican and Puritan understandings of the regulative principle with the following diagram.[13]

The Regulative and Normative Principles Contrasted

The Puritan View

[11] G. I. Williamson, *The Westminster Confession of Faith for Study Classes* (Philipsburg, NJ: P&R Publishing, 1964), 162. Some might complain that Williamson's statement requires explicit commands for anything done in corporate worship. I do not think this is his intent. He simply means to clearly contrast the two views. At any rate, I should make clear that I do not think that to justify a part of worship an explicit command is necessary. If the regulative principle is true and thus was practiced in scriptural examples of proper worship, then a scriptural example or precedent would be sufficient. Such an example or precedent would then assume an implied command.

[12] Bannerman, *The Church of Christ*, 1: 339-40.

[13] Williamson, *The Westminster Confession of Faith for Study Classes*, 160. A correspondent complained that the following diagram misrepresents the Anglican view by asserting that they might introduce absolutely anything not forbidden into corporate worship. Of course, it is unlikely that Anglicans would do this. But the reason would be that it contradicts their reason and not because they have a biblical reason not to do so.

True Worship

(Only What Is Commanded)

False Worship
(Anything Not Commanded)

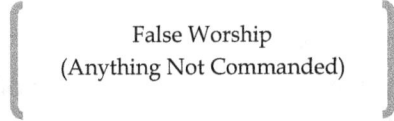

The Anglican View

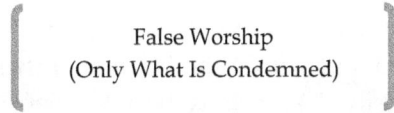

True Worship

(What Is Commanded, Plus Anything Not Expressly Forbidden)

False Worship
(Only What Is Condemned)

The difference between Puritans and Anglicans may be helpfully illustrated by means of two builders intent on building the temple of God. Mr. Anglican must use the materials of the Word of God, but has no blueprint and may use other materials. Mr. Puritan must use only materials of the Word of God and has a blueprint. It takes no special genius to discern that the two completed buildings will differ drastically or to discern which will be more pleasing to God.[14]

---

[14] Some have reacted with doubt to my assertion that Anglicans have no blueprint for the temple of God. Surely godly Anglicans would not say this, they think! On the contrary, I believe Richard Hooker's statement of Anglican views in his *The Laws of Ecclesiastical Polity* confirms my assertion. Hooker does not believe we have a biblical blueprint for worship or church government. This is why Hooker then and the Anglican Peter Toon today (in the four views book, *Who Runs the Church?* [Grand Rapids: Zondervan, 2004], 21-41, especially 23) believe that reason and the church councils of the first five centuries must be used in addition to the Bible to create an adequate or complete church government.

Ecclesiastical Framework

In speaking of the ecclesiastical framework of the regulative principle, I come to one of the matters in the Reformed tradition which I believe is in need of some clarification. The clarification which follows will, I think, help defenders of the regulative principle better defend and apply it. At the same time, it will expose the problems with a controversial, modern affirmation of the regulative principle.

The common name given to the principle under discussion is "the regulative principle of worship." I propose to clarify this principle by calling it *the regulative principle of the church.* Implicit in historical discussions of the regulative principle is a distinction between worship and the rest of life. This distinction is given acute expression in Williamson's description of the principle cited above: "What is commanded is right, and what is not commanded is wrong." If this is an apt description of the regulative principle, and I think it is, it underscores the idea that God regulates his worship in a way which differs from the way in which he regulates the rest of life. In the rest of life, God gives men the great precepts and general principles of his Word and within the bounds of these directions allows them to order their lives as seems best to them. He does not give them minute directions as to how they shall build their houses or pursue their secular vocations. The regulative principle, on the other hand, involves a limitation on human initiative and freedom not characteristic of the rest of life. It says of a certain slice of life called worship that it is regulated in a more restrictive and defined way than the rest of life.

The WCF at 20.2 provides further evidence for a view of the regulative principle which restricts it to something less than all of life. Notice the part of that paragraph I have placed in bold italics below:

> God alone is Lord of the conscience, and hath left it free from the doctrines and commandments of men, which are, in anything, contrary to his Word; *or beside it, if matters of faith, or worship.* So that, to believe such doctrines, or to obey such commands, out of conscience, is to betray true liberty of conscience: and the requiring of an implicit faith,

and an absolute and blind obedience, is to destroy liberty of conscience, and reason also.[15]

According to this statement, *sola Scriptura* has a different application to matters of faith and worship than it does to the rest of life. In the rest of life it means that we are free from the commands of men that are contrary to the Word. In matters of faith and worship it means that we are even free from the commands of men that are beside the Word. This area of life is different.

I will argue, however, that there is a better and more accurate way to describe the aspect of life governed by the regulative principle than "worship." This description of the proper application of the principle is both too vague in certain ways, too broad in some ways, and paradoxically also too restrictive a description of its proper application. The proper scope or application of the regulative principle may be clarified if we squarely ask the question, "What distinction is it that gives rise to the special, more restrictive, and more defined regulation of the aspect of life under discussion?" The answer to this question is suggested by an attribute of the church ascribed to it in the Nicene Creed. We believe one, *holy*, catholic, apostolic church. The church is holy in a way that the rest of life is not. It has a distinctive relationship to God that even other divine institutions like the family and the state do not have. It is the special holiness of the church that gives rise to and necessitates the special regulation of the church embodied in what has been called the regulative principle of

---

[15] It is true that the words in bold italics are missing in the Savoy Declaration and the 2LCF. Some have opined that this is because the framers of these Confessions did not hold the distinction they assume. John Owen was one of the framers of the Savoy and held to the distinction between the church's worship and the rest of life. Cf., for example, *The Works of John Owen* (London: Banner of Truth Trust, 1960), 15:445-530. It is very unlikely, then, that Owen did not hold this distinction. The deletion of the words in question is, however, difficult. Their absence raises difficult questions about the legitimacy of commands not contained in the Bible of human authorities like the state or family. Perhaps the framers of the Savoy felt that this possible misunderstanding was addressed by the statement later in the paragraph that such commands were not to be obeyed "out of conscience," that is, perhaps, out of conscience toward God, but merely out of respect for human authority. In my view the deletion of these words raise unnecessary questions, should have been included, and are needed to make the idea of the paragraph clear.

worship.

I think this distinction is assumed in many traditional treatments of the regulative principle of worship. It is even suggested, I think, by the Confession itself. As I will explain below, it is commonly acknowledged that an important supplement and clarification of the regulative principle is stated in the Confession's discussion of the sufficiency of Scripture in the second half of chapter 1 and paragraph 6. Here is what both the Westminster and the 2LCF say at that point:

> . . . there are some circumstances concerning the worship of God, and government of the church, common to human actions and societies, which are to be ordered by the light of nature and Christian prudence, according to the general rules of the Word, which are always to be observed.

In this statement of clarification with regard to the circumstances of the worship of God, it is to be noted that the government of the church is also and immediately mentioned. The suggestion is, thus, present that the government of the church is like the worship of God to be governed by the regulative principle except with regard to the matter of its "circumstances." It is also clear from the statement of 1.6 that the worship in view here in this qualifying statement with regard to the regulative principle is the corporate worship of the church (at least primarily). This provides, I believe, some justification for the clarification I am suggesting. John Frame, however, rejects completely both the restriction of the regulative principle to corporate worship and to the church. Yet he himself testifies to the historical propriety of this restriction. He notes:

> In the Presbyterian tradition, the regulative principle has been typically discussed in the context of "church power." . . . For them the issue of the regulative principle was the issue of church power: what may the church require worshipers to do? And the Puritan-Presbyterian answer was, quite properly, only what Scripture commands. . . . This position on church power, however, led some theologians to distinguish sharply between worship services that are "formal" or "official" (i.e., sanctioned by the ruling body of the church), and other

meetings at which worship takes place, such as family devotions, hymn sings at homes, etc., which are not officially sanctioned. Some have said that the regulative principle properly applied only to the formal or official services, not to other forms of worship. But that distinction is clearly unscriptural. . . . On the Puritan view, the regulative principle pertains primarily to worship that is officially sanctioned by the church. . . . I therefore reject the limitation of the regulative principle to official worship services. In my view, the regulative principle in Scripture is not about church power and officially sanctioned worship services.[16]

As a matter of fact, and as I said above, the Anglican views against which the Puritans launched the regulative principle argued that church government as much as church worship was subject to supplementation by the traditions of men. This reality gives a context to the debate over the regulative principle which forces us also in the direction of including the government of the church under the regulative principle.

It seems to me that one of the major intellectual stumbling-blocks which hinders men from embracing the regulative principle is that it involves the idea that the church and its worship is ordered and regulated in a way different from the rest of life. In the rest of life, as mentioned above, God gives men the great precepts and general principles of his Word and within the bounds of these directions allows them to order their lives as seems best to them. He does not give them the same kind of detailed directions as to how they shall build their houses or pursue their secular vocations, as we assert that he does with regard to the church.

The regulative principle, on the other hand, involves a limitation on human initiative and freedom not characteristic of the rest of life. It clearly assumes that there is a distinction between the way the church and its worship is to be ordered and the way the rest of human society and conduct is to be ordered. Thus, the regulative principle is liable to strike men as oppressive, peculiar, and, therefore, suspiciously out of accord with God's dealings with mankind in the rest of life. The distinction between the church and the rest of life which I am

---

[16] Frame, *Worship in Spirit and Truth*, 43-44.

suggesting means that *sola Scriptura* has a different application to the church, than it does to the rest of life.[17]

This peculiarity of the regulative principle makes it absolutely necessary to commence our study of its biblical foundations by opening up its ecclesiastical framework. In other words, we must begin by clearly stating and showing that there is a reality unique to the church and its worship which demands that it be specially ordered in the way that the regulative principle assumes. That unique ecclesiastical reality is that the church is the place of God's special presence and is, therefore, the house or temple of God, and as such is holy in a distinct way that the rest of life is not. Once we understand the peculiar closeness of the church to God, and the special holiness of the church as compared to the rest of human society, we will not be surprised by the fact that it is specially regulated by God. Rather, it will seem eminently appropriate that the church as God's own house should be regulated by the immediate directives of God. It will seem most suitable that the church as God's holy temple should be subject to a special and detailed regulation by his Word.

1. The special character of the church of God as the place of his special presence (Matthew 18:20)

Matthew 18:15-20 is one of the first two passages in the New Testament where the term church is used; and it contains the first explicit mention of the local church in the New Testament. It culminates in the great promise of verse 20. Very obviously this is a promise of the special presence of Christ. The promise of verse 20 comes attached to a very plain condition or limitation, *"For where two or three have gathered together in my name, I am there in the midst of them."* The stated limitation found in these words is the assembling of the local church, the formal or public gathering of the people of God. Upon what grounds do I assert that these words specify such an assembly? Let me set out four grounds for this assertion.

The first is the context assumed in verse 20a. The passage from verse

---

[17] This seems a problem or objection to some, but I will deal with it in my excursus on the contemporary objections to the regulative principle to be published in *JIRBS* 2016.

17 and following deals with the local church. Several exegetical details in the passage underscore this contextual connection between verses 19-20 and verses 15-18. The use of "again" at the beginning of verse 19 emphasizes it. This word often bears the meaning of "furthermore." In the context of the entire Gospel of Matthew and especially in light of the closely paralleled use of "again" in Matthew 19:23-24, it clearly connects the preceding context to the interpretation of this promise. Alfred Plummer remarks on verse 19, "By his 'Again' . . . Mt. couples the second 'I say unto you' with the former one (v. 18) . . . The connection is that God is sure to ratify the decision of the congregation . . ."[18]

Another significant reason for interpreting this promise as a reference to the special presence promised to the local church is that there is an actual web of parallels between this promise and what has gone before. Lenski suggests the parallel between the two or three of verse 20 and the two or three of verse 16. He remarks on verse 20:

> Since He is thus in the assembly of the church or present when two or three are convicting a brother of sin, it is he himself who acts with his church and its members when they carry out his Word by invoking also his presence and his help.[19]

Verse 19 repeats the reference of verse 18 to the heaven and earth which speaks of the discipline of the church on earth being confirmed in heaven. Hendriksen remarks, "note anything that they may ask relates especially to prayer for wisdom in dealing with matters of discipline."[20] The promise of the special presence of Christ is given pursuant to the promise of verse 18 that church discipline finds a heavenly or divine confirmation.

There are also conceptual connections between verses 19-20 and verses 15-18. A church or Christian synagogue is (to transliterate the

---

[18] Alfred Plummer, *An Exegetical Commentary on the Gospel according to St. Matthew* (London: Robert Scott Roxburghe House Paternoster Row, 1928), 254.

[19] R. C. H. Lenski, *The Interpretation of St. Matthew's Gospel* (Minneapolis: Augsburg, 1943), 707.

[20] William Hendriksen, *Exposition of the Gospel according to Matthew* (Grand Rapids: Baker, 1973), 702.

Hebrew word often translated by *ekklesia* in the LXX) a QAHAL, a Hebrew word for assembly. God's QAHAL is an assembly that gathers around himself as Israel gathered around Yahweh in the day of the church or assembly (QAHAL) at Mount Sinai. This same Old Testament imagery is present in the two or three that gather around Jesus in verse 20. There is an allusion to the QAHAL of Israel gathered around Yahweh. The smallest conceivable or possible assembly is the gathering of two or three people.

We must read the Bible contextually and not as providing mottoes for our living room walls with no context to fix their meaning. The two or three mentioned in verse 20, then, is simply a graphic way of emphasizing that even the smallest conceivable local church possesses this great promise of Christ.

The second is the verb used in verse 20a. While by itself the verb used is not conclusive, it bears mentioning that the words "have gathered together" are a translation of the verbal root from which both in English and in Greek the word synagogue is derived. The Christian church is, in fact, called a synagogue in James 2:2, where the same verbal root is used: "For if a man comes into your assembly (or synagogue) . . ." Though this verbal root may be and often is used more broadly of other gatherings, in this context (as noted above) its use is suggestive and forms part of a cumulative argument for the idea that the gathered church is in view.

The third ground upon which I assert that the words of verse 20a designate the formal gathering of the local church is the qualification given in verse 20a. I am referring to the words "in my name." Matthew 10:41 provides a parallel use of this phrase. To receive a prophet in the name of a prophet means to receive him in his official character as a prophet, to receive him because he is a prophet. It is, therefore, not any gathering of men, or even any gathering of Christians which forms the specified condition of this promise, but the gathering in Christ's name. This phrase has reference to the gathering of Christ's people in their official character as his church and under his authority. It designates the gathering in view as one which is officially and formally and intentionally a gathering of Christ's people under his authority. One commentator has clearly seen the significance of this phrase when he says that gathering in Christ's name "is a synonym for the new society. The ecclesia is a body of men gathered together by a common relation to the name of Christ: a Christian synagogue."[21]

Let me illustrate the significance of this phrase. A number of years ago, I worked in a large warehouse with a number of other Christians. The warehouse was owned and operated by Amway Corporation. At lunch we would eat together. We often opened lunch with prayer and spent the whole time discussing biblical issues. There were more than two or three of us. That lunch gathering was, however, not a gathering in Christ's name according to the meaning of this text. It was a gathering of Christians, true enough, but it was a gathering of Christians in the name of Amway Corporation and because of hunger, not in the name of Christ. We were gathered as Amway employees and not as Christ's official people. We could not by any biblical right claim the promise of Matthew 18:20. The specified limitation of this promise is the assembling of the local church officially in Christ's name, because they are a church, and in their character as a church. That is the condition which must be met for the claiming of this promise.[22]

The fourth reason for seeing verses 19-20 as closely connected to verse 15-18 are the parallels between this passage and the other major passage on church discipline in the New Testament, 1 Corinthians 5:1-13. The parallels between the Matthew 18:15-20 and 1 Corinthians 5:4 are striking. Here is 1 Corinthians 5:4: "In the name of our Lord Jesus Christ, when you are gathered together, along with my spirit, with the power of our Lord Jesus Christ . . ." The parallels between this passage and Matthew 18:15-20 are striking, and unavoidable, and they provide a *Pauline and biblical* interpretation of Jesus' words in Matthew 18:20. Just as Paul's words in Ephesians 2:20 exegete Matthew 16:17-18, so Paul's words here exegete Matthew 18:15-20. What are the parallels I have in mind?

- Both passages are treating the subject of church discipline.
- Both call for this discipline to be enacted by a formal

---

[21] *The Expositor's Greek Testament* (London: Hodder and Stoughton), 1:241.

[22] One correspondent disagreed that gathering in Jesus' name refers to the church and argued that we can pray in Jesus' name anywhere. We can certainly pray in Jesus' name anywhere. It does not take a gathering of the church to be able to pray in Jesus' name. Praying in Jesus' name and gathering in Jesus' name are, however, not the same thing. They are clearly different and should not be confused.

gathering of the church.

- Both use the same word to speak of this gathering. Cf. 1 Cor. 5:4 with Matt. 18:20.
- Both describe this gathering as taking place in the name of the Lord Jesus. Cf. 1 Cor. 5:4 with Matt. 18:20.
- Both speak of the authority of this gathering to exercise church discipline as consisting of the special presence of the Lord Jesus Christ. If Christ's power is especially present, then he is especially present. Cf. 1 Cor. 5:4 with Matt. 18:20.

John Owen is one of the progenitors of our Reformed Baptist polity and the regulative principle. In his "Brief Instruction on the Worship of God," he reads Matthew 18:20 in exactly the way I here defend. He says:

> . . . so the Lord Jesus Christ hath promised his presence to the same ends and purposes, unto all them that assemble together in his name for the observation of the worship which in the gospel he hath appointed: Matthew 18:20.[23]

Here is my simple point. The Apostle Paul supports the interpretation of Matt. 18:19-20 offered here.

2. **The distinctive regulation of the church of God as the place of his special presence (1 Tim. 3:15)**

First Timothy 3:15 is, of course, a key text for the doctrine of the church:

> But if I am delayed, I write so that you may know how you ought to conduct yourself in the house of God, which is the church of the living God, the pillar and ground of the truth.

You will notice that in this text the special character or unique identity of the church is emphasized by means of three descriptions. It is "the house of God, the church of the living God, and the pillar and support

---

[23] Owen, *Works*, 15:475.

of the truth." Our particular interest is in the first two of these three descriptions.

The church is, first, the house or household of God. The term, house, used here may refer to the church as God's family (1 Tim. 3:5, 12) or the church as God's temple (1 Pet. 2:5). In either case the special and close relation of the church to God is emphasized.

Second, the house of God is identified in this text as "the church of the living God." The term, church, identifies the new covenant people of God as an organized and governed assembly. This word in Greek culture was used of the official assembly of the Greek city-state. This word in the Greek translation of the Old Testament was used to describe the QAHAL of Israel, the official civil and religious assembly of the nation of Israel. Both of these backgrounds serve to emphasize the formal, official, or organized nature of the assembly to which reference is made.

But this church is described as the church *of the living God.* "The living God" is the one described in Psalm 115:1-8. The significance of the use of this description here is to emphasize the idea that this church is dominated by the Word and presence and power of God. It is the church in which he dwells, in which he is active, in which he rules. Now what is the reason for this tremendous emphasis on the unique identity of the church in this verse? I believe that the stated concern of this verse provides the answer. Paul says that he is writing to Timothy "so that [he] may know how one ought to conduct himself in the household of God, which is the church of the living God, the pillar and support of the truth." What is Paul's point? It is that there is a special conduct demanded by the special character of that church in which Timothy moves as Paul's apostolic delegate or representative. The unique identity of the church requires a unique regulation of Timothy's conduct in it. Timothy was not ignorant of the laws of God. He was not even ignorant of the regulations which had governed the Old Testament worship. From childhood he had known the sacred writings (2 Tim. 3:15). Why, then, did Paul have to write to Timothy and carefully instruct him concerning proper conduct in the house of God? The reason is plainly that with the coming of a new temple, there come new regulations for its ordering and worship. Hebrews 9:1 asserts that "even the first covenant had regulations of divine service and the earthly sanctuary." The implication of such a text is that the new covenant with its true tabernacle also has such regulations as are fitting for the divine worship conducted in the church.

When we understand the unique identity of the church as the new tabernacle and temple of God, it will not seem far-fetched to us to see an application to the church in Exodus 26:30 where Moses was strictly charged, "And you shall raise up the tabernacle according to its pattern which you were shown on the mountain." The substance of this command is often repeated in the Bible (Exod. 25:9, 40; Heb. 8:5). Exodus 39 records Moses' careful obedience to the detailed divine commands regarding the construction of the Lord's house. All was completed "as the Lord had commanded Moses" (v. 1). This statement is repeated in verses 5, 7, 21, 26, 29, 31, 32, 42, and 43. What is the application today of these emphases of the Old Testament? God specially regulates the construction and worship of his house-temple. Nothing short of the precise and complete obedience to those special regulations which was exemplified in Moses is required.

God never told Moses precisely how to construct Moses' tent. God never told Moses precisely how to regulate his family. Those tasks he left to the discretion of Moses because it was Moses' tent and Moses' family. But it is for that very reason that God exercises such pervasive control over the tabernacle and its worship. The tabernacle was God's tent; it ministers to his family. Thus, he rules its worship with a special and detailed set of regulations to which he expects precise obedience. As God told Moses when he appeared to him at the burning bush, and as God told Joshua when he appeared to him outside the city of Jericho, the place of God's special presence is holy ground and requires the removal of one's sandals from one's feet. Just so the church is holy ground, and this requires a unique mindset and special regulation of one's conduct.

Similarly in the New Testament special and even unique regulations are given for God's new covenant house. Some illustrations of this are the following. Regulations are given for the speaking and keeping silent of prophets, tongue-speakers, and women which only apply to the meetings of the church and not necessarily to other non-church gatherings (1 Cor. 14:27-40; cf. esp. the threefold emphasis on the church as the defined scope of the regulation given about women in vv. 33-35; 1 Tim. 2:1-13). Regulations are given for matters unique to the local church: church discipline (Matt. 18:15-17; 1 Cor. 5:1-13); the Lord's Supper (1 Cor. 11:17-34); the number, nature, qualifications, appointment, support, and protection of church officers (1 Tim. 3:1-13; 5:17-22; Phil. 1:1; Tit. 1:5-9); and the specific arrangements for the conduct of church prayer meetings (1 Tim. 2:1-13). The major elements of the worship of the church are designated (Acts 2:42; 1 Cor. 14; 1 Tim. 2). This detail of regulation for the church is unparalleled with regard to other divine institutions like the family or the state. Of course, both the Old and New Testaments contain divine regulations for the family and the state, but the focus of biblical concern is on the regulation of the covenant community. In the new covenant, this community is in a new way different from the old Israel, fundamentally distinct from both the family and the state.

I do not put all of this forward as my main argument for the regulative principle of the church. All of this does, however, provide the proper framework in which the scope, force, and application of those arguments are best appreciated. Having looked, then, at the theological framework of the regulative principle, let us come to those arguments which form its main biblical support.

Biblical Support

Four biblical arguments for the Puritan regulative principle of the church and its worship will now be presented.[24]

1. It is the prerogative of God alone to determine the terms on which sinners may approach him in worship.

Bannerman eloquently states this first argument:

> The fundamental principle that lies at the basis of the whole argument is this, that in regard to the ordinance of public

---

[24] I am aware that there are objections to the way I will expound and apply the various scriptural passages which support the regulative principle of the church. For clarity of treatment, I will address these under Contemporary Objections in *JIRBS* 2016.

worship it is the province of God, and not the province of man, to determine both the terms and the manner of such worship . . . The path of approach to God was shut and barred in consequence of man's sin: it was impossible for man himself to renew the intercourse which had been so solemnly closed by the judicial sentence which excluded him from the presence and favour of his God. Could that path ever again be opened up, and the communion of God with man and of man with God ever again be renewed? This was a question for God alone to determine. If it could, on what terms was the renewal of intercourse to take place, and in what manner was fellowship of the creature with his Creator again to be maintained? This, too, was a question no less than the former for God alone to resolve.[25]

But not only does God possess this prerogative, the Bible shows that he exercises it! Genesis 4:3-5 records the first instance of formal worship in the Bible. It is clear from this passage that it is not merely the persons of Cain and Abel that determined God's acceptance of Abel's offering and the rejection of Cain's. The text is clear. It is both Abel *and his offering* that are accepted and Cain *and his offering* that are rejected. Sometimes it is assumed that, because there is no mention previously of any particular requirements for such offerings that there could have been nothing more acceptable about Abel's offering than Cain's. But there are several problems with this assumption. First, the slaughter of animals to provide skin coverings for Adam and Eve in Genesis 3:21 is suggestive of the appointment of animal sacrifice. Second, the mention in Genesis 4:4 of "the firstborn of the flock and of their fat" anticipates later appointments of the sacrificial laws. For the sacrificial significance of the firstborn notice Leviticus 27:26. For the sacrificial significance of the fat notice Exodus 23:18; 29:13, 22 and Leviticus 3:3-4, 9-10; 7:3-4, 23-24. The likelihood is that Moses intends us to think of these later appointments. Thus, it is not implausible to understand Moses in Genesis 4:4 as intending us to conclude that both Cain himself and his sacrifice were unacceptable to God (1 John 3:12). Exodus 20:4-6 is often cited as grounding the regulative principle in the Reformed tradition. It also makes clear that God exercises his

---

[25] Bannerman, *The Church of Christ*, 1:340-41.

prerogative to control how human beings bring worship to him. How arrogant for man to think that he has the right to determine how God will be worshipped and served!

2. The introduction of extra-biblical practices into worship inevitably tends to nullify and undermine God's appointed worship.

Matthew 15:3 suggests the inevitable tendency of following human traditions: "And He answered and said to them, 'Why do you yourselves transgress the commandment of God for the sake of your tradition?'" Second Kings 16:10-18 is a penetrating moral tale and striking illustration of what happens to the ordinances when human invention intrudes itself into the ordained worship of God. If you read the story, you will notice that the altar of the Lord is not replaced by the new altar. It is only displaced. This is the usual subtlety of human error. *We would never dream of getting rid of God's ordinances. We will treat them with great respect. But they will not have the central place in our worship. That will be occupied by the inventions of our wisdom.* This tendency is illustrated in evangelical churches today where mundane or silly announcements in the middle of worship, the unwise tradition of hand-shaking in the middle of worship, badly organized testimony times, clown shows, mime, liturgical dance, movies, and drama completely replace or severely restrict the clearly ordained parts of worship. These and other traditions of men, for instance, often leave only 15-20 minutes for preaching. Similarly worship bands and the predominance of special music can push congregational singing into the corner of corporate worship.

3. The wisdom of Christ and the sufficiency of the Scriptures is called into question by the addition of un-appointed elements into worship.

The reasoning behind the addition of un-appointed elements in worship illustrates how this happens. John Owen remarks:

Three things are usually pleaded in the justification of the observance of such *rites* and ceremonies in the worship of God: — First, That they tend unto the furtherance of the *devotion* of the worshippers; secondly, That they render the worship itself *comely* and beautiful; thirdly, that they are the preservers of *order* in the celebration thereof. And therefore on these accounts they may be instituted or appointed by some, and observed by all.[26]

Reasoning such as Owen describes impugns the wisdom of Christ. With all our weakness, sin, and folly, will Christ leave us without an adequate guide in the most important matter of worship? Has he left us who are natively in such a spiritual condition without a sufficiently devotional, beautiful, and orderly worship of God? Says another Puritan:

For he that is the wisdom of the Father, the brightness of his glory, the true light, the word of life, yea truth and life itself, can he give unto his Church (for the which he paid the ransom of his blood) that which should not be a sufficient assurance for the same?[27]

Not only is such reasoning out of accord with our needy spiritual condition, not only does it, therefore, bespeak not a little spiritual pride, but such reasoning also impugns the sufficiency of Scripture (2 Tim. 3:15-17). Dr. Tulloch, an opponent of the regulative principle, attempts to evade this charge that his view denies the sufficiency of Scripture by arguing that the Bible was never intended to be a rule of church polity. He remarks:

The Christian Scriptures are a revelation of divine truth, and not a revelation of church polity. They not only do not lay down the outline of such a polity, but they do not even give the adequate and conclusive hints of one.[28]

---

[26] Owen, *Works*, 15:467.

[27] *The Reformation of the Church*, selected with introductory notes by Iain Murray (London, The Banner of Truth Trust, 1965), 75.

[28] *The Reformation of the Church*, 44.

The key biblical text on the sufficiency of Scripture provides us with explosives necessary to destroy Dr. Tulloch's view of Scripture. Second Timothy 3:16-17 is that text. The sufficiency of the Scriptures spoken of in this text is its sufficiency precisely for the man of God. The man of God is the person charged to order and lead the people of God.[29] Second Timothy 3:16-17 requires us to raise this question to those who think like Dr. Tulloch: Is ordering the church for the glory of God a good work which the man of God is peculiarly required to perform? Then, the Scriptures are able to thoroughly equip the man of God for this task. They teach the man of God an adequate form of biblical church order and the essential elements of the worship of the church.

4. The Bible explicitly condemns all worship that is not commanded by God (Lev. 10:1-3; Deut. 4:2; 17:3; 12:29-32; Josh. 1:7; 23:6-8; Matt. 15:13; Col. 2:20-23).

Three of these passages deserve special comment. Deuteronomy 12:29-32 in its original context is addressed precisely to the question of how God should be worshipped (v. 30). The rule given here in answer to this issue is very clear: "Whatever I command you, you shall be careful to do; you shall not add to nor take away from it" (v. 32). This clearly implies that it is a great temptation for God's people to see how the world worships and to allow that to have a formative impact on our attitudes about worship. Such an attitude is explicitly forbidden for God's people.

Colossians 2:23 condemns what may be literally translated as "will worship." Herbert Carson states the unavoidable implication of this phrase: "The words . . . imply a form of worship which a man devises for himself."[30]

Leviticus 10:1-3 is the frightening account of what happened to

---

[29] I assume here, what I believe careful exegesis will prove, that the man of God is not every Christian, but the leader or pastor of God's people. Both the OT use of the phrase, man of God, and the context of its use by Paul in 1 Tim. 6:11 support this identification. Of course, I do not deny that there is an important application of the sufficiency of the Scriptures to every Christian.

[30] Herbert Carson, *Tyndale New Testament Commentaries: The Epistles of Paul to the Colossians and Philemon* (Grand Rapids: Wm. B. Eerdmans Co., 1976), 79.

Nadab and Abihu when they displeased God in the way they worshipped him. What was it that brought upon them such a shocking judgment? Verse 1 is explicit. They "offered strange fire before the Lord." The meaning of the phrase, "strange fire," is expounded in the following clause. It is not fire which God had forbidden. The Hebrew clearly and literally reads that it was fire "which He had not commanded them." The mere fact that they dared to bring "unauthorized fire" (the translation of the NIV) brought fiery death upon them.

Multifaceted Function

A clear understanding of and a thorough commitment to the regulative principle of the church is, I am convinced, absolutely crucial if biblical church reformation is ever to become a reality in churches. The regulative principle is intended, as we have seen, to govern the whole of the church's life both as an institution and as an assembly. G. I. Williamson summarizes the regulative principle, as we have seen, with a pithy sentence: *What is commanded is right, and what is not commanded is wrong*. Using this as a simple summary of the regulative principle, we can see that this principle has a proper and important application to four areas of church life.

1. The doctrine of the church

The doctrine of the church must be governed by the regulative principle. In other areas of life we are allowed to believe what we think true as long as it does not contradict Scripture. So long as our political, scientific, or other views do not contradict the teaching of Scripture, we are allowed to believe as we think right. But this is not the case with regard to the church's doctrine. With regard to the doctrine of the church, there must be clear and compelling biblical support. With regard to this 2LCF 1.6 is clear:

> The whole counsel of God concerning all things necessary for his own glory, man's salvation, faith and life, is either

expressly set down or necessarily contained in the Holy Scripture: unto which nothing at any time is to be added, whether by new revelation of the Spirit, or traditions of men.

This statement is, of course, in its historical context intended to combat Rome, on the one hand, and certain Anabaptists' claims to new revelation on the other. Extra-biblical tradition, contrary to Rome, can form no part of the basis for the church's doctrine. Similarly, extra-biblical revelations, contrary to the claims both of some Anabaptists then and some Charismatics today, can form no part of the basis of the confession or creed of the church. The church's doctrine must be (to quote the language of the WCF parallel to that of the 2LCF quoted just above) "either expressly set down in Scripture, or by good and necessary consequence may be deduced from Scripture." The doctrine of the church may not be constructed on the basis of what the Scripture says plus what the church decrees. It must be constructed on the basis of the regulative principle.

2. The government of the church

Puritans (holding the regulative principle) have historically been committed to the *jus divinum*. In other words, they have been committed to the concept that there is a divinely ordained form of church government given us in the Bible. Historically, Anglicans (beginning with Hooker's treatise on the government of the Church of England) and many others since then have argued that God has left the church free within very general principles to construct its own government. Richard Hooker, in his work *Of the Laws of Ecclesiastical Polity*, expressly denies the regulative principle of the Puritans. One writer says, "Its object is to assert the right of a broad liberty on the basis of Scripture and reason."[31]

Hooker's views have simply anticipated the views of many evangelicals today. But such views can only be entertained while one remains in ignorance of the identity of the church as the house of God

---

[31] *The New Schaff-Herzog Encyclopedia of Religious Knowledge* (New York: Funk & Wagnalls, 1909), 5:360.

and the special regulative principle appropriate to the house of God. Once these things are understood, the superficial and even profane character of the view espoused by Hooker is obvious.

The fact that the regulative principle controls both the worship and government of the church is suggested by the way in which the second paragraph of 2LCF 1.6 qualifies the sufficiency of Scripture. It lumps together the worship and government of the church when it qualifies the regulative principle:

> . . . there are some circumstances concerning the worship of God, and government of the church, common to human actions and societies, which are to be ordered by the light of nature, and Christian prudence, according to the general rules of the Word, which are always to be observed.

Thus, when the Confession affirms the sufficiency of Scripture as the regulative principle of the church, it also makes clear that this refers not to the circumstances (detailed applications) of the government of the church, but to the basic parts or elements of church order.

If we are to remember that the church is the house of God and conscientiously endeavor to order it according to the mind of Christ, we must believe that the Word of God is a sufficient revelation of the way the church is to be ordered. Only a deep-rooted confidence in Scripture will make us search the Scriptures as we must so that our ministry will properly order the church of Christ.

3. The tasks of the church

The church is subject to the special regulation of the Word of God precisely because of its unique identity in human society. In the language of the early creeds, the church is *holy* in a way that no other institution of human society is. Neither the family, nor even the state, is subject to the regulative principle summarized above in the words of Williamson: *What is commanded is right, and what is not commanded is wrong.* The unique identity of the church directly leads us to the unique identity of its functions or tasks in the world.

It is not my purpose to expound in detail or even identify the tasks of the church. If, however, the distinctive tasks of the church are specified by the regulative principle, this suggests to me three plain duties of the church. First, it requires that the church carefully fulfill its distinct tasks. The church must clearly define and understand the peculiar functions God has given it. The church must put forth its resources and strength in the completion of those tasks.

Second, the church must carefully avoid usurping or having thrust upon it functions that are properly those of the state or the family. The danger is precisely the same as that pointed out in one of the arguments for the regulative principle. The introduction of extra-biblical practices into worship inevitably tends to nullify and undermine God's appointed worship. In the same way the introduction of extra-biblical functions into the church inevitably tends to nullify and undermine God's appointed tasks. If the temple of God feels a need to function as a political party or as a general educational institution, there will be an inevitable tendency to forget its unique and exalted identity as the temple of God.

Third, the church must carefully refrain from abdicating its own peculiar tasks and permitting other spheres of society to fulfill its own unique functions. This is the great principle on the basis of which our attitudes to parachurch organizations must be formed. We are told constantly today that the church cannot do the things that God has ordained that it should do. I do not believe it. Only the church can maintain the public worship of God. Only the church can fulfill the Great Commission. Only the church can disciple, baptize, and teach the disciples to observe all Christ's commandments. Only the church can properly train its own leadership.

4. The worship of the church

The regulative principle of the church has historically been identified as the regulative principle of worship. While this is not the only application of the regulative principle, it is a major application. Here it is helpful to recall that, in the New Testament, church has two related but distinct meanings. *Sometimes the church is institution or organization.* In Acts 20:17 where Paul is said to call for the elders of the church, the text means the leaders of a certain institution or organization. *Sometimes the church is the actual meeting of the church.* For instance, in

Matthew 18:17 where Jesus commands that something be "told to the church," and in 1 Corinthians 14:34-35 where Paul requires that women keep silent in the church, it is clearly the actual meeting of the church that is in view.

Keeping these two distinct meanings of the word in mind, we can see that the regulative principle of the church governs the church in both meanings. With regard to the church as an institution, its tasks, government, and doctrine are governed by the regulative principle. But the church's formal meetings or worship is also governed by it. It is the regulative principle *of the church.*

The regulative principle of worship is often seen as repressive and negative. In actuality, it is positive and liberating. It requires that the great and spiritually invigorating elements of gospel worship ordained in the Word of God have central place in the worship of the church. Some feel that their worship is dull, lifeless, and traditional and search everywhere for some new ceremony, program, or innovation to liven things up. How sad! The way to life and power and reality in the worship of God is not the way of innovation and novelty. It is the way back to a zealous and believing practice of the great, central requirements of biblical gospel worship.

Necessary Limitation

Chapter 1, paragraph 6 of the Confession provides an important clarification of the regulative principle.

> . . . there are some circumstances concerning the worship of God, and government of the church, common to human actions and societies, which are to be ordered by the light of nature and Christian prudence, according to the general rules of the Word, which are always to be observed.

When the Confession affirms, therefore, that what is not commanded in public worship is forbidden, we are speaking of the *substance* and *parts* of worship, not its circumstances. Note the emphasis on the parts of worship in paragraphs two through six of Chapter 22 and especially paragraphs 2, 3, and 5.

While the parts and substance of public worship are divinely limited, God has left the circumstances of worship to be determined by the light of nature, Christian prudence, and the general rules of Scripture. This distinction naturally and necessarily suggests this question: How may we distinguish between the parts of worship and its circumstances? This is a difficult and important question. Much of the contemporary opposition to and revision of the regulative principle is based on problems and objections raised by the distinction between the parts and circumstances of worship.[32] To it I have several responses. First, Bob Fisher in his unpublished teaching on this subject points out that 2LCF 1.6 limits these "circumstances concerning the worship of God, and government of the church" to things "common to human actions and societies." We have seen that it is the unique identity of the church which requires its special regulation. It makes sense, then, that those things which the church has in common with other societies should be regulated in the same way that those societies are governed. Pastor Fisher mentions the times of the meetings (as long as the Lord's Day is observed), the place of the meetings, the posture in which people attend the meetings, whether standing or seated on the floor or on chairs, the order of the meetings, if the meeting involves singing whether that singing is accompanied by a piano or a pitch-pipe or a flute as illustrations of such circumstances.

Second, 1 Corinthian 14 contains two examples of such general rules which God demands that we apply to our specific circumstances. They are the rules of edification and order (vv. 26 and 40). God demands that these two rules be followed, but he has not given us a detailed list of what they mean in every situation and culture.

Third, the circumstances of corporate worship and church government must be understood in light of what we believe to be the parts or elements of worship. Once those parts or elements of worship are defined, it becomes much easier to see what things are the circumstances required to carry out or implement those elements of worship. For instance, once we understand that corporate worship requires the assembly of the church for, among other things, the

---

[32] Gore in *Covenantal Worship*, 47-51, rejects the regulative principle partly because of difficulties he sees with this distinction. Frame in *Worship in Spirit and Truth*, 40-41, bases much of his revision of the principle on similar difficulties.

hearing of the proclamation of the Word of God, it will follow that such circumstances as place, posture, and time will have to be worked out in such a way as to best implement that part of worship. In my view, as well, once it is determined that singing the praise of God is a part of worship (as I believe it to be[33]), then the issues of circumstance which must be decided become clear. Will there be musical accompaniment? Who will lead the singing? How will everyone know what to sing? Will a song sheet, hymnal, overhead projector, or power-point be used? How long shall we sing? How many songs shall we sing?

Fourth, churches may differ as to where the line is drawn between circumstances and parts of worship without ceasing to be true churches or engaging in long polemics with one another. Just as churches may differ on certain doctrinal matters without becoming heretical, so also some differences on this issue of the regulative principle ought not to be a cause of division between churches. Reasonable differences should not be made the source of division. Let the elders of each church be fully assured in their own mind. Differences in application of the regulative principle may be tolerated as long as each church recognizes its unique identity as the house of God and holds seriously to the regulative principle. We may be charitable in such things, as long as the substance of the regulative principle is sincerely embraced.

Fifth, a godly fear will result from a genuine embrace of the principle that we must worship corporately only as God has appointed. This must certainly inject an attitude of caution and conservatism into what we justify as legitimate circumstances of corporate worship. Such caution must not, however, lead us to adopt the strictest and most conservative application of the regulative principle. Such a reactionary position often leads to the violation of other principles of Scripture.

---

[33] Interestingly, Frame does not believe it to be a part of worship, but believes it is a kind of mode by which we do other parts of worship. Cf. *Worship in Spirit and Truth*, 57.

Chapter 17

New Covenant Worship

Hebrews 2:12 and the Real Presence of Christ

Donald R. Lindblad[*]

"I will declare thy name unto my brethren,
In the midst of the congregation will I sing thy praise."
Hebrews 2:12[1]

Blessed Jesus, at thy word
We are gathered all to hear thee;
Let our hearts and souls be stirred
Now to seek and love and fear thee,
By thy teachings sweet and holy,
Drawn from earth to love thee solely.[2]

Recently, the invitation came to contribute an essay to a contemplated volume in honor of Dr. James M. Renihan on the occasion of his 60th birthday. Since 1998 he has served faithfully and energetically as president, dean, and professor (now Professor of Historical Theology) of the Institute of Reformed Baptist Studies (IRBS) at Westminster Seminary California. It did not take me long to answer affirmatively, for the following reasons.

First, apart from a brief interruption a few years ago, I have served continuously as trustee of IRBS. From the earliest days of my

---

[*] Donald R. Lindblad is a pastor of Trinity Reformed Baptist Church, Kirkland, WA.

[1] Unless part of a citation, Scripture references are from the American Standard Version (ASV), 1901.

[2] Tobias Clausnitzer, "Blessed Jesus at Thy Word," in *Trinity Hymnal — Baptist Edition* (Suwanee, GA: Great Commission Publications, Inc., 1995), 220.

association and friendship with Jim Renihan, the subject of worship, particularly preaching and the ministry, have been a regular part of our conversation. I remember very well a particular occasion, when we were driving together over the mountains, discussing the ministry and the centrality of preaching. In a day when multiplied ministries and other forms of communicating truth compete with and have replaced the ministry of the Word in many churches, this particular discussion was mutually encouraging. For Dr. Renihan, the ministry of the Word has a central place in the worship of the people of God.

Second, much of Dr. Renihan's public ministry has been devoted to an emphasis upon worship and the place of the ordinary means of grace. Preaching, the sacraments, and prayer are the ordinary means whereby God communicates the benefits of saving grace to his people. For example, Question 93 of *The Baptist Catechism* asks:

> What are the outward means whereby Christ communicateth to us the benefits of redemption? A. The outward and ordinary means whereby Christ communicateth to us the benefits of redemption are His ordinances, especially the Word, baptism, the Lord's Supper, and prayer; which means are made effectual to the elect for salvation.[3]

If any question remains as to how the Word is made effectual to salvation, Question 94 supplies the answer:

> How is the Word made effectual to salvation? A. The Spirit maketh the reading, but especially the preaching of the Word, an effectual means of convincing and converting sinners, and of building them up in holiness and comfort through faith unto salvation.[4]

---

[3] *The Baptist Confession of Faith of 1689 & The Baptist Catechism* (Vestavia Hills, AL: Solid Ground Christian Books and Carlisle, PA: Reformed Baptist Publications, 2010), 116. Proof texts cited are Matthew 28:19, 20; Acts 2:42, 46, 47.

[4] *The Baptist Catechism*, 116. Proof texts cited are Nehemiah 8:8; Acts 26:18; Psalm 19:8; Acts 20:32; Romans 1:15, 16; 10:13-17; 15:4; 1 Corinthians 15:24, 25; 1

Preaching, then, is a unique form of communication, something *The Baptist Catechism* and *The Baptist Confession of Faith of 1689* maintain.[5] In support of this position, I have in my files a number of papers delivered by Dr. Renihan on the ministry of the Word as necessary to the life of the church.[6]

Third, when it came time to choose a seal for IRBS, given the focus of the Institute and Dr. Renihan's ministry, the unanimous decision was *Praedicatio Verbi Dei Verbum Dei Est*, The Preaching of the Word of God is the Word of God, taken from the *Second Helvetic Confession of Faith*.[7] It is not that the preacher is inspired, but that when the minister preaches faithfully, he preaches authoritatively. He becomes the voice of Christ to the congregation. Such is the grandeur and the importance of preaching.

While he is much too young for anyone to deduce definitively what Dr. Renihan's legacy will be, it is not too soon to conclude what a major part of it will be. It certainly will include the recovery and definition of a robust Reformed confessionalism, with a particular focus (though not exclusively) on the public means of grace. He has done as much or more than anyone else in our generation to restore an emphasis on public worship and the ordinary means of grace. In other words, not only have I profited greatly and have learned from him, but so have a growing number of his students, as well as his hearers in congregations throughout the world. An essay on some aspect of public worship, preaching, and the ordinary means of grace is certainly fitting in a *festschrift* for Dr. Renihan on such a special occasion.

Timothy 3:15-17.

[5] See, for example, 2LCF, 14:1.

[6] Dr. Renihan's IRBS inaugural address subsequently was published as James M. Renihan, "The Ministry of the Word, Part 1," *The Banner of Truth*, Issue 491-2, (2004): 37-45; James M. Renihan, "The Ministry of the Word, Part 2," *The Banner of Truth*, Issue 493 (2004): 15-22. See also unpublished *The ordinary Means of Grace: Exposition*, IRBS Convocation, November 2003 and *Ordinary Means: 26 Theses*, same date.

[7] *The Second Helvetic Confession of Faith*, "Chapter 1. Of the Holy Scripture Being the True Word of God," paragraph 4. For the text see John Leith, ed., *Creeds of the Churches*, 3rd. (Atlanta: John Knox Press, 1982), 133. Also cited by J. Mark Beach, "The Real Presence of Christ in Preaching," *Mid-America Journal of Theology*, 10 (1999): 77-78. The subtitle comes from Heinrich Bullinger's heading of the paragraph. Bullinger was the author.

There is another reason why this essay has particular relevance. Many professing Christians—and others—have an altogether different litmus test for the public worship of God. Preference takes precedence over principle. It is subjective experience that matters most for many. Contrariwise, those committed to Reformed Christianity, at least historically, have come to appreciate the Bible's teaching that God's worship must be conducted in God's way. Public worship is central to the Christian life, and to please God that worship must be regulated according to God's Word. In other words, worship is for God and it must conform to the truth of God. In deference to the people of God who worship, it should also be added that right worship ought to have a profound effect upon the worshipper as well.

The so-called worship wars have divided the field hopelessly, almost to the point that it is impossible to discuss worship with others in any meaningful way without the heat rising and tempers flaring. Perhaps it has always been that way, since three different viewpoints have prevailed through the centuries. Rome's view may justly be called the *inventive principle*. According to this perspective, the church, or magisterium, may get as inventive as desired, even, apparently, prescribing elements contrary to the teaching of Scripture itself. The church, in this view, has authority over worship. Luther and others rejected this perspective and implemented what may be called the *normative principle*. If God has not prohibited a practice, that practice is allowed if it allegedly edifies. General *norms* are revealed, but not specifics. This probably reflects the prevailing view among most evangelicals today. The Reformed were much more rigorous in their understanding and implementation, advocating the *regulative principle*. Whatever is not commanded is forbidden. To put it differently, what God commands alone is permitted, taking seriously the words of Jesus, that worship must be "in spirit and truth" (John 4:23). The 2LCF puts it well and with biblical accuracy:

> The light of nature shows that there is a God who hath lordship and sovereignty over all; is just, good and doth good to all; and is therefore to be feared, loved, praised, called upon, trusted in, and served, with all the heart and all

the soul, and with all the might. But the acceptable way of worshipping the true God, is instituted by Himself, and so limited by His own revealed will, that He may not be worshipped according to the imagination and devices of men, nor the suggestions of Satan, under any visible representations, or any other way not prescribed in the Holy Scriptures. (2LCF 22:1)[8]

Introduction

Since worship that is acceptable to God must be far less *will-driven* and far more *Word-driven*, this essay will examine a particular text devoted to the matter of public worship and seek to expound it. It is not my intention to rehearse much of the fine material already written on a theology of worship or to reexamine the more common texts that have been expounded in sermons, books, and journals (e.g., Rom. 10:14, 17; 2 Cor. 5:20, 21, etc.). Rather, the intent is to explore a key passage that is devoted to new covenant worship in which Christ is both the *accent* (the center) of Christian worship and is also *active* in the believer's worship (who is really, though not carnally, present). Christ is both mediator to ensure our worship and leader of our worship; he is both the preacher and the principal who leads our praise. Much has been written about the real spiritual presence of Christ in the Lord's Supper, but far less has been produced about the equally real spiritual presence of Christ in our preaching and in our singing. Without taking away from the Reformed and confessional perspective on the real spiritual

---

[8] For further study, see John Calvin, "The Necessity of Reforming the Church" in *Tracts and Treatises on the Reformation of the Church*, 3 vols. (1844; reprint, Grand Rapids: Eerdmans, 1958), 1:121-234; William Cunningham, "The Reformers and the Regulative Principle" in *The Reformation of the Church: A Collection of Reformed and Puritan Documents on Church Issues* (London: The Banner of Truth Trust, 1965), 38-50; William Cunningham, "Obligation of Apostolic Practice," in *Historical Theology: A Review of the Principal Doctrinal Discussions in the Christian Church Since the Apostolic Age*, 2 vols. (London: The Banner of Truth Trust, 1960, 1969), 1:64-73; Terry L. Johnson, "The Regulative Principle," in *The Worship of God: Reformed Concepts of Biblical Worship* (Ross-shire, Scotland: Christian Focus Publications, 2005), 29; D. G. Hart and John R. Muether, *With Reverence and Awe: Returning to the Basics of Reformed Worship* (Phillipsburg, NJ: P&R Publishing, 2002), 75-87.

presence of Christ in the Supper, it is hoped this essay will contribute something to an understanding and appreciation of the real spiritual presence of Christ in our proclamation and in our praise.

Dr. Sinclair Ferguson, preaching to the congregation assembled in the historic Tenth Presbyterian Church, Philadelphia, on Reformation Day 2010, introduced his sermon on Hebrews 2:12 by asking the congregation to think of Hebrews 8:1-2. Here, he claimed, was a clue to what is being said in Hebrews 2:12. "We have such a high priest, who sat down on the right hand of the throne of the Majesty in the heavens." In verse 2, this high priest, the Lord Jesus, is described as "a minister of the sanctuary and of the true tabernacle, which the Lord pitched, not man." The word translated "minister," as Ferguson rightly points out, is the Greek word λειτουργὸς, our "liturgy" or "liturgist." Again, as Ferguson suggests, "We have such a high priest, a worship leader in the holy places, in the true tent that the Lord set up, not man."[9]

In verse 6, the writer uses the word, λειτουργίας, translated "ministry." The author now relates this heavenly ministry of our high priest to the new covenant. This heavenly priest applies the benefits of the new covenant effectually to sinners.

> In classical Greek the verb λειτουργεῖν and its cognates had no religious content, but Hebrews reflects the LXX, where the verb and its substantive were given a cultic nuance and were used for divine service only.[10]

This high priest makes real the benefits of the new covenant: transformation, communion, pardon, and inheritance—a truly effectual covenant. Jesus Christ is central to the new covenant, to our acceptance before God and to our worship. Christ's ministry forms a part of a new and better order, coordinating the two,

---

[9] Sinclair Ferguson, "When Jesus Is the Worship Leader," www.sermonaudio.com/tenth (Accessed June 26, 2015).

[10] William L. Lane, *Word Biblical Commentary, Hebrews 1-8* (Grand Rapids: Zondervan, 1991), 208. See also Strathmann, "D. λειτουργέω and λειτουγία in the New Testament," in *Theological Dictionary of the New Testament,* 12 vols., ed. Gerhard Kittel and trans. Geoffrey W. Bromiley (Grand Rapids: Wm. B. Eerdmans Publishing Company, 1967), 4:226, 28.

priestly ministry and covenant.

With Hebrews 8 in mind, and as something of a backdrop for our study, we turn now to our text, Hebrews 2:12, where we discover that this high priest, though in heaven, is in some sense present in our worship and the precentor (i.e., one who facilitates) of our public worship. He is in the midst and he leads, in proclamation and in praise. He is present among his people as they worship and he leads them in their worship, which has profound implications for how we understand the church, her Head, and her worship. As one author put it, "It is the writer's hope and prayer to encourage more awareness of the precious truth that the Lord Jesus is living and active in our midst as the Mediator of God's truth and the Leader of our worship."[11]

New Covenant Worship and the Person of Christ

1. The speaker

It is Christ who speaks in our text. The background to the immediate speech is the incarnation and the humiliation of Christ, which the author begins to unpack as far back as 2:5. When he comes to verse 11, the writer selects three Old Testament texts to prove Christ's solidarity with his people, that "For both he that sanctifieth and they that are sanctified are all of one: for which cause he is not ashamed to call them brethren" (2:11). John Brown writes, "The inspired writer now proceeds to quote a variety of passages from the Old Testament in proof of his assertion, that both the sanctified and the Sanctifier are of one common nature."[12]

It is the first of these texts that supports our interest for this essay. Verse 12 begins with the word, "saying," λέγων. The one who is not ashamed to call those whom he has redeemed his brethren speaks. And what he speaks firstly is what we discover in the rest of verse 12, which is a direct quotation of Psalm 22:22 from the

---

[11] Ron Man, *Proclamation and Praise: Hebrews 2:12 and the Christology of Worship* (Eugene, Oregon: Wipf & Stock Publishers, 2007), xi.

[12] John Brown, *Hebrews* (Edinburgh: The Banner of Truth Trust, 1961), 117.

Septuagint (LXX, 21:23). The only difference is that Hebrews replaces the διηγήσομαι of the LXX with ἀπαγγελῶ. While scholars advance a number of reasons for the change, there is no satisfying answer. There does not seem to be any substantive difference or significance in the change of verbs, with the author of Hebrews selecting the more common New Testament term for authoritative proclamation.[13]

Jesus takes up the words of this psalm, making them his own, as an expression of his experience on the cross and beyond. As F. F. Bruce writes, "It is the psalm whose opening words Jesus took upon His lips as the expression of His own experience in the hour of dereliction on the cross, 'My God, my God, why hast thou forsaken me?'"[14]

2. The source

Historically, the original speaker was David. It therefore initially reflects the experience of David; however, there is nothing in his life recorded in the Scriptures that approximates the tragedy or later the triumph of this psalm. In particular, there is nothing either personally or politically that comes even close to matching the horrific description of suffering in the first half of the psalm. As B. F. Westcott remarks, "The ground of the application in the first case lies in the fact that language goes beyond the actual experience of David, or of any righteous sufferer."[15]

Derek Kidner, in his commentary on the psalms, likewise remarks:

> No incident recorded of David can begin to account for this. As A. Bentzen points out, it is "not a description of illness, but of an *execution*"; and while David was once threatened

---

[13] Peter T. O'Brien, *The Letter to the Hebrews*, The Pillar New Testament Commentary, gen. ed. D. A. Carson (Grand Rapids, Wm. B. Eerdmans Publishing Company, 2010), 110, n. 147.

[14] F. F. Bruce, *The Epistle to the Hebrews*, The International Commentary on the New Testament (Grand Rapids: Wm. B. Eerdmans Publishing Company, 1964), 45.

[15] B. F. Westcott, *The Epistle to the Hebrews* (Grand Rapids: Wm. B. Eerdmans Company, 1965), 50.

with stoning (1 Sa. 30:6), this is a very different scene . . . Whatever the initial stimulus, the language of the psalm defies a naturalistic explanation; the best account is in terms used by Peter concerning another psalm of David: "Being therefore a prophet . . . he foresaw and spoke of . . . the Christ" (Acts 2:30f.).[16]

In introducing all three quotations used by the author of Hebrews to support his thesis, Philip Hughes confirms the above conclusion by writing:

Hebrew Christians who, as reverent and assiduous students of the Old Testament Scriptures, would readily recognize the appropriateness of the context from which these quotations are derived . . . The first of these quotations comes from a psalm which was of special messianic significance in the apostolic church, namely, Psalm 22.[17]

3. The substance

The psalm is made up of three parts: *tragedy, entreaty,* and *victory.* The first part is a lament, a lament for the absence of God and the presence of evil human beings. It begins with a cry of dereliction in verse 1, "My God, my God, why hast thou forsaken me." These are the opening words of anguish which Jesus uttered on the cross (Matt. 27:46; Mark 15:34). The rest of the section (through v. 21), however, continues to expose the ugly details of the events attending Christ's crucifixion. Peter T. O'Brien comments:

The first part of the psalm (vv. 1-21), which is a righteous man's cry for deliverance, provides graphic parallels to the events surrounding Christ's crucifixion: the words of vv. 7-8,

---

[16] Derek Kidner, *Psalms 1-72, An Introduction and Commentary,* gen. ed. D. J. Wiseman, Tyndale Old Testament Commentaries (Leister, UK: Inter-Varsity Press, 1973), 105.

[17] Philip Edgcumbe Hughes, *A Commentary on the Epistle to the Hebrews* (Grand Rapids: Wm. B. Eerdmans Publishing Company, 1977), 107.

in which the righteous man is taunted ("He trusts in the Lord; let the Lord rescue him."), reflect the ridicule of the religious leaders around the cross (Matt. 27:43), while vv. 16-18 speak explicitly of the piercing of the righteous one's hands and feet, the wholesomeness of his bones, and the dividing of his garments by casting lots (Matt. 27:35; John 19:23, 31-36). This psalm as a whole clearly fits the author's wider concern with Jesus' suffering death on the cross.[18]

As F. F. Bruce observes with regard to Heb. 2:12:

> The first quotation (Psa. 22:22) is taken from a psalm in which no Christian in the first century would have failed to recognize Christ as the speaker. . . . Practically the whole of the lament to which the first part of the psalm is devoted was used in the Church from very early times as a *testimonium* of the crucifixion of Christ; not only is it expressly quoted, but its language has been worked into the very fabric of the New Testament passion narratives, especially in the First and Fourth Gospels.[19]

Following a prayer for deliverance (vv. 20-21), lament changes to thanksgiving. Tragedy and aversion are exchanged for triumph and elation. God answers the prayer of the righteous man and "the righteous man's lament changes to thanksgiving as he responds joyfully to the Lord's vindication and exaltation after his suffering and affliction."[20]

> It is most natural, then, that when the psalmist's lament gives way to the *public* [emphasis mine] thanksgiving of which the second part of the psalm consists, the same speaker should be recognized, and the one crucified, now exalted Christ should be heard saying: "I will declare thy name unto my brethren; in the midst of the congregation will I sing thy praise."[21]

---

[18] O'Brien, *Hebrews*, 110-11.

[19] Bruce, *Hebrews*, 45.

[20] O'Brien, *Hebrews*, 111.

[21] Bruce, *Hebrews*, 45.

Calvin puts it simply and profoundly, "These things are accomplished only in Christ, who enlarged the kingdom of God not over a small space, as David did, but extended it over the whole world; it was before confined as it were within narrow limits."[22]

New Covenant Worship and the Power of Christ

1. Solidarity and its identity

Psalm 22 is cited by the author of Hebrews in a context of suffering and exaltation for Christ. It is the exalted one who addresses his brethren. "The connection between ἀδελφούς αὐτούς καλεῖν ('to call them brothers,' v. 11) and τοῖς ἀδελφοῖς μου ('to my brothers,' v. 12) is both obvious and significant."[23] Jesus' promise to declare his name to his brethren demonstrates his solidarity with them. They have a common origin and a common relation. They have a common humanity and a common destiny. As Hughes writes:

> The Messiah's *brethren*, as we have previously explained, are those, his fellow men by incarnation and his fellow heirs by reconciliation and adoption, whom he has redeemed by his sacrifice of himself on the cross.[24]

To broaden our horizon, we cast a backward glance over the preceding verses. The writer begins his introduction to this great salvation from which the Christian professor must not drift away (2:1-4), by citing Psalm 8:4ff. (Heb. 2:5-8) and identifying the fulfillment of the psalm with the coming of Jesus Christ. The new world order has been inaugurated by the coming of Christ into the world. He identifies the man of Psalm 8 not with the first Adam but with the last Adam.

---

[22] John Calvin, *Commentaries on the Epistle of Paul the Apostle to the Hebrews*, trans. and ed. Rev. John Owen, *Calvin's Commentaries*, 22 vols. (1843; reprint, Grand Rapids: Baker Books, 2009), 22:65.

[23] O'Brien, *Hebrews*, 111, n. 148.

[24] Hughes, *Hebrews*, 108.

In verses 9-11, the passage goes on to describe the career of this man through whom salvation has come. He is marked by present exaltation, but only after his humiliation, incarnation, suffering and death, through which he tasted death for all he came to save, those many sons brought to glory. It was this act of redemption that rendered him perfect as mediator, not that he could be made perfect ontologically, for he was already the perfect Son of God; rather, that his suffering and death fully equipped him to be a faithful Savior.[25] Here is the means of bringing many sons to glory. The focus is on the humanity of Jesus (his human name, v. 9). As Hughes writes on 2:9, "Hence the expression marks the reality both of the humanity and the dying of Jesus."[26] Hughes continues with:

> . . . first the Cross, then the Crown: the exaltation of Jesus was the consequence of his humiliation, not, however, merely the humiliation of his incarnation, but especially the humiliation of the cross; for the incarnation was the means to 'the suffering of death' as the end for which he came, and Calvary accordingly is both the explanation and the fulfilment of Bethlehem.[27]

2. Solidarity and its integrity

There is some debate among commentators at two points: the nature of this sanctification and what it means that both are "of one." As to the first, the word can have at least two senses: separation for special use and moral change or holiness. As to the second, the "one" can be either masculine or neuter. If masculine, suggestions have ranged from God, to Adam, to Abraham; if neuter, it would refer to our Lord's human nature. Space does not permit entering into the debate. For our purposes, and in keeping with the majority of commentators, it seems best to adopt the following.

---

[25] O'Brien, *Hebrews*, 107. On τελειῶσαι, O'Brien says, "Although this has been interpreted in telic, cultic, and ethical terms, a vocational understanding of the perfecting of Christ best fits the immediate context of Hebrews and is consistent with other instances in Hebrews."

[26] Hughes, *Hebrews*, 91.

[27] Hughes, *Hebrews*, 88.

The one who sanctifies and the ones who are sanctified are timeless present participles used as nouns. Textually, sanctification describes the persons who are brought to glory and are the objects of this redemption. Biblically, to sanctify or sanctification means two things: separation or dedication to God, to belong exclusively to God, and to purify from sin. Sanctification, then, is both cultic and ethical. The ones set apart for God are set apart for worship and service, as well as in their character (cf. Num. 16:5; John 17:17-19, for the former; 1:3; 9:14, for the latter). Sanctification has implications that are *liturgical* (Heb. 12:22-24) and *ethical*.[28]

"Of one" is a matter of dispute both as to gender and to reference, as noted above. If the gender is masculine, references have been made to God, to Adam, even to Abraham (v. 16). If neuter, it refers generically to human nature. The latter fits the context best. That is the point of comparison. Jesus and those he saves are of the same stock, human stock. Jesus was a real man, who, though God, took on human flesh and in his humiliation lived and died for those he came to save.[29] John Owen says it well:

> It is, then, one common nature that is here intended. He and they are of the same nature, of one mass, of one blood. And hereby he came to be meet to suffer for them, and they to be in a capacity of enjoying the benefit of his sufferings; which how it answers the whole design of the apostle in this place doth evidently appear.[30]

3. Solidarity and its intimacy

The redeemed are called brethren. The persons so called sustain the closest possible relation to the one who is the author of their

---

[28] For a helpful expansion, see Paul Ellingworth, *The Epistle to the Hebrews: a Commentary on the Greek Text*, eds. I. Howard Marshall and W. Ward Gasque, The New International Greek Testament Commentary (Grand Rapids: Wm. B. Eerdmans Publishing Company, 1993), 163-64.

[29] Ellingworth, *Hebrews*, 164-65. For an alternate view, that reference is to God, i.e., both have the same origin in God, see O'Brien, *Hebrews*, 108-09.

[30] John Owen, *An Exposition of the Epistle to the Hebrews* in *The Works of John Owen*, 23 vols. (1854, reprint, Edinburgh: The Banner of Truth Trust, 1991), 19:418, vol. 3 of the Hebrews commentary.

salvation.[31] They are brethren in view of his incarnation, humiliation, and victorious exaltation, an exaltation that provides benefits for "brethren."

> The *main* point of the quotation is the word ἀδελφός. This expresses Christ's identification with Christians, the oneness of ὁ ἁγιαζων and οἱ ἁγιαζόμενοι, which thus depends, not on an abstract ontological principle (as if v. 11a stood in isolation), but on a voluntary act of Christ (v. 14a), culminating in his death (vv. 10, 14b) within the purpose of God (ἔπρεπεν, v. 10; ὤφειλεν, v. 17).[32]

As Arthur Pink put it:

> But more: not only did the 22nd Psalm announce beforehand the sufferings of the Messiah; it also foretold his victory. Read again the last clause of v. 21; "Save me from the lion's mouth; for thou *hast* heard me." Christ *was* "saved," not from death but out of death, cf. Heb 5:7. Now what is the very next thing in Psalm 22? This: "I will declare thy name unto My brethren" (v. 22). Here the Saviour is seen on resurrection ground, victorious over every foe. It is this which the apostle quotes in Heb. 2:12.[33]

And Pink again:

> Now that which it is particularly important to note is that in this verse from Psa. 22 Christ is heard saying He would declare the Father's name unto his "brethren." *That* would only be possible on resurrection ground.[34]

---

[31] Hughes, *Hebrews*, 100, n. 88. "The noun ἀρχηγός is difficult to translate satisfactorily. It signifies one who is both the source or initiator and the leader (ἀρχη, plus ἄγω), one who first takes action and then brings those on whose behalf he has acted to the intended goal. The same designation is applied to Jesus in 12:2 below and also in Acts 3:15 and 5:31, where, as ἀρχηγὸς τῆς ζωῆς, he is both the source and the means of life."

[32] Ellingworth, *Hebrews*, 166.

[33] Arthur W. Pink, *An Exposition of Hebrews* (Grand Rapids: Baker Book House, 1954), 122.

[34] Pink, *Hebrews*, 122.

New Covenant Worship and the Preaching of Christ

1. The teacher

The "who" of the text is Jesus. He is the one who teaches, who preaches, who makes authoritative announcements to his brethren. Jesus is the one who preaches to his people. Jesus Christ is central to preaching and teaching.

2. The time

The "when" of the text is *now*. The author of the epistle cites Psalm 22, which historically has to do with David. David worshiped in the tabernacle; he declared God's name in the psalms he wrote. When did or does Jesus do this? Jesus too proclaimed God's name in the temple and in the synagogues during his earthly ministry. He was found in the temple teaching when he was just a boy (Luke 2:47); his first sermon was preached as a young man in the synagogue at Nazareth (Luke 4:16ff.); throughout his earthly life he preached and held crowds spellbound; he taught the Twelve throughout the years of his public ministry; in the final week of his life, he preached in the temple. Clearly, Jesus declared God's name throughout his life. "Here in Hebrews he boldly declares God's name in the assembly of those who need strength."[35]

In addition Christ instructed his apostles in all things his church needed to know. Paraphrasing William Gouge, our Lord said to the Twelve in the Upper Room, ". . . for all things that I heard from my Father I have made known to you" (John 15:15b). Likewise, he commanded his apostles "to teach people to observe all things whatsoever he had commanded them" (Matt. 28:20). Subsequently, he gave ministers of the Word, pastors and teachers, after apostles, for the edification of the church (Eph. 4:11-12). These stand in Christ's place, commanding reconciliation (2 Cor. 5:21).[36]

---

[35] O'Brien, *Hebrews*, 112.

[36] William Gouge, *Commentary on Hebrews: Exegetical and Expository — Volume One, Chapters 1-7* (1866; reprint, Birmingham, AL: Solid Ground Christian Books,

While some have located this preaching in the parousia, there seems good reason to reject this view and to see 2:12 as referring to the ongoing ministry of Jesus in the "already," this church age. As one writer has said, this view has been variously and convincingly defended. Note the following:

Quite apart from quotations and allusions to Ps. 22 in the Gospel passion narratives, the reference in Ps. 22:30f. to a "coming generation" and a "people yet to be born" may have impressed the author of Hebrews as pointing towards fulfilment in Christ and in his Church. If so, this fact may have contributed to his decision to quote v. 22b. (LXX 23b) as referring to the Church. It also suggests that the time perspective of the quotations in Heb. 2:12f. is that of realized eschatology. . . . From the time of Christ's exaltation and the establishment of the Christian ἐκκλησία, the future tenses in the quotation, though still quoted as such, have become present reality.[37]

2006), 1:151.

[37] Ellingworth, *Hebrews*, 167-68.

3. The task

The "what" of the text is the present ministry of Christ: his declaring or preaching. It is the exalted Christ who should be heard. A number of texts highlight the present ministry of Christ in preaching,[38] and Reformed theology has long recognized what might be called the real presence of Christ in preaching. That is, that Christ is really, though not physically or carnally, present in the church when the Word is preached by those appointed and authorized to do so. Jesus Christ, the God-Man, is in heaven, but he ministers through his servants by the Holy Spirit. Specific texts support this view, and therefore classic, confessional, Reformed Theology endorses it. A sentence from *The Second Helvetic Confession* was cited briefly at the beginning of this essay. Now note its fuller expression:

> Wherefore when this Word of God is now preached in the church by preachers lawfully called, we believe that the very Word of God is preached, and received of the faithful, and that neither any other Word of God is to be feigned or to be expected from heaven: and that now the Word itself which is preached is to be regarded, not the minister that preaches, who, although he be evil and a sinner, nevertheless the Word of God abides true and good.[39]

Since the days of the Reformation, Reformed theology has maintained a high view of preaching. Preaching plays a prominent

---

[38] For example, Romans 10:14 is often understood to say, ". . . how shall they believe in him of whom they have not heard"; however, the word "of" is not in the Greek text. Rather, the verse reads, "how shall they believe him whom they have not heard" (πῶς δὲ πιστεύσωσιν οὗ οὐκ ἤκουσαν). For further study, see C. E. B. Cranfield, *The Epistle to the Romans*, International Critical Commentary, 2 vols. (Edinburgh: T & T Clark Limited, 1979), 2:534; Leon Morris, *The Epistle to the Romans*, The Pillar New Testament Commentary (Grand Rapids: Wm. B. Eerdmans Publishing Company, 1988), 389-90; John Murray, *The Epistle to the Romans*, The New International Commentary on the New Testament, 2 vols. (Grand Rapids: Wm. B. Eerdmans Publishing Company, 1965), 2:58.

[39] *The Second Helvetic Confession* (1566), 1:4.

and conspicuous role in the life of the church. As J. Mark Beach writes, citing *The Second Helvetic Confession*:

> What is more, according to the classic Reformed tradition, the preaching of the Word of God *is* the Word of God. Or, to state it more accurately, preaching, when accompanied by the Spirit's presence and power, is Christ's living voice to the church and world today. Christ is really present in the preaching of the gospel.[40]

We may rightly speak, then, of the real presence of Christ in preaching. Beach writes, "In this connection, some scholars believe there is a link between Calvin's conception of the divine presence in preaching and his understanding of that presence in the sacraments."[41] "In preaching, the Holy Spirit uses the words of the preacher as an occasion for the presence of God in grace and mercy."[42] Preaching, then, is more than a lecture, more than merely conveying information. In preaching, Christ meets with us in a unique and powerful way. He speaks; he is the preacher. And he does so through the mediation of men. There is a union between the work of God and the work of men in preaching. Beach asserts:

> Preaching finds its sanction not because it is the most effective means to educate or reform the church; rather, it finds its sanction in the will of God itself. God wants to build his church by this means. Thus nothing may be substituted for it, even if other means would prove to be more popular or useful. The preacher, Calvin dared to say, was the mouth of God, "for God does not wish to be heard but by the voice of his ministers." Preaching should therefore be undertaken, and the preacher's words should be heard, as Christ making himself present with the gospel; in this way the recipients of the sermon come to hear his voice through the voice of the

---

[40] Beach, "Real Presence," 77-78.

[41] Beach, "Real Presence," 93.

[42] John H. Leith, "Calvin's Doctrine of the Proclamation of the Word and Its Significance for Today in the Light of Recent Research," *Review and Expositor* 86 (Winter 1989): 31, cited in Beach, "Real Presence," 93.

minister.[43]

Preaching then is a means of grace. It is the means the Spirit uses in the salvation of sinners and the nourishment of God's people. Yet, where faithfulness to the written Word is lacking, preaching ceases to function as God's Word. That noted, preaching is still applicable and appropriate where faithfulness is present. The ministry of Christ through his servants is still verbal, despite the claim of many today who wish to shift the focus back to an Old Testament emphasis on the visual.

Interestingly, T. H. L Parker observes that those with a low view of the sacraments tend to have a low view of preaching:

> It is not just coincidence that those who held a "Zwinglian" view of the Sacraments held also the view of preaching which we have been expounding, for preaching and Sacraments are the two parts of the one action; a "low" view of either must result in a "low" view of the other.[44]

According to Calvin, then, preaching so to say "borrows" its status of "Word of God" from Scripture. It is the Word of God inasmuch as it delivers the Biblical message, which is God's message or Word. But "God's Word" means, for Calvin, that which is spoken by God; not simply in its first giving but in its every repetition. It does not somehow become weakened by repetition so as to become less and less God's Word.[45]

Returning to our text, listen to Calvin:

> We must further notice the office which Christ assumes, which is that of *proclaiming the name of God* ; and this began to be done when the gospel was first promulgated, and is

---

[43] Beach, "Real Presence," 96. "Preaching is therefore human in its instrumentality but divine in its efficacy."

[44] T. H. L. Parker, *Calvin's Preaching* (Edinburgh: T & T Clark, 1992; first American edition Louisville: Westminster/John Knox Press), 22.

[45] Parker, *Calvin's Preaching*, 23-24.

now done daily by the ministry of pastors. . . . And this is what Paul says, for he declares that he and others were ambassadors for Christ ; and he exhorted men as it were in the name of Christ. (2 Cor. v. 20.) And this ought to add no small reverence to the gospel, since we ought not so much to consider men as speaking to us, as Christ by his own mouth; for at the time when he promised to publish God's name to men, he had ceased to be in the world; it was not however to no purpose that he claimed this office as his own; for he really performs it by his disciples.[46]

New Covenant Worship and the Praise of Christ

1. The liturgist

Interestingly, and contrary to popular practice, Jesus is also the worship leader of his people. According to our text, worship is not actually led by a song leader or by an enthusiastic worship team, but it is led by Jesus, the one who redeemed his people. Pink writes, "The position in which Jesus Christ is here viewed is very blessed, 'in the midst': it is the Redeemer leading the praises of his redeemed."[47]

Just as Jesus preached during the period of his incarnation, so he sang. Edmund Clowney puts it this way:

> In the New Testament, Jesus Christ comes as the Son of David, the sweet singer of Israel, to reveal God's love. In the upper room, Jesus sang with his disciples before he went out to the Garden of Gethsemane. On the cross, he uttered the opening cry of Psalm 22, "My God, my God, why have you forsaken me?" Hebrews attributes to Christ a later verse from the same psalm: "I will declare your name to my brothers; in the presence of the congregation I will sing your praises." (Heb. 2:12; Ps. 22:22).

---

[46] Calvin, *Hebrews*, 23:66.
[47] Pink, *Hebrews*, 123.

Jesus who voiced the opening plea of dereliction, also utters the cry of triumph in the same psalm, and now sings in the midst of the congregation as he pays his vow of praise. Our triumphant King is a singing Saviour. He sings with us here on earth, and we with him in the assembly of heaven. Jesus is the heavenly Choirmaster, the Lord's Anointed (2 Sa. 23:1).[48]

Jesus sang then, but Jesus sings now. Calvin asserts both Christ's incarnational example and present leadership in praise:

It hence appears still more plainly, that the proclamation of God's praises is always promoted by the teaching of the gospel; for as soon as God becomes known to us, his boundless praises sound in our hearts and in our ears; and at the same time Christ encourages us by his own example publicly to celebrate them, so that they may be heard by as many as possible. For it would not be sufficient for each one of us to thank God himself for benefits received, except we testify openly our gratitude, and thus mutually stimulate one another. And it is a truth, which may serve as a most powerful stimulant, and may lead us most fervently to praise God, when we hear that Christ leads our songs, and is the chief composer of our hymns.[49]

Richard D. Phillips in a volume of sermons on Hebrews confirms, with this:

This reminds us that Jesus is the true singer of the Psalms; they were written first and foremost for him, and it is always with him in mind that we sing most truly. But this psalm also makes an important theological point: Christ died and rose again not merely to save us but to make us worshipers of his Father. This is fulfilled in our churches today; literally, Hebrews 2:12 concludes, "I will sing hymns in the church."[50]

---

[48] Edmund P. Clowney, *The Church*, Contours of Christian Theology, ed. Gerald Bray (Downers Grove, IL: InterVarsity Press, 1995), 134-35.

[49] Calvin, *Hebrews*, 23:66-67.

2. The liturgy

More precisely, what about the songs sung in the church? The first Christians took their lead from the simple service of the synagogue, which included the singing of psalms. In Acts 4:23-31, the church's prayer service began with the congregation singing psalms. First Corinthians 14:26 records Paul's instruction to the church for the singing of psalms when they gather for worship. Paul writes to the churches in Ephesus and Colossae and encourages the singing of "psalms, hymns, and spiritual songs." Hughes Oliphant Old connects the singing of psalms and the ministry of the Spirit:

> The psalms of the Old Testament were considered perfectly acceptable for Christian worship. They were the songs of the Holy Spirit. The first Christians were particularly conscious of the presence of the Holy Spirit in their worship. It was the Spirit who inspired their worship. Their preaching and their interpretation of the Scriptures was the work of God's Spirit crying out within them. The Spirit within them bore witness that Jesus was the Christ, the Lord's anointed. The same Holy Spirit moved them to praise. Often the mention of singing psalms and hymns in the New Testament is accompanied by references to the Holy Spirit. For example, Paul admonishes the Ephesians to be filled with the Holy Spirit, to sing psalms and spiritual songs, making melody in their hearts (Eph. 5:18-20). In Acts 4 we find another example. We read the congregation, "lifted up their voices together." Then a line from Psalm 146 is quoted and after that several lines from Psalm 2. What is of particular interest is that Psalm 2 is introduced by a benediction very similar in literary form to the benediction used to introduce psalmody in the synagogue, "[T]he mouth of our father David, thy servant, didst say by the Holy Spirit . . ." (Acts 4:25). Quite obviously for the first Christians this was an important

---

[50] Richard D. Phillips, *Hebrews*, Reformed Expository Commentary (Philipsburg, NJ: P&R Publishing, 2006), 74.

consideration. When they sang the Psalms, the Holy Spirit was praising the Father within their hearts.[51]

While the psalms formed the basic hymn book for early Christians, a number of passages suggest that the earliest Christians sang praises in addition to the 150 canonical psalms. As Hugh Oliphant Old points out:

> In the first place, we find a number of Christian psalms such as the Song of Mary (Luke 1:46-55); the Song of Zechariah (Luke 1:68-79), and the song of Simeon (Luke 2:29-32). These are clearly Christian psalms written in the literary genre of the Hebrew votive thanksgiving psalms.[52]

In addition, there are at least two places elsewhere in the New Testament that indicate the development of hymns. In the epistles of Paul there are two hymns to Christ: the Christological hymn of Philippians 2:5-11 and a similar hymn-like passage in Colossians 1:15-20. Finally, in Revelation we discover the worship of heaven (Rev. 4:8; 15:3).[53]

3. The litmus test

While this writer is not prepared to plead for exclusive psalmody, the singing of the psalms only in public worship, even this narrow study of an exposition of Hebrews 2:12 suggests that the psalms are important for the public praise of the people of God. Jesus leads his people in worship, and the proof text for this truth is a quotation in the New Testament epistle of Hebrews from the Old Testament book of Psalms.

For hundreds of years, the psalms comprised the only hymn book of the people of God. Jesus sought to prove to the two on the

---

[51] Hughes Oliphant Old, *Worship: Reformed According to Scripture*, Revised and Expanded Edition (Louisville/London: Westminster John Knox, 2002), 36-37.

[52] Old, *Worship*, 37.

[53] Old, *Worship*. 37-38. For an elaboration of my paragraph, see his development.

road to Emmaus all that had happened to him, ". . . from all the scriptures . . ." The psalms too are Christ-centered and may be sung by the people of God in this age and ought also to be used as a litmus test for what is appropriate to sing in public worship. After all, if Christ leads us in worship, then certainly what we sing about must be full of him and have his approval. The psalms, then, give to us helpful guidelines if we choose to sing hymns other than the psalms, and if we choose to compose them for the church today. A number of books have been written on the subject, but a very helpful place to begin is with "Statement of Principle for Music in the Church," found in The Psalter Hymnal, published by the Christian Reformed Church in 1976.[54] It contains a list of ten principles, easily read and digested, that will set the reader in a biblical direction for making decisions regarding singing in the church.

To round off this section, consider the words of Spurgeon:

It is so here this evening; Christ is praising God in this congregation. . . . Behold, then, in your midst, O Church of God, in the days of his flesh there stood this glorious One whom angels worship, who is the brightness of his Father's glory in the very heaven of heavens; yet when he stood here, it was to join in this worship of his people, declaring the Father's name unto his brethren, and with them singing praises unto the Most High. Does not this bring him very near to you? Does it not seem as if he might come at any moment, and sit in that pew with you; I feel as if already he stood on this platform side by side with me; why should he

---

[54] "Statement of Principle for Music in the Church," in *The Psalter Hymnal: Doctrinal Standards and Liturgy of the Christian Reformed Church* (Grand Rapids: Board of Publications of the Christian reformed Church, 1976) v. Among many fine resources on worship, two stand out: Eds. Frank J. Smith and David C. Lachman, *Worship in the Presence of God: A Collection of Essays on the Nature, Elements, and Historic Views and Practice of Worship* (Greenville, SC: Greenville Presbyterian Theological Press, 1992); Eds. Greenville Presbyterian Seminary, *The Worship of God: Reformed Concepts of Biblical Worship* (Ross-shire, Scotland: Christian Focus Publications, 2005). See also four tests for appropriate music in the church introduced by Terry Johnson: Is it singable; biblically and theologically sound; biblically and theologically mature; emotionally balanced, cited in Hart and Muether, *With Reverence and Awe*, 172-73.

not? Oh, happy hour, if we could but see him in very flesh and blood among us! Yet, we know that he is here, even if we cannot see him, for he has said, "Lo, I am with you alway even unto the end of the world."[55]

New Covenant Worship and the Prosecution of Christ

1. Dialogue

Jesus Christ presides over the worship of his brethren in two ways: he speaks for God *to* us, declaring authoritatively his name; he speaks to God *with* and *for* us, leading us in our praises. He is both prophet and priest to his people. We may justly call this conversation *dialogue*.

This principle of dialogue is reinforced when we consider that the relevant context of Psalm 22:22 was in the mind of the author of Hebrews as he mentions Christ singing in the midst of the congregation. In order to clarify the point, Ron Man states:

> However, it is better to see in this verse a *synthetic* parallelism, with two halves regarded as complementary but *in opposite directions*. . . . [It] is best to interpret the two halves of Hebrew 2:12 as referring to two quite distinct, though marvelously complementary, activities: the declaration of God's praiseworthiness to the people (12a.) and the appropriate praise then lifted to God in response (12b.).[56]

Man continues:

> [M]uch of the second section of Psalm 22 consists of a call by the vindicated one to His brethren to join in with Him in praise to God. That includes the very next verse after the one

---

[55] C. H. Spurgeon, "All of One," Sermon on Hebrews 2:11-13, *Metropolitan Tabernacle Pulpit*, vol. 41, 1895 (1895; reprint, Pasadena, TX: Pilgrim Publications, 1975, 1995) 295.

[56] Man, *Proclamation and Praise*, 30.

quoted: "You who fear the Lord praise Him. And stand in awe of Him, all you descendents of Israel" (22:23). Certainly the one praising God in 22:22 (and the one quoted in Hebrews 2:12) intends to draw others into praise with Him![57]

Peter C. Craigie, in his commentary on the Psalms, reinforces the above conclusion:

> The opening words of praise and thanksgiving are addressed to God (v. 23) [v. 22 in English]; the remaining and major portion of the declaration is addressed to the congregation as a whole (vv. 24-27). Because the worshiper has received the assurance of God's response in the context of congregational liturgy, his immediate response is to say to God that he will offer him praise in that same congregation. Thus, the praise of God that follows is not addressed to God in a vacuum; it is addressed to God through the congregation, with the invitation that they too honor and praise God.[58]

R. B. Kuiper put it this way:

> Since corporate worship is offered to God in a meeting of God and His people, it must consist of two sorts of transactions. In some, as the reading of Scripture, the preaching of the Word and the benediction, God addresses His people and they worship by reverently attending. In others, as prayer, song, and the offering of gifts, they respond in holy fear to what God has spoken. In every part of their worship God's people either listen to God or reply to God.[59]

How lofty a conception of corporate worship Scripture

---

[57] Man, *Proclamation and Praise*, 31.

[58] Peter C. Craigie, *Word Biblical Commentary, Psalms 1-50* (Nashville: Thomas Nelson, Inc., 2004), 19:200-01.

[59] R. B. Kuiper, *The Glorious Body of Christ: A Scriptural Appreciation of the One Holy Church* (London: The Banner of Truth Trust, First British Edition, 1967), 348.

presents! When God's people assemble for worship they enter into the place where God dwells. God meets them, and they meet God. They find themselves face to face with none other than God Himself. Their worship is an intimate transaction between them and their God. If the church were fully conscious of that truth, what dignity and reverence would characterize its worship! Of levity and frivolity there would be not a trace. The worshipers would exclaim, as did Jacob at Bethel: "How dreadful is this place! This is none other than the house of God and this is the gate of heaven" (Genesis 28:17).[60]

The principle of dialogical worship is under attack today. According to Hart and Muether, several recent studies on worship have challenged the God-centered and vertical approach to worship, insisting that worship be both vertical and horizontal. In the vertical we do things that honor and glorify God, and in the horizontal we do things that "edify" the people. But, the principle of dialogue illustrated by our text challenges this distinction by maintaining that all worship is vertical. Besides, even the casual observer will note that the word "edify" in the context of modern worship takes on a rather fluid meaning. Hart and Muether respond to this challenge:

> [Worship] is a holy transaction or conversation between God and his people. It is not a conversation among God's people. When we greet our neighbors in the next pew or when we listen to testimonies, we are not worshiping God. As edifying as these activities may be, and as encouraging as they are in the appropriate setting, corporate worship is a time when the dialogue goes back and forth between God and his people.[61]

2. Deduction

---

[60] Kuiper, *Glorious Body*, 345.
[61] Hart and Muether, *With Reverence and Awe*, 96.

If Jesus leads his brethren, the church, in praise, then the New Testament puts a premium on congregational singing. Singing in the church is not for the purpose of entertainment, equally not intended as a personal emotional jolt. Music, or song, does arouse emotion, but it is intended in the church for praise. This is not to say, once again, that good music does not bless the worshipers. True worship certainly does bless and satisfy. However, there is a God-centeredness about praise to God, which all too often is marginalized by a focus on the horizontal. Jesus, as song-leader, leads the congregation in praise to God. God is the recipient of our praise. Those who are the brethren of Jesus ought to give careful attention to Jesus as a model, who sang God's praises himself, and as the leader who guides by his Word and Spirit in singing the praises of God.

New Covenant Worship and the People of Christ

1. The constitution of the church

There is a readily apparent correlation in the text between the brethren of Jesus and the congregation (ASV). As we have seen, his brethren are those who are one with him in his humanity and who have come to share in the benefits of his salvation for them. Now, he speaks of the same persons as belonging to the congregation, literally, church. The word used is the word used commonly throughout the New Testament, ἐκκλησία. He will sing God's praise in the midst of the church, in the context of his brethren. As F. F. Bruce writes:

> The employment of this word in synonymous parallelism with 'brethren' in a Christian context indicates that those whom the Son of God is pleased to call his brethren are the members of his church.[62]

---

[62] Bruce, *Hebrews*, 46.

Interestingly, this is the same word, ἐκκλησία, used by the LXX for the Hebrew, קָ,הָ,ל, often translated "assembly." In both passages the Scriptures assume that the redeemed, his brethren, will identify with God's people in the church. Neither David nor Jesus have in view a privatized faith that ignores the assemblies of God's people, the church. Whatever value private devotion has, and it certainly has great value and is a necessary part of Christian experience, both Psalm 22 and Hebrews 2 place the spotlight on corporate worship. Corporate worship, hearing the Word from faithful ministers and singing the praises of God, both in the context of the real presence of Christ, is at the center of Christian experience and necessary to a vital Christian life.

Public worship is at the center of Christian life and experience. Jesus, the ideal man, the Last Adam, became man that he might identify with man in leading many sons to glory. Through his human activity he became one with man to sanctify him and ultimately make him a worshiper of God. God saved us that we might become worshipers of him. Note the words of the Puritan William Gouge: "That which is principally here intended is, that Christ would set forth God's praise publicly, among the people of God, and not in a private corner, or among a few of them, but in the midst of them, so as all might hear."[63] He goes on to write:

> The foresaid practice of Christ is of use to stir up people to frequent public assemblies where God's praise is sounded forth, that so they may join with such as sing praises to God, and reap the benefit of the mysteries that are there revealed concerning God's name. Christ hath promised his presence in such places, Matt. 28:20.[64]

2. The vocation of the church

The vocation, the calling, the purpose of the church is worship. "The *position* in which Christ is here viewed is very blessed, 'in the midst': it is the Redeemer leading the praises of His redeemed."[65]

---

[63] Gouge, *Hebrews*, 153.
[64] Gouge, *Hebrews*, 154.

Craigie puts it this way:

> The mixture of forms and types of language suggests
> strongly that the text of Ps 22 is the basis of a liturgy, in
> which the worshiper moves from lament, to prayer, to praise
> and thanksgiving. The psalm should probably be interpreted
> primarily as an individual psalm, though the liturgy sets the
> problem of the individual in the context of the community as
> a whole, thus, the liturgy was clearly a communal affair.[66]

Craigie again says:

> Yet the psalm differs finally from the record of the
> experiences of Job and Jeremiah by virtue of its liturgical
> character; the liturgy immediately sets the loneliness of
> dying into the context of a caring community. And the
> worshiper, who begins his words in utter desolation, ends
> by having his fellow-worshipers to join in the praise of God
> (22:23) [v. 22 in English]. The agent of the deliverance from
> desolation is God himself, but the context in which that
> deliverance is declared is none other than the community of
> God's people.[67]

3.   The position of the church

The church is the place of God's special presence when Christ's
brethren gather for public worship, which occurs when the Word is
preached and praises are sung, led by Christ himself through the
ministry of his Spirit. There is no bifurcation, as moderns often
argue, between teaching on the one hand and worship, defined as
singing, on the other. No, Christ declares God's Word and leads his
people in praise to God. Owen argues the same in the following
citations:

---

[65] Pink, *Hebrews*, 123.

[66] Craigie, *Psalms 1-50*, 19:197-98.

[67] Craigie, *Psalms 1-50*, 19:202.

[on Psa. 22:23, praise in the temple] And this was a type of the whole church of the elect under the new testament. The Lord Christ, in his own person, by his Spirit in his apostles, by his word, and by all his messengers unto the end of the world, setting forth the love, grace, goodness, and mercy of God in him the mediator, sets forth the praise of God in the midst of the congregation.[68]

This, then, being that which he principally aimed at, this design must needs be greatly in his mind. He took care that so great glory, built on so great a foundation as his incarnation and mediation should not be lost.[69]

In brief, the gathering of his church, the setting up of his kingdom, the establishment of his throne, the setting of his crown upon his head, depend wholly on his declaring the name of God in the preaching of the gospel. Seeing, therefore, that the glory of God which he aimed at, the salvation of the sons which he sought for, and the honour of his kingdom which was promised unto him, do all depend on this work, it is no wonder if his heart were full of it, and that he rejoiced to be engaged in it.[70]

Moreover, the Lord Christ, by declaring that he will set forth the praise of God in the church, manifests what is the duty of the church itself, namely to praise God for the work of his love and grace in our redemption by Christ Jesus. *This he promiseth to go before them in; and what he leads them unto is by them to be persisted in.* This is indeed the very end of gathering the church, and of all the duties that are performed therein and thereby.[71]

New Covenant Worship and the Prerogative of Christ

---

[68] Owen, *Hebrews*, 3:426.
[69] Owen, *Hebrews*, 3:427.
[70] Owen, *Hebrews*, 3:428.
[71] Owen, *Hebrews*, 3:428-29, emphasis mine.

Psalm 22:22 and Hebrews 2:12 have far reaching implications for the church of Jesus Christ. In other words, these texts point in the direction of particular pastoral application. As noted previously, corporate worship is far less a matter of preference and far more an insistence upon principle. Reformed Christianity takes seriously the Word of God and the prerogative or endorsement of Christ as revealed in that Word for all things, including worship. With regard to the public worship of the people of God, Christ is prominent and preeminent in new covenant worship. Without unnecessary repetition, note the following implications from Hebrews 2:12.

1. Biblical worship is founded upon the Word of God.

The Word of God regulates our worship. Biblical worship begins with a high view of the Bible. There is only one inspired and inscripturated Word that is preached, is sung, and is the basis of our song. Hart and Muether write, "The Word not only directs our worship, as we have seen, but it also comprises our worship. It is read, it is sung, and it is preached."[72]

Despite differences with regard to the Lord's Supper, both Luther and Calvin held a high view of preaching, so much so that Luther insisted that the church ought to be a "mouth-house rather than a pen-house."[73] The irony is not lost on the writer of an essay devoted in part to the importance of preaching!

2. Biblical worship is centered in God.

Biblical worship is God-centered; it is vertical, not vertical and horizontal. As noted previously, whatever legitimate value there is in the horizontal for Christians, it is not part of public worship. Edification and encouragement, as brothers and sisters interact with one another in their common life, is a great benefit to the Christian. But public worship is different: the worshiper listens to God and the

---

[72] Hart and Muether, *With Reverence and Awe*, 184.
[73] Cited in Mark Beach, "The Real Presence of Christ in Preaching," 82.

worshiper speaks to God in praise. Hart and Muether report:

> John Murray described Reformed piety as God-consciousness, "an all-pervasive sense of God's presence." This spirituality should characterize all of life, but especially the gathering of the saints for public worship. "Adoration springs from the apprehension of God's majesty," Murray continues, "and where this is, there is reverence, that is, godly fear. Here again much of our worship falls under the charge of irreverence and therefore under condemnation. There is a place in life for jollity and jollification. But how alien to the worship of God would this be in the sanctuary."[74]

3. Biblical worship is dialogical.

Biblical worship is conversational. It has God at the center, but it includes God speaking to man and man speaking back to God in response. It begins and it ends with God. Our text does not include all the elements of worship, but it does address this principle of dialogue.

> Worship is a meeting between God and his people. Believers come at his invitation, are welcomed into his presence . . . The service is a holy conversation between heaven and earth. It cannot be repackaged as a form of entertainment or congregational meeting.[75]

4. Biblical worship is focused on Christ.

Biblical worship is nothing without the mediation of Christ, hence the placement of Hebrews 2:9-11 before verse 12. Worship is no mere formality, sentimentality, morality, ritual, magic, or a mystical experience of receiving new revelation, but it is about Christ who

---

[74] Hart and Muether, *With Reverence and Awe*, 185. Citing John Murray, "Worship," in *Collected Writings of John Murray*, 4 vols. (Edinburgh: Banner of Truth Trust, 1976), 1:167.

[75] Hart and Muether, *With Reverence and Awe*, 185.

New Covenant Worship: Hebrews 2:12 and the Real Presence of Christ

mediates our salvation and our worship. Without the gospel of Christ there can be no new covenant worship.

5. Biblical worship is effectual because of the real presence of Christ.

When we speak of the real presence of Christ in our worship, in the preaching and in our praise, we must not think in carnal or material terms. It is a spiritual presence, meaning that the Spirit of God is present in the faithfully preached Word and in the praise of God's people. Preaching, for example, does not depend upon oratorical skill, and the view of preaching defended in this essay does not lead to authoritarianism, or even a new word from God; rather, just the opposite. Preaching must be faithful to God's Word. Only then is it the authoritative word about Christ, by Christ. While this view of preaching may appear presumptuous, if not dangerous, once again, the opposite is true. True preaching conforms to the Word. Faithful preaching never adds to the Word of God, or exceeds its bounds; it is but the administration of that true Word and derivative of it. Faithfully rendered, it is speech possessing the authority of Christ. It comes to us as Christ himself addressing us. Consider the following:

> Thus from one perspective the human work of the sermon is critically important. The sermon's fidelity to Scripture, the skill of the syntax and rhetoric, the liveliness of the delivery are of a fundamental importance that ought not to be minimized. From another perspective a sermon is a work of the Spirit of God which may make a "poor" sermon the occasion of God's presence and a brilliant sermon barren of power.[76]

Likewise in our praise, Jesus is present. Jesus, our ascended Savior, still wearing our humanity as our representative before the heavenly Father says to his heavenly Father in the midst of the congregation, "I will sing your praise."[77] Ferguson exhorts us as follows:

---

[76] Leith, *Calvin's Doctrine*, 117, cited in Beach.
[77] Ferguson, *When Jesus is the Worship Leader*.

The author of Hebrews is saying to them, "Fix your gaze upon what God has given you in the gospel because what God has given you in the gospel is nothing less than the very presence of the Lord Jesus Christ among you as the liturgist, as the worship leader of the congregation. And if you gaze not on the things that are seen but on the one who is unseen, who keeps his promise that where two or three gather in his name he will be there in the midst of them, then it will dawn on you that you have privileges way beyond anything you ever knew in the past."[78]

6. Biblical worship is met with a sense of expectancy and urgency.

If Christ is present in our worship, as we have noted the Scriptures promise, then public worship ought to be a priority for God's people, and it ought to be anticipated with a sense of expectation. Pastors should not feel embarrassed to urge attendance at all of the stated meetings of the church for worship. As well, God's people should be eager to gather for worship without feeling under pressure to do so. After all, Christ is present! We meet with him. He speaks to us God's Word of assurance and forgiveness. He leads us in praise to God. He is in heaven, but his Spirit is here with us. Here is a bit of heaven before we get to heaven. Why would we exchange the verbal for the visual? Why would we be drawn to self-help guidance and moralizing sermons telling us we can do better? We have the privilege of communing with the living God himself! As William Perkins noted, "God is nearer to us in the presence of his ordinances such as his word, his sacraments, and public worship in the congregation."[79]

Michael Horton says it profoundly:

Proclamation does involve doctrinal and ethical instruction, of course. The law and the gospel not only kill and make

---

[78] Ferguson, *When Jesus Is the Worship Leader.*

[79] William Perkins, *The Art of Prophesying* (Edinburgh: The Banner of Truth Trust, 1996), 79.

alive; they direct our life and doctrine. However, we must come to church expecting nothing less than God's gracious assault on the citadels of our autonomy, our supposing that we could ascend to God by our theological acumen any more than by our actions. This confrontation occurs not only in the sermon but in the entire liturgy, including the singing, whose purpose is "to let the word of Christ dwell in you richly, teaching and admonishing one another in all wisdom, singing psalms and hymns and spiritual songs, with thankfulness in your hearts to God" (Col. 3:16). While carefully distinguishing the Spirit's illumination of the preached Word from the Spirit's inspiration of the canonical word, we can affirm that the content—Christ and all his benefits—is exactly the same. This should create a sense of urgency and expectancy in our public assembly, as God addresses us here and now.[80]

Conclusion

The great Puritan preacher of the late sixteenth century in England, William Perkins, was known for advocating a plain style in preaching. He advocated an approach to preaching that was without artifice, so common in his day. An "open manifestation of the truth" is what he believed should characterize preaching. Preaching was aimed at the mind in order to reach the conscience, not to entertain or to impress. He once wrote the following, which is about as plain as it can be made. Perhaps this is all that needs to be said:

> The heart of the matter is this:
> Preach one Christ,
> by Christ,
> to the praise of Christ.[81]

---

[80] Michael Horton, *The Christian Faith: A Systematic Theology for Pilgrims on the Way* (Grand Rapids: Zondervan, 2011), 763.

[81] Perkins, *Art of Prophesying*, 79.

Tributes

I met Dr. James Renihan just before my career at Westminster Seminary and IRBS, where he was to be my teacher in all things Baptist. As I sat in his classes, it became clear that the man had a passion for theology, but also for the practice and pastoral implications which follow there from. I quickly learned how good a theologian and effective a teacher Dr. Renihan was, as I found those very truths and convictions impressed upon me. His courses never seemed a mere academic exercise. He taught me God's truth in a way that weighed upon my heart, and led to my own passion for things like preaching and the practice of the regulative principle. I have personally witnessed and can testify that Dr. Renihan, as a theologian and a teacher, is daily concerned with God's glory and worship according to truth. And that's the best thing you can say about a creature.

But more than a teacher, Dr. Renihan has been a pastor to me. He has patiently listened to my tearful confessing; he has reminded me of the gospel when I needed it; he has edified me with encouraging words, and has constantly been to me an example of a godly servant. He is truly a man worthy of double honor, and I heartily affirm and rejoice that the Lord has gifted him to us. As a pastor and a man, Dr. Renihan has been a mentor and a father to me, so I thank God for him in my prayers. May the Lord continue to bless and delight in Doc, our beloved pastor and teacher.

Gatlin Bredeson
Assistant to the Dean of the Institute of Reformed Baptist Studies
Bonney Lake, WA

The Apostle Paul said that ministers of the gospel are gifts given by Christ to the church (Eph. 4:11). One particular gift is Dr. James M. Renihan. Reformed Baptists as a whole have been helped greatly by the scholarship and godliness of Dr. Renihan. His work on the 2nd London Confession of Faith of 1677/1689 has been of tremendous benefit in bringing to light the original context and meaning of our Confession. For those who have benefited from knowing Dr.

Renihan on a personal level, it is obvious that he strives after the glory of God through the pursuit of doctrinal precision, but a precision that takes seriously the maintenance of ecclesiastical peace and unity. I had the privilege of working with Dr. Renihan on a theology committee and was provided with a model for how the theological enterprise must be pursued with respect to precision and unity. I count myself blessed to have benefited both from Dr. Renihan's teaching and from his godly example. May Christ the Lord continue to use this particular gift to further the cause of God and truth in our churches. And may Christ the Lord continue to bless the good Doctor in his personal and family life.

Pastor James P. Butler
Free Grace Baptist Church
Chilliwack, B.C

Many pastors and theologians have influenced me throughout my lifetime, but none as much as Dr. James Renihan. His commitment to Scripture, our Confession of Faith, and Reformed theology have profoundly impacted my life and ministry. There are four emphases that center his ministry. First, his overarching focus is the ministry of the Word of God. Whatever else he has done, accomplished, or taught, it is his calling as a minister of the gospel that is most important to him and encouraged most in his students. Second, his emphasis upon the means of grace. His commitment to the truth that God has ordained means in the spread of the gospel and our growth in grace guides all else. Third, he has an unwavering commitment to sound theology. This is a commitment which manifests itself both in endeavoring to be biblical, orthodox, and Reformed, while also exhaustive and nuanced. Finally, there is a great emphasis upon the catholicity of the church. While maintaining strong commitments to our orthodox, and confessional Reformed theology, he also endeavors to pass on a love for the church catholic, and a desire for unity in the body of Christ as well as love for all the saints. These four commitments have given a balance in ministry and teaching that has made him a gift not only to the Reformed Baptist community but the broader church of

Christ. I praise the Lord that he has allowed me to learn from Dr. Renihan. I look forward to many more years of benefit as he continues to serve the church of Christ.

Rev. Robert E. Cosby
2009 Graduate of the Institute of Reformed Baptist Studies
and Westminster Seminary California
Pastor of Tucson Reformed Baptist Church
Tucson, AZ

It has been my privilege and joy to have met Dr. Jim Renihan and work with him in the city of Donestk, Ukraine. I have benefited from observing and listening to him present biblical, expositional sermons to pastors and church workers who have never had theological training. Jim used his theological gifts with pastoral care and sensitivity to a foreign culture. I also watched many Ukrainian pastors deeply appreciate the lectures and personally thank brother Jim.

Being far away from home, for a long week of teaching and preaching, I especially appreciated my friendship with Jim. We would discuss many things and cover many topics such as: our families, seminary life, pastoral ministry, and even sports teams from Boston. Jim lifted my tired mind from jet lag, and long days in a crowded church building. One memorable, and humorous occasion (at least to us), is when we were listening to a Russian song being sung and he translated the chorus line to what it sounded like to him in English, "salsa in a leaky boat." When the song was sung, I still can see Jim's smile as we turned and looked at each other, tempted to sing our own English version, but we didn't. I don't think transposing or transliterating Russian songs is in the future for Jim. And that is just fine, because he has many other ministry gifts to use for the edification of Christ's church.

Jim has a book that he wrote based on 1 Corinthians 13 on love. It really is a blessing to know an author who doesn't just write books, or a professor who doesn't just give fine lectures, but who by the grace of God, lives a life of Christian love and Christ-centered ministry! I pray and wish much joy for Jim and an awareness that

God has and still is using him to bless God's people and further the kingdom of Christ through his ministry, near and far away!

> Rev. C. J. den Dulk
> Pastor of Trinity CRC
> Sparta, MI

It was not until 1997 that I met Jim Renihan while he was pastoring a church in Worcester, MA. We have been good friends ever since.

Of the many things that stand out about Jim, there are three things that I appreciate so much about this man. First, there is his humility. Jim is never one to call attention to himself or to his accomplishments. Proverbs 27:2 says, "Let another praise you, and not your own mouth; a stranger, and not your own lips." You won't hear Jim tooting his own horn or see him patting himself on the back. He is a very humble person. Second, Jim is a man of gratitude. Humble people are always thankful people who are quick to express appreciation. If you do something for him or give something to him, he will acknowledge it and thank you for it. In Jim's book, *Edification and Beauty*, he devotes eight paragraphs of acknowledgements to everyone who helped and supported him. He is a very thankful person. Third, Jim is extremely gracious and charitable toward others. He and his doctrines have come under attack in the past, yet Jim has always responded with grace and respect. Jim may disagree with an opponent but he is never contentious. He has few enemies but many, many friends. His graciousness also shines through when he offers correction, which makes for a great seminary professor and friend.

Jim was a pastor before he became a professor and his pastor's heart remains at the surface of all that he does. After eighteen years of service on campus, he continues to be loved and highly respected by the WSC faculty in Escondido. Jim has been a tremendous blessing to our Association of Reformed Baptist Churches. Since 1998 he has faithfully served ARBCA with distinguishing honor as Dean and Professor of our Institute of Reformed Baptist Studies. Through his service at IRBS, our Association has benefitted over the years as well-trained men enter into pastoral ministry, thus strengthening our churches and planting new ones.

Jim may be turning 60, but that is still low-mileage as far as this man is concerned. He has squeezed a lot of good into his 60 years but by God's grace he is just hitting his stride. May the Lord be pleased to grant Jim the health and stamina to serve God's kingdom for many years to come.

John Giarrizzo
Pastor of Grace Covenant Church, Gilbert, AZ
Interim Coordinator of ARBCA
Friend of Jim Renihan

I count it a great privilege to number Dr. James M. Renihan among my close friends. Over the years since we first met (about ten years ago), every interaction has strengthened my regard for him and has been a means of immeasurable blessing to me, whether sitting under his ministry at our annual School of Theology in Palmerston North, driving through the scenic countryside of New Zealand discussing a range of subjects from the sublime to the ridiculous, staying in his home in Escondido enjoying the company of his family, or walking the campus of Westminster Seminary California hearing him tell the history of IRBS and the excellent relationship he enjoys with the Westminster faculty. Jim has modeled for me grace, wisdom, patience, generosity, constancy, love, and so much more in these diverse settings.

Through these years Jim has also made a quiet but real contribution to the Reformed Baptist "movement" in New Zealand: he is respected, loved, and welcomed here, and his self-sacrificial and warmhearted contribution to our churches and fellowship has been greatly appreciated. In Jim we have witnessed one whose manner of life is worthy of the gospel of Jesus Christ as he has worked side by side with us for the faith of the gospel (Phil. 1:27). To God be the glory for raising up and equipping this man whose ministry in both word and life is a gift of God to the churches!

Dafydd Hughes
Crosspoint Church, Palmerston North, New Zealand
(Dafydd has been involved in church planting and pastoral ministry for 19 years in New Zealand, first in Christchurch and currently in

Palmerston North, where the church is a member of the Fellowship of Reformed Baptist Churches of New Zealand and hosts an annual School of Theology at which Dr Renihan has taught on seven occasions.)

Our church has been a member of ARBCA from its inception (and RBMS before that). When it was announced that IRBS would be forming, I was excited, but when Dr. Renihan was announced as the key man chosen to lead IRBS, I only had a passing knowledge of him, since I knew mostly west coast men.

I now know Dr. Renihan well. He is an east coast man, a west coast man, a fly-over country man, and a world-traveler, taking IRBS/ARBCA literally around the globe. He has been tireless in his efforts to advance God's truth, and his efforts at home and abroad have been greatly used of the Lord.

It was a brave step of faith to lead his family to relocate from Worcester, MA, those many years ago. It has been a personal joy to witness all that has taken place since. It has been my privilege to audit all the classes offered at IRBS; some of them twice. They are that rich and full! I have also witnessed the Doctor as a Pastor and it has been exciting to see the growth and blessing Christ Reformed Baptist Church has been to the students attending IRBS and also the greater community of Vista/Escondido.

Thank you Dr. Renihan for the goldmine of scholarly and practical truths you have uncovered from our past. We have profited much and learned much from your digging into our Confessional roots. Our movement has benefited greatly and a solid foundation is being laid for Confessional Baptists for years to come.

Pastor Steve Marquedant
Sovereign Grace Baptist Church
Ontario, California

I count it a great privilege to know Dr. Jim Renihan and to have worked with him closely on more than one project and to have him as a dear friend. I would like to draw attention to one great quality, among many, that sets Jim apart. Jim is a man of integrity. He is a man of integrity at home, in the academy and in the church.

I have experienced and observed Jim's integrity in his home. I have stayed in his home for several weeks total over the years and have observed him in his family life. His home life is a joy to behold and participate in. He and his dear helpmate, Lynne, practice hospitality that is always warm and inviting and frequently sacrificial. I love being in his home with his family. He is in his home what he professes to be in public—a Christian man, husband and father, pastor and scholar. He is at home what he is in public—thoughtful, kind, fun and warmly a Christian man. Lynne is a perfect complement for Jim and a true asset to his ministry. He could not have accomplished what he has over the years without her practical and logistical support.

I have sat under Jim's teaching and preaching ministry many times and always with great edification. In the classroom he is a clear teacher with important content. And he models for me the pastoral care for his students (whether in their 20s or the "over the hill gang" of pastors who are blessed to call him friend). I have seen him tested and challenged and responding in a measured and gracious way. His commitment to *ad fontes,* the original sources, means that Jim is committed to the truth, biblically and historically. I deeply admire him for that. His scholarship is impeccable but I have never sensed that it was done in the service of Jim's academic career but for the churches he loves and serves.

I have admired how much Jim is a churchman. He loves Christ's church and the saints—even ones like me who are not always lovable! He has opened up the wells of Baptist church history that the Philistines had stopped up (Gen. 26:18-19).

He has repeatedly taken us back to the Bible and our seventeenth-century Baptist fathers. He has taught us well and we shall ever be in his debt.

I return to my original commendation—Jim is a man of great integrity whose persona as a Christian gentleman, husband, father, pastor and scholar are all intertwined to make him who he is. Brother, we salute you and thank God for you!

Steve Martin
Retired ARBCA pastor

There are a few of us who have a saying that goes something like this: *"If anyone doesn't like Jim Renihan, then there's something wrong and it ain't with Jim!"* This acknowledges not some general personality trait summed up in *"he's a super nice guy"* but the reality that in Jim a number of emulation-worthy superlatives coalesce to make him an exemplar for men presently in, and men seeking to join, the Christian ministry. He is a steadfast adherent to biblical and confessional doctrine, holding to the things most surely believed among us with a tenacious grip and an apologetic vigor. He is a man that you would want on your team in any engagement of Christian discourse or debate where the truth is at stake. He is a man rich with theological acumen, scriptural knowledge, and historical insight. For many this would be enough, but all these things come further tempered by a Christocentric love of the gospel of sovereign grace, an obvious joy for the rehearsal and propagation of the truth, the refreshing absence of abrasiveness and one-upmanship in theological discourse, a desire to see Christ's churches full, and that with peace and unity, a good teacher's exuberance, a kind father's patience, and a true pastor's heart.

To know Jim, however, even for a minute, is to know that he would much rather hear how you were doing in Christ and life than to hear others applaud his character, list his accolades, and rehearse his contributions. This simply demonstrates the Christian man of precedent he is—an object lesson for those seeking to humbly serve in the church of Christ. No doubt when Jim is gone there will be in ink a long catalog of invaluable impressions left by him upon our good Baptist way, yet in the service of his legacy (if I may speak before the time) might we who have known him, in whatever capacity, make his indelible mark to be that we love his God, that we preach his Christ, and that we defend the old paths where the good way is.

Pastor Cameron G. Porter
Free Grace Baptist Church
Chilliwack, B.C

I count it a great privilege to have been asked to write a few words about my good friend, Jim Renihan. Our church counts Dr. Renihan among our dearest friends. He has ministered to us faithfully on multiple occasions. It has been our delight to host several classes (i.e., Baptist Symbolics twice and Puritanism in Context) for pastors in which Jim was the professor. These have been profitable times as we have partaken of the fruit of his gifts and disciplined labors in the doctrine we hold in common.

During these times, Jim has usually stayed in our home. Because of this interaction through the years, our friendship has grown and involved many times of enjoyable fellowship around the table or fire, in the living room or on the porch. Our brother Jim has made himself a close and true friend. He has persevered in faithfulness to our triune God, to the Scriptures, to his church, to our Confession, to his school, to his family, and to his many friends. We give praise to our Father in heaven for him and the grace of God that we see in him. What better thing can a man say about another man?

Jim is also one of those men I'd like to lock in a room and require him to write, allowing him occasional recesses, so that he will produce good books for current and future pastors and Reformed Baptists. While we love benefitting from his labors and know that much of his thinking is instilled in his students, we pray that the things he has studied and taught will be preserved for future generations. There is a current glut of evangelical books, but his will be of lasting value long after we are gone from this earth and in the presence of the church in heaven worshiping the Lord God.

Pastor Larry Vincent
Heritage Baptist Church: A Reformed Baptist Congregation
Mansfield, TX

To some, Dr. James M. Renihan is "Prof" and "Doc," but for me, Jim is brother and friend. The first time I met Jim was in the Philippines in 2004 at a Pastors' Conference. He was the main speaker and I was one of the other speakers. As we were going for dinner after the first day of the conference, he expressed his disapproval of my message.

That was how our friendship started! The second time was in 2014 whereby I was privileged to spend nearly three weeks of my Sabbatical staying in his home, interacting with him outside the classroom and pulpit, eating and drinking and talking with his family. From these two extended periods of interaction with him, one thing comes across strongly to me: *Jim is human.* He is the human face of the 1677/89 Baptist Confession. To many, he is the "expert" in matters concerning the Baptist Confession. To me, he is the "visible, human expression" of how the doctrines of the Baptist Confession are and should be lived out. While I greatly appreciate his scholarly contributions, I am most thankful to God for how he set the example for me in expressing these beliefs in his talk and walk. Thank you, brother and friend. All praise to Jesus the Christ, your Savior-Lord and mine!

Pastor Wei En Yi
Shalom Church
Singapore

Appendix:

Education, Academic Career and Pastoral Ministry,

and a Bibliography of the Publications of

James M. Renihan

compiled by Micah Renihan

Education

- B.S., Liberty Baptist College
- Letter of Recognition, Trinity Ministerial Academy
- M.Div., Seminary of the East
- Ph.D., Trinity Evangelical Divinity School

Academic Career and Pastoral Ministry

- Pastor, Mohawk Valley Bible Church, Herkimer, NY, 1984-87.
- Pastor, Grace Reformed Baptist Church, Amesbury, MA, 1987-92.
- Doctoral Fellow in Church History, Trinity Evangelical Divinity School, Deerfield, IL, 1993-94.
- Pastor, Heritage Baptist Church, Worcester, MA, 1995-98.
- Adjunct Professor of Church History, The Southern Baptist Theological Seminary, Northeast Extension Campus, Northborough, MA, 1996.
- Dean, Institute of Reformed Baptist Studies, Escondido, CA, 1998-present.
- Associate Professor of Historical Theology, Institute of Reformed Baptist Studies, Escondido, CA, 1998-2006.

- Elder, Christ Reformed Baptist Church, Vista, CA, 1999-present.
- Professor of Historical Theology, Institute of Reformed Baptist Studies, Escondido, CA, 2006-present.
- Visiting Professor of Church History, Westminster Seminary California, Escondido, CA, 2008-present.
- External Graduate Faculty, University of Maine, Orono, ME, 2011-present.
- Visiting Lecturer in Church History, Sunshine Coast Theological College, Buderim, Queensland, Australia, 2012.

Books

- *Daily Treasure: 366 Daily Readings from Charles Spurgeon's Treasury of David* (Evangelical Press, 2000), editor (Translated into Dutch, French and Russian).
- *Denominations or Associations? Essays on Reformed Baptist Associations* (Calvary Press, 2001), editor, contributor.
- *Covenant Theology from Adam to Christ* (Reformed Baptist Academic Press, 2005), editor.
- *True Confessions: Baptist Documents in the Reformed Family* (Reformed Baptist Academic Press, 2007).
- *Edification and Beauty: The Practical Ecclesiology of the English Particular Baptists, 1675-1705* (Paternoster, 2008).
- *True Love: Understanding the Real Meaning of Christian Love* (Evangelical Press, 2010).
- *Confessing the Impassible God: The Biblical, Classical, and Confessional Doctrine of Divine Impassibility* (RBAP, 2015), editor, contributor.

Articles, Chapters, and Pamphlets

- "An Examination of the Possible Influence of Menno Simons' *Foundation Book* upon the Particular Baptist Confession of 1644," *American Baptist Quarterly* XV:3 (September 1996): 190-207. 1995 Torbet Prize winning essay.

- "An Annotated Bibliography of Important Reading and Study Materials Concerning British Particular Baptists," *Baptist Review of Theology/La Revue Baptiste de Théologie* VI.1 (Spring 1996): 62-66.
- "Henry Danvers' *A Treatise of Baptism*: A Study in Seventeenth-Century Historiography," *Baptist Review of Theology/La Revue Baptiste de Théologie* VII.1-2 (Spring/Fall 1997): 27-47.
- *A Tale of Two Associations* (Reformed Baptist Publications, n.d.).
- "Church Planting and the London Baptist Confessions of Faith" in *The Founders Journal* 37 (Summer 1999): 10-19.
- "Caterpillars and Butterflies: A Review of *New Covenant Theology* by Tom Wells and Fred Zaspel," *Reformation Today* 195 (September-October 2003): 23-26.
- "Out from Hyper-Calvinism: Andrew Fuller and the Promotion of Missions," *Reformed Baptist Theological Review* I.1 (January 2004): 45-66.
- "Thomas Collier's Descent into Error: Collier, Calvinism, and the Second London Confession," *Reformed Baptist Theological Review* I.1 (January 2004): 67-84.
- "The Increase of Faith: The Ordinary Means of Grace in the Second London Confession," *Reformed Baptist Theological Review* I.2 (July 2004): 74-94.
- "The Ministry and the Church" Parts 1 & 2, *Banner of Truth* (Issue 491-92, August-September 2004): 37-45; (Issue 494, November 2004): 15-22.
- *The Baptist Catechism* (Reformed Baptist Publications, n.d.), editor and foreword.
- "Foreword," in H. F. Stander and J. P. Louw, *Baptism in the Early Church* (Reformation Today Trust, 2004), 7-11.
- "Reforming *The Reformed Pastor*: Baptism and Justification as the Basis for Richard Baxter's Pastoral Method," *Reformed Baptist Theological Review* II:1 (January 2005): 111-34.
- "Theology on Target: The Scope of the Whole (Which is to Give all Glory to God)," *Reformed Baptist Theological Review* II:2 (July 2005): 36-53.

- "Introduction: Why is this reprint important?" and "An Excellent and Judicious Divine: Nehemiah Coxe," in Nehemiah Coxe and John Owen, *Covenant Theology From Adam to Christ*, edited by Ronald D. Miller, James M. Renihan, and Francisco Orozco (Reformed Baptist Academic Press, 2005), 1-4 and 7-24.
- "The Gifts for Church Government: Elders and Deacons," *The Gospel Witness* (October 2005): 8-10.
- "Confessing the Faith in 1644 and 1689," *Reformed Baptist Theological Review* III.1 (January, 2006): 48-76.
- "Bound To Keep the First Day: Covenant Theology, the Moral Law, and the Sabbath among the first English Particular Baptists," *Reformed Baptist Theological Review* III:2 (July, 2006): 51-76.
- "Introduction to This New Edition," in Benjamin Beddome, *A Scriptural Exposition of the Baptist Catechism* (Solid Ground Classic Reprints, 2006), xi-xiv.
- "How Will I Understand Unless Someone Guides Me?: Helps for Interpreting Our Confession of Faith," *Reformed Baptist Theological Review* IV.1 (January 2007): 43-58.
- "An Excellent and Judicious Divine: Nehemiah Coxe," *Reformed Baptist Theological Review* IV:2 (July, 2007): 61-78.
- "Foreword," in Micahel A. G. Haykin and Steve Weaver, editors, *Devoted to the Service of the Temple: Piety, Persecution, and Ministry in the Writing of Hercules Collins* (Reformation Heritage Books, 2007), xiii-xiv.
- "Baptist Theological Controversies," in *Baptist History Celebration — 2007* (Particular Baptist Press, 2008), 513-37.
- "'Truly Reformed in a Great Measure'" A Brief Defense of the English Separatist Origins of Modern Baptists," *The Journal of Baptist Studies* 3 (2009): 24-32.
- "Ecclesiology in Debate: 'Whether Iesus Christ Shall Be a King Or No,'" *Reformed Baptist Theological Review* VII.2 (Fall 2010): 41-72.
- "Foreword," in *The Baptist Confession of Faith & The Baptist Catechism* (Solid Ground Christian Books, 2010), vii-x.
- "'An Ingenuous Unfolding of Our Principles:' Confessionalism among 17th Century Particular Baptists," in

Thomas K. Ascol and Nathan A. Finn, editors, *Ministry by His Grace and for His Glory: Essays in Honor of Thomas J. Nettles* (Founders Press, 2011), 249-63.

- "Person and Place: Two Problems with Biblicism" and "'Good and Necessary Consequence' or 'Necessarily Contained': Toward a Particular Baptist Method of Theology," in Richard C. Barcellos, editor, *Southern California Reformed Baptist Pastors' Conference Papers* Volume 1, 2012, 111-52.
- "Introduction" and "Covenant Theology in the First and Second London Confessions of Faith," in Richard C. Barcellos, editor, *Recovering a Covenantal Heritage* (RBAP, 2014), 13-18; 45-70.
- "'That Stronghold of Their Common Faith:' Salvation in Christ Alone among Seventeenth-Century Baptists," *Journal of the Institute of Reformed Baptist Studies* (2014): 69-94.
- "Foreword," in Richard C. Barcellos, *The Lord's Supper As a Means of Grace: More Than a Memory* (Mentor, 2014), 11-14.
- "Foreword," in Hercules Collins, *An Orthodox Catechism*, edited by Michael A. G. Haykin and G. Stephen Weaver, Jr. (RBAP, 2014), 7-8.
- "Sufficient, Certain, and Infallible: The Inscripturated Word," *Journal of the Institute of Reformed Baptist Studies* 2015: 43-62.
- "An Introduction to the Doctrine of Divine Impassibility: Why is this Doctrine Important" and "Confessional Theology and the Doctrine of Divine Impassibility" in Ronald S. Baines, Richard C. Barcellos, James P. Butler, Stefan T. Lindblad, and James M. Renihan, editors, *Confessing the Impassible God: The Biblical, Classical, & Confessional Doctrine of Divine Impassibility* (RBAP, 2015), 33-46; 353-72.